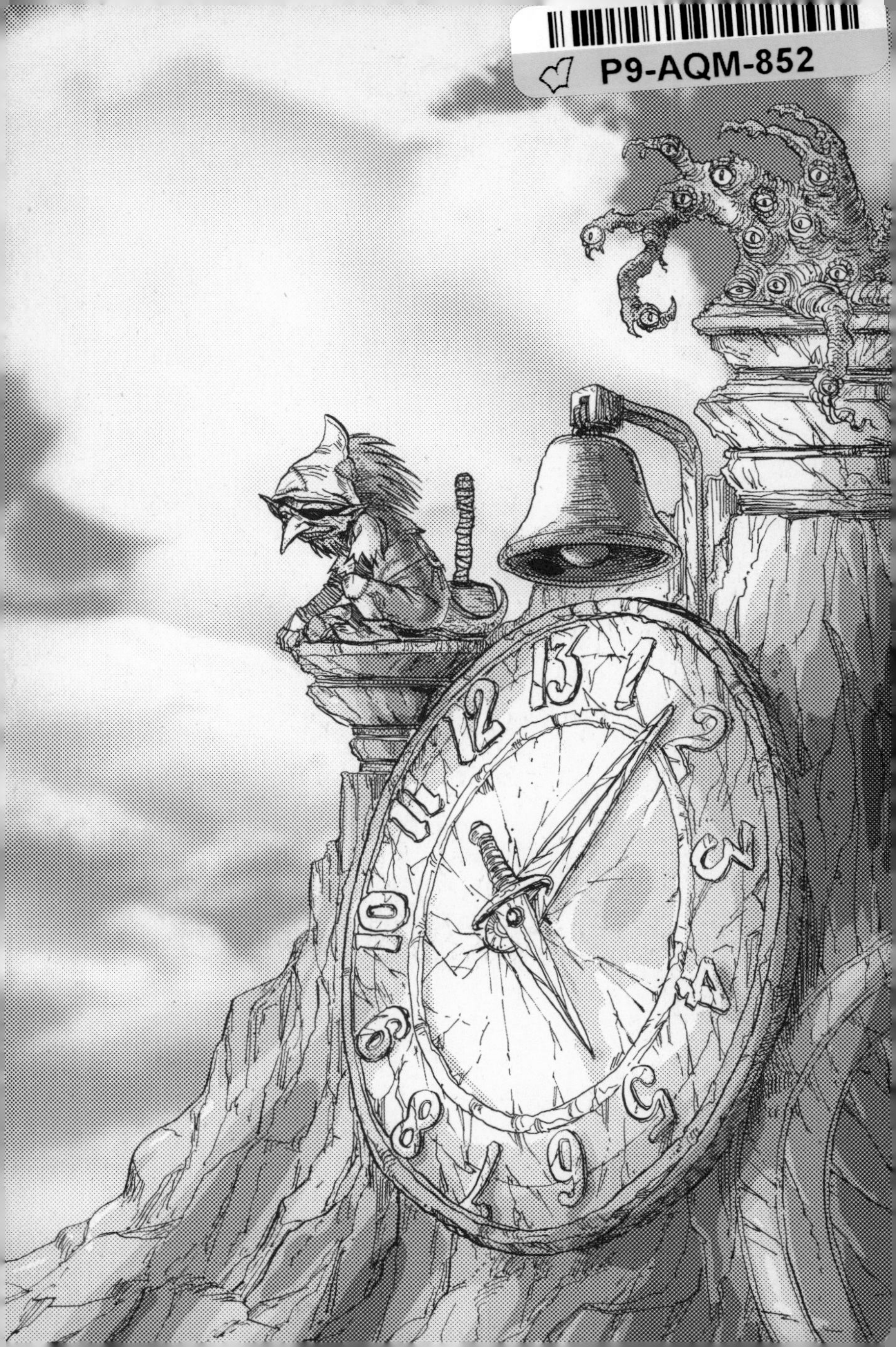

Jim Henson's Return to Labyrinth Vol. 1

Inkers - Jeremy Freeman
with Robert Grabe, Alex McCaffrey
Tyler Niccum & Em Stone
Toner - Erfan Fajar Studio
Layout and Lettering - Lucas Rivera
Cover Design - Anne Marie Horne & Kyle Plummer

Consulting Editor
for the Jim Henson Company - Michael Polis
Contributing Editors - Tim Beedle & Luis Reyes

Editor - Rob Valois
Digital Imaging Manager - Chris Buford
Pre-Production Supervisor - Lucas Rivera
Art Director - Anne Marie Horne
Managing Editor - Elisabeth Brizzi
Editorial Director - Jeremy Ross
VP of Production - Ron Klamert
Editor-in-Chief - Rob Tokar
Publisher - Mike Kiley
President and C.O.O. - John Parker
C.E.O. and Chief Creative Officer - Stuart Levy

A TOKYOPOP® Manga

TOKYOPOP Inc.
5900 Wilshire Blvd. Suite 2000
Los Angeles, CA 90036

E-mail: info@TOKYOPOP.com
Come visit us online at www.TOKYOPOP.com

ISBN: 978-1-59816-725-2

First TOKYOPOP printing: August 2006

10 9 8 7 6 5 4 3 2

Printed in the USA

Jim Henson's RETURN TO LABYRINTH

Volume 1

Written by Jake T. Forbes
Illustrated by Chris Lie
Cover Art by Kouyu Shurei

Based on the feature film "Labyrinth"
Directed by Jim Henson
Story by Dennis Lee and Jim Henson
Screenplay by Terry Jones

Original designs by Brian Froud

TOKYOPOP®

HAMBURG // LONDON // LOS ANGELES // TOKYO

Contents

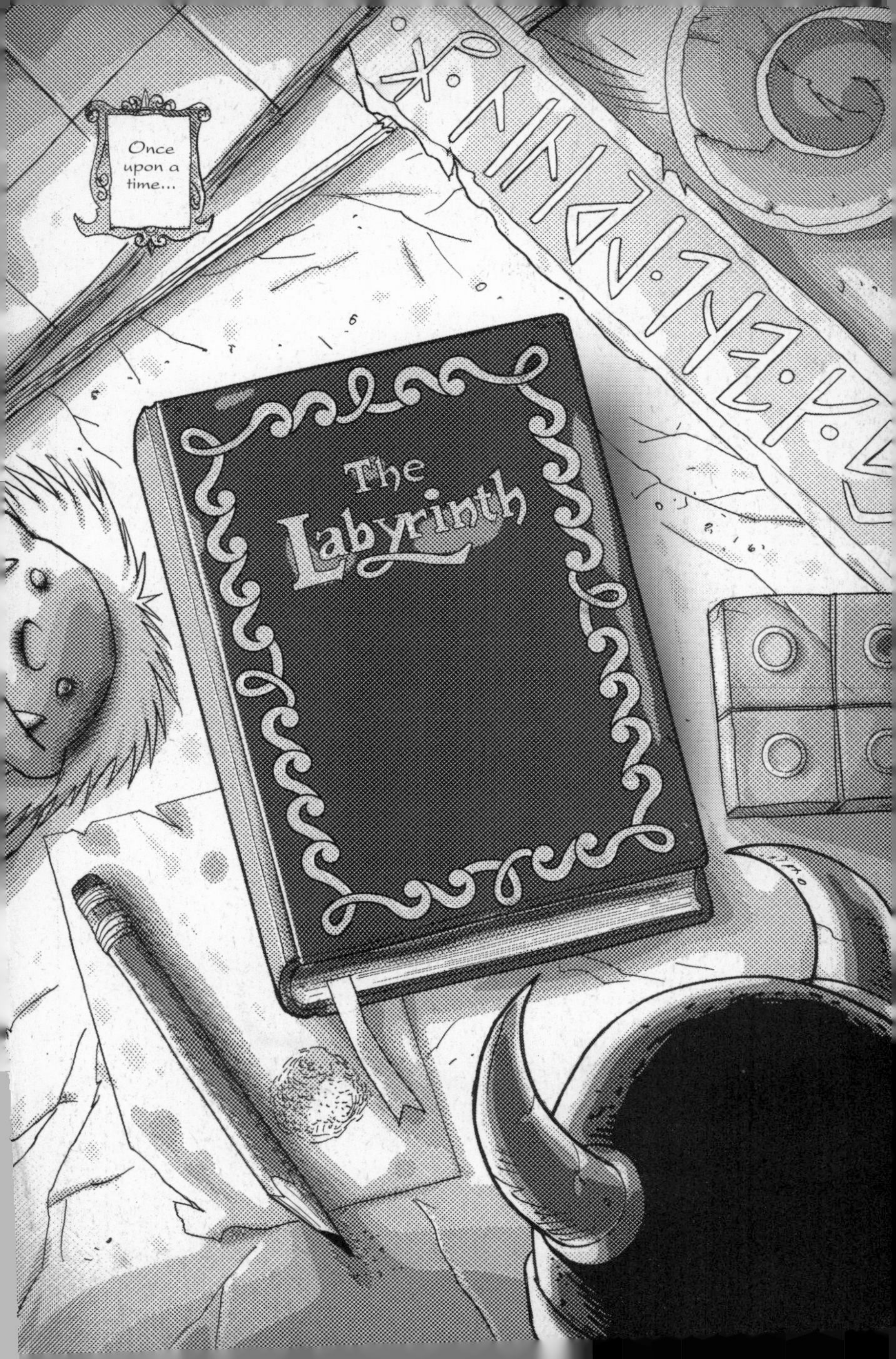
Once upon a time...
The Labyrinth

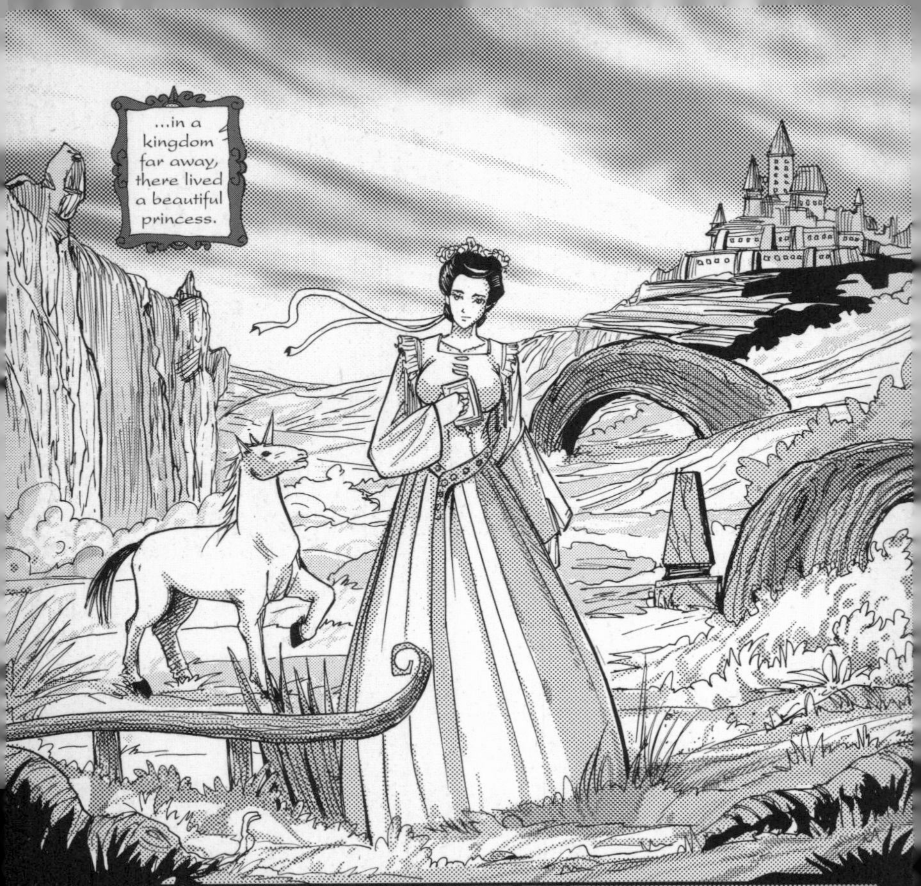
...in a kingdom far away, there lived a beautiful princess.
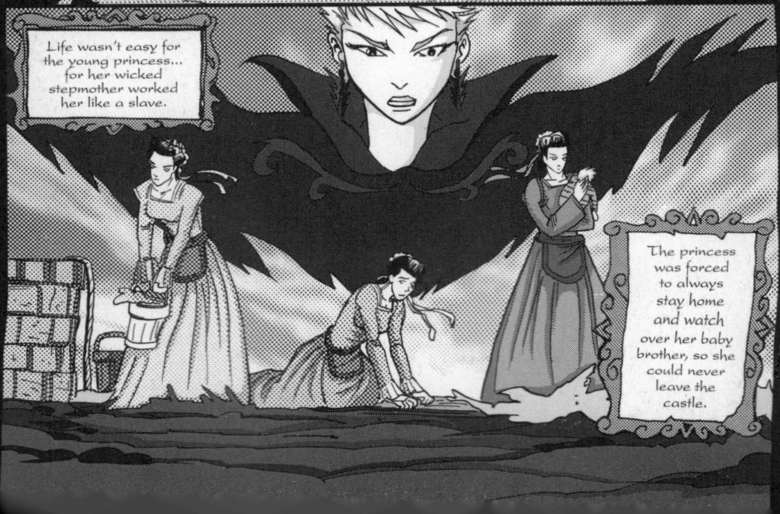
Life wasn't easy for the young princess... for her wicked stepmother worked her like a slave.
The princess was forced to always stay home and watch over her baby brother, so she could never leave the castle.

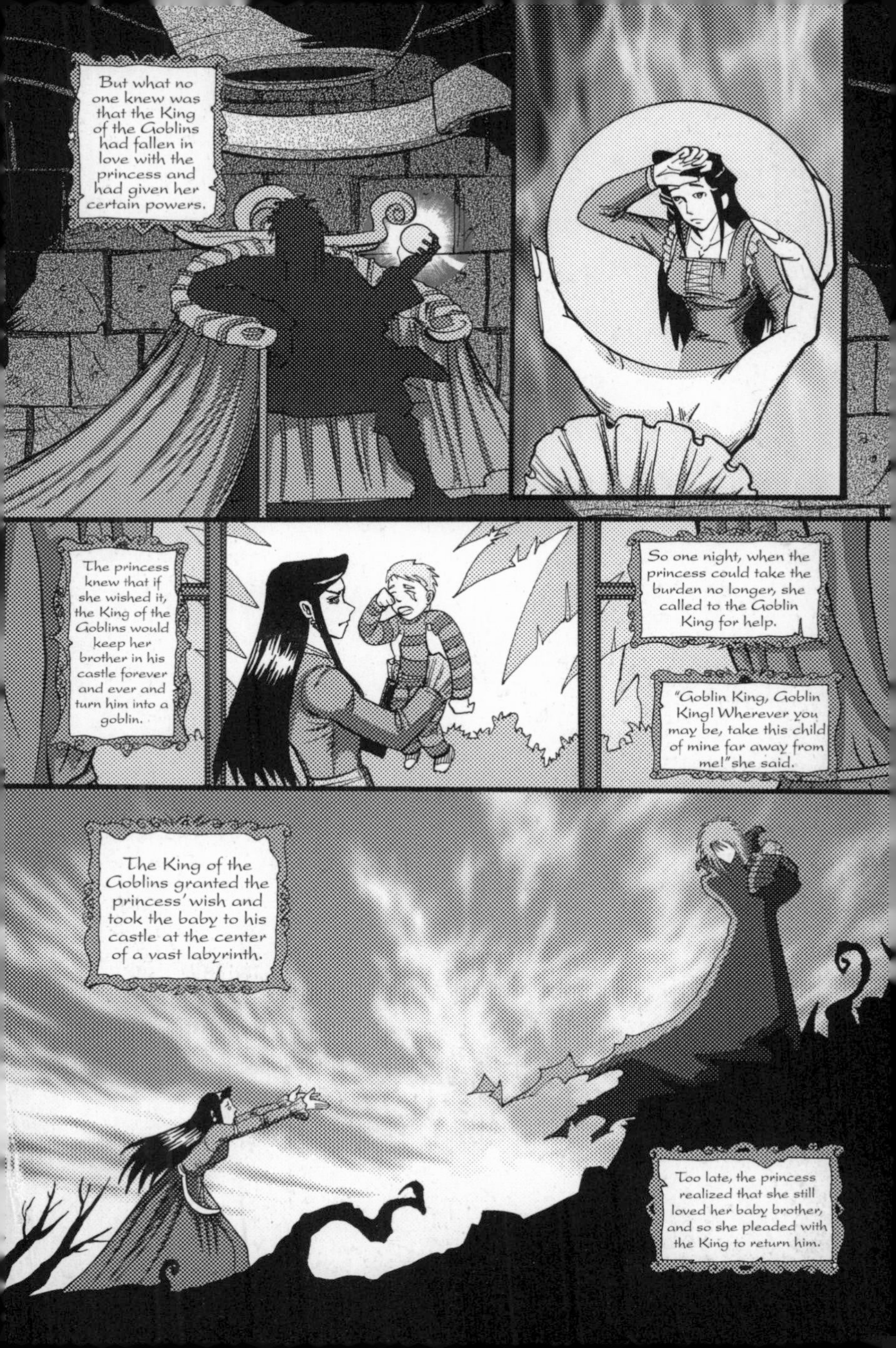
But what no one knew was that the King of the Goblins had fallen in love with the princess and had given her certain powers.
The princess knew that if she wished it, the King of the Goblins would keep her brother in his castle forever and ever and turn him into a goblin.
So one night, when the princess could take the burden no longer, she called to the Goblin King for help.
"Goblin King, Goblin King! Wherever you may be, take this child of mine far away from me!" she said.
The King of the Goblins granted the princess' wish and took the baby to his castle at the center of a vast labyrinth.
Too late, the princess realized that she still loved her baby brother, and so she pleaded with the King to return him.

"What's said‍ä
is said," the‍ä
Goblin King‍ä
responded,‍ä
for he took‍ä
his promises‍ä
very‍ä
seriously.

But the Goblin King did not have
it in his heart to refuse the Princes‍
for he still loved her a great dea‍
"You have thirteen hours in which
solve the Labyrinth before your b‍o
brother becomes one of us foreve‍

Through dangers untold
and hardships unnumbered,
she fought her way to the
castle beyond the Goblin
City to take back the ·
child that he had stolen.

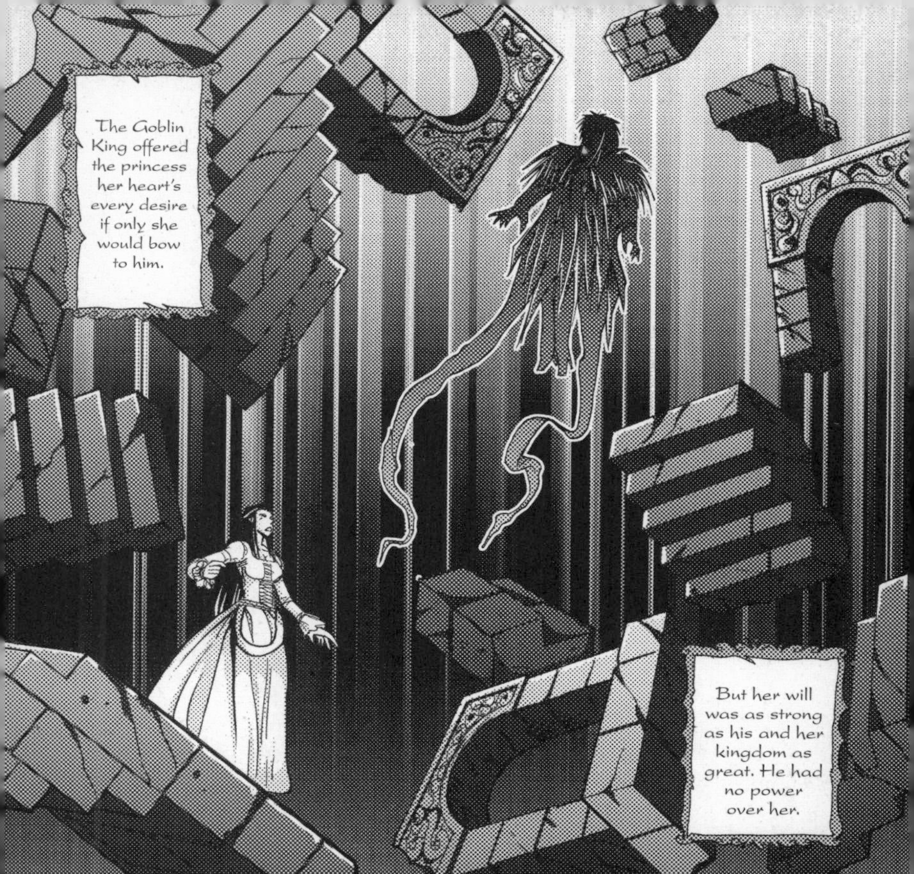
The Goblin King offered the princess her heart's every desire if only she would bow to him.
But her will was as strong as his and her kingdom as great. He had no power over her.
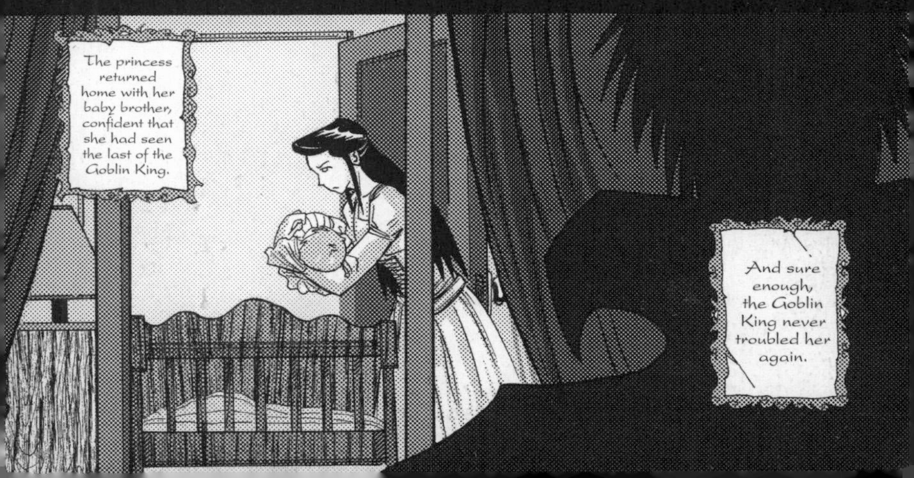
The princess returned home with her baby brother, confident that she had seen the last of the Goblin King.
And sure enough, the Goblin King never troubled her again.

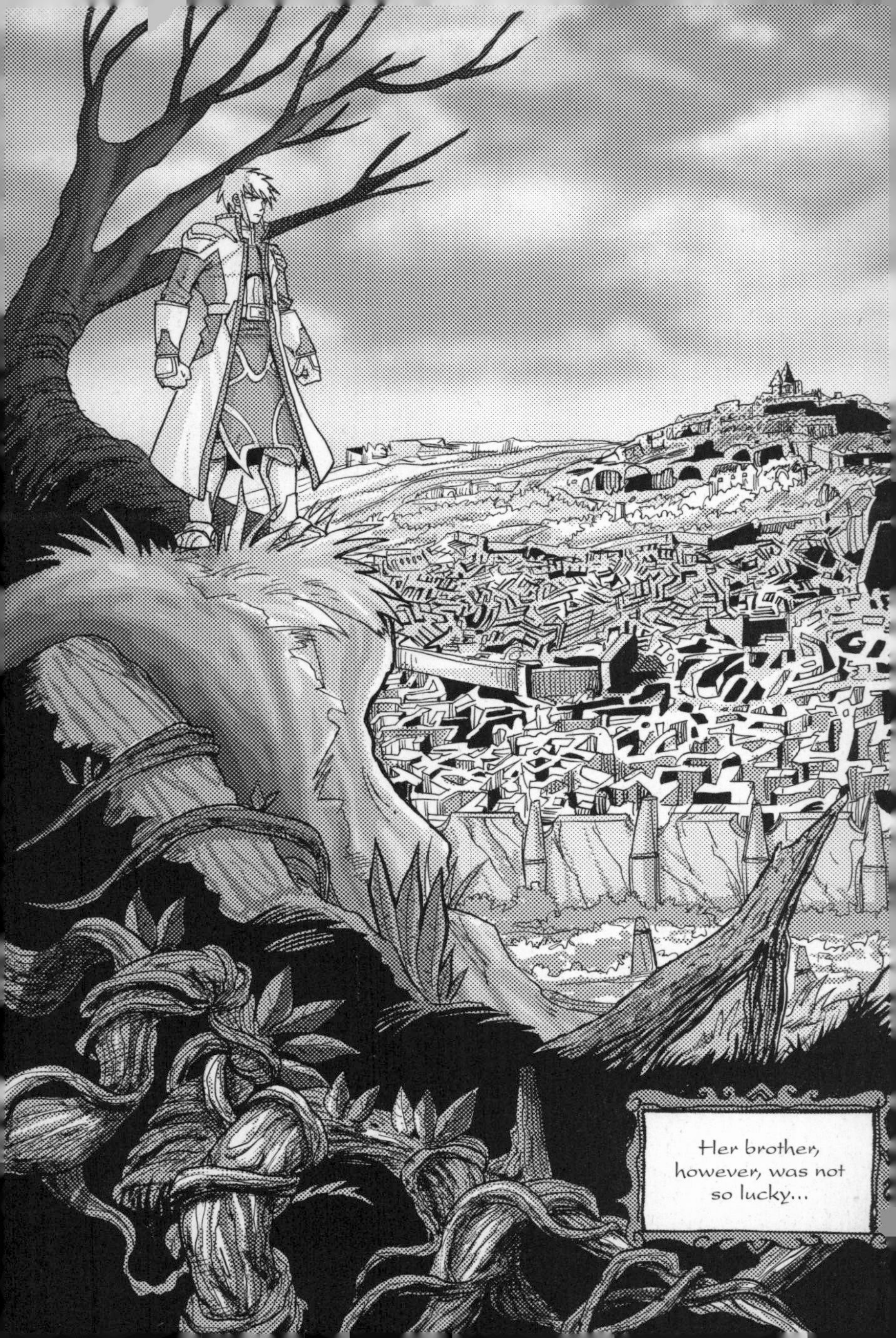
Her brother, however, was not so lucky...

Chapter 1
Bad Luck

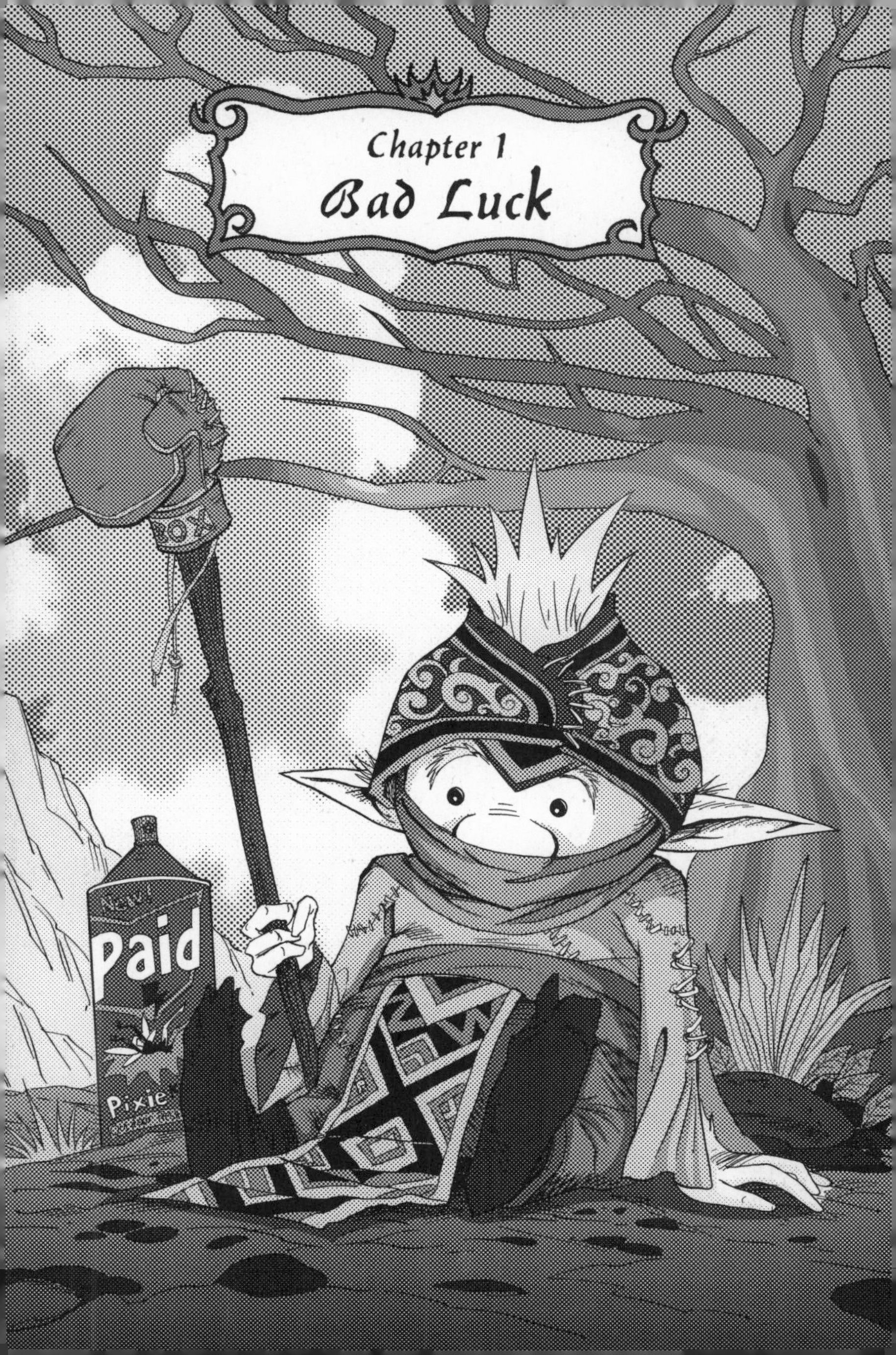
Paid
Pixie

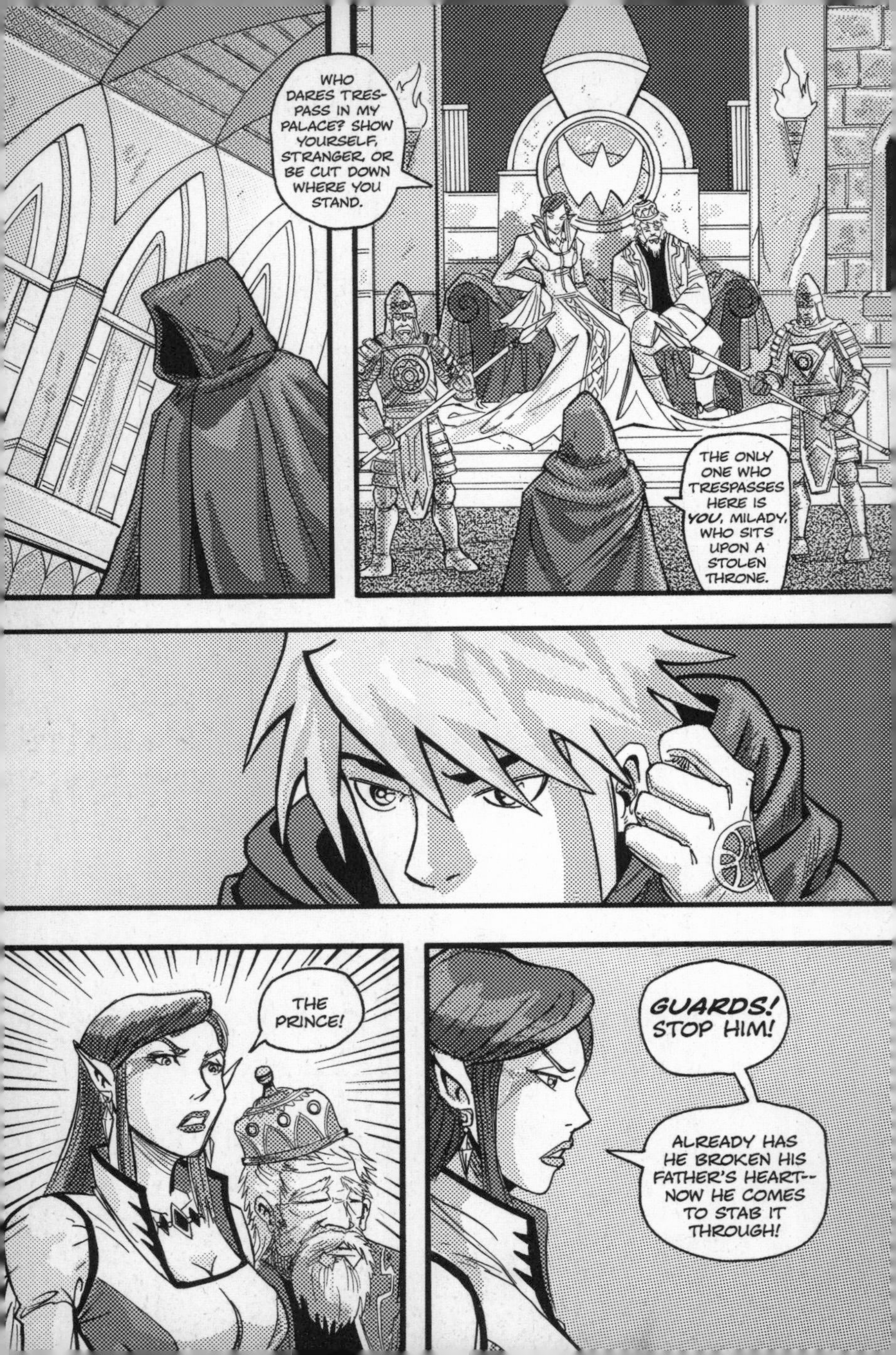
WHO DARES TRES-PASS IN MY PALACE? SHOW YOURSELF, STRANGER, OR BE CUT DOWN WHERE YOU STAND.
THE ONLY ONE WHO TRESPASSES HERE IS *YOU*, MILADY, WHO SITS UPON A STOLEN THRONE.
THE PRINCE!
GUARDS! STOP HIM!
ALREADY HAS HE BROKEN HIS FATHER'S HEART-- NOW HE COMES TO STAB IT THROUGH!

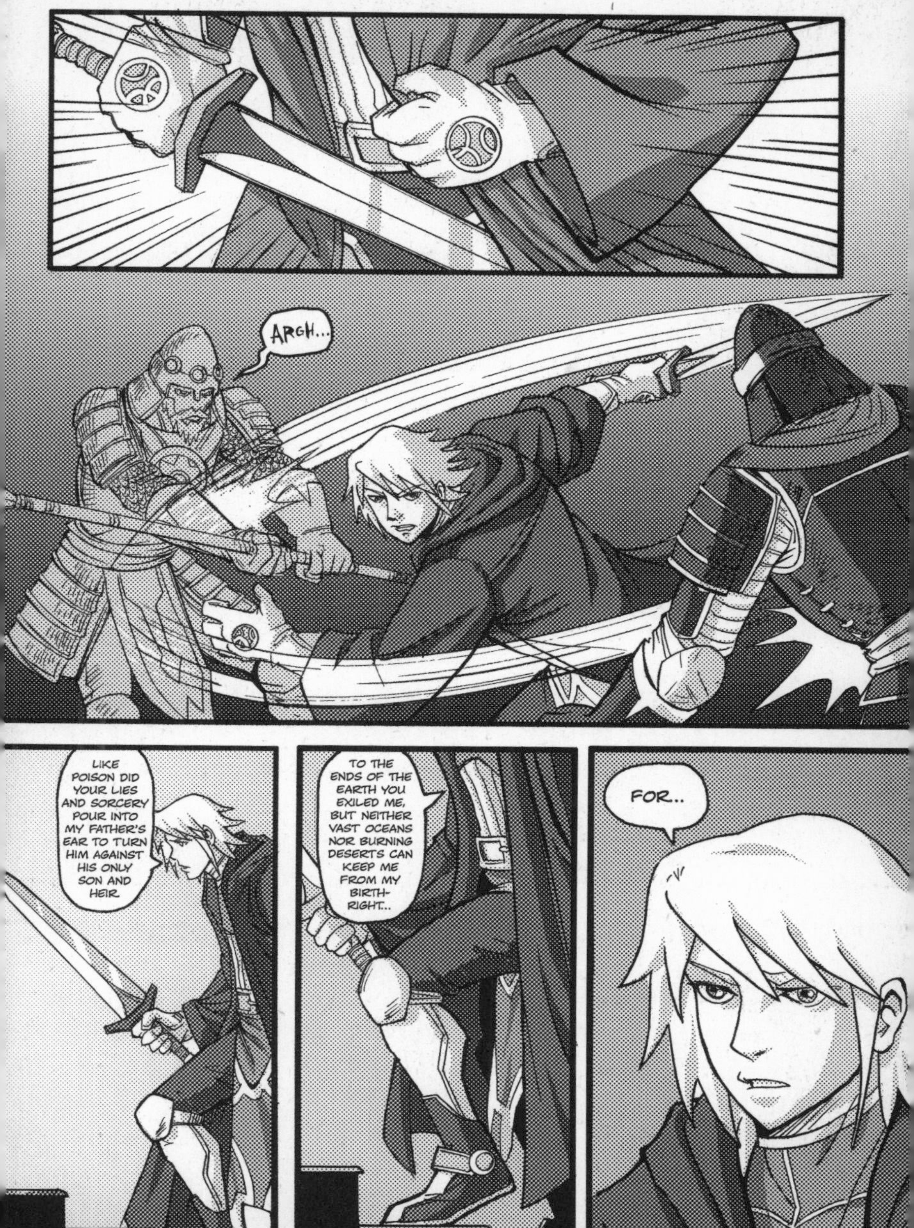
ARGH...
LIKE POISON DID YOUR LIES AND SORCERY POUR INTO MY FATHER'S EAR TO TURN HIM AGAINST HIS ONLY SON AND HEIR
TO THE ENDS OF THE EARTH YOU EXILED ME, BUT NEITHER VAST OCEANS NOR BURNING DESERTS CAN KEEP ME FROM MY BIRTH-RIGHT...
FOR..

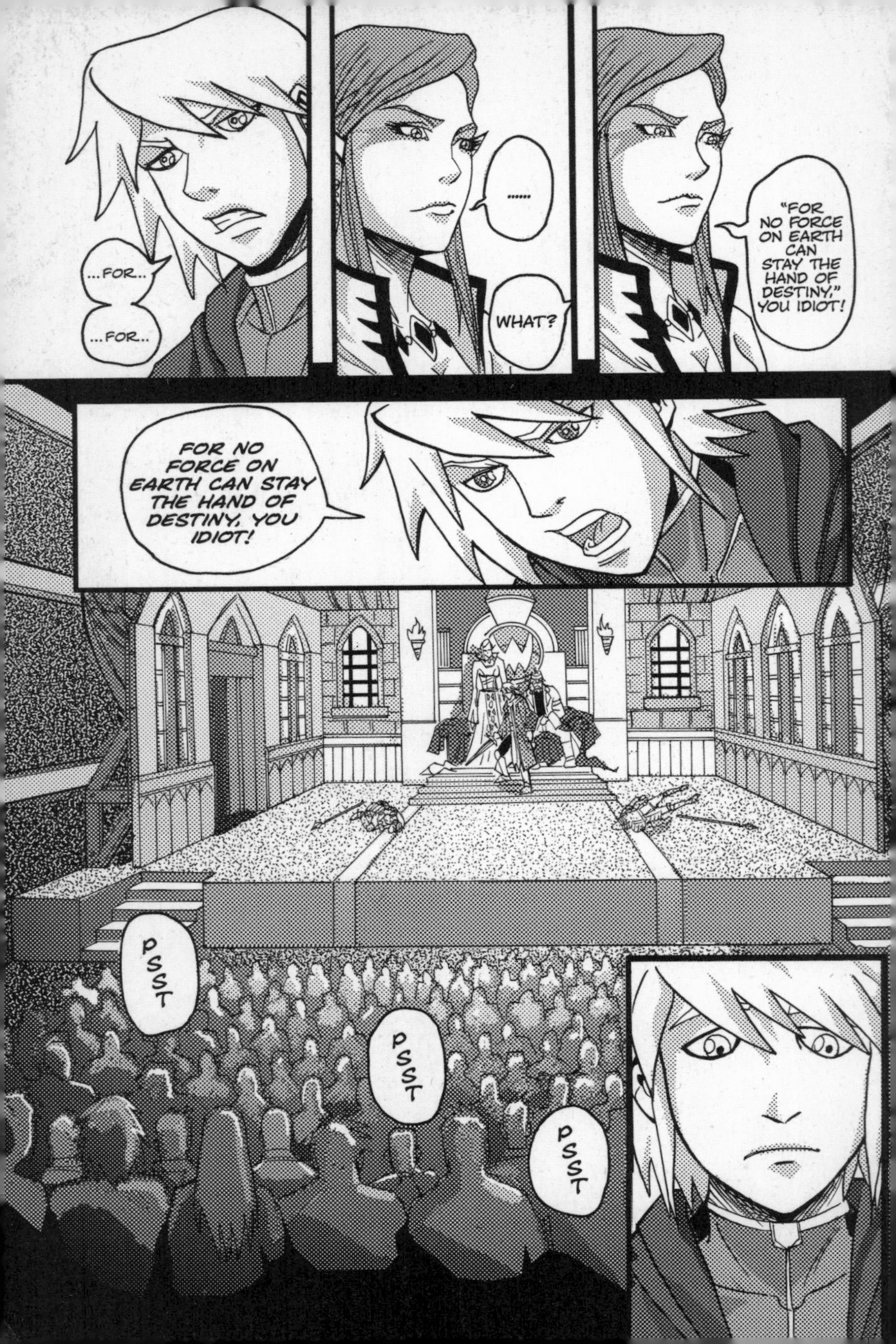
...FOR...
...FOR...
......
WHAT?
"FOR NO FORCE ON EARTH CAN STAY THE HAND OF DESTINY," YOU IDIOT!
FOR NO FORCE ON EARTH CAN STAY THE HAND OF DESTINY, YOU IDIOT!
PSST
PSST
PSST

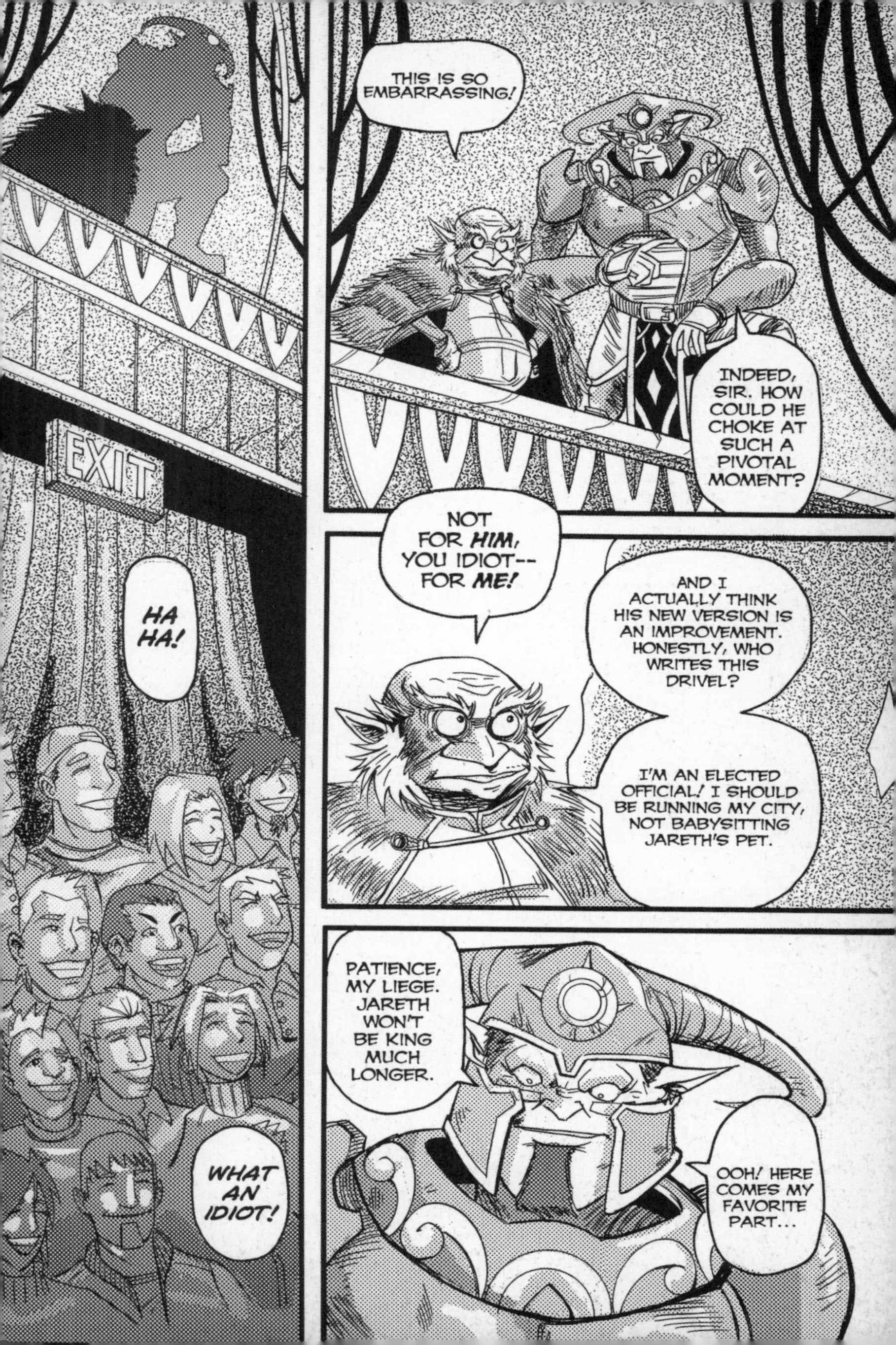
EXIT
HA HA!
WHAT AN IDIOT!
THIS IS SO EMBARRASSING!
INDEED, SIR. HOW COULD HE CHOKE AT SUCH A PIVOTAL MOMENT?
NOT FOR *HIM*, YOU IDIOT-- FOR *ME!*
AND I ACTUALLY THINK HIS NEW VERSION IS AN IMPROVEMENT. HONESTLY, WHO WRITES THIS DRIVEL?
I'M AN ELECTED OFFICIAL! I SHOULD BE RUNNING MY CITY, NOT BABYSITTING JARETH'S PET.
PATIENCE, MY LIEGE. JARETH WON'T BE KING MUCH LONGER.
OOH! HERE COMES MY FAVORITE PART...

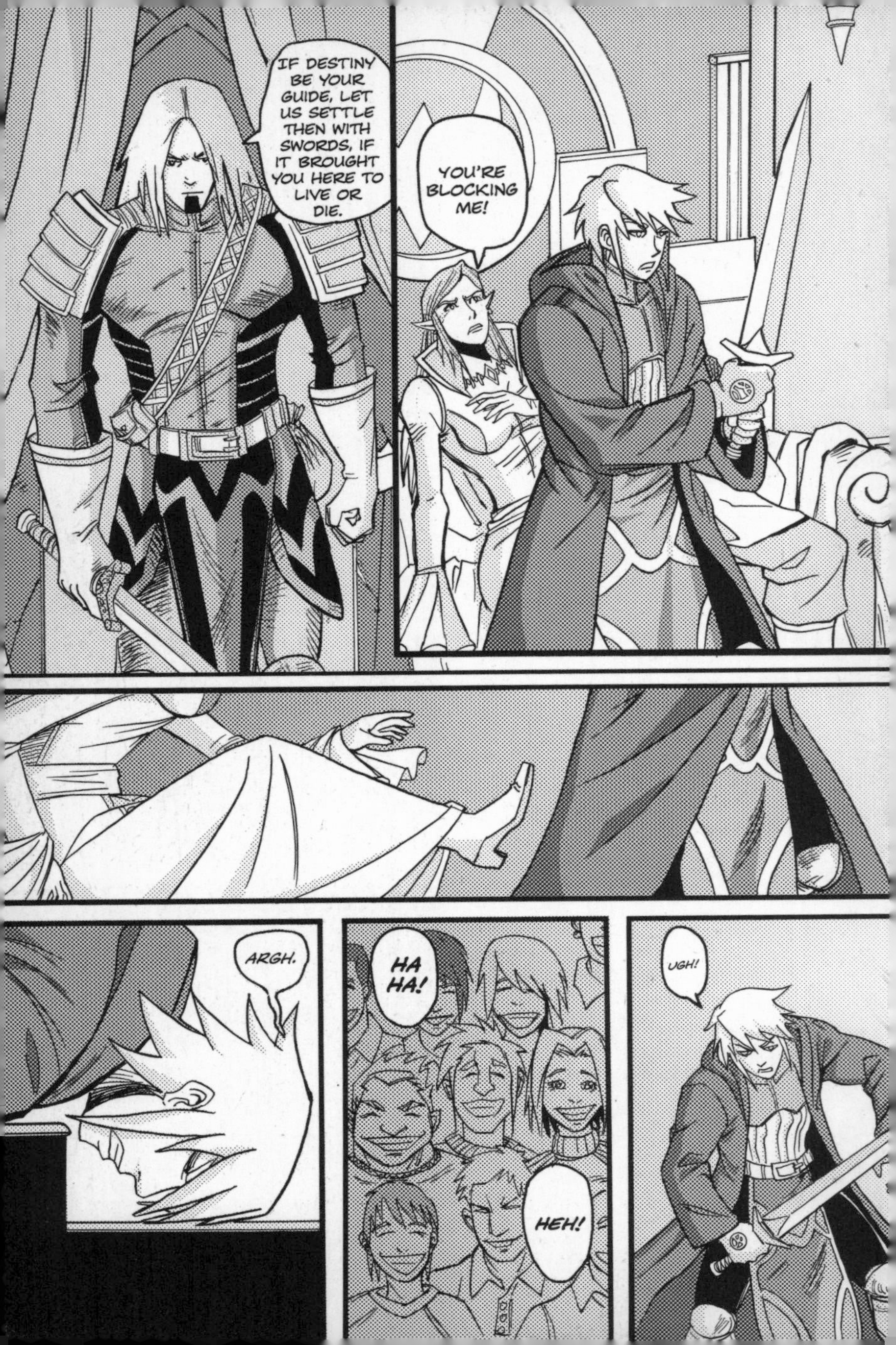
IF DESTINY BE YOUR GUIDE, LET US SETTLE THEN WITH SWORDS, IF IT BROUGHT YOU HERE TO LIVE OR DIE.
YOU'RE BLOCKING ME!
ARGH.
HA HA!
HEH!
UGH!

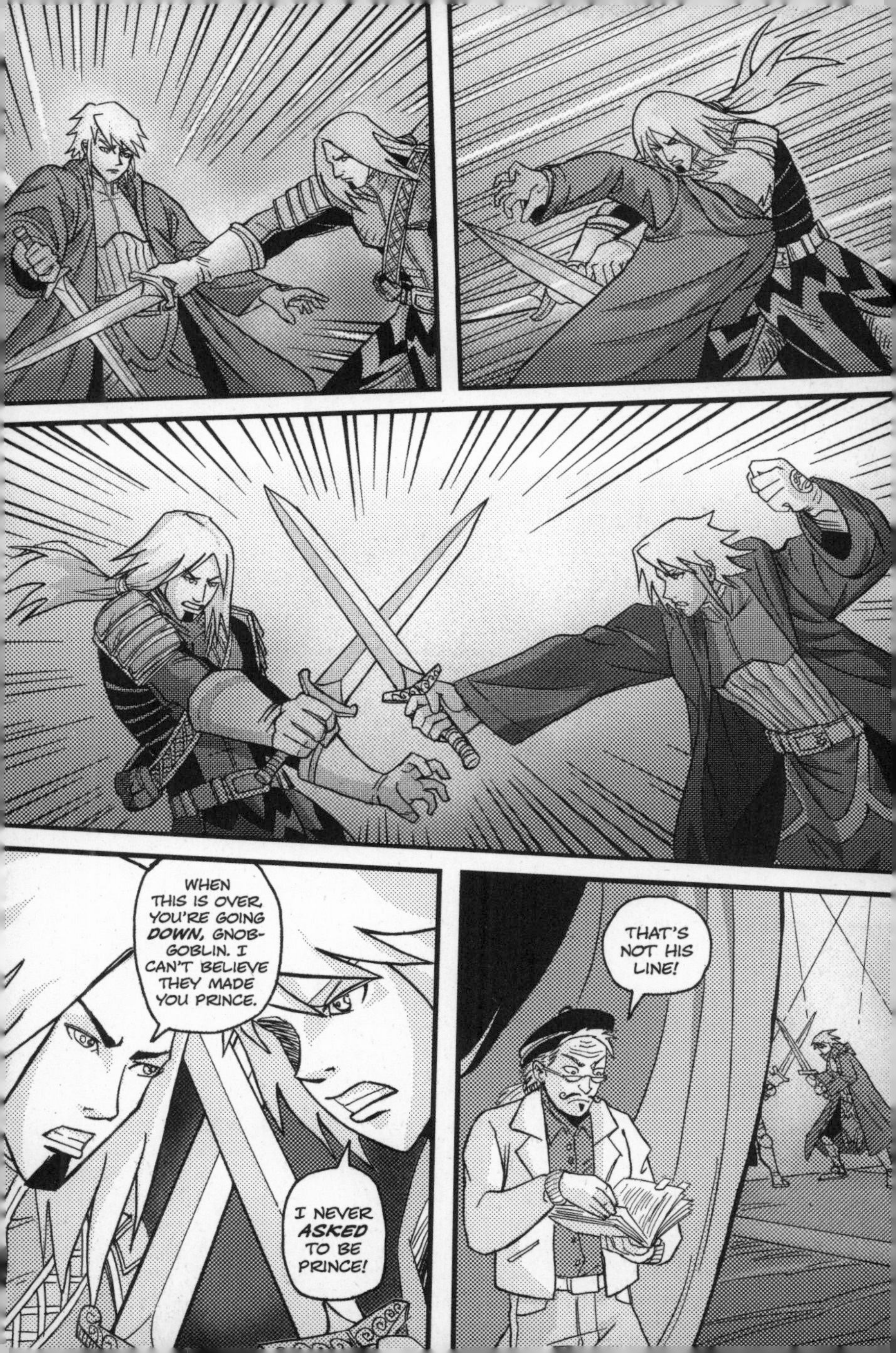
WHEN THIS IS OVER, YOU'RE GOING DOWN, GNOB-GOBLIN. I CAN'T BELIEVE THEY MADE YOU PRINCE.
I NEVER ASKED TO BE PRINCE!
THAT'S NOT HIS LINE!

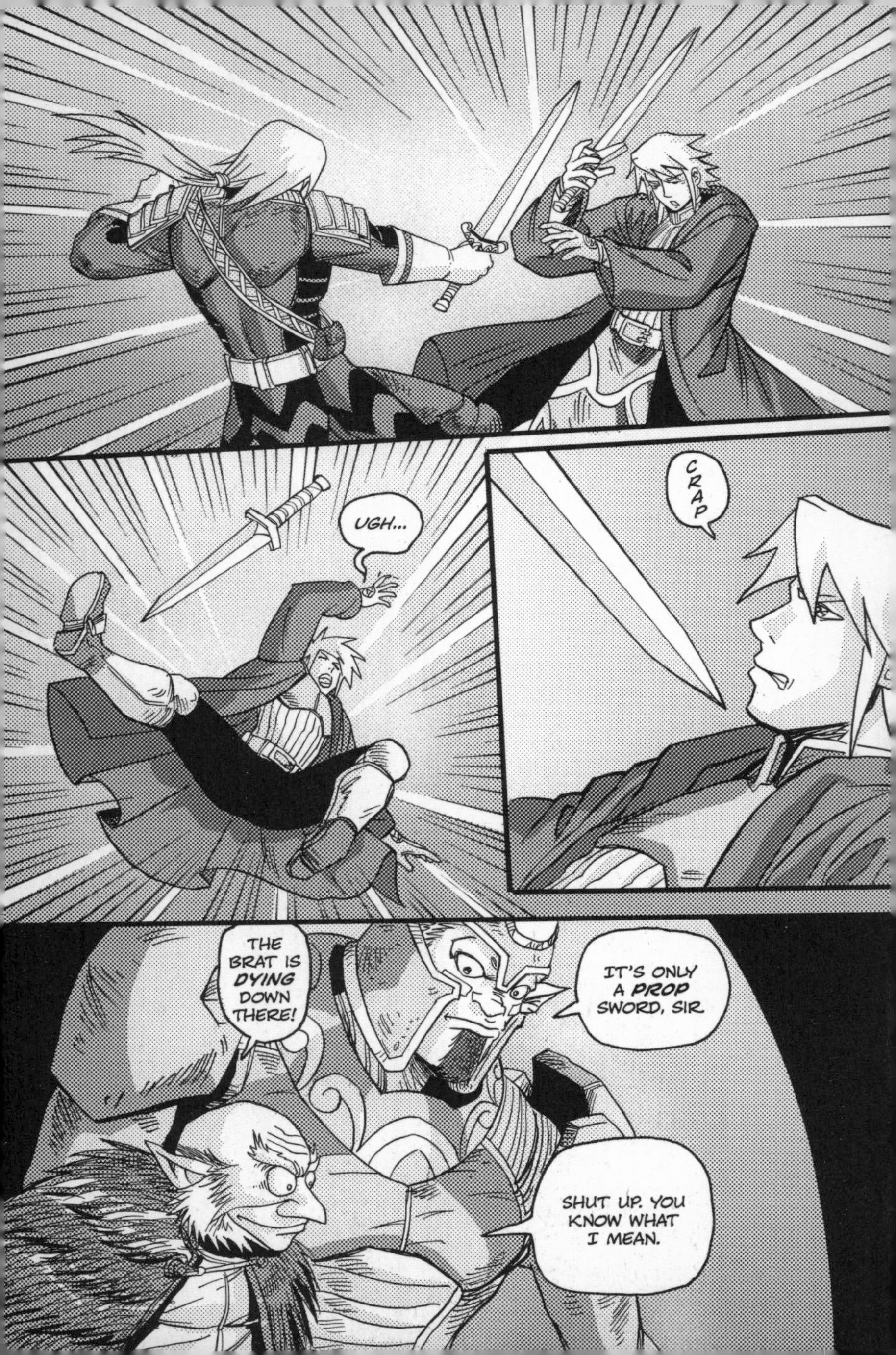
UGH...
CRAP
THE BRAT IS DYING DOWN THERE!
IT'S ONLY A PROP SWORD, SIR
SHUT UP. YOU KNOW WHAT I MEAN.

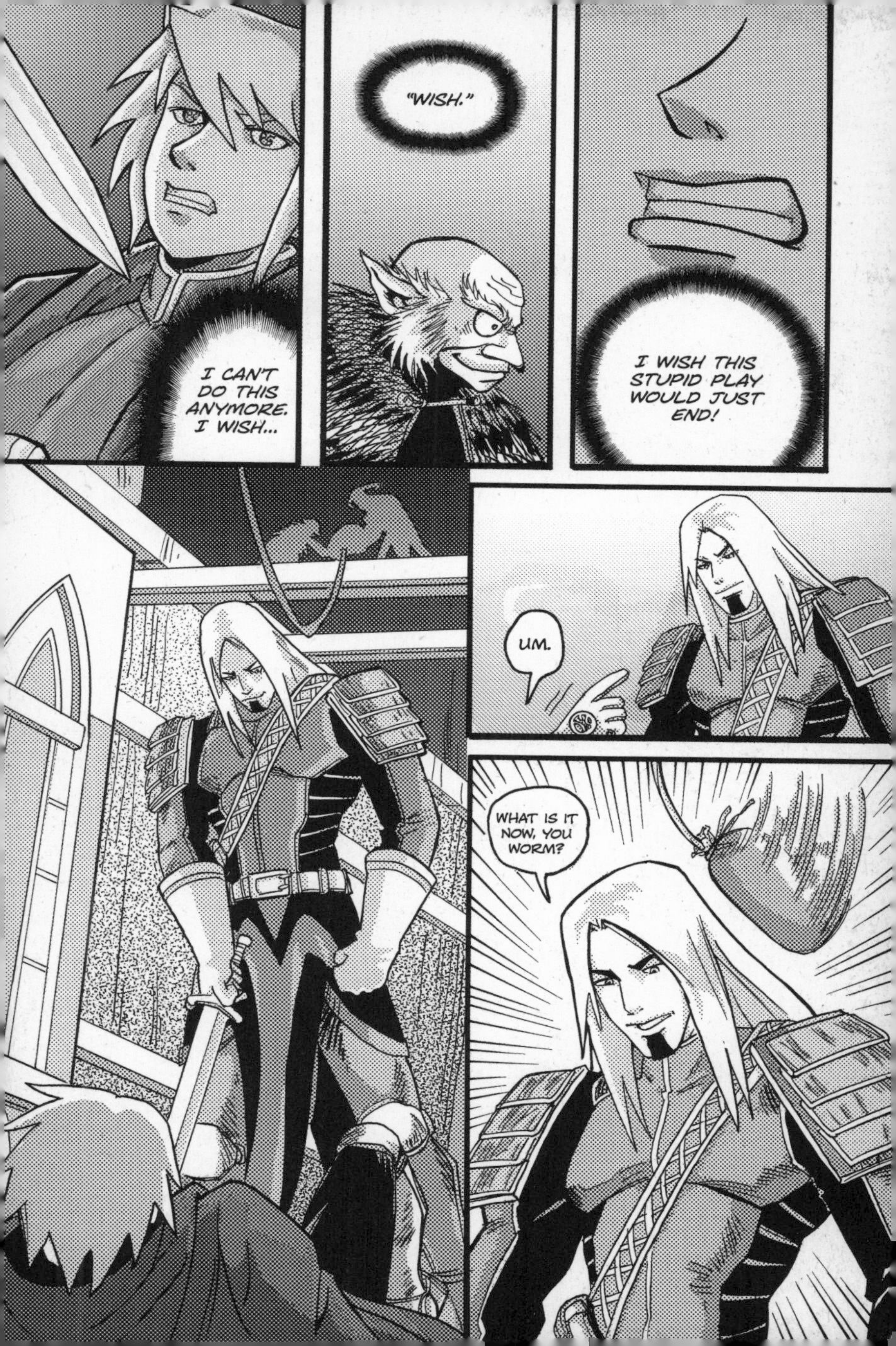
I CAN'T DO THIS ANYMORE. I WISH...
"WISH."
I WISH THIS STUPID PLAY WOULD JUST END!
UM.
WHAT IS IT NOW, YOU WORM?

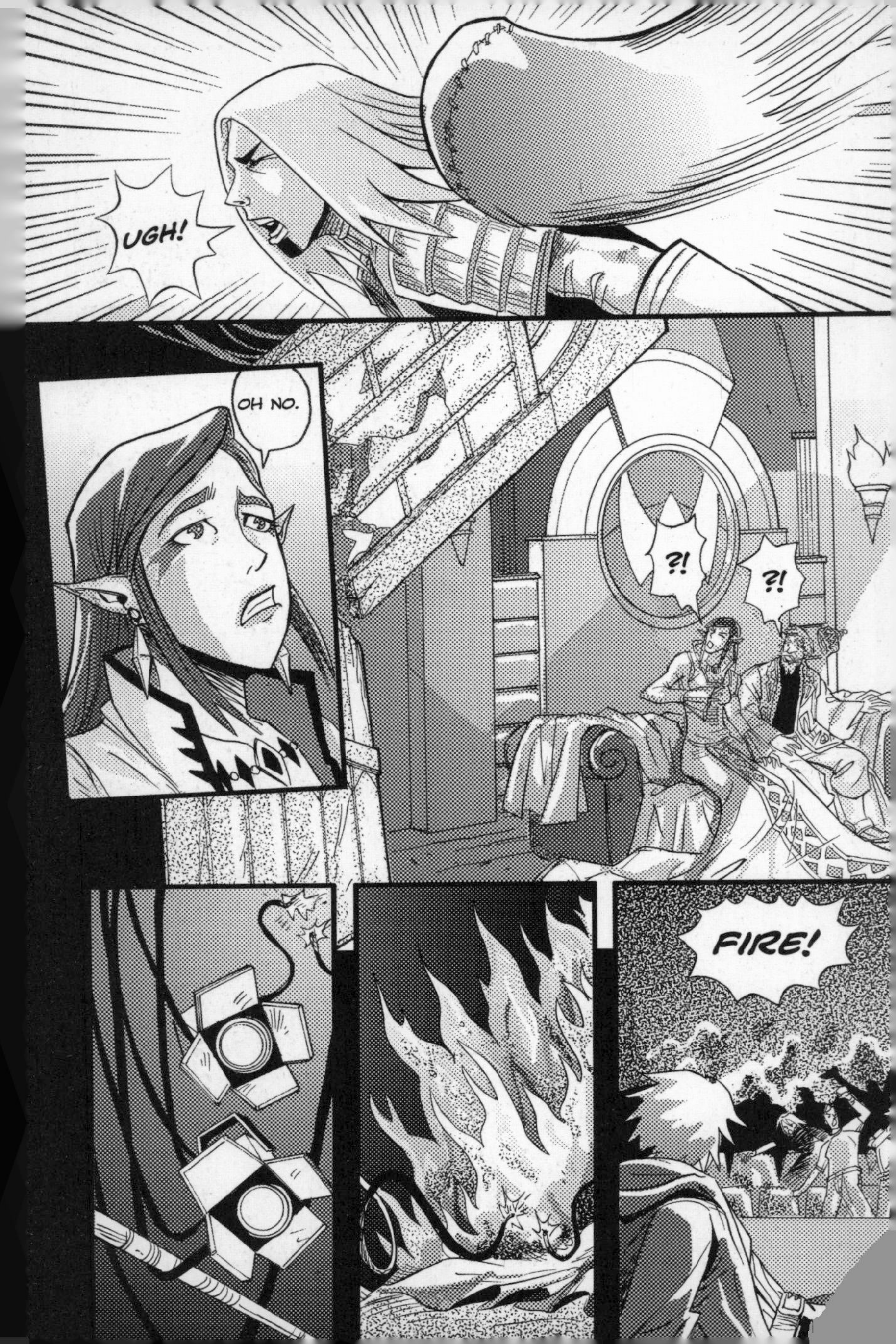
UGH!
OH NO.
?!
?!
FIRE!

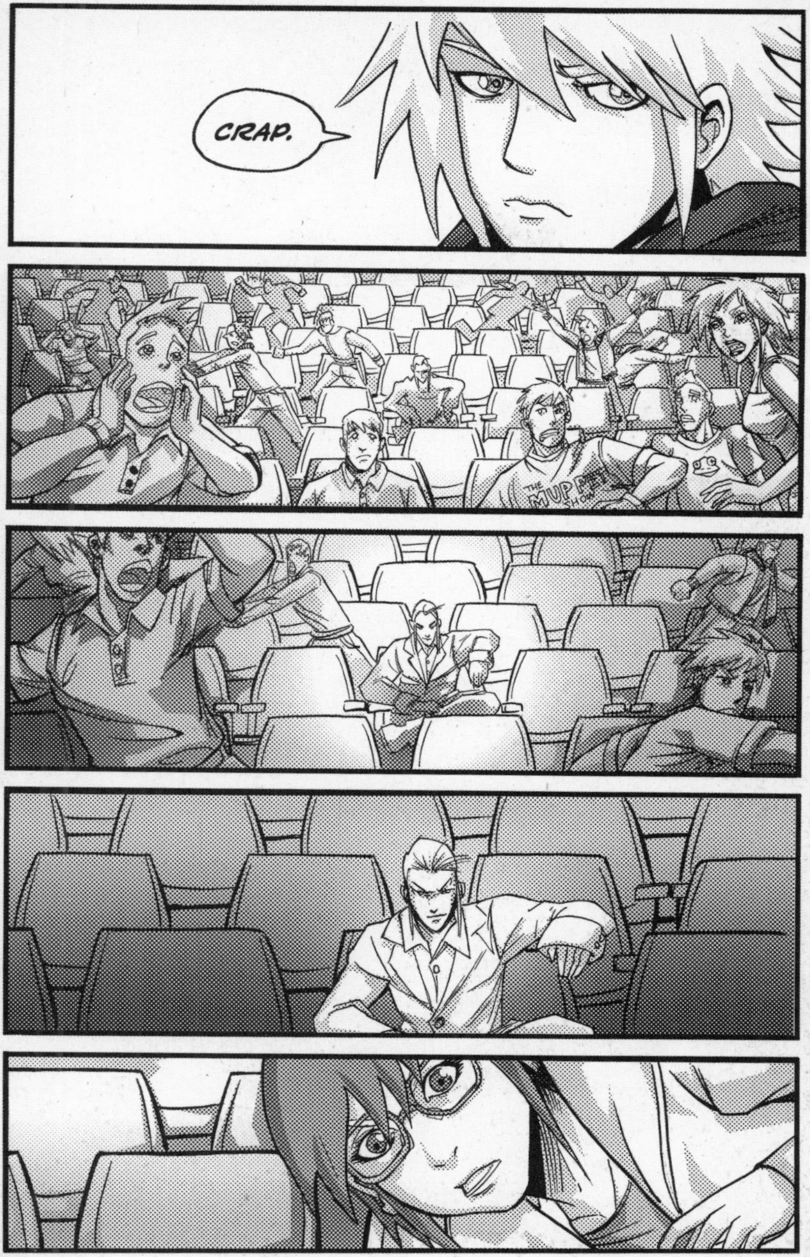
CRAP.

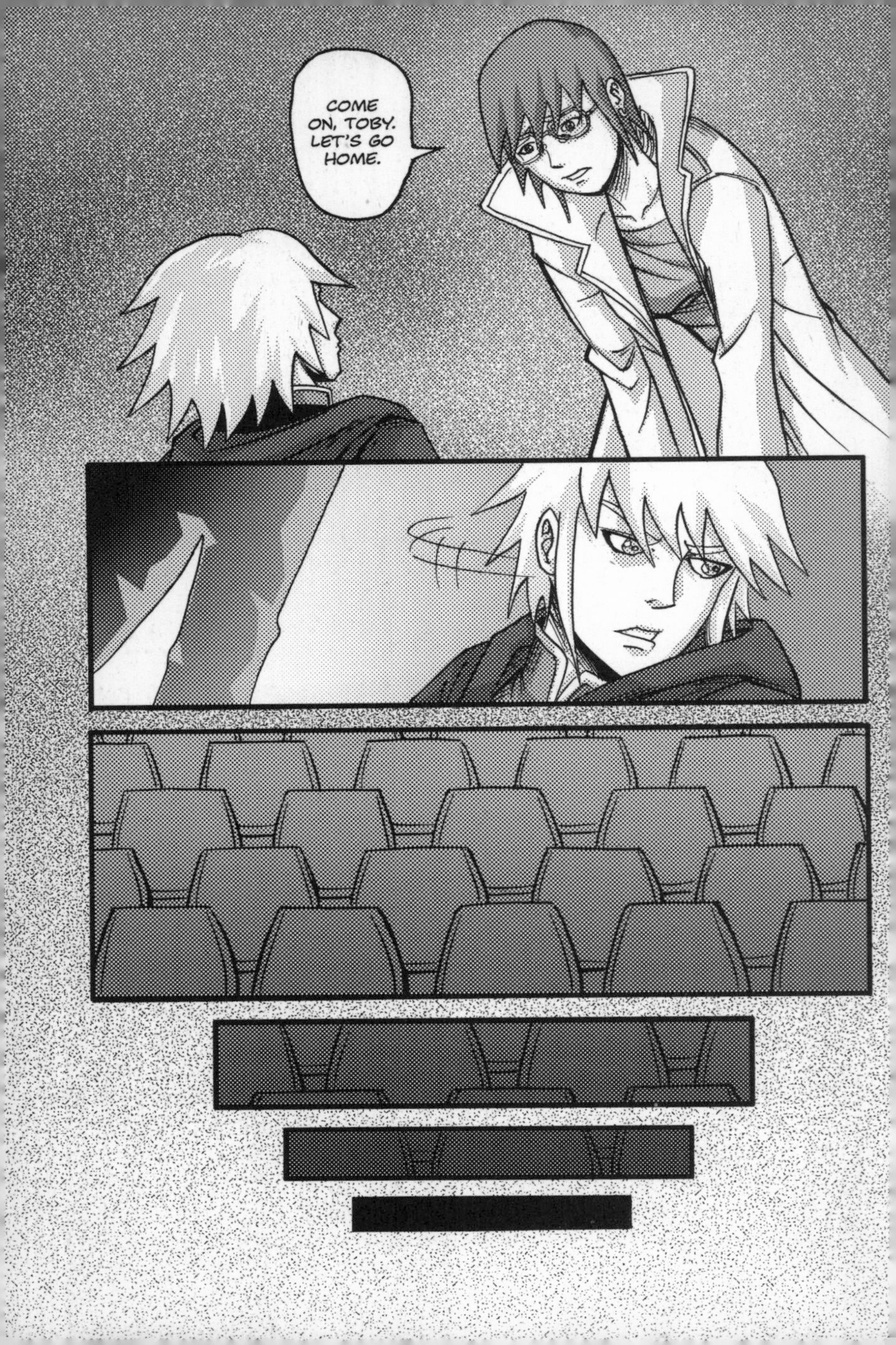
COME ON, TOBY. LET'S GO HOME.

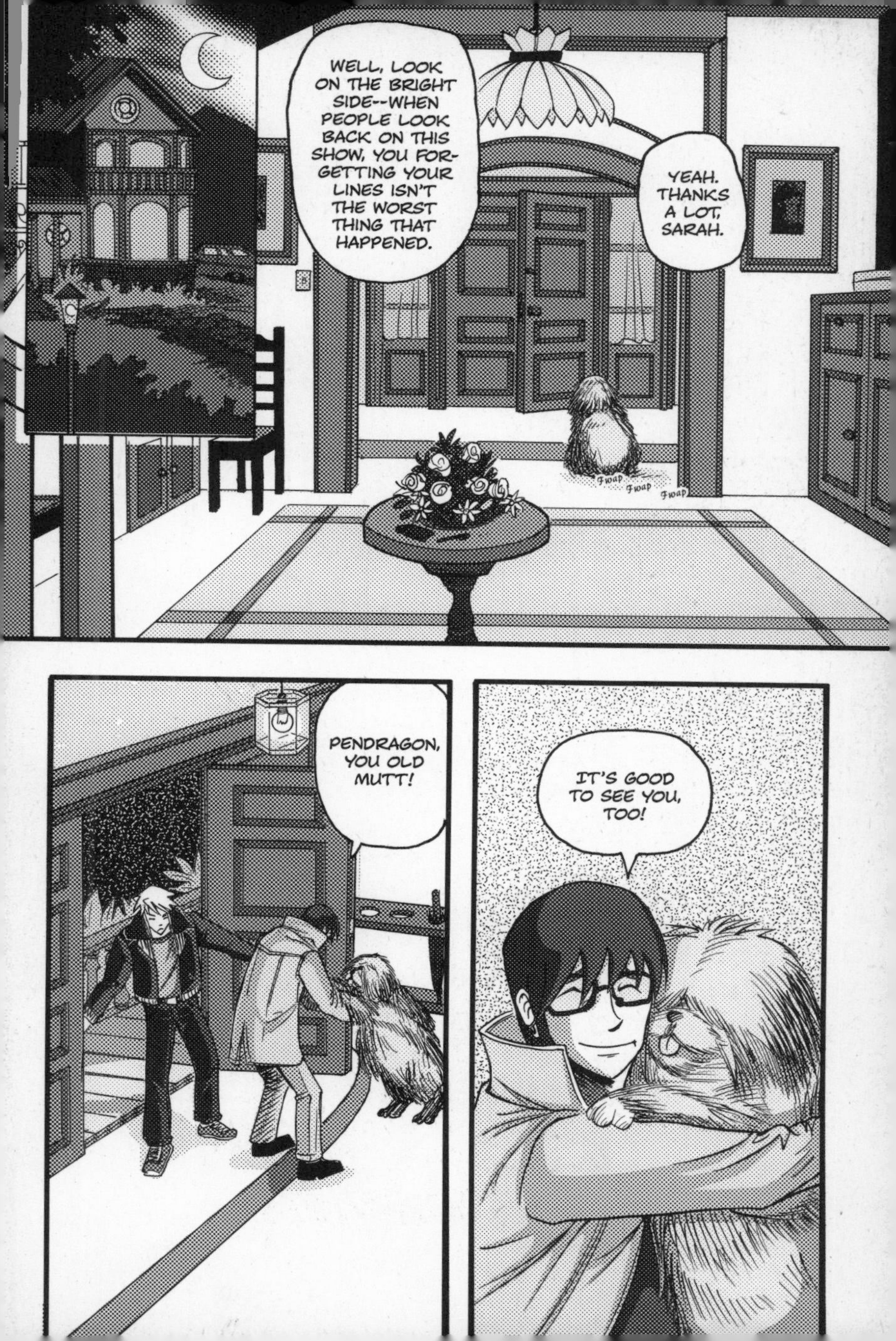
WELL, LOOK ON THE BRIGHT SIDE--WHEN PEOPLE LOOK BACK ON THIS SHOW, YOU FOR-GETTING YOUR LINES ISN'T THE WORST THING THAT HAPPENED.
YEAH. THANKS A LOT, SARAH.
Fwap
Fwap
Fwap
PENDRAGON, YOU OLD MUTT!
IT'S GOOD TO SEE YOU, TOO!

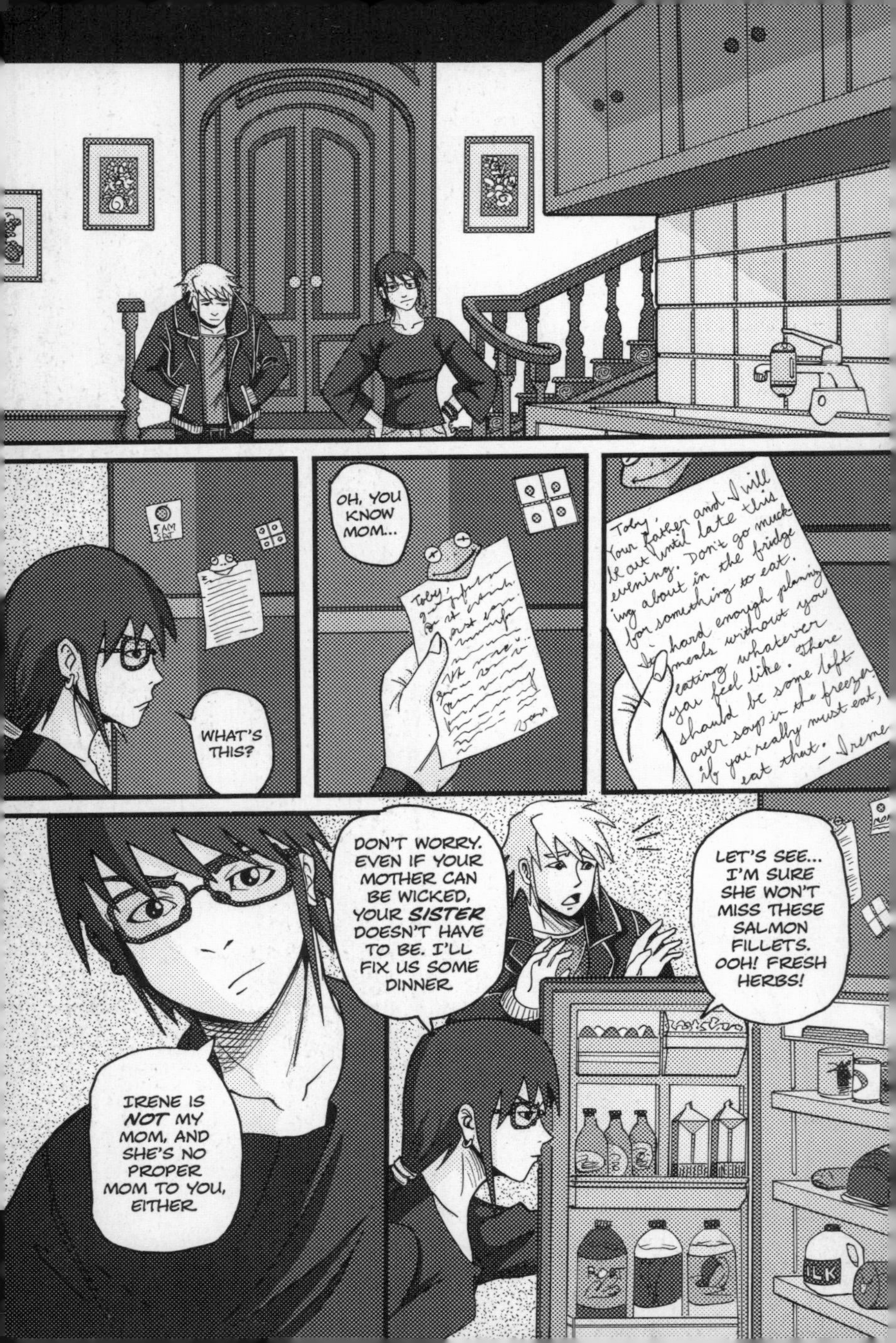
WHAT'S THIS?
OH, YOU KNOW MOM...
Toby,
Your father and I will be out until late this evening. Don't go mucking about in the fridge for something to eat. It's hard enough planning meals without you eating whatever you feel like. There should be some left over soup in the freezer. If you really must eat, eat that. —Irene
IRENE IS NOT MY MOM, AND SHE'S NO PROPER MOM TO YOU, EITHER
DON'T WORRY. EVEN IF YOUR MOTHER CAN BE WICKED, YOUR SISTER DOESN'T HAVE TO BE. I'LL FIX US SOME DINNER
LET'S SEE... I'M SURE SHE WON'T MISS THESE SALMON FILLETS. OOH! FRESH HERBS!

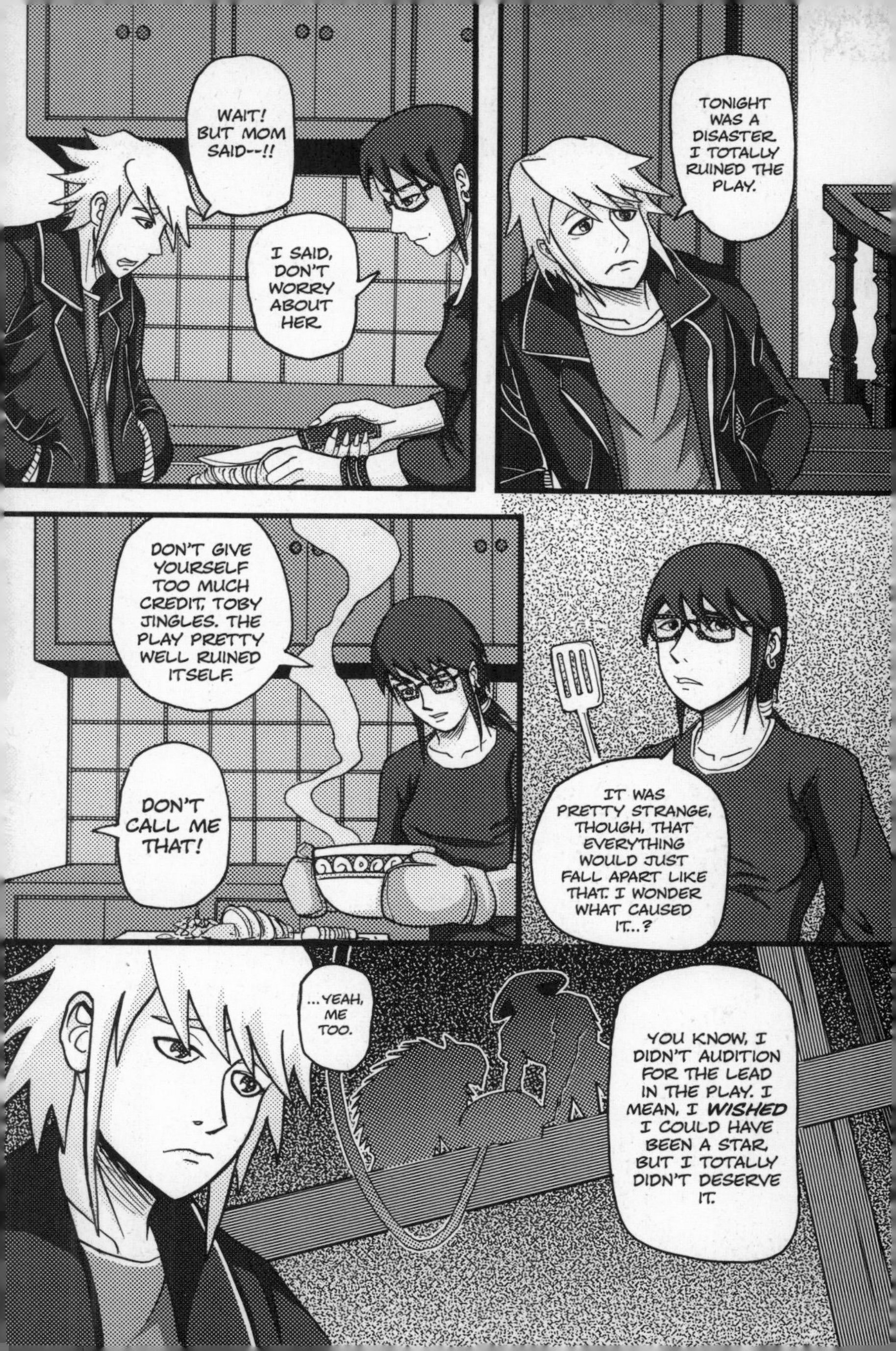
WAIT! BUT MOM SAID--!!
I SAID, DON'T WORRY ABOUT HER
TONIGHT WAS A DISASTER. I TOTALLY RUINED THE PLAY.
DON'T GIVE YOURSELF TOO MUCH CREDIT, TOBY JINGLES. THE PLAY PRETTY WELL RUINED ITSELF.
DON'T CALL ME THAT!
IT WAS PRETTY STRANGE, THOUGH, THAT EVERYTHING WOULD JUST FALL APART LIKE THAT. I WONDER WHAT CAUSED IT...?
...YEAH, ME TOO.
YOU KNOW, I DIDN'T AUDITION FOR THE LEAD IN THE PLAY. I MEAN, I *WISHED* I COULD HAVE BEEN A STAR, BUT I TOTALLY DIDN'T DESERVE IT.

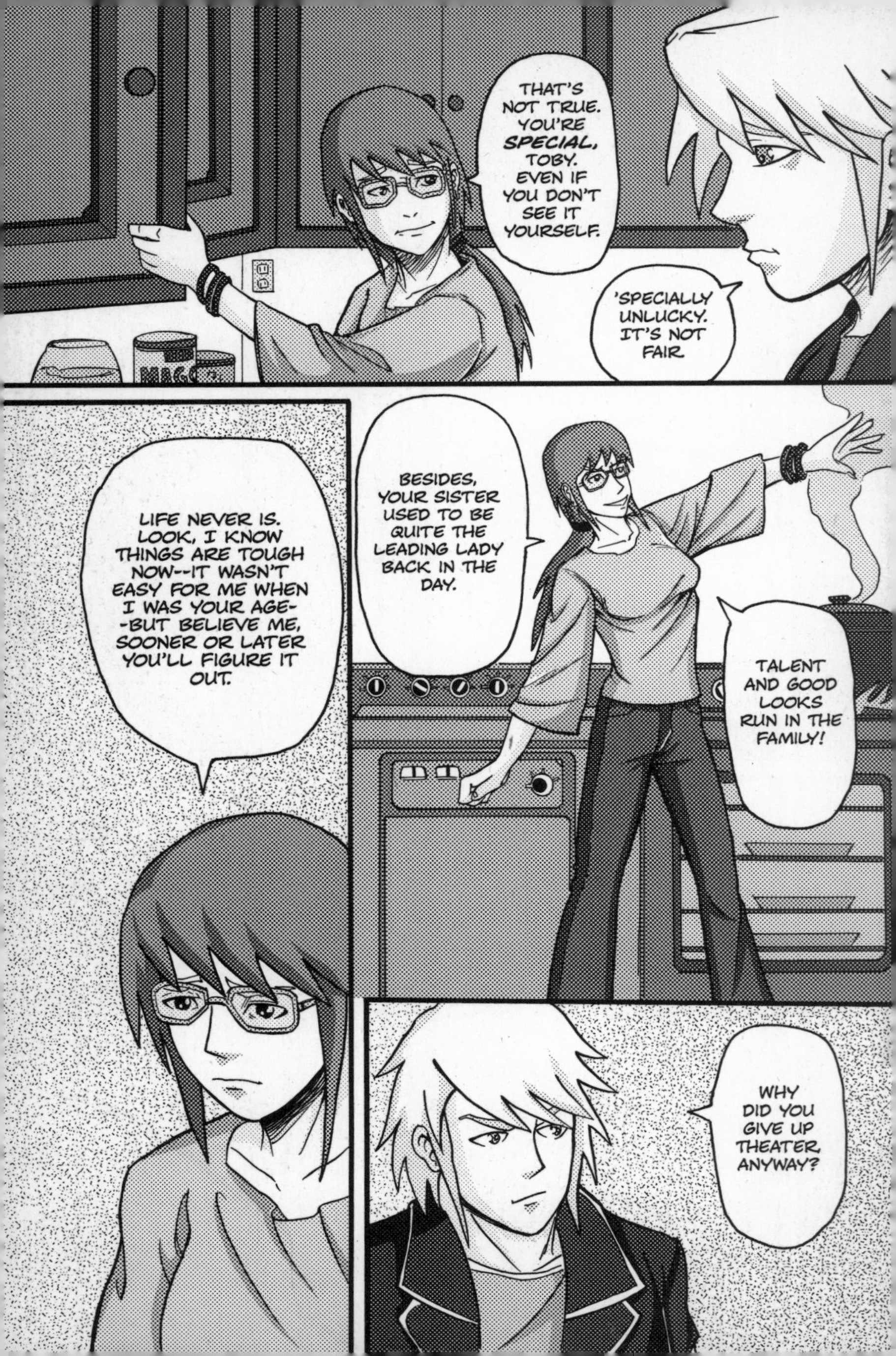
THAT'S NOT TRUE. YOU'RE *SPECIAL,* TOBY. EVEN IF YOU DON'T SEE IT YOURSELF.
'SPECIALLY UNLUCKY. IT'S NOT FAIR
LIFE NEVER IS. LOOK, I KNOW THINGS ARE TOUGH NOW--IT WASN'T EASY FOR ME WHEN I WAS YOUR AGE--BUT BELIEVE ME, SOONER OR LATER YOU'LL FIGURE IT OUT.
BESIDES, YOUR SISTER USED TO BE QUITE THE LEADING LADY BACK IN THE DAY.
TALENT AND GOOD LOOKS RUN IN THE FAMILY!
WHY DID YOU GIVE UP THEATER, ANYWAY?

...I GUESS I JUST GREW UP. YOU CAN'T LIVE IN A FAIRY TALE FOREVER

VOILA! A MEAL FIT FOR A *PRINCE.*

YOU'RE SUCH A DORK, SARAH.

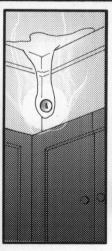

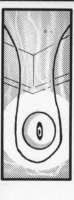

27

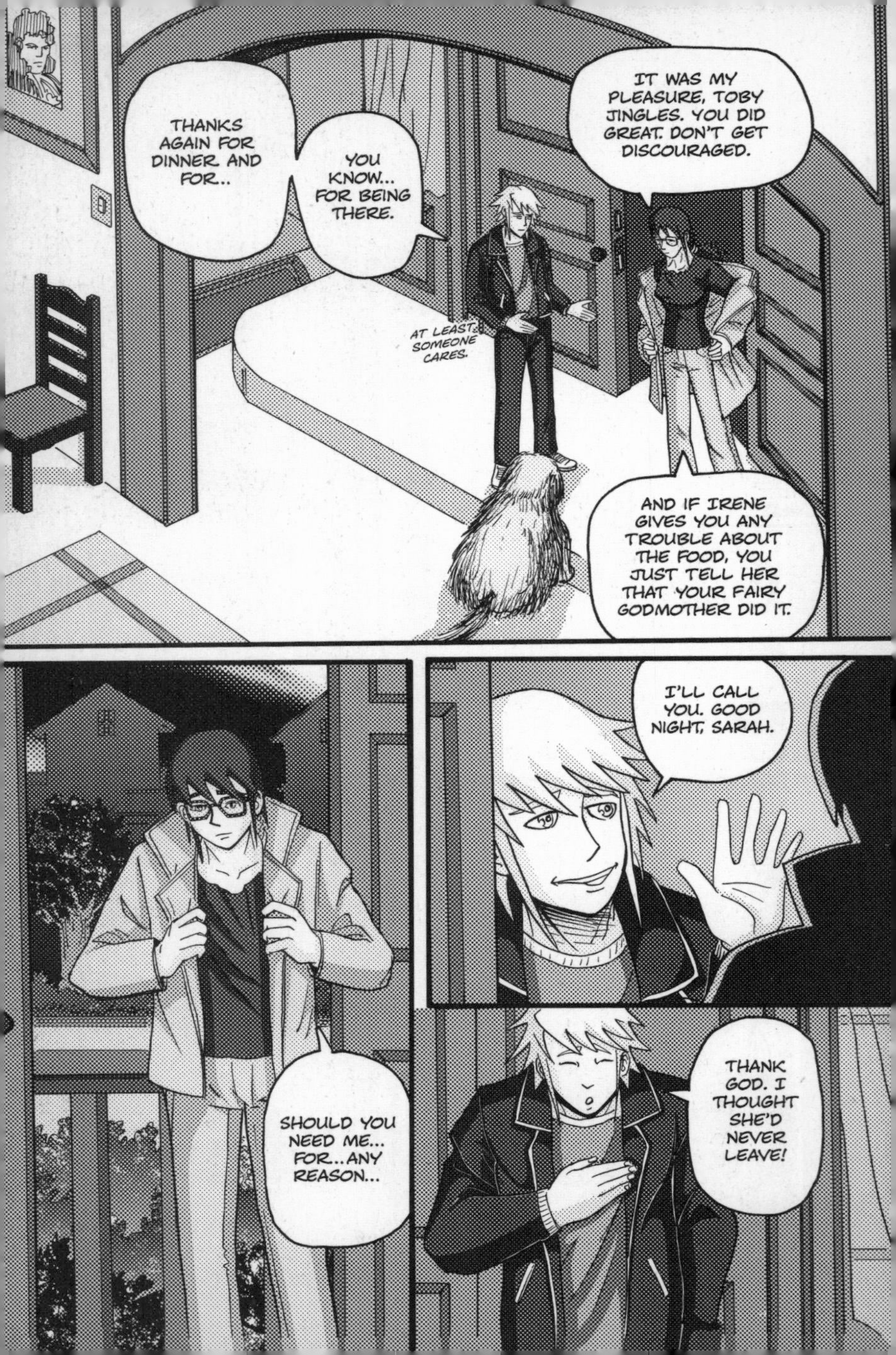
THANKS AGAIN FOR DINNER AND FOR..
YOU KNOW... FOR BEING THERE.
AT LEAST SOMEONE CARES.
IT WAS MY PLEASURE, TOBY JINGLES. YOU DID GREAT. DON'T GET DISCOURAGED.
AND IF IRENE GIVES YOU ANY TROUBLE ABOUT THE FOOD, YOU JUST TELL HER THAT YOUR FAIRY GODMOTHER DID IT.
SHOULD YOU NEED ME... FOR...ANY REASON...
I'LL CALL YOU. GOOD NIGHT, SARAH.
THANK GOD. I THOUGHT SHE'D NEVER LEAVE!

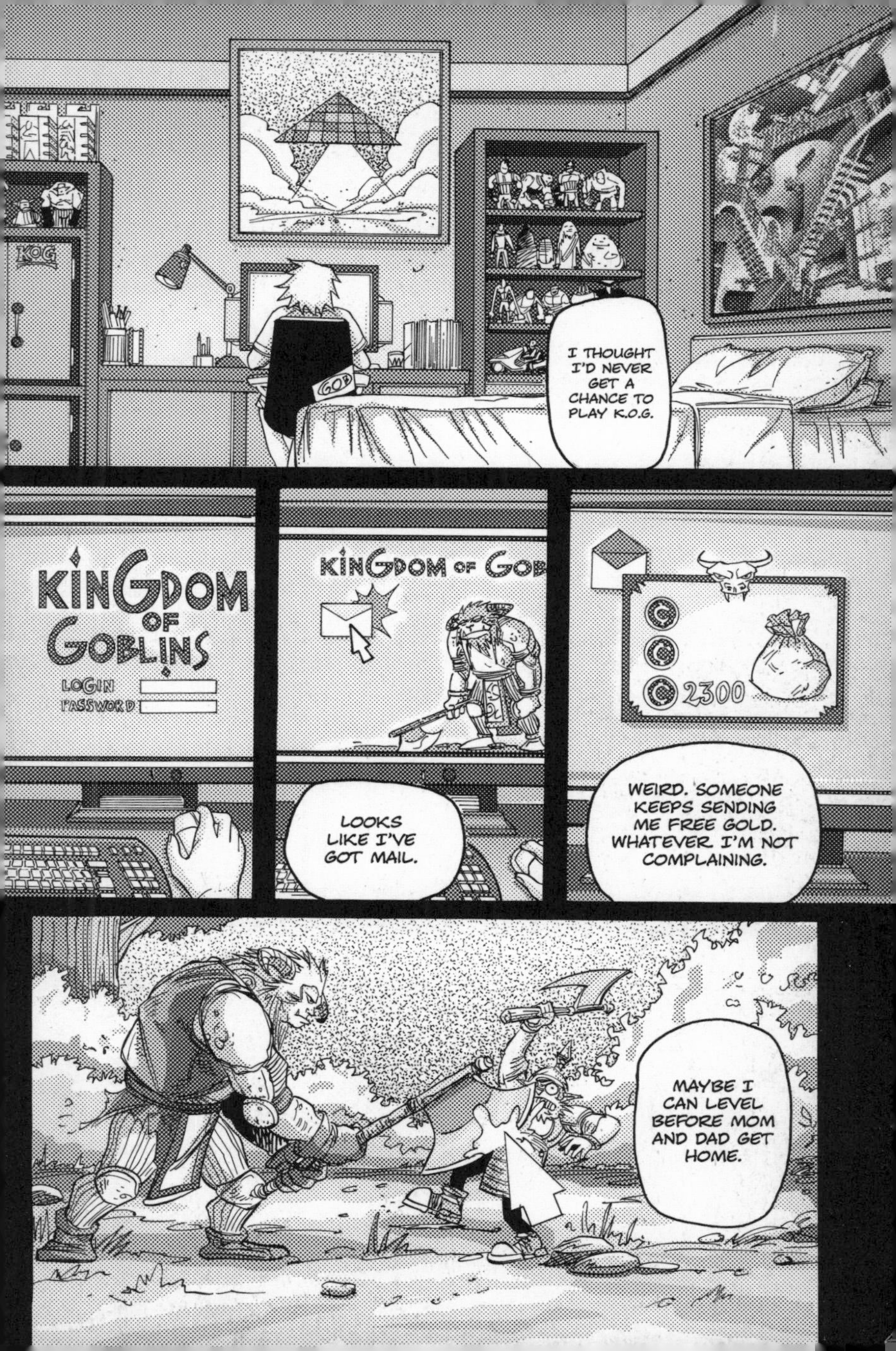
KOG
GOB
I THOUGHT I'D NEVER GET A CHANCE TO PLAY K.O.G.
KINGDOM OF GOBLINS
LOGIN
PASSWORD
KINGDOM OF GOB
LOOKS LIKE I'VE GOT MAIL.
2300
WEIRD. SOMEONE KEEPS SENDING ME FREE GOLD. WHATEVER I'M NOT COMPLAINING.
MAYBE I CAN LEVEL BEFORE MOM AND DAD GET HOME.

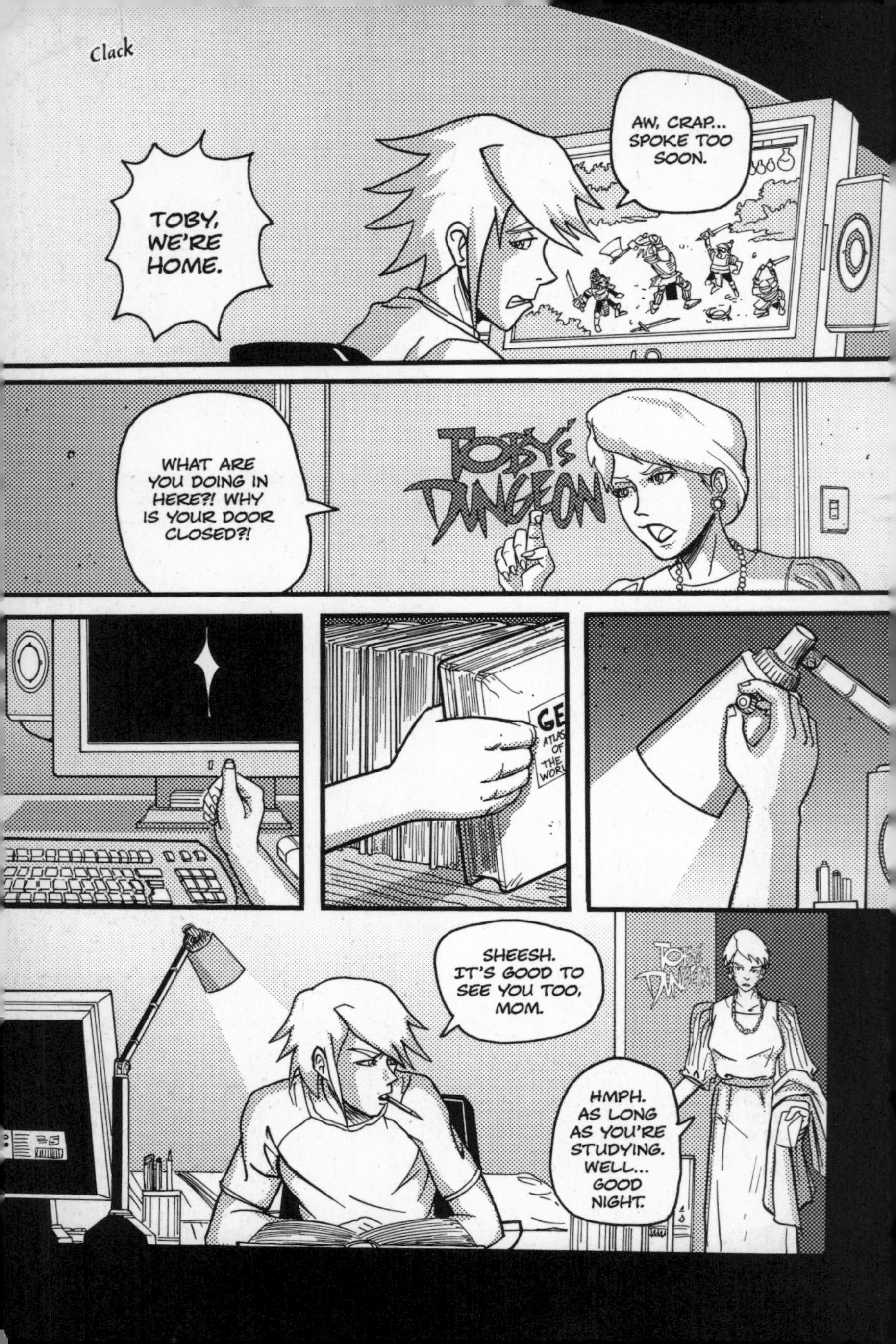
Clack
TOBY, WE'RE HOME.
AW, CRAP... SPOKE TOO SOON.
WHAT ARE YOU DOING IN HERE?! WHY IS YOUR DOOR CLOSED?!
TOBY'S DUNGEON
GE ATLAS OF THE WORL
SHEESH. IT'S GOOD TO SEE YOU TOO, MOM.
HMPH. AS LONG AS YOU'RE STUDYING. WELL... GOOD NIGHT.

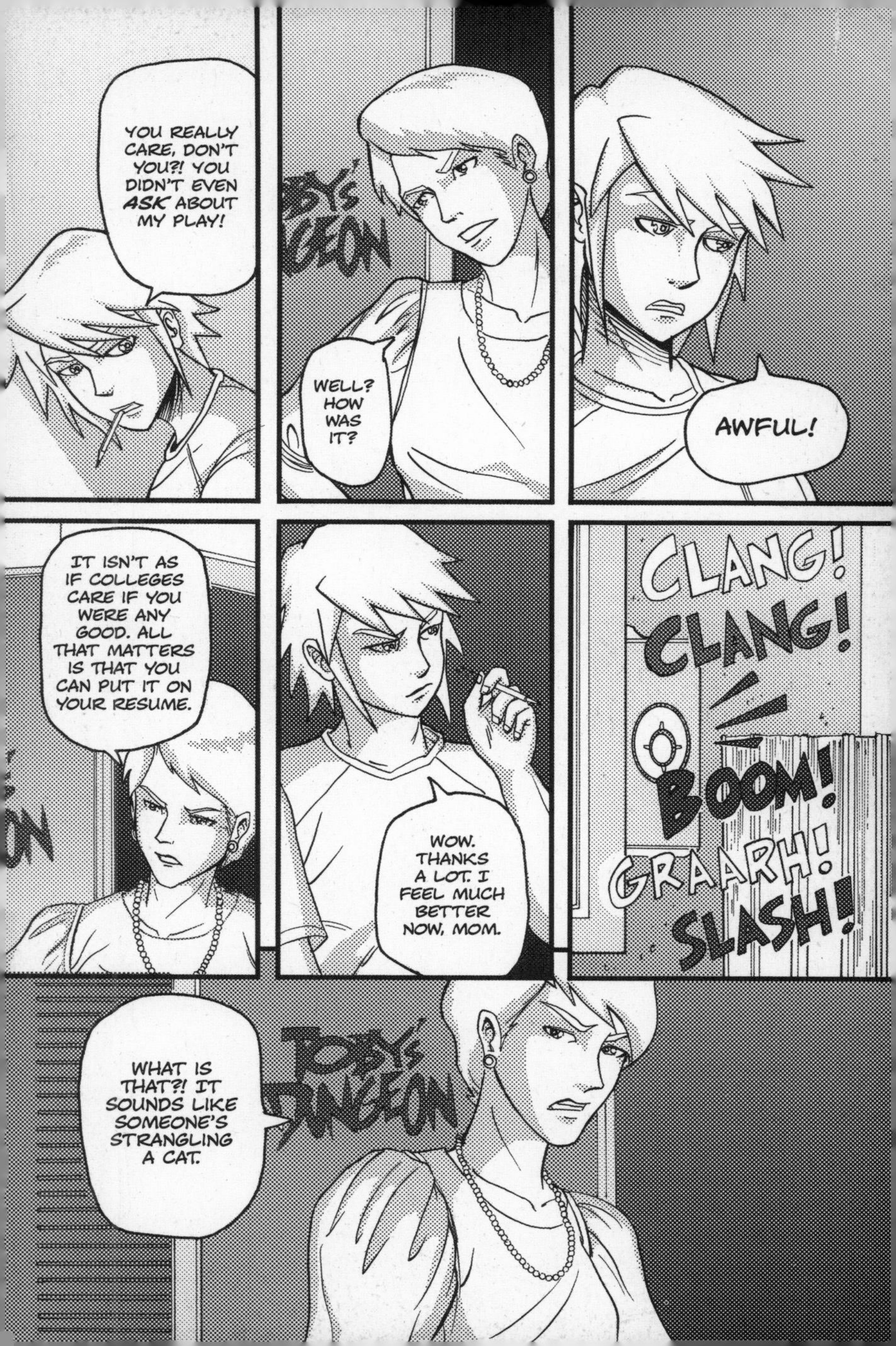
YOU REALLY CARE, DON'T YOU?! YOU DIDN'T EVEN ASK ABOUT MY PLAY!
WELL? HOW WAS IT?
AWFUL!
IT ISN'T AS IF COLLEGES CARE IF YOU WERE ANY GOOD. ALL THAT MATTERS IS THAT YOU CAN PUT IT ON YOUR RESUME.
WOW. THANKS A LOT. I FEEL MUCH BETTER NOW, MOM.
CLANG! CLANG!
BOOM!
GRAARH!
SLASH!
TOBY'S DUNGEON
WHAT IS THAT?! IT SOUNDS LIKE SOMEONE'S STRANGLING A CAT.

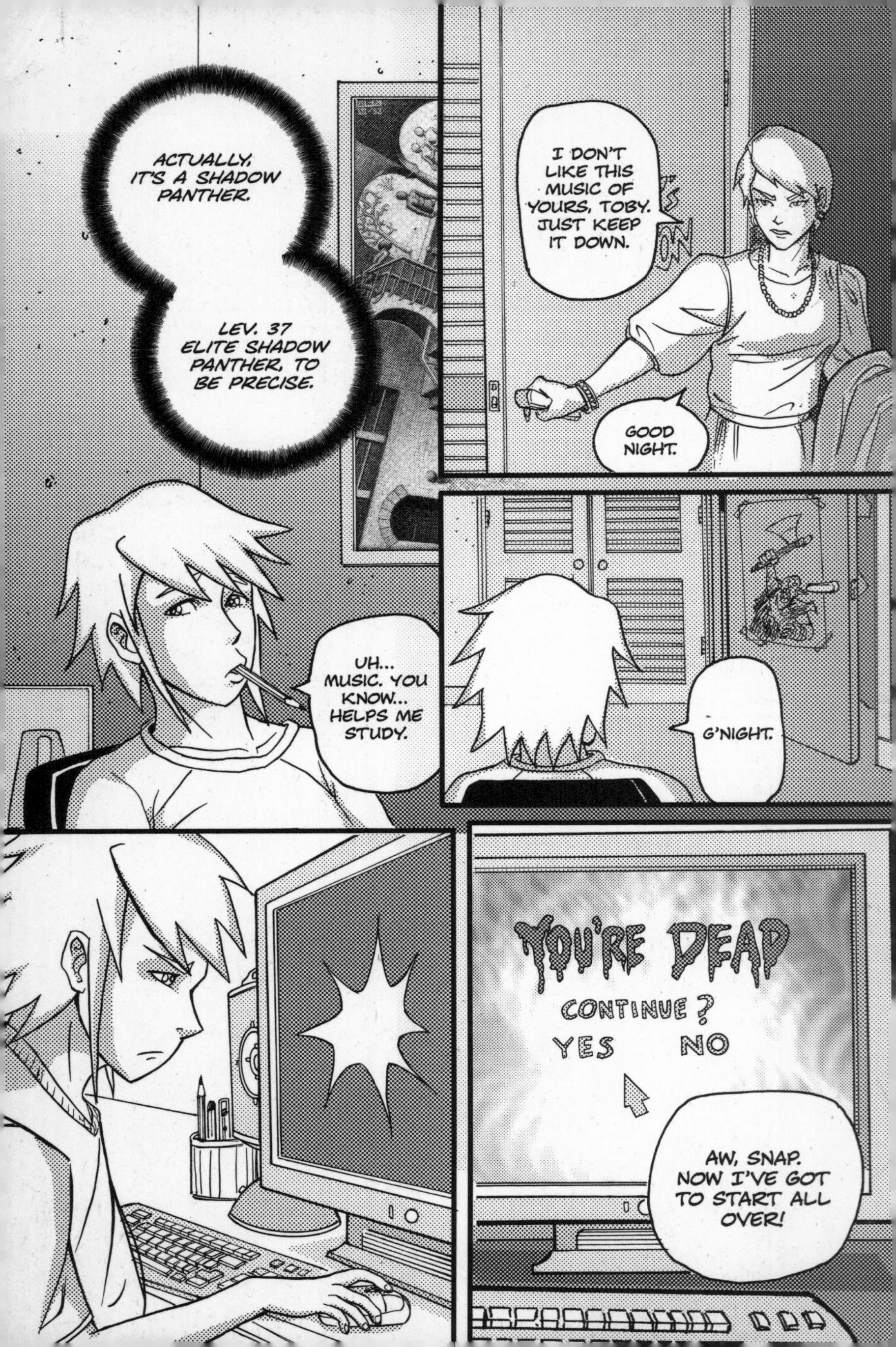
ACTUALLY, IT'S A SHADOW PANTHER.
LEV. 37 ELITE SHADOW PANTHER, TO BE PRECISE.
UH... MUSIC. YOU KNOW... HELPS ME STUDY.
I DON'T LIKE THIS MUSIC OF YOURS, TOBY. JUST KEEP IT DOWN.
GOOD NIGHT.
G'NIGHT.
YOU'RE DEAD
CONTINUE ?
YES NO
AW, SNAP. NOW I'VE GOT TO START ALL OVER!

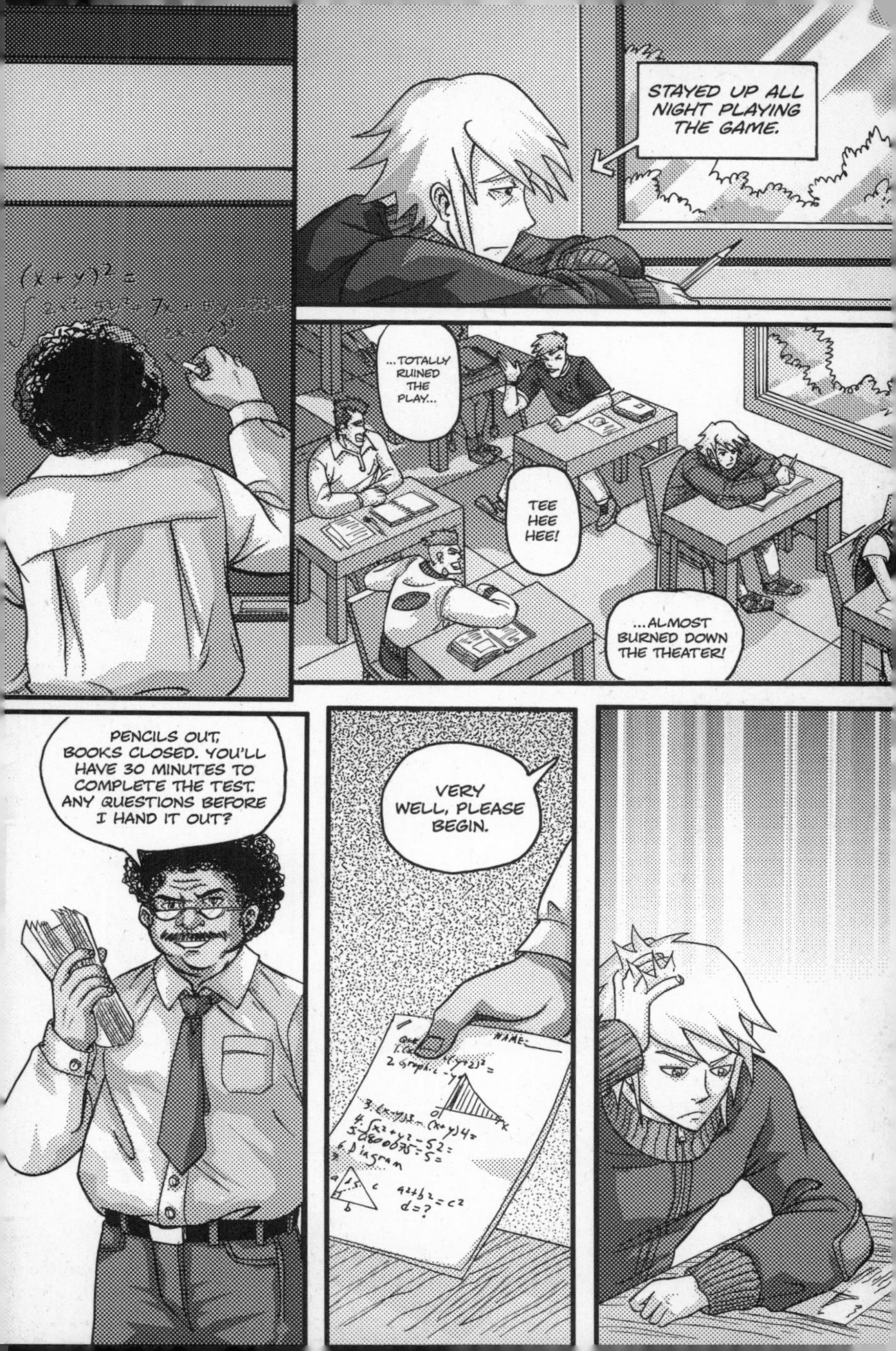
STAYED UP ALL NIGHT PLAYING THE GAME.
...TOTALLY RUINED THE PLAY...
TEE HEE HEE!
...ALMOST BURNED DOWN THE THEATER!
PENCILS OUT, BOOKS CLOSED. YOU'LL HAVE 30 MINUTES TO COMPLETE THE TEST. ANY QUESTIONS BEFORE I HAND IT OUT?
VERY WELL, PLEASE BEGIN.

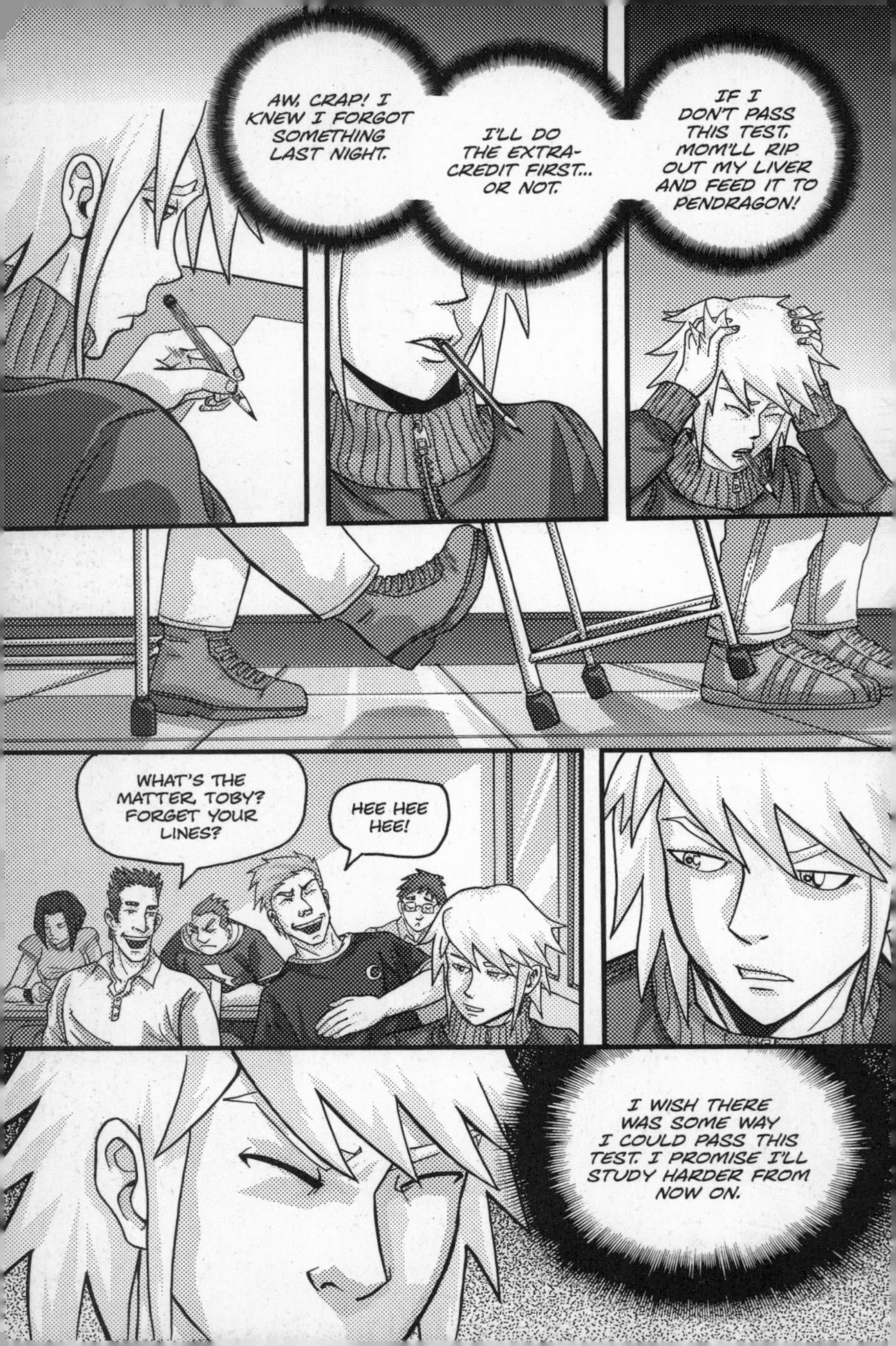
AW, CRAP! I KNEW I FORGOT SOMETHING LAST NIGHT.
I'LL DO THE EXTRA-CREDIT FIRST... OR NOT.
IF I DON'T PASS THIS TEST, MOM'LL RIP OUT MY LIVER AND FEED IT TO PENDRAGON!
WHAT'S THE MATTER, TOBY? FORGET YOUR LINES?
HEE HEE HEE!
I WISH THERE WAS SOME WAY I COULD PASS THIS TEST. I PROMISE I'LL STUDY HARDER FROM NOW ON.

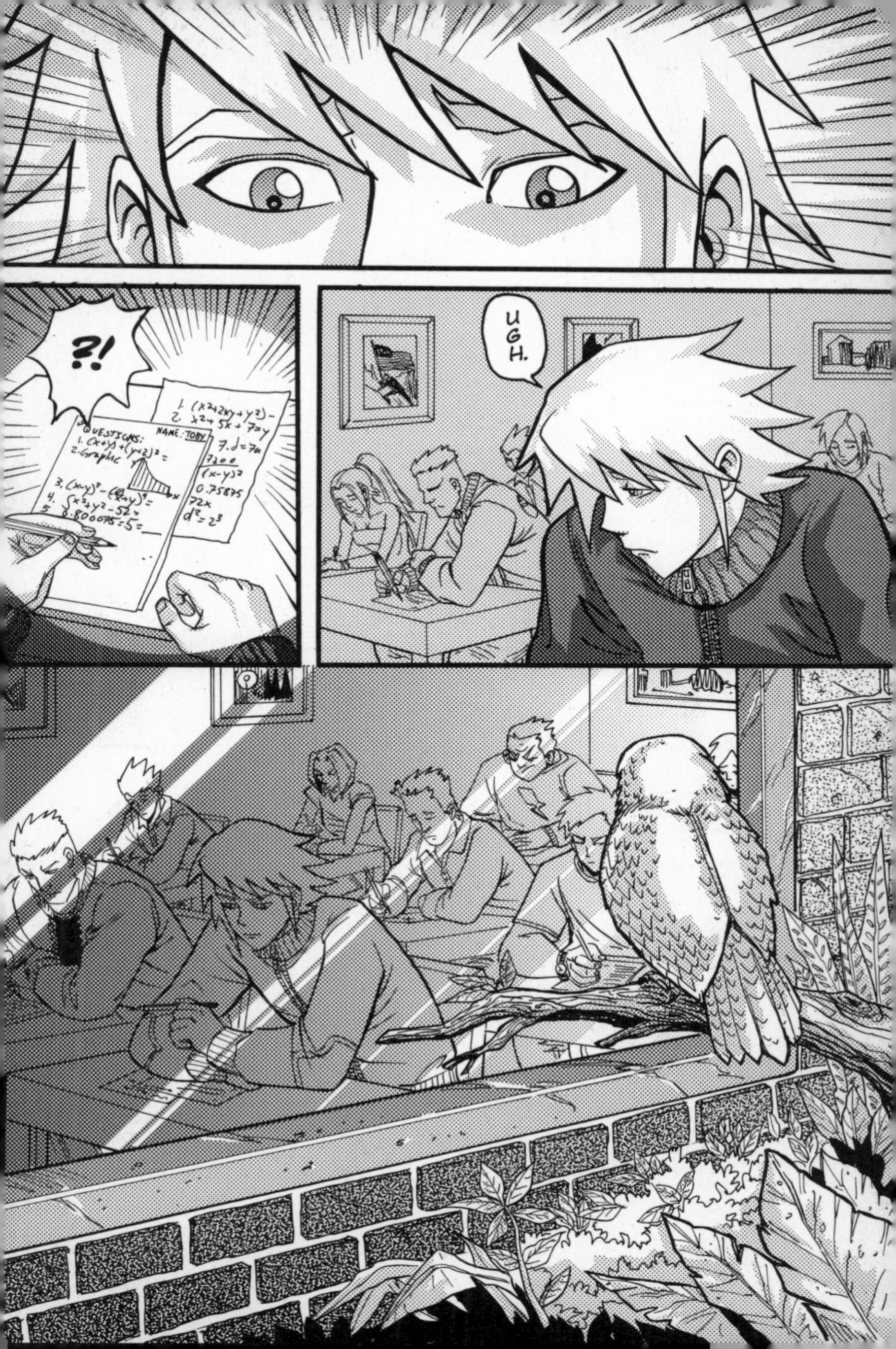
?!
QUESTIONS:
NAME: TOBY
1. (x+y)+(y+z)² =
2. Graphic
3. (x-y)³-(x+y)⁴ =
7. d = 7
7200
(x-y)²
0.75875
72x
d² = 2³
UGH.

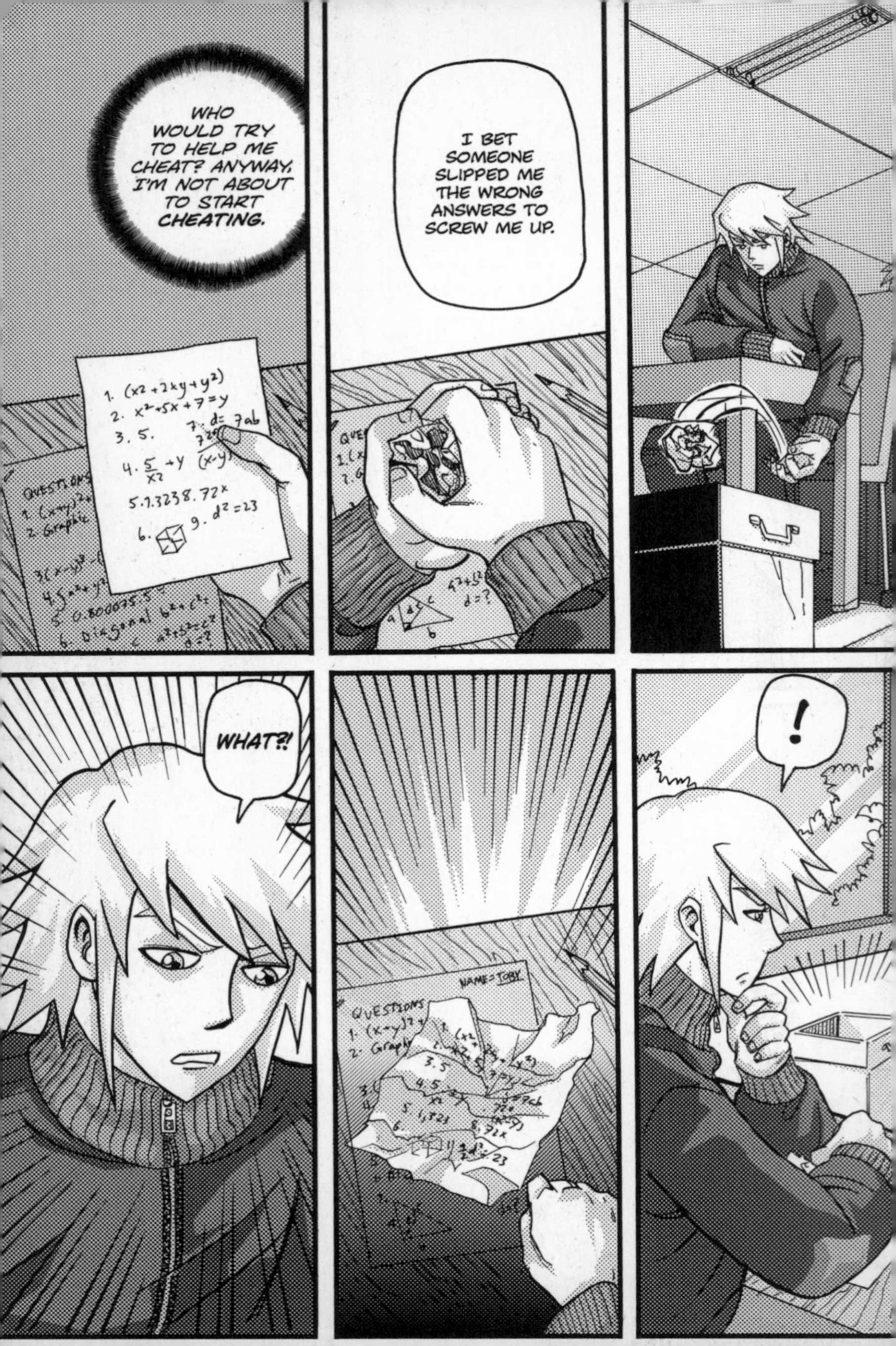
WHO WOULD TRY TO HELP ME CHEAT? ANYWAY, I'M NOT ABOUT TO START CHEATING.
I BET SOMEONE SLIPPED ME THE WRONG ANSWERS TO SCREW ME UP.
WHAT?!
!

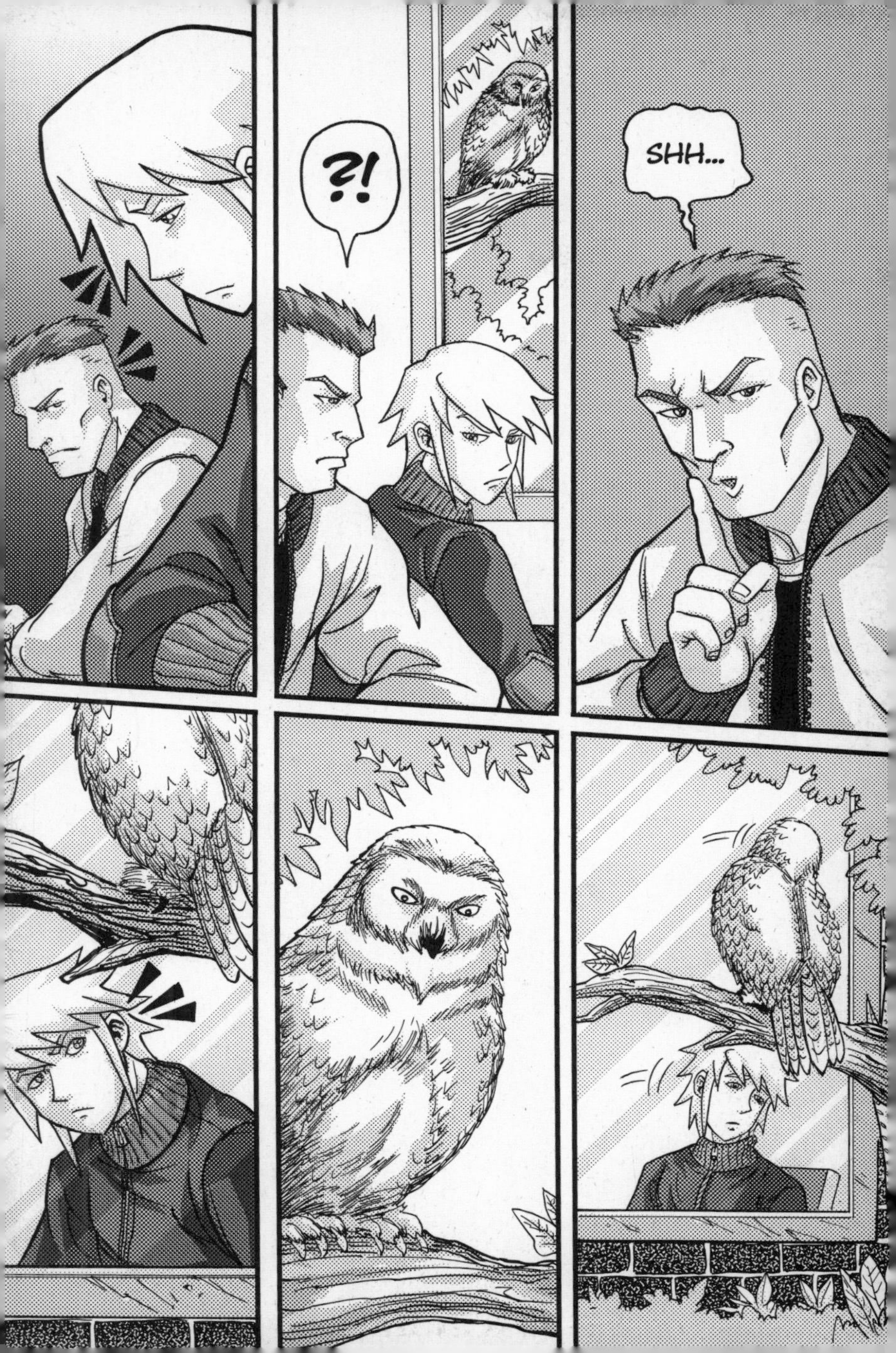
?!
SHH...

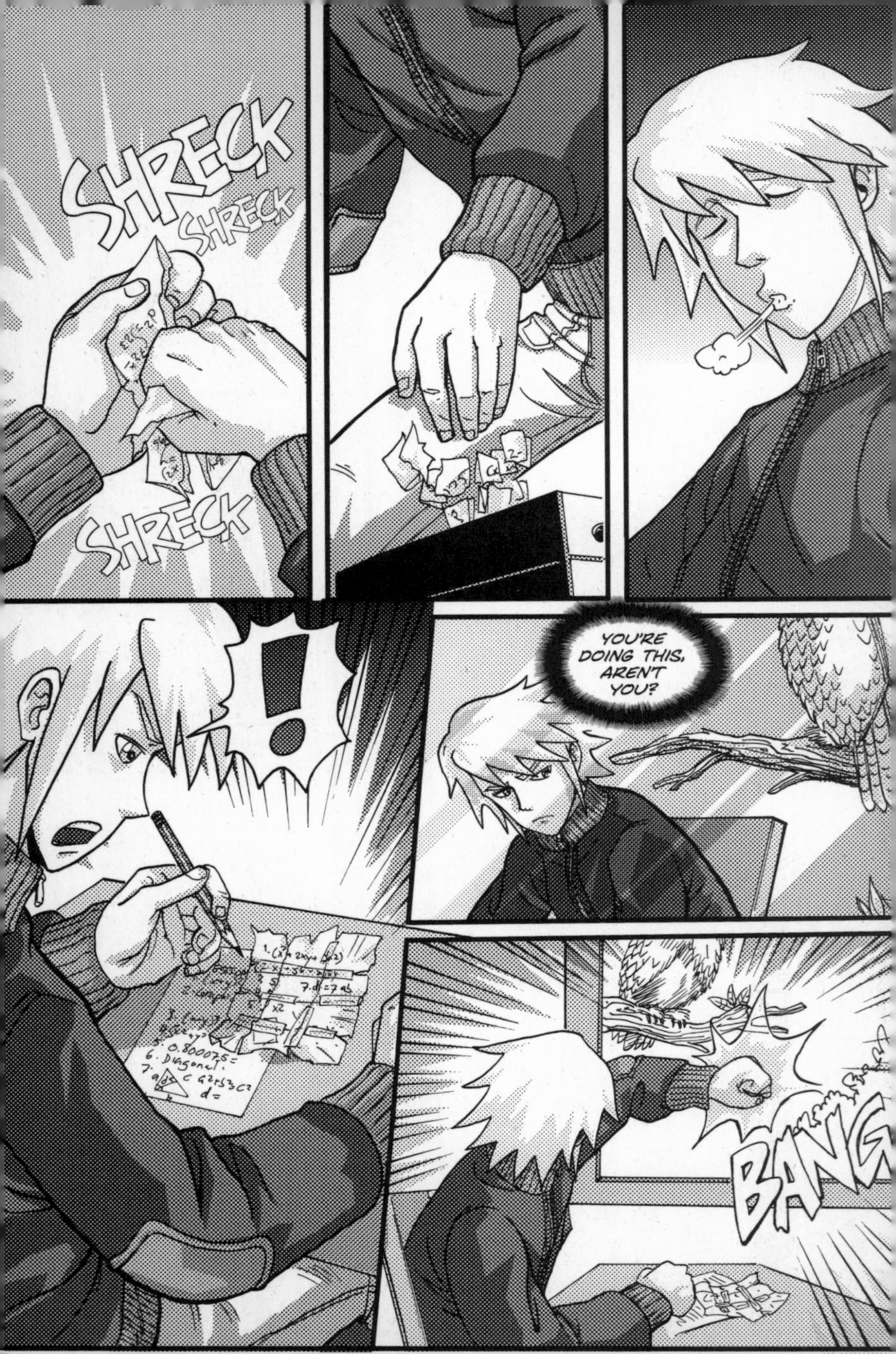

SHRECK
SHRECK
SHRECK
!
YOU'RE DOING THIS, AREN'T YOU?
BANG

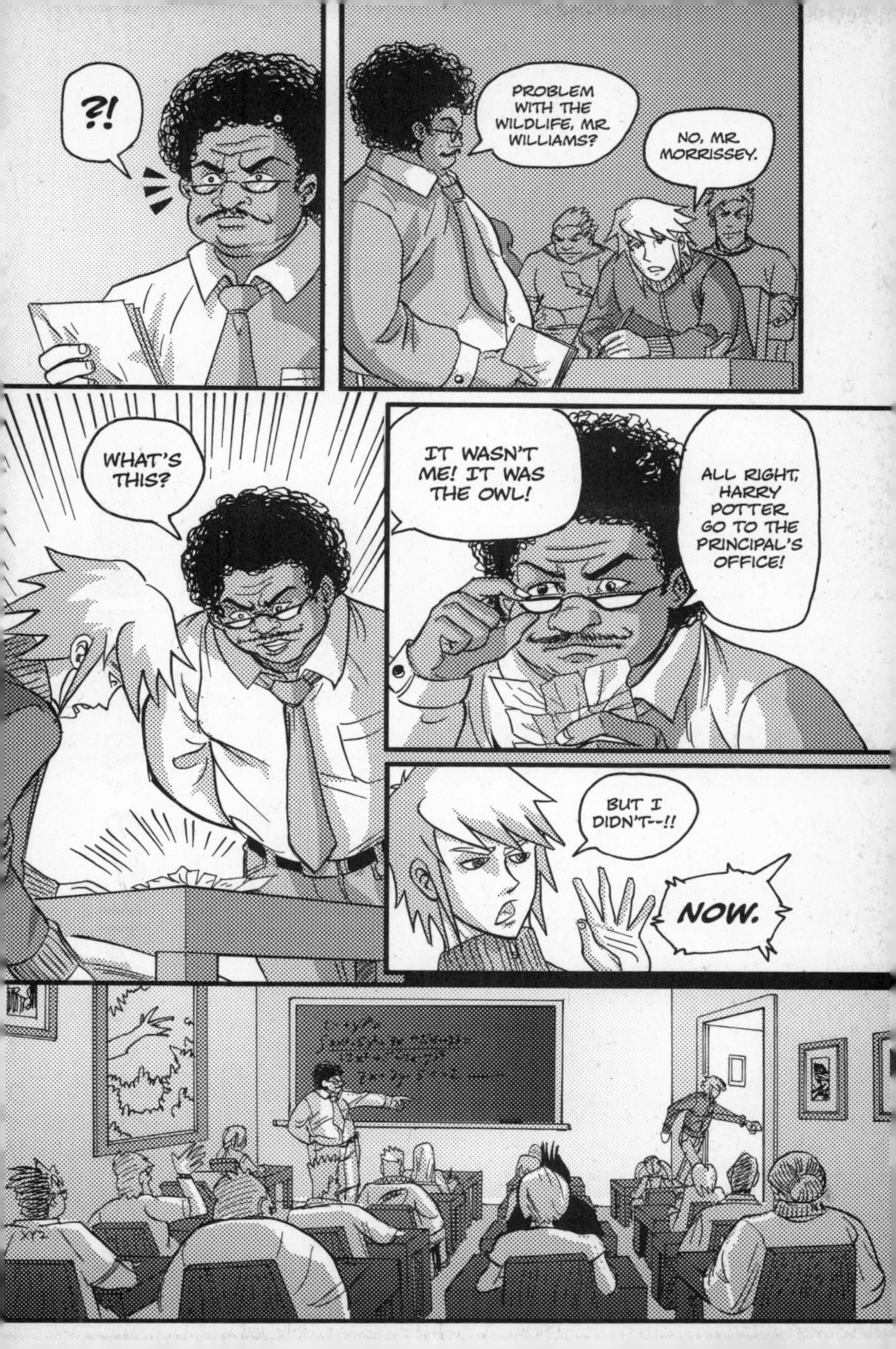
?!
PROBLEM WITH THE WILDLIFE, MR WILLIAMS?
NO, MR MORRISSEY.
WHAT'S THIS?
IT WASN'T ME! IT WAS THE OWL!
ALL RIGHT, HARRY POTTER GO TO THE PRINCIPAL'S OFFICE!
BUT I DIDN'T--!!
NOW.

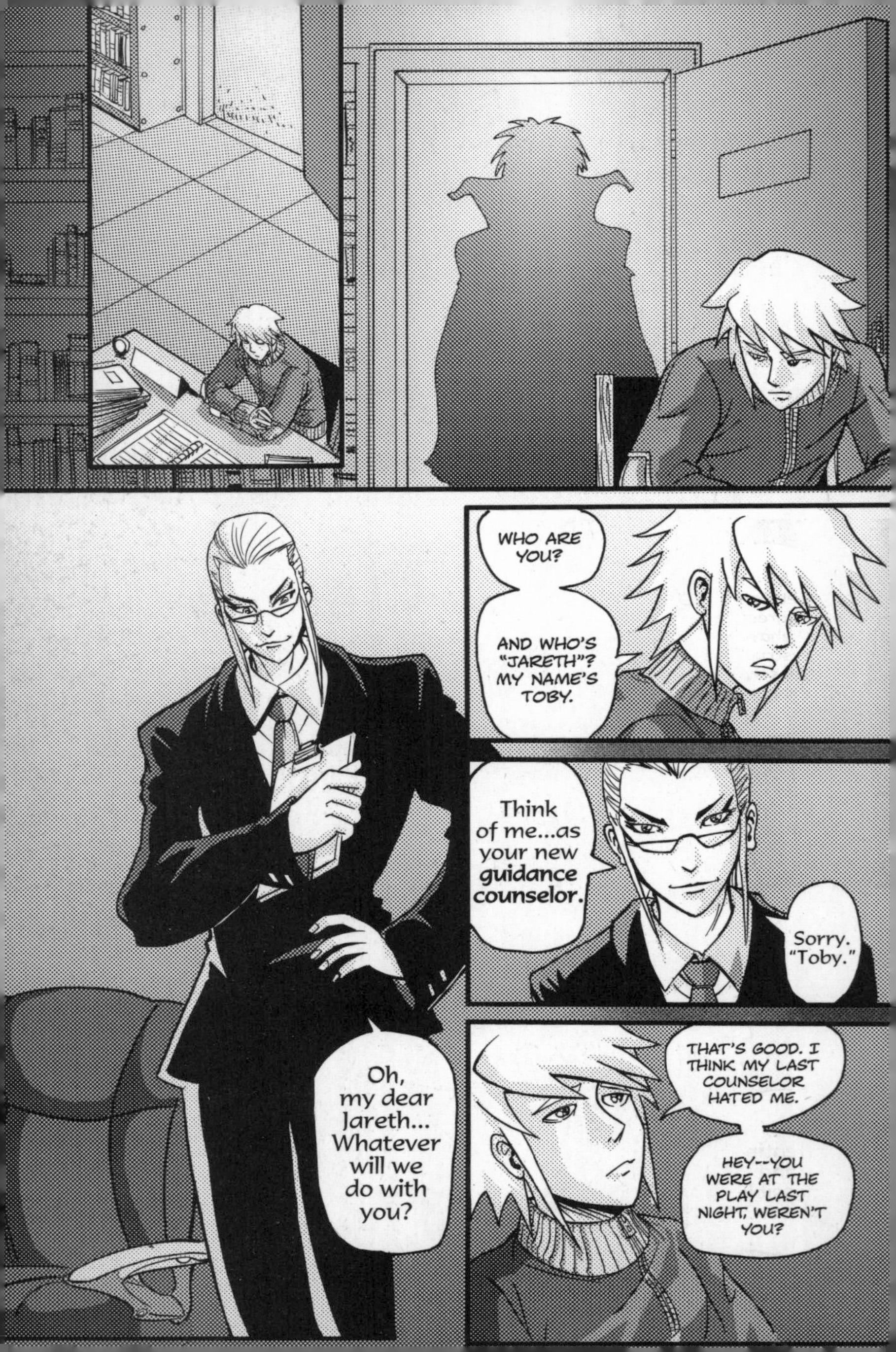
Oh, my dear Jareth... Whatever will we do with you?
WHO ARE YOU?
AND WHO'S "JARETH"? MY NAME'S TOBY.
Think of me...as your new **guidance counselor.**
Sorry. "Toby."
THAT'S GOOD. I THINK MY LAST COUNSELOR HATED ME.
HEY--YOU WERE AT THE PLAY LAST NIGHT, WEREN'T YOU?

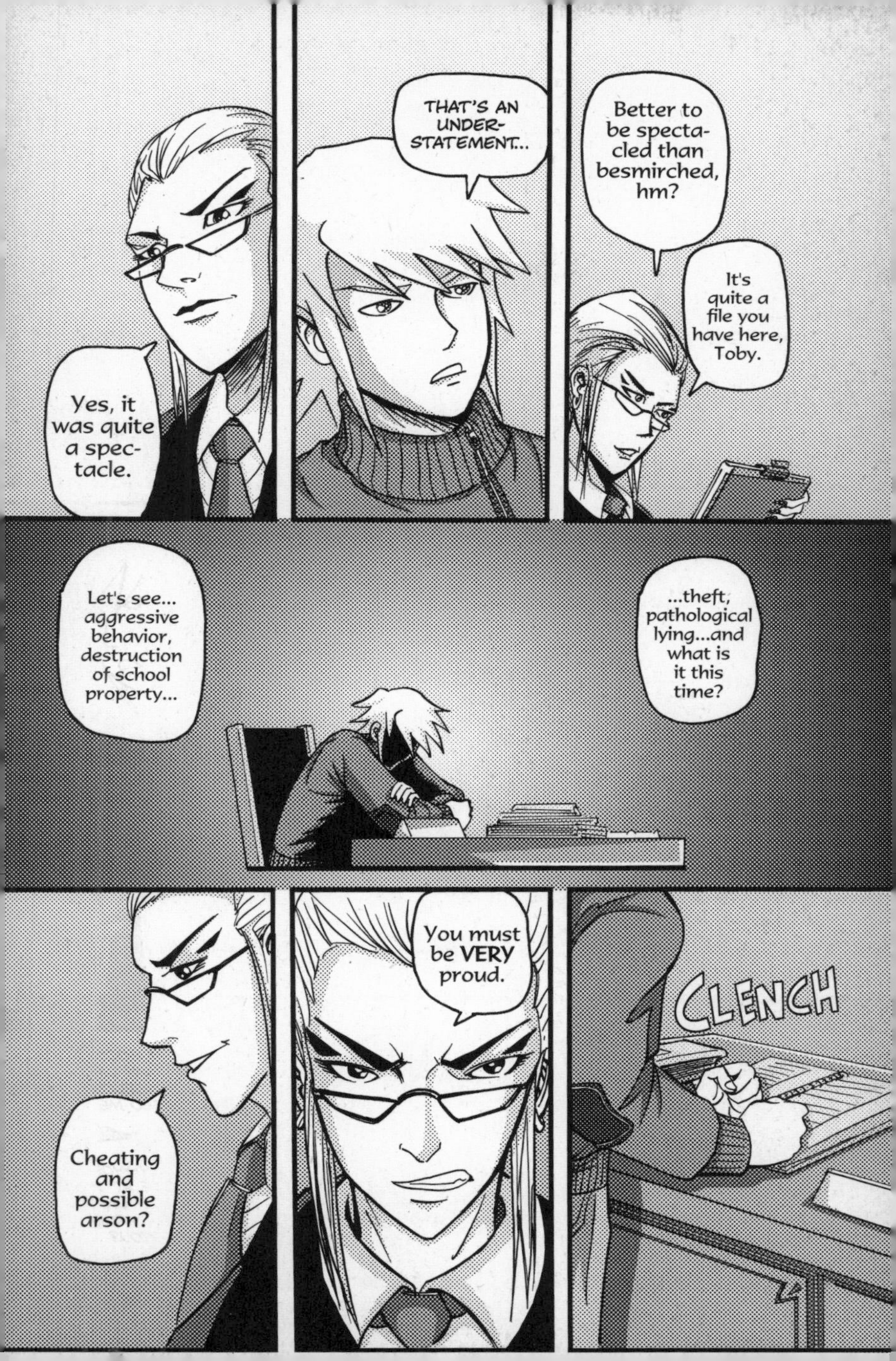
Yes, it was quite a spec-tacle.
THAT'S AN UNDER-STATEMENT...
Better to be specta-cled than besmirched, hm?
It's quite a file you have here, Toby.
Let's see... aggressive behavior, destruction of school property...
...theft, pathological lying...and what is it this time?
Cheating and possible arson?
You must be **VERY** proud.
CLENCH

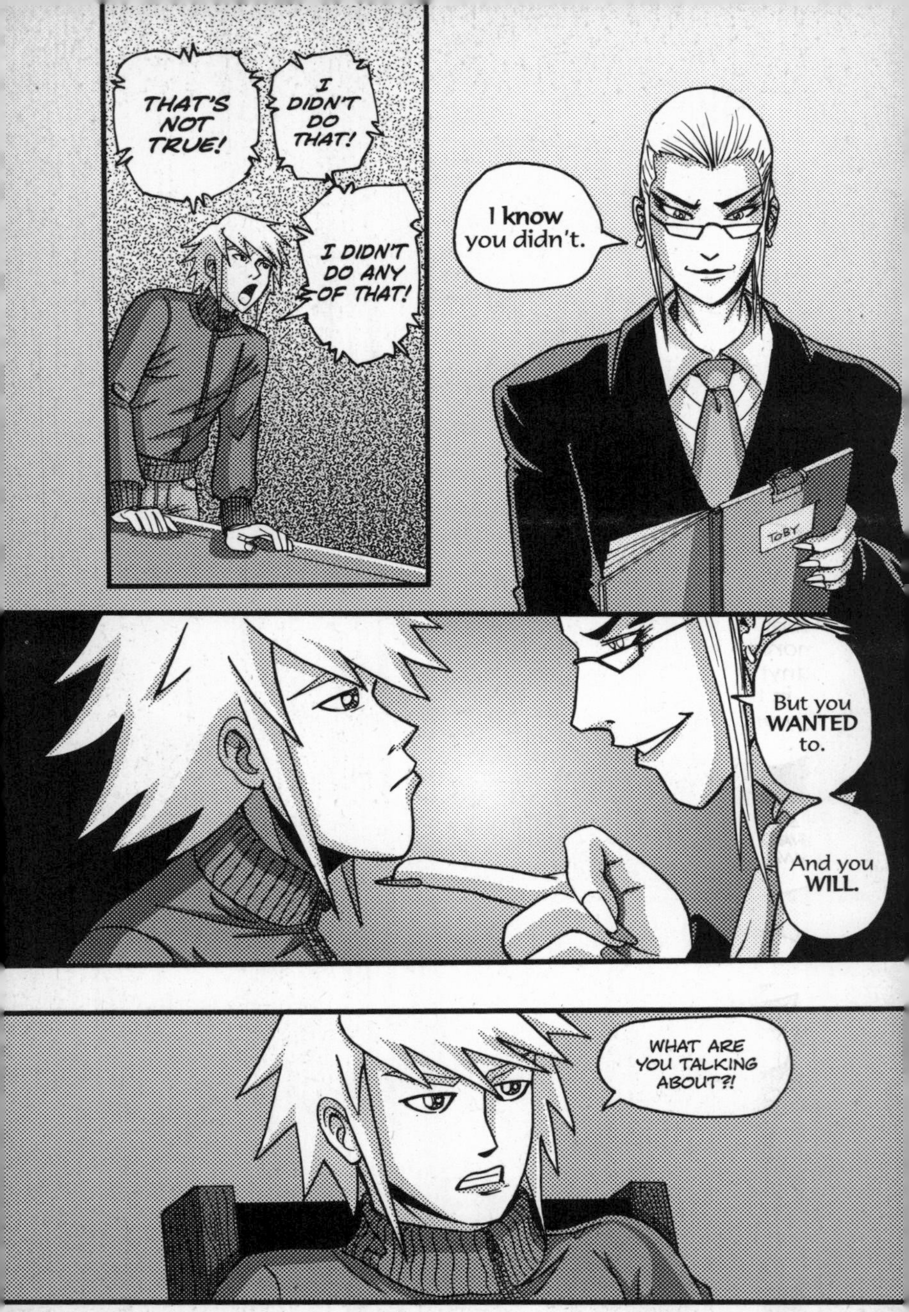
THAT'S NOT TRUE!
I DIDN'T DO THAT!
I DIDN'T DO ANY OF THAT!
I know you didn't.
TOBY
But you WANTED to.
And you WILL.
WHAT ARE YOU TALKING ABOUT?!

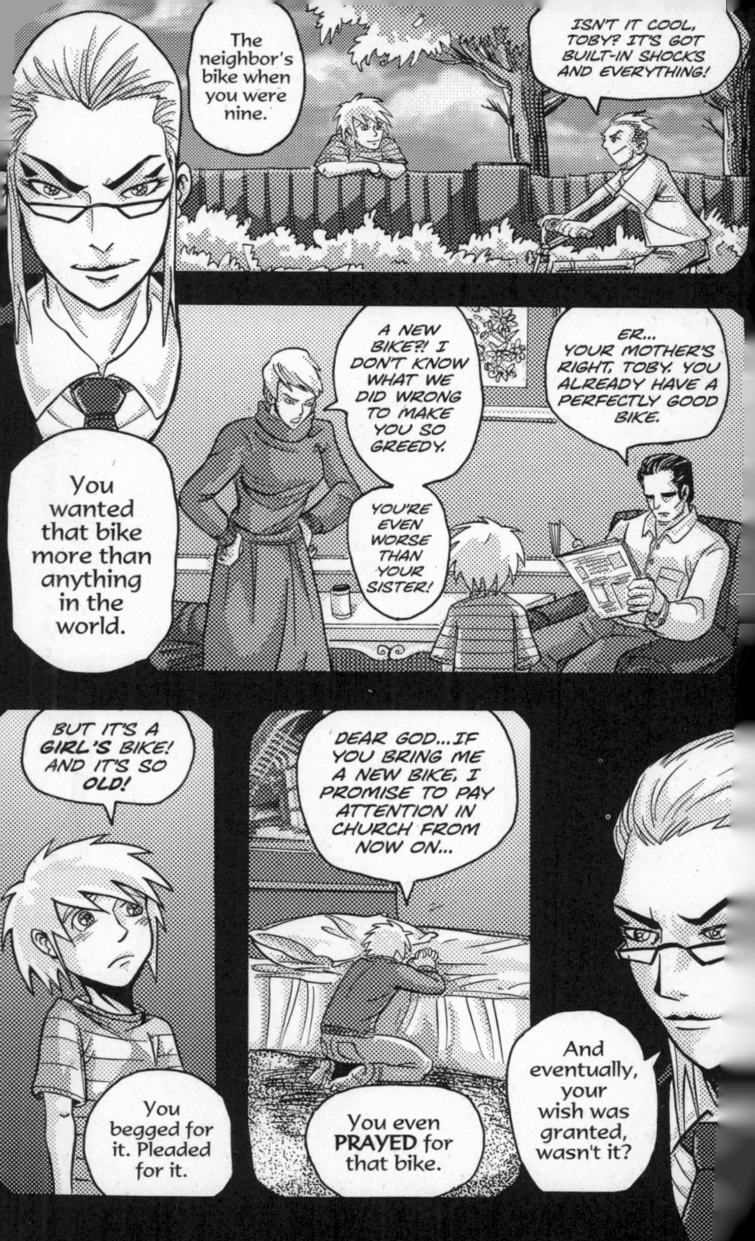

The neighbor's bike when you were nine.
ISN'T IT COOL, TOBY? IT'S GOT BUILT-IN SHOCKS AND EVERYTHING!
You wanted that bike more than anything in the world.
A NEW BIKE?! I DON'T KNOW WHAT WE DID WRONG TO MAKE YOU SO GREEDY.
YOU'RE EVEN WORSE THAN YOUR SISTER!
ER... YOUR MOTHER'S RIGHT, TOBY. YOU ALREADY HAVE A PERFECTLY GOOD BIKE.
BUT IT'S A **GIRL'S** BIKE! AND IT'S SO **OLD**!
You begged for it. Pleaded for it.
DEAR GOD...IF YOU BRING ME A NEW BIKE, I PROMISE TO PAY ATTENTION IN CHURCH FROM NOW ON...
You even **PRAYED** for that bike.
And eventually, your wish was granted, wasn't it?

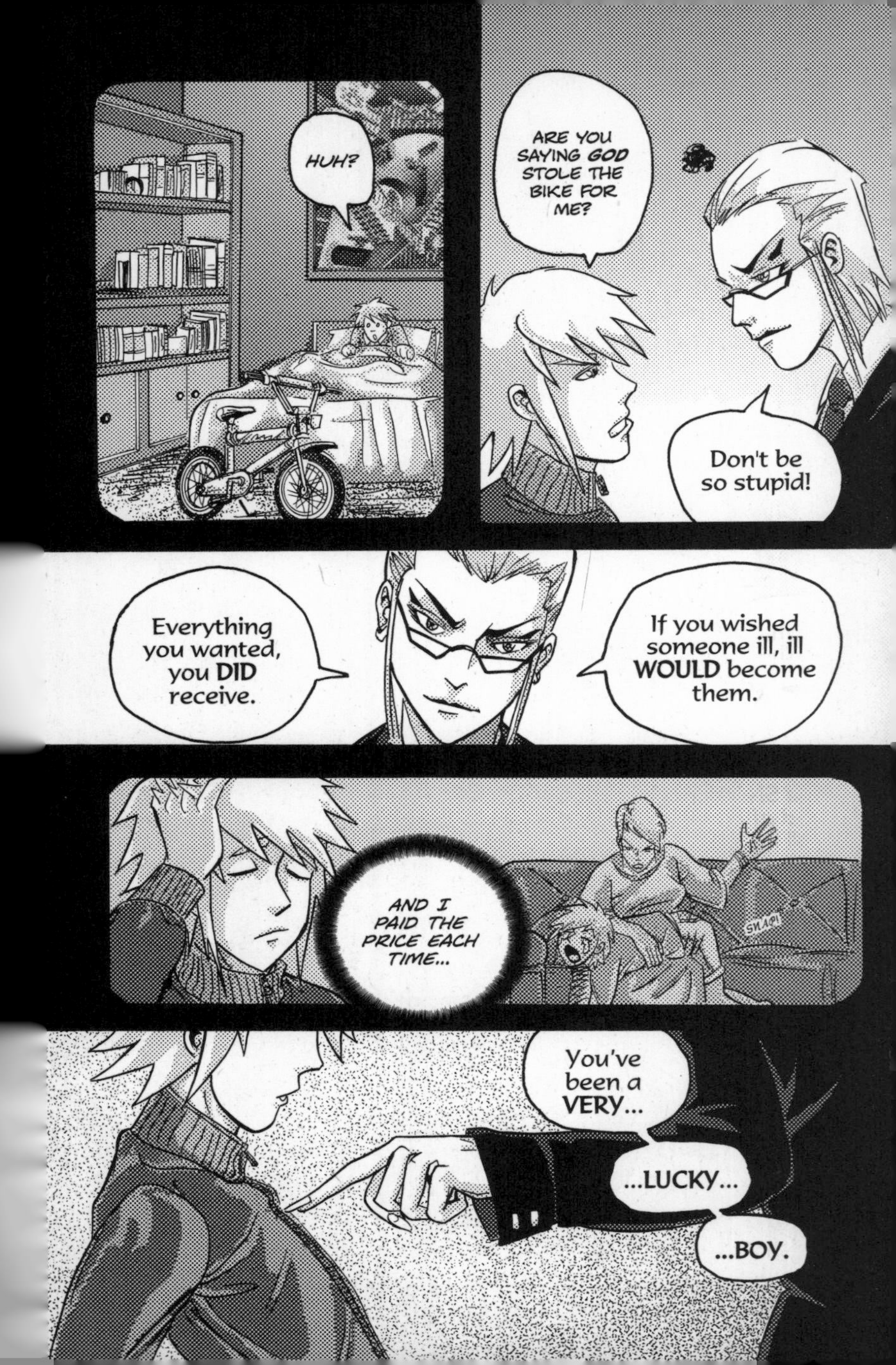
HUH?
ARE YOU SAYING GOD STOLE THE BIKE FOR ME?
Don't be so stupid!
Everything you wanted, you **DID** receive.
If you wished someone ill, ill **WOULD** become them.
AND I PAID THE PRICE EACH TIME...
SNAP!
You've been a **VERY**...
...**LUCKY**...
...**BOY.**

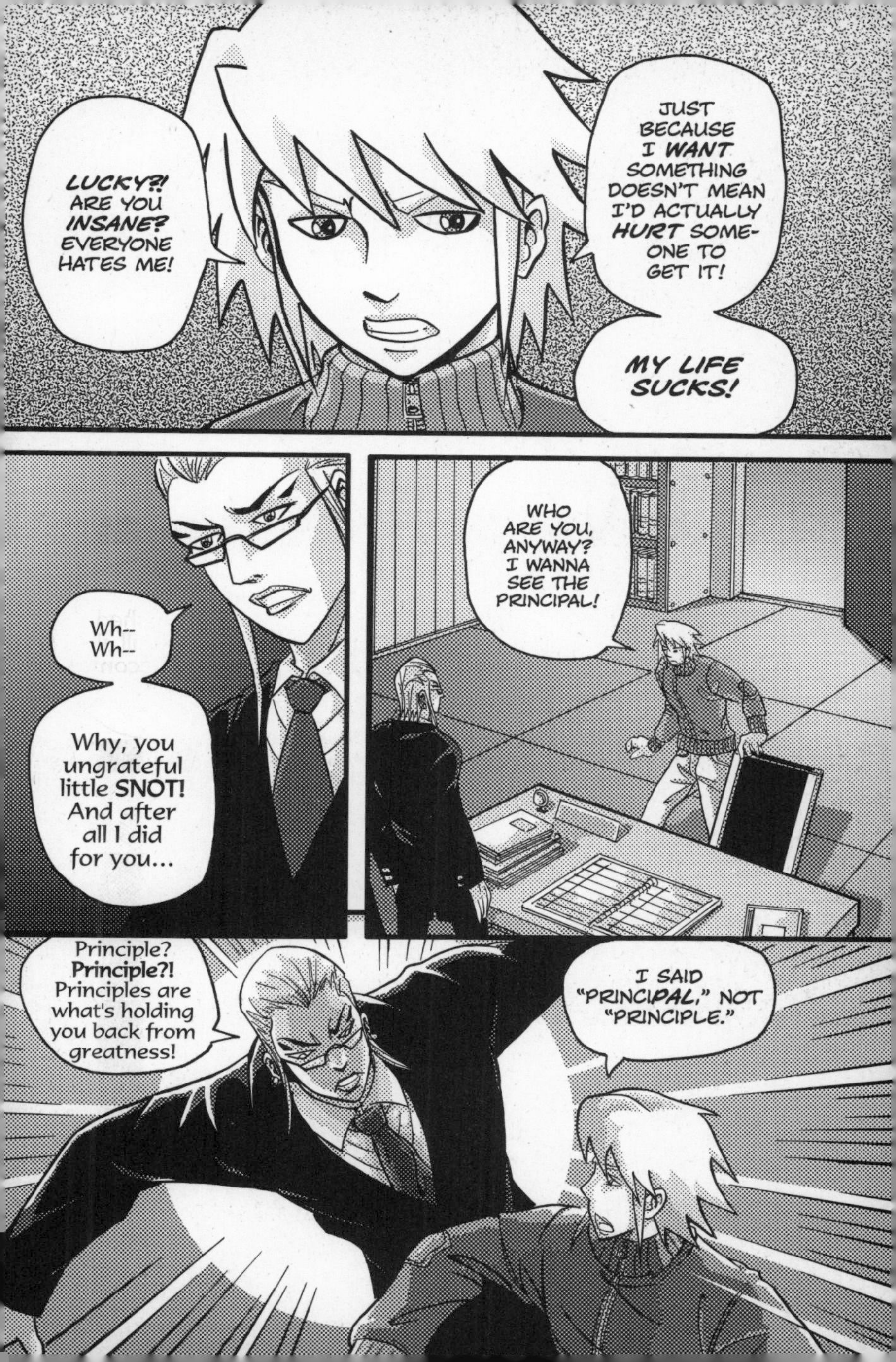
LUCKY?! ARE YOU INSANE? EVERYONE HATES ME!
JUST BECAUSE I WANT SOMETHING DOESN'T MEAN I'D ACTUALLY HURT SOME-ONE TO GET IT!
MY LIFE SUCKS!
Wh-- Wh--
Why, you ungrateful little SNOT! And after all I did for you...
WHO ARE YOU, ANYWAY? I WANNA SEE THE PRINCIPAL!
Principle? Principle?! Principles are what's holding you back from greatness!
I SAID "PRINCIPAL," NOT "PRINCIPLE."

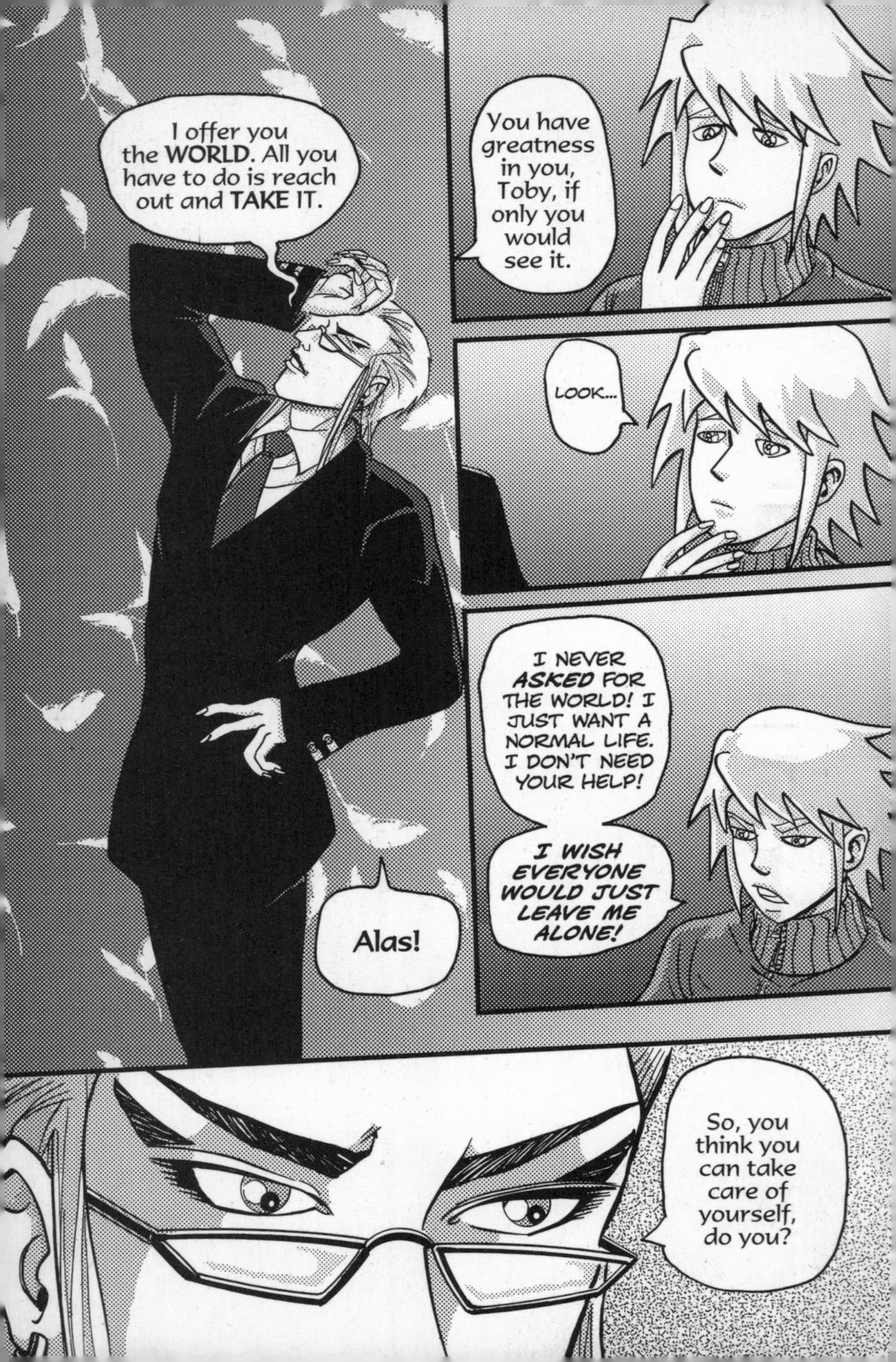
I offer you the WORLD. All you have to do is reach out and TAKE IT.
Alas!
You have greatness in you, Toby, if only you would see it.
LOOK...
I NEVER ASKED FOR THE WORLD! I JUST WANT A NORMAL LIFE. I DON'T NEED YOUR HELP!
I WISH EVERYONE WOULD JUST LEAVE ME ALONE!
So, you think you can take care of yourself, do you?

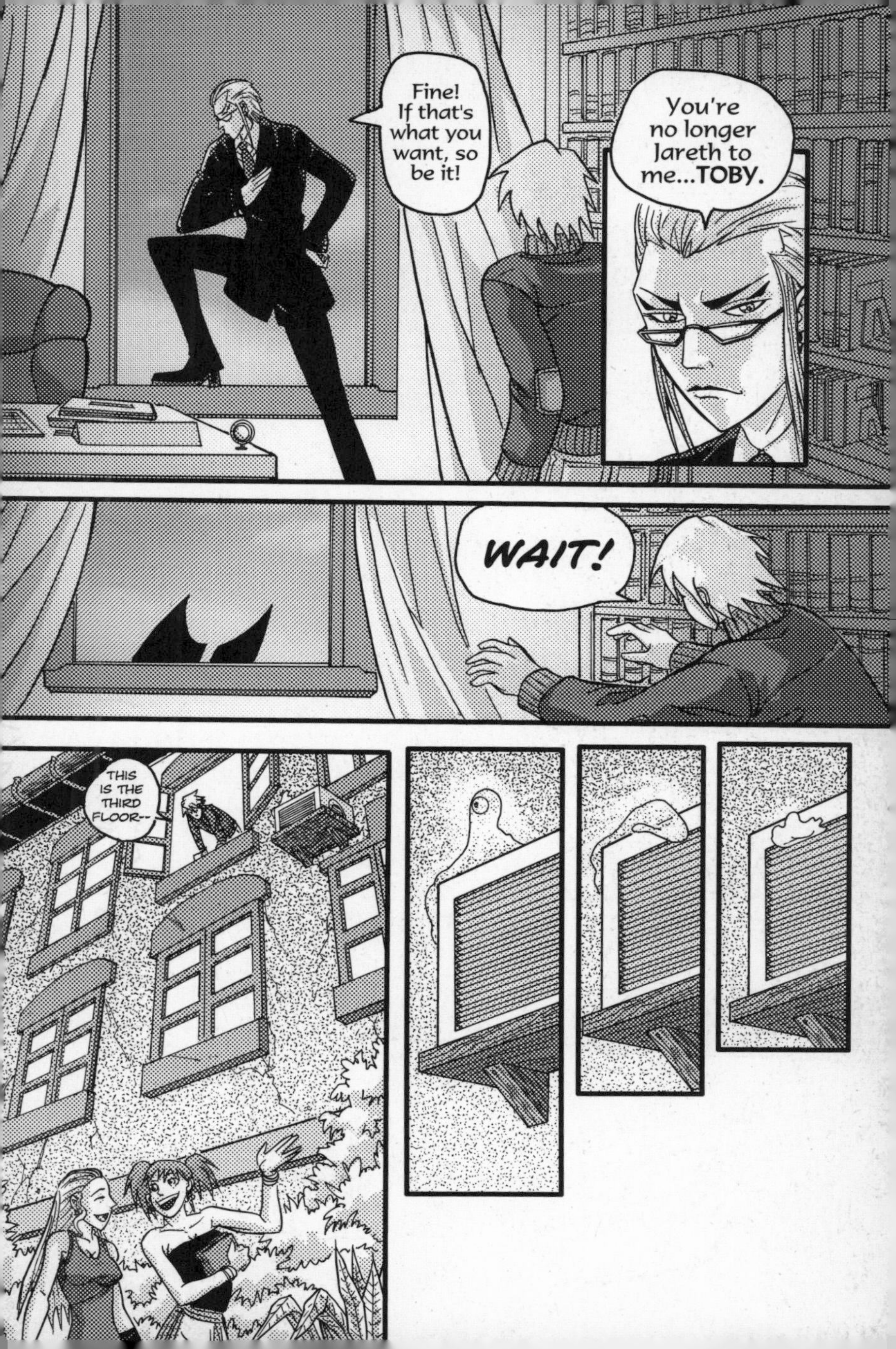
Fine! If that's what you want, so be it!
You're no longer Jareth to me...TOBY.
WAIT!
THIS IS THE THIRD FLOOR--

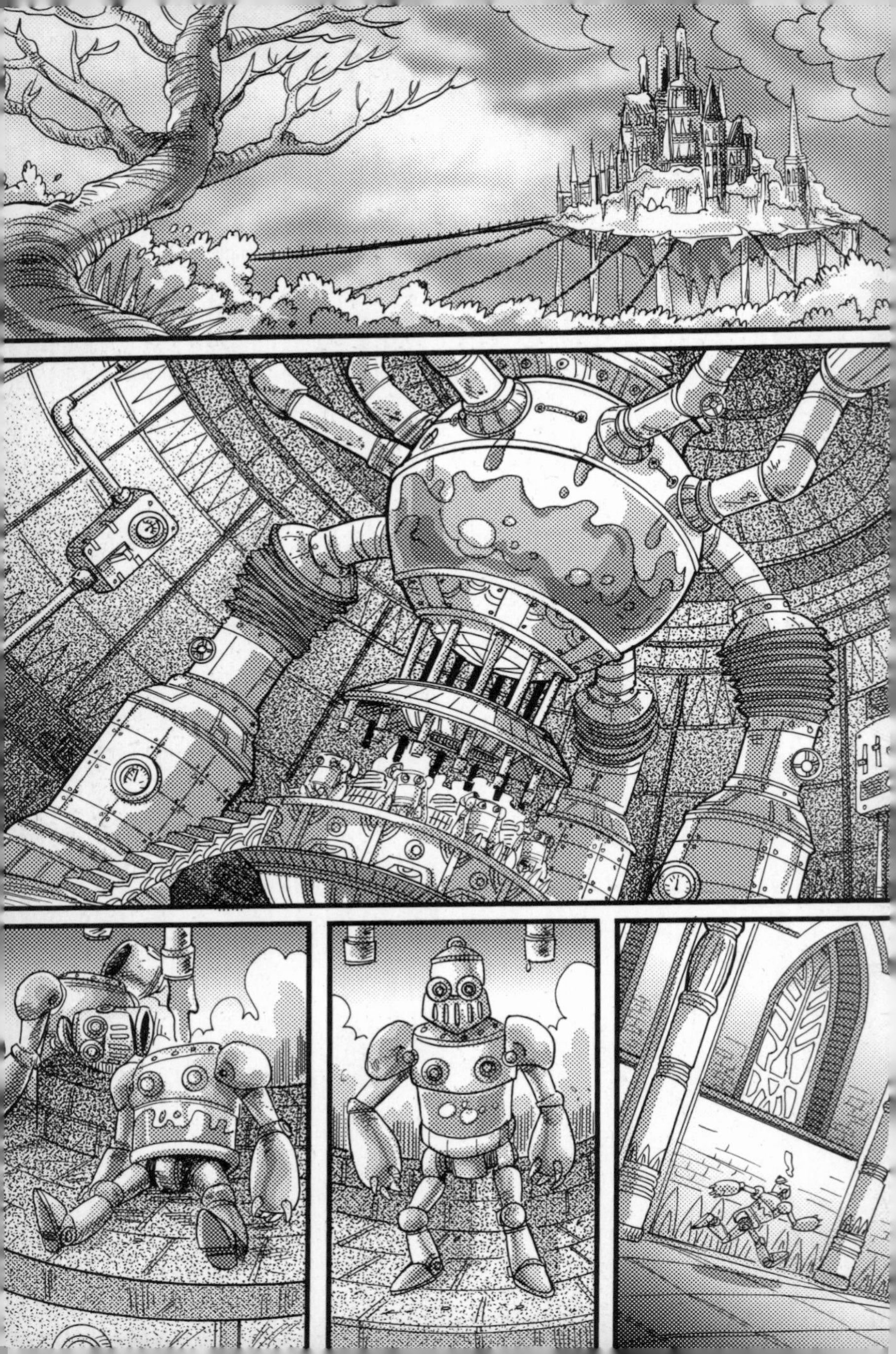

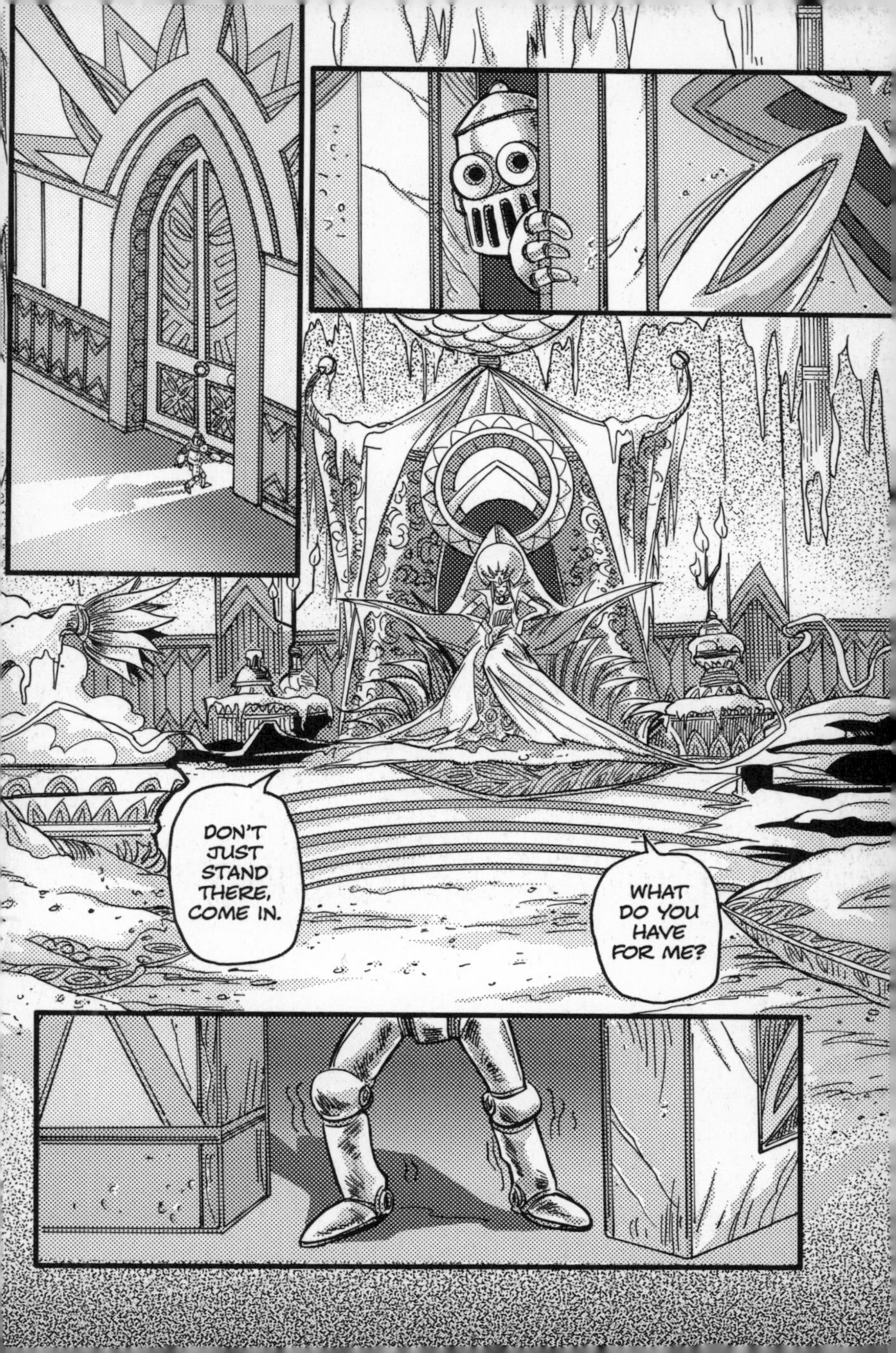
DON'T JUST STAND THERE, COME IN.
WHAT DO YOU HAVE FOR ME?

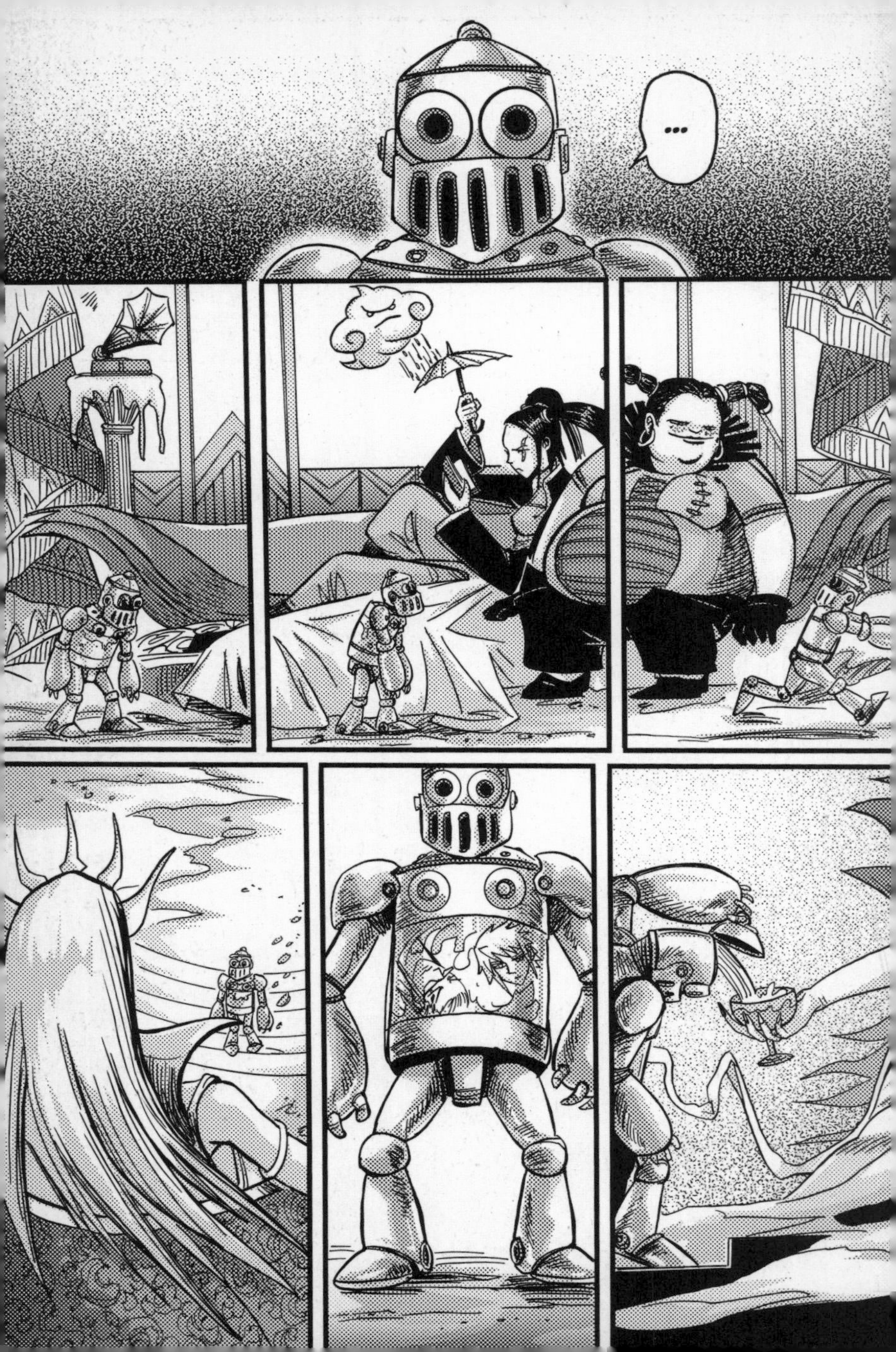
...

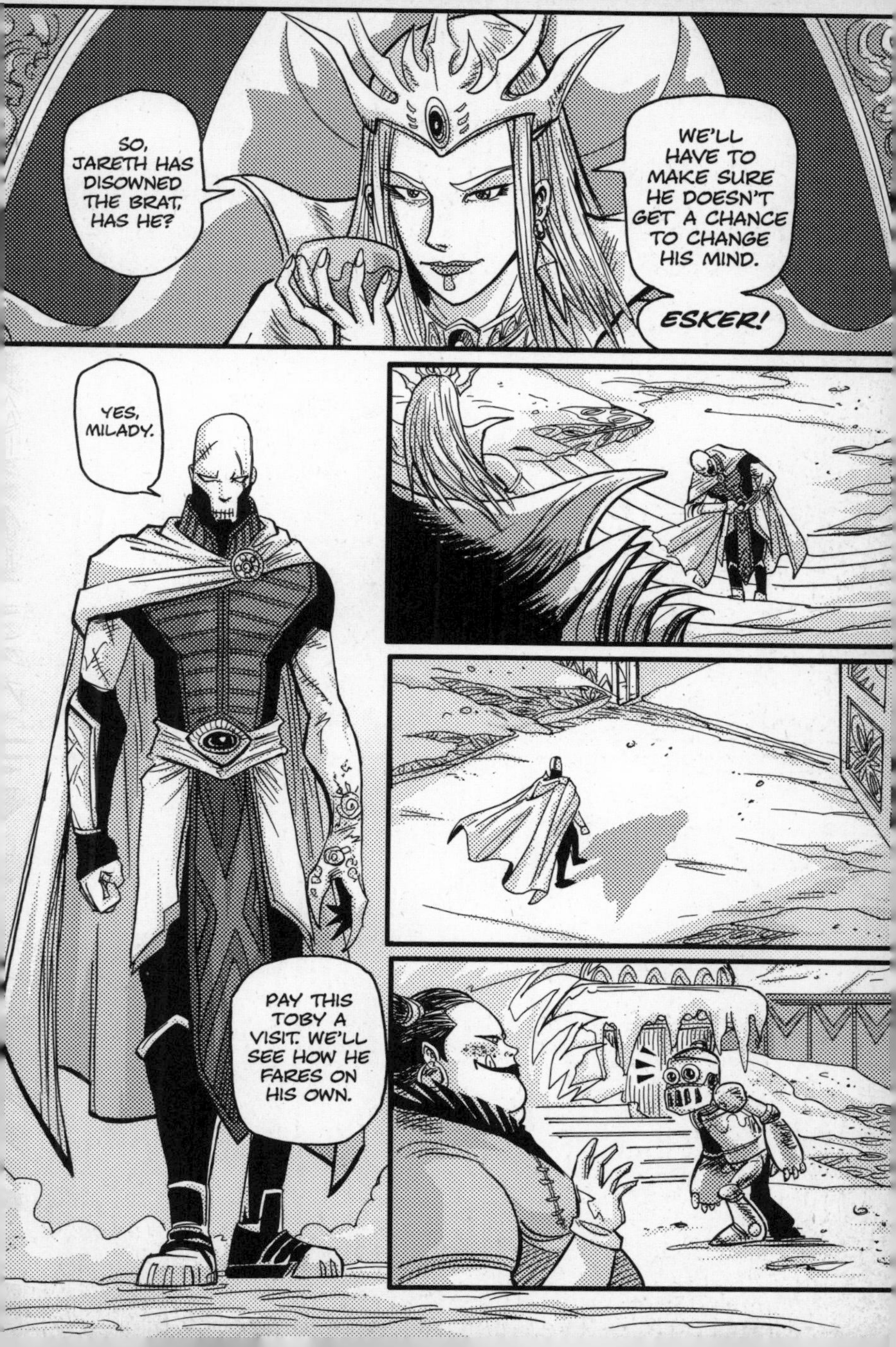
SO, JARETH HAS DISOWNED THE BRAT, HAS HE?
WE'LL HAVE TO MAKE SURE HE DOESN'T GET A CHANCE TO CHANGE HIS MIND.
ESKER!
YES, MILADY.
PAY THIS TOBY A VISIT. WE'LL SEE HOW HE FARES ON HIS OWN.

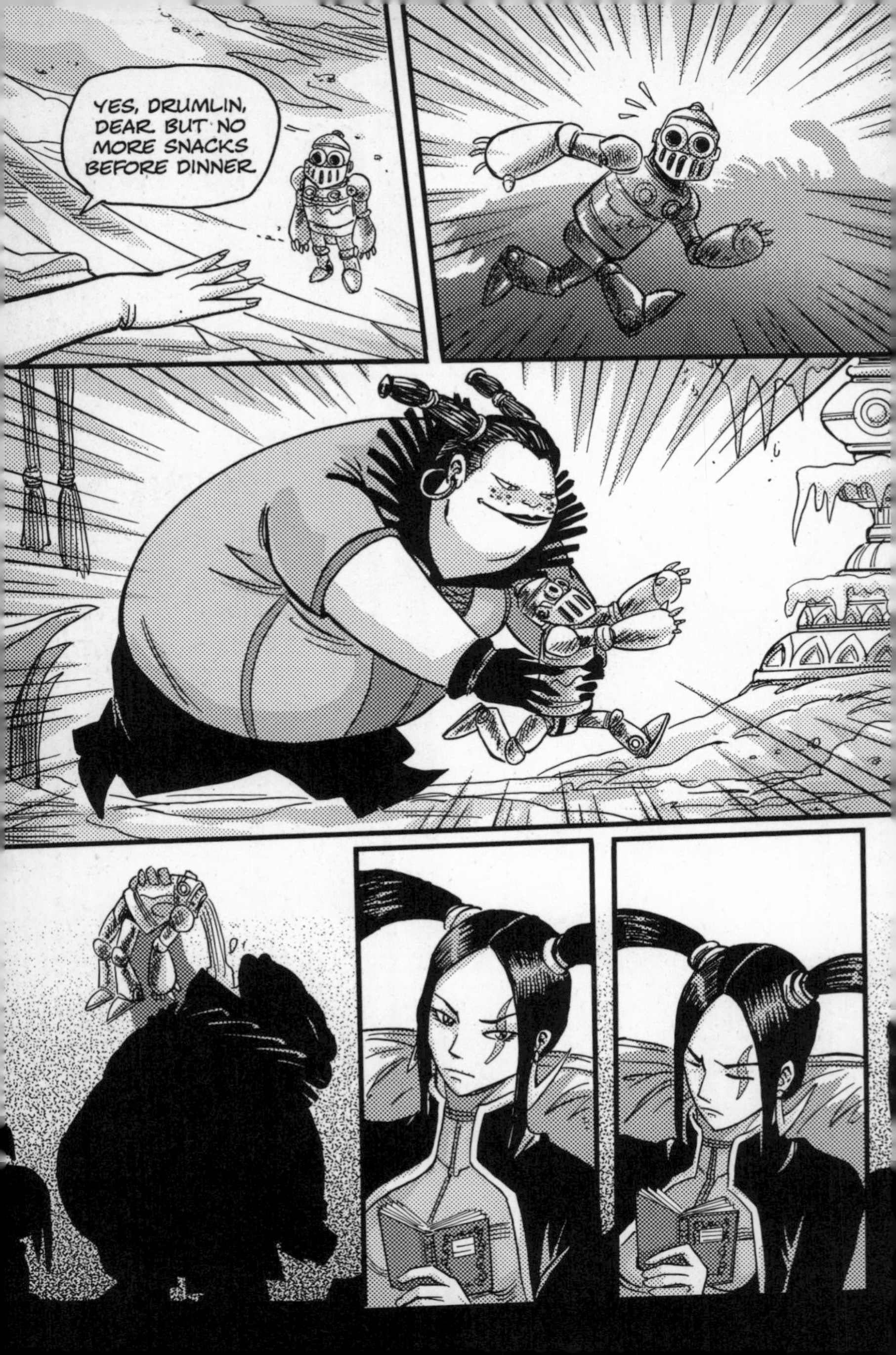
YES, DRUMLIN, DEAR BUT NO MORE SNACKS BEFORE DINNER

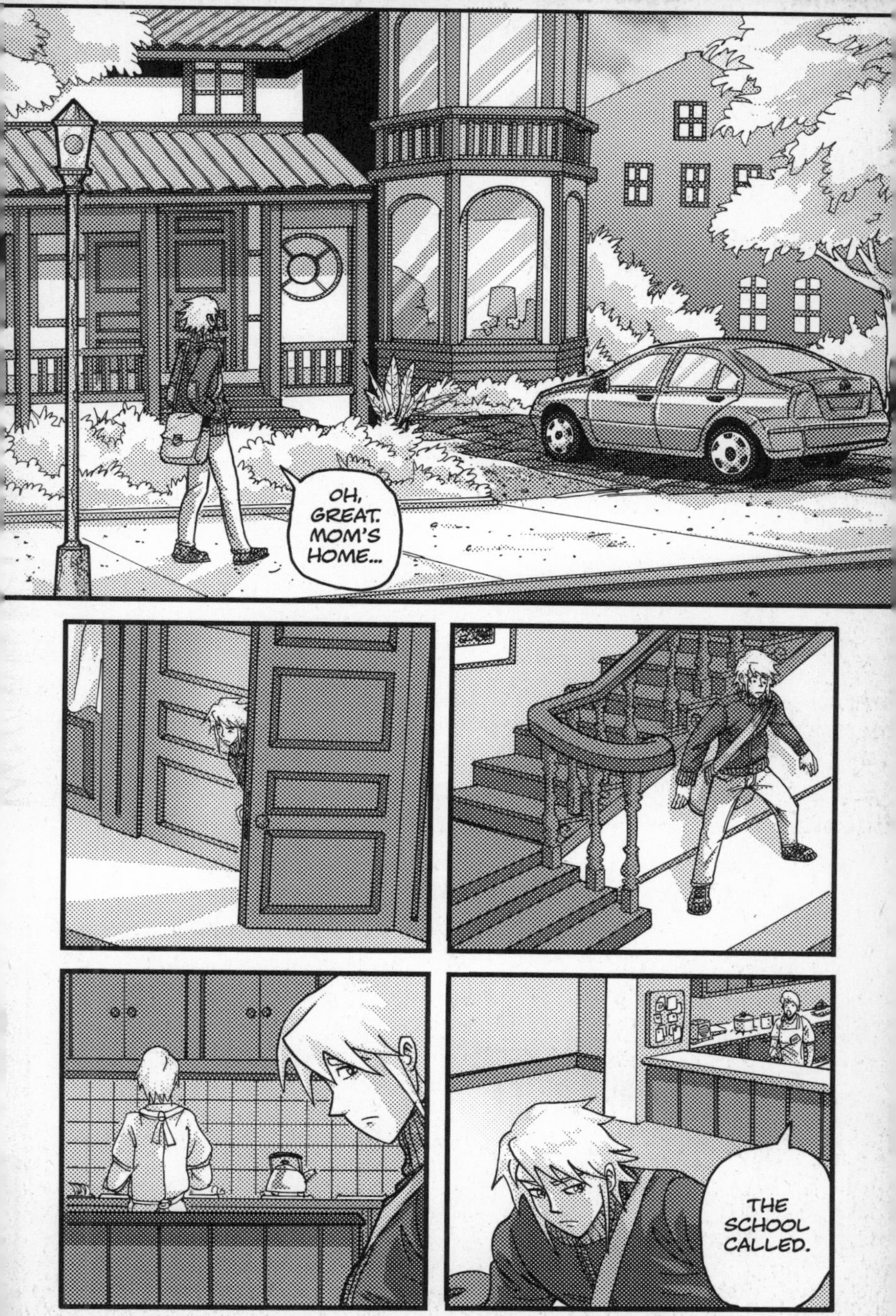
OH, GREAT. MOM'S HOME...
THE SCHOOL CALLED.

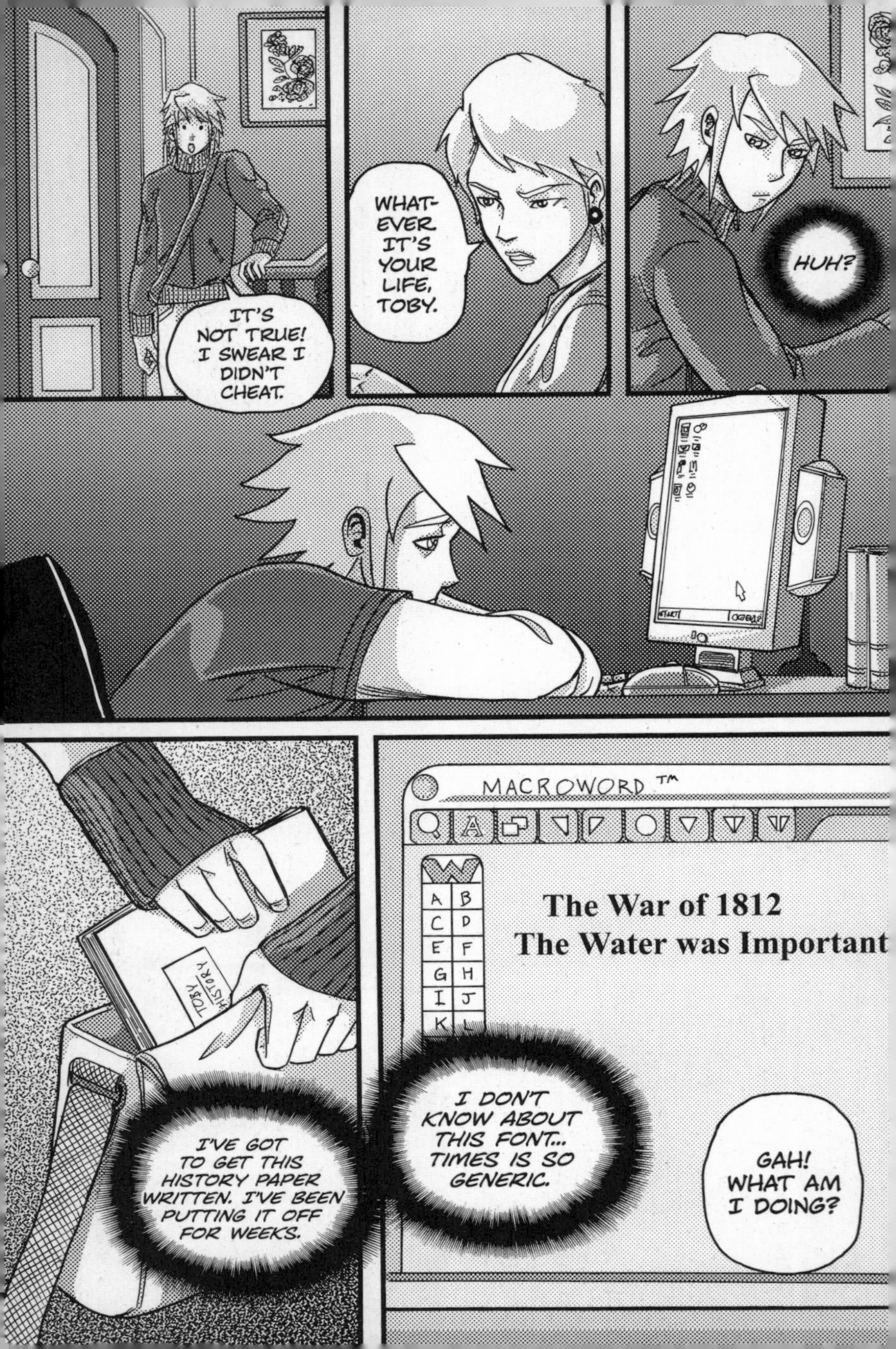

IT'S NOT TRUE! I SWEAR I DIDN'T CHEAT.
WHAT-EVER IT'S YOUR LIFE, TOBY.
HUH?
TOBY HISTORY
MACROWORD ™
The War of 1812
The Water was Important
I'VE GOT TO GET THIS HISTORY PAPER WRITTEN. I'VE BEEN PUTTING IT OFF FOR WEEKS.
I DON'T KNOW ABOUT THIS FONT... TIMES IS SO GENERIC.
GAH! WHAT AM I DOING?

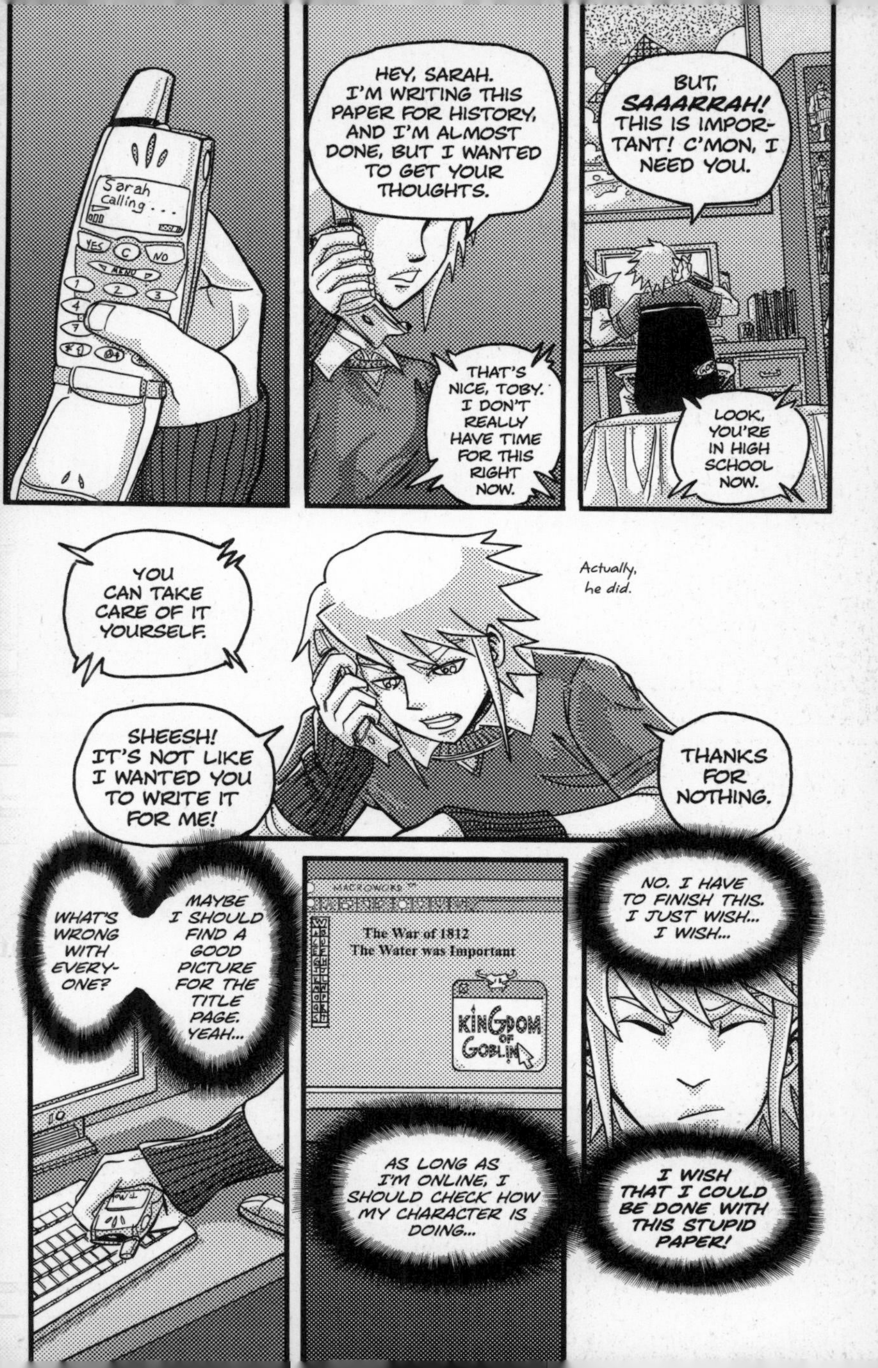
Sarah calling...
YES
C
NO
MENU
HEY, SARAH. I'M WRITING THIS PAPER FOR HISTORY, AND I'M ALMOST DONE, BUT I WANTED TO GET YOUR THOUGHTS.
THAT'S NICE, TOBY. I DON'T REALLY HAVE TIME FOR THIS RIGHT NOW.
BUT, *SAAARRAH!* THIS IS IMPORTANT! C'MON, I NEED YOU.
LOOK, YOU'RE IN HIGH SCHOOL NOW.
YOU CAN TAKE CARE OF IT YOURSELF.
SHEESH! IT'S NOT LIKE I WANTED YOU TO WRITE IT FOR ME!
Actually, he did.
THANKS FOR NOTHING.
WHAT'S WRONG WITH EVERYONE?
MAYBE I SHOULD FIND A GOOD PICTURE FOR THE TITLE PAGE. YEAH...
MACROWORD
The War of 1812
The Water was Important
KINGDOM OF GOBLIN
AS LONG AS I'M ONLINE, I SHOULD CHECK HOW MY CHARACTER IS DOING...
NO. I HAVE TO FINISH THIS. I JUST WISH... I WISH...
I WISH THAT I COULD BE DONE WITH THIS STUPID PAPER!

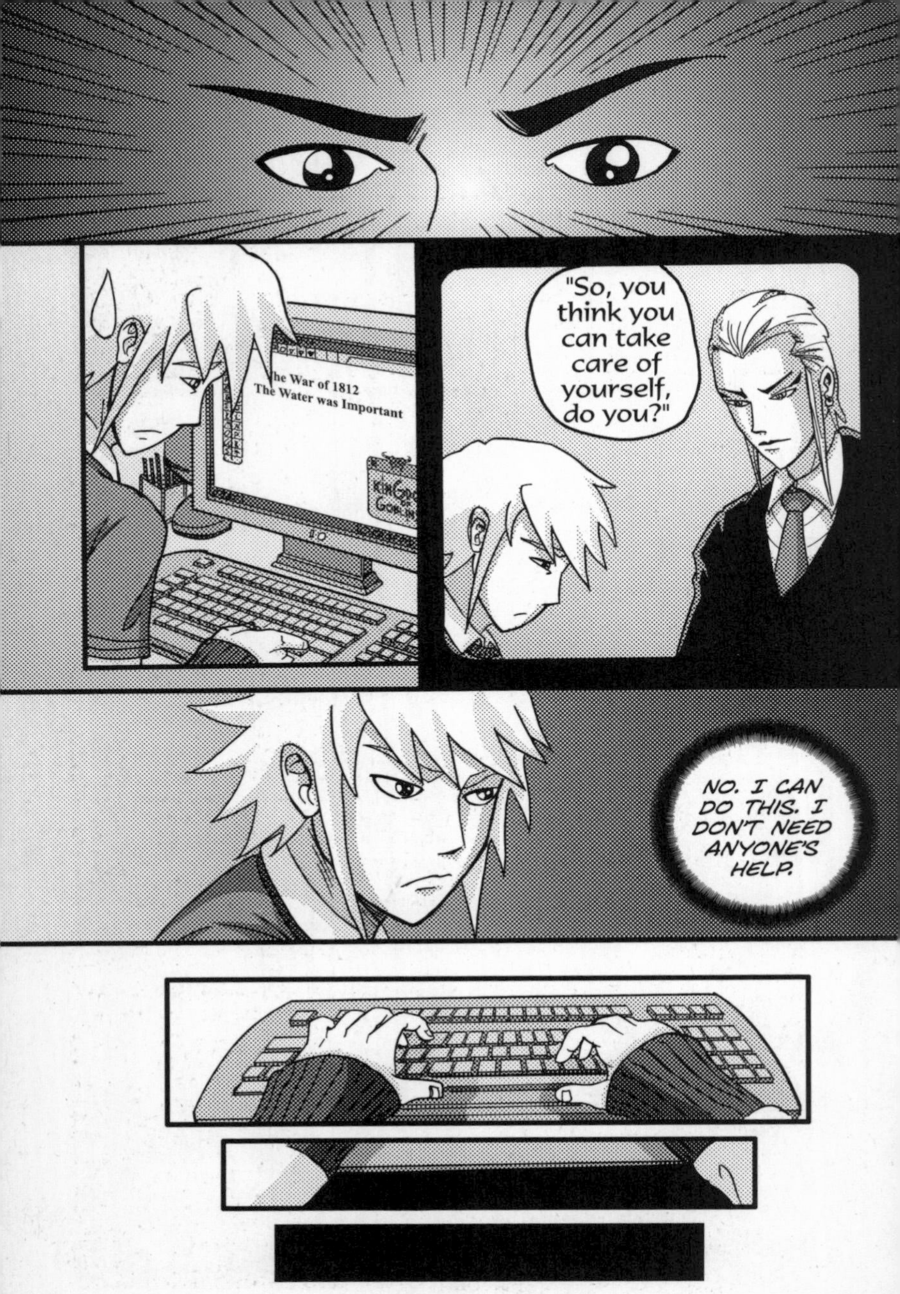
he War of 1812
The Water was Important
"So, you think you can take care of yourself, do you?"
NO. I CAN DO THIS. I DON'T NEED ANYONE'S HELP.

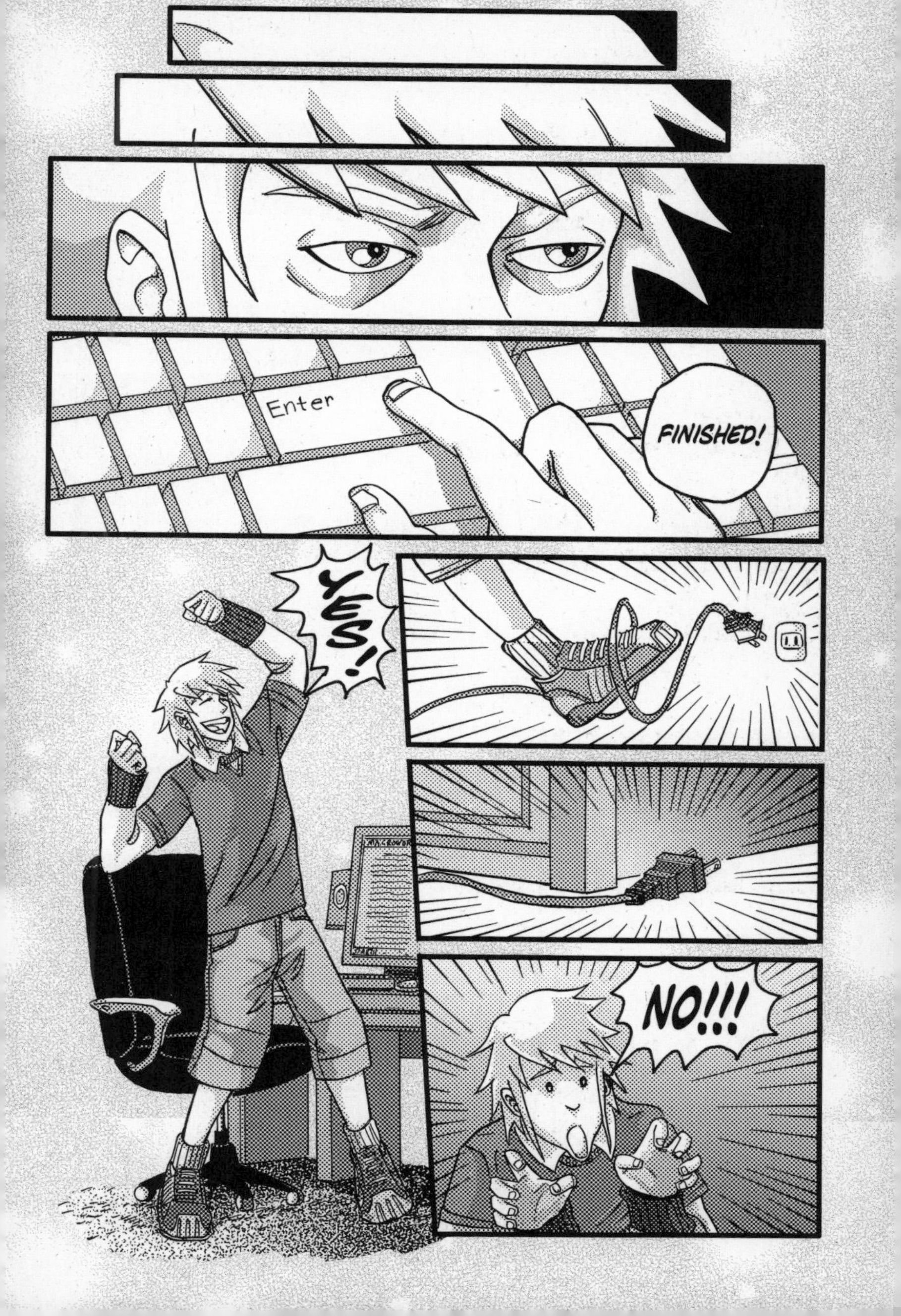
Enter
FINISHED!
YES!
NO!!!

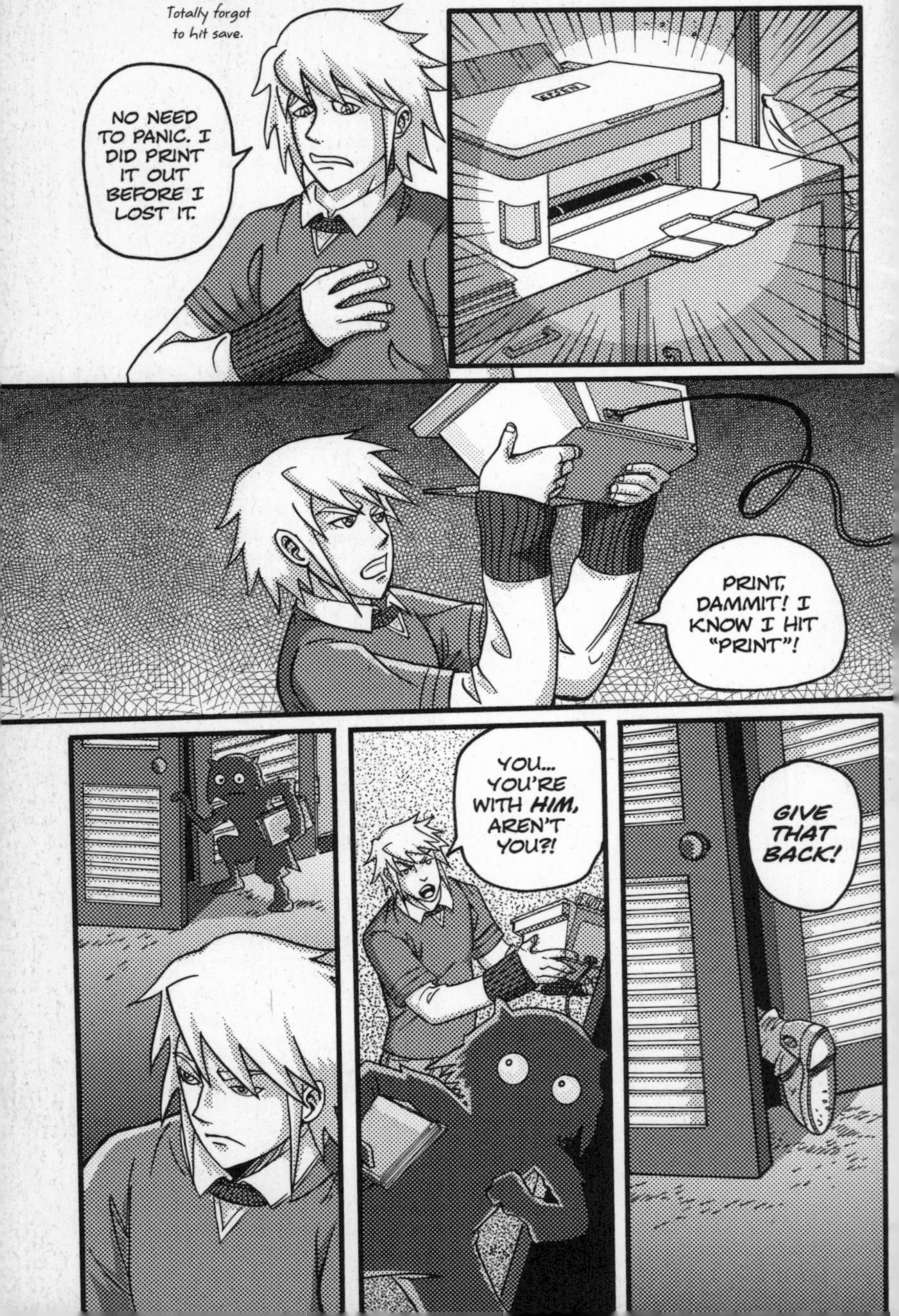
Totally forgot to hit save.
NO NEED TO PANIC. I DID PRINT IT OUT BEFORE I LOST IT.
PRINT, DAMMIT! I KNOW I HIT "PRINT"!
YOU... YOU'RE WITH ***HIM***, AREN'T YOU?!
GIVE THAT BACK!

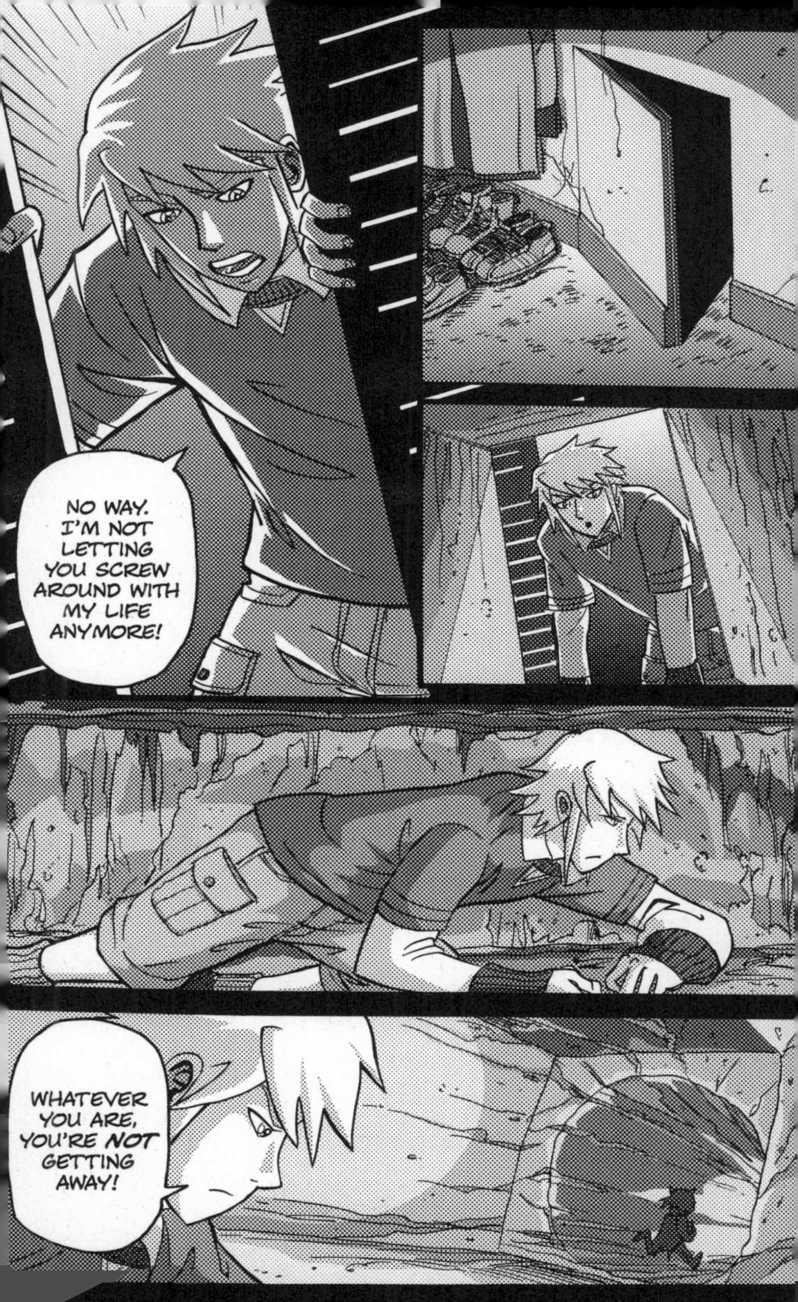
NO WAY. I'M NOT LETTING YOU SCREW AROUND WITH MY LIFE ANYMORE!
WHATEVER YOU ARE, YOU'RE *NOT* GETTING AWAY!

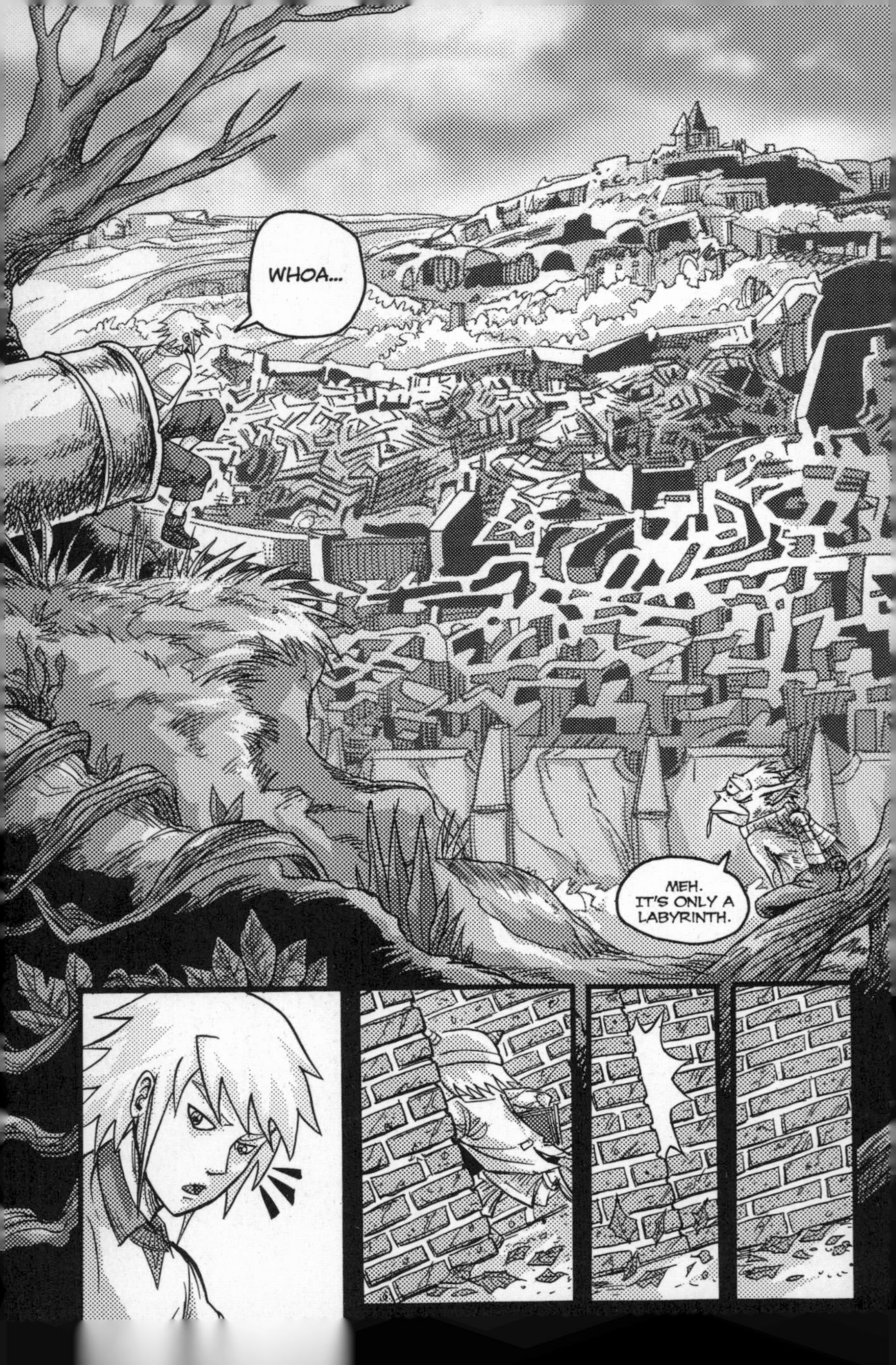
WHOA...
MEH. IT'S ONLY A LABYRINTH.

Chapter 2

INTO THE LABYRINTH

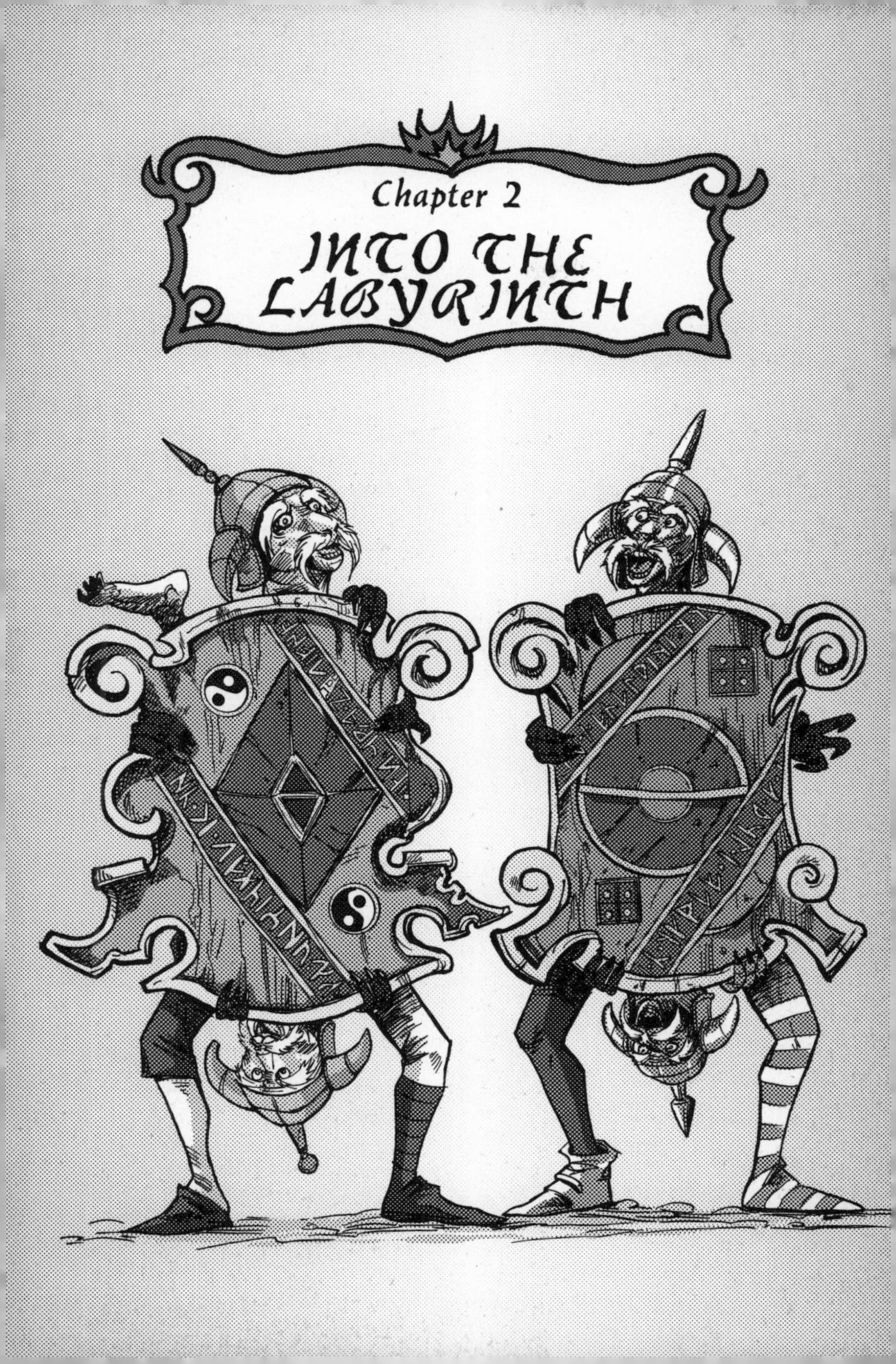

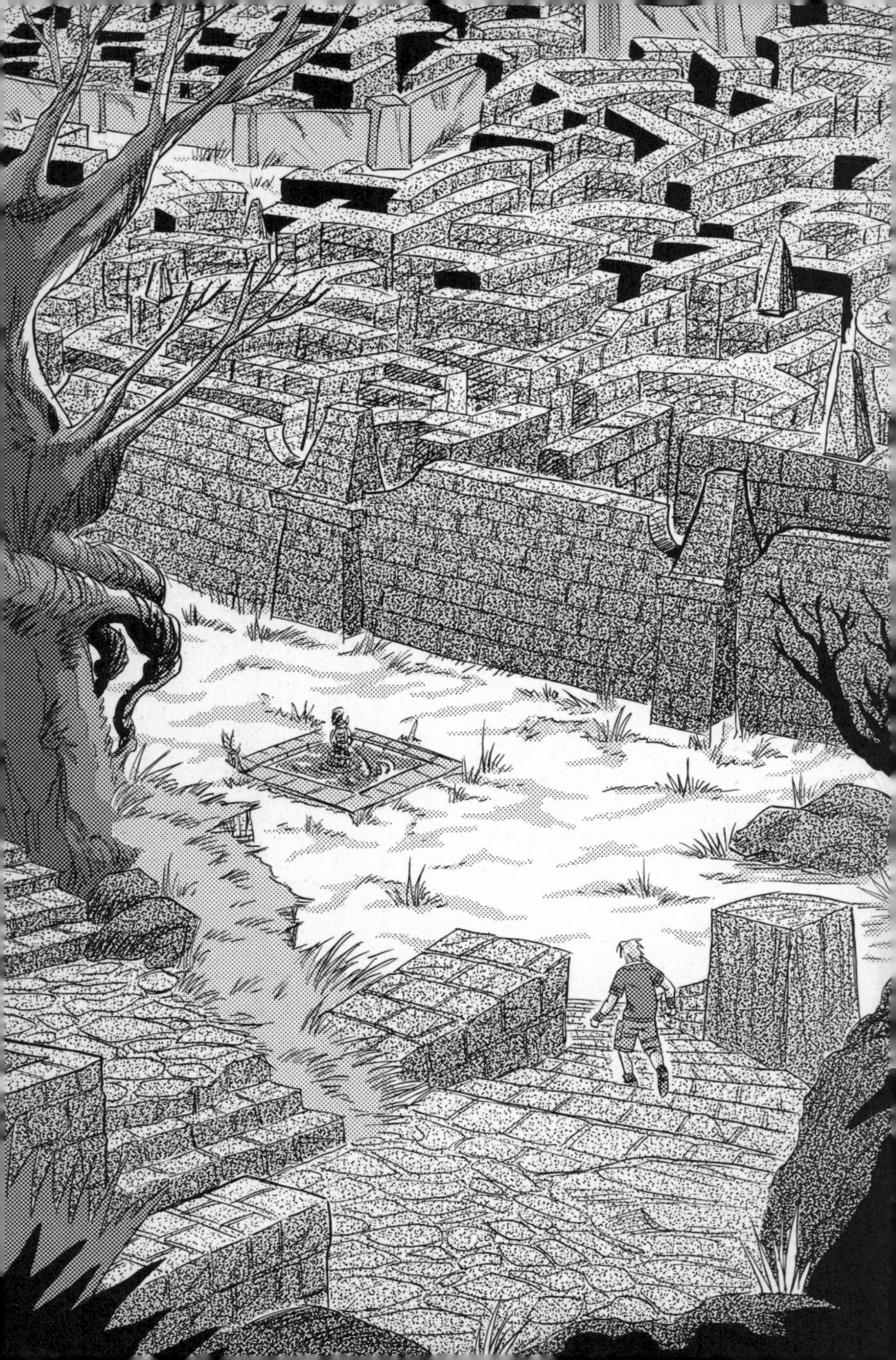

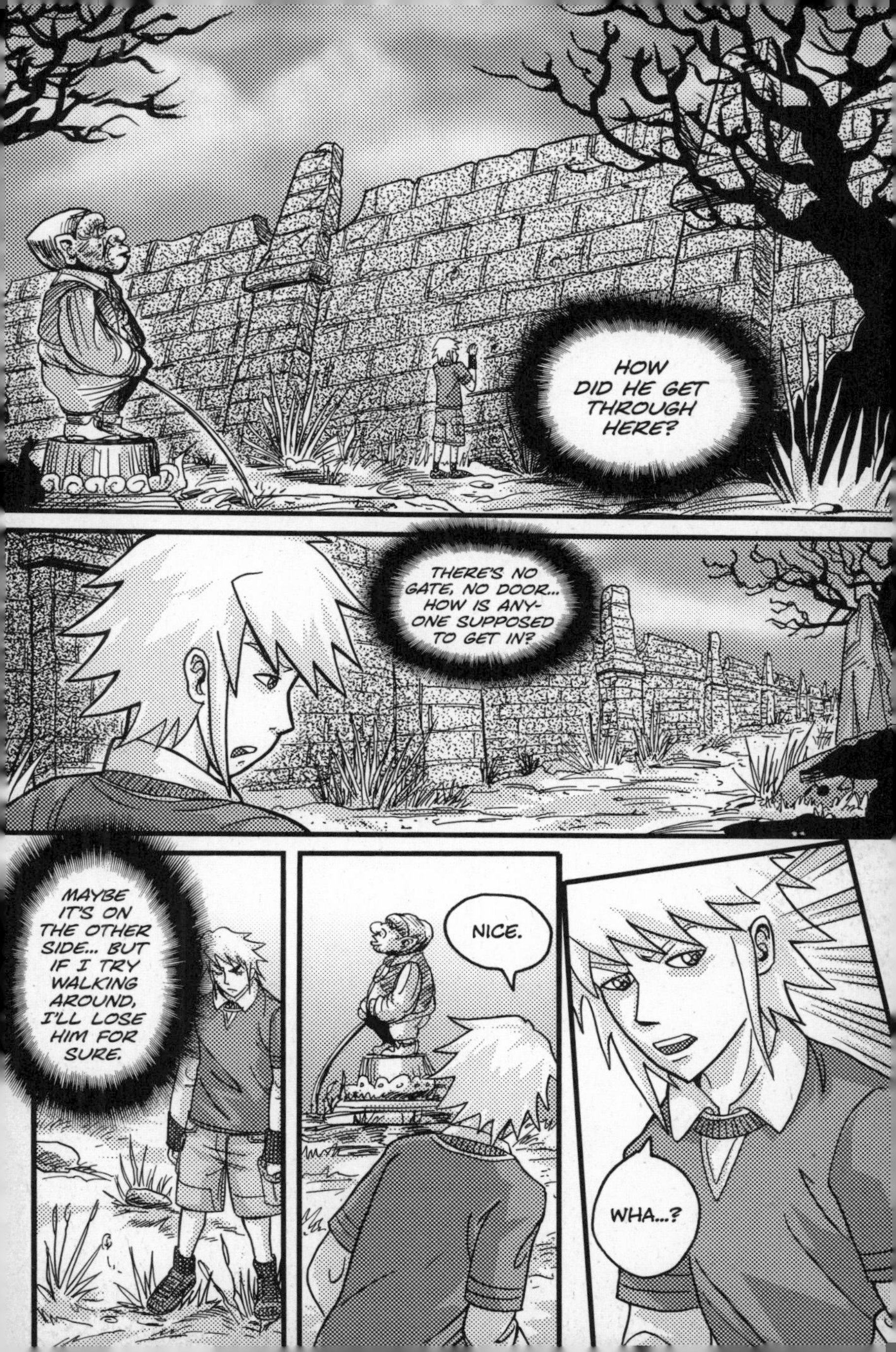
HOW DID HE GET THROUGH HERE?
THERE'S NO GATE, NO DOOR... HOW IS ANY-ONE SUPPOSED TO GET IN?
MAYBE IT'S ON THE OTHER SIDE... BUT IF I TRY WALKING AROUND, I'LL LOSE HIM FOR SURE.
NICE.
WHA...?

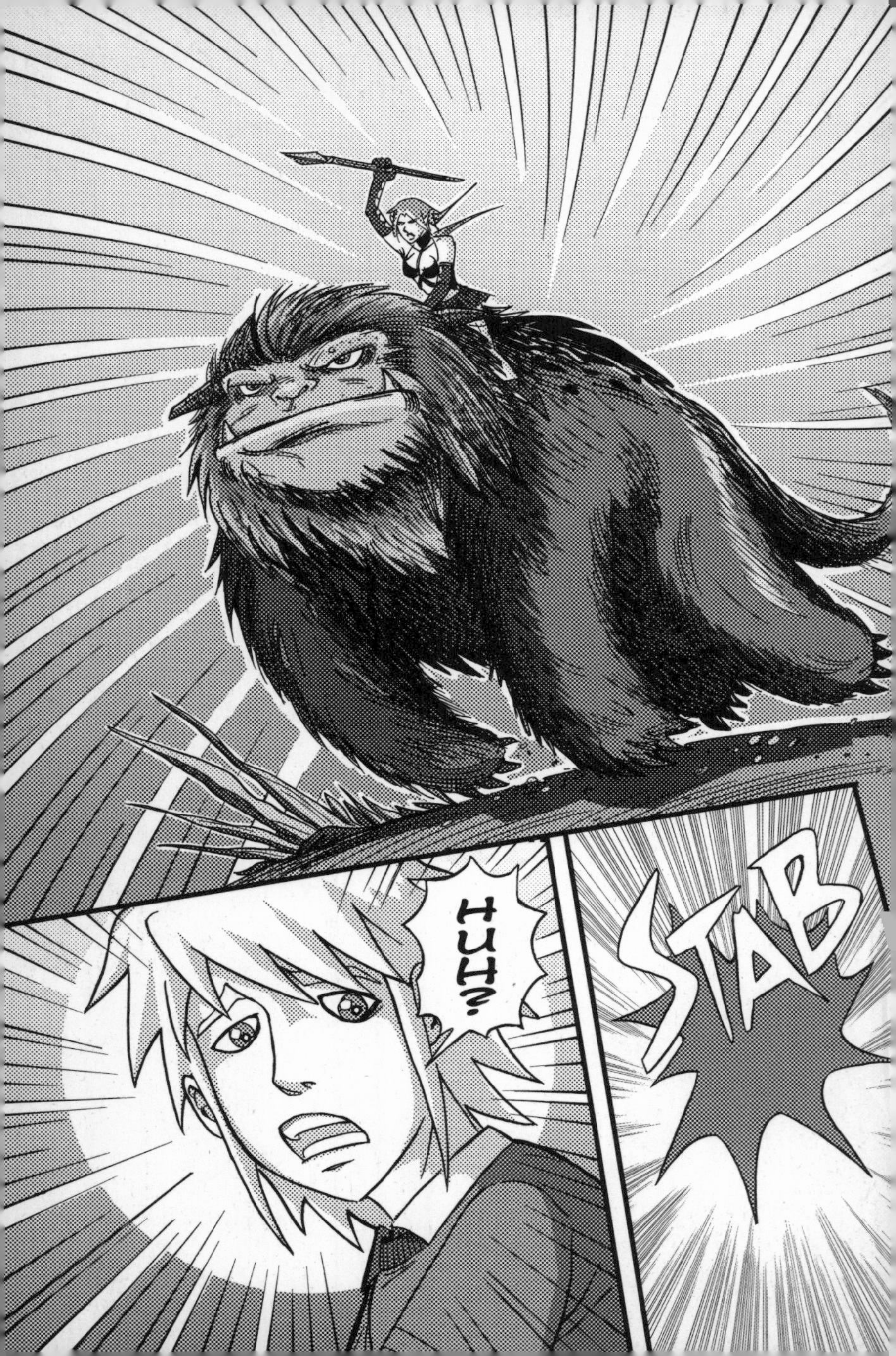
HUH?
STAB

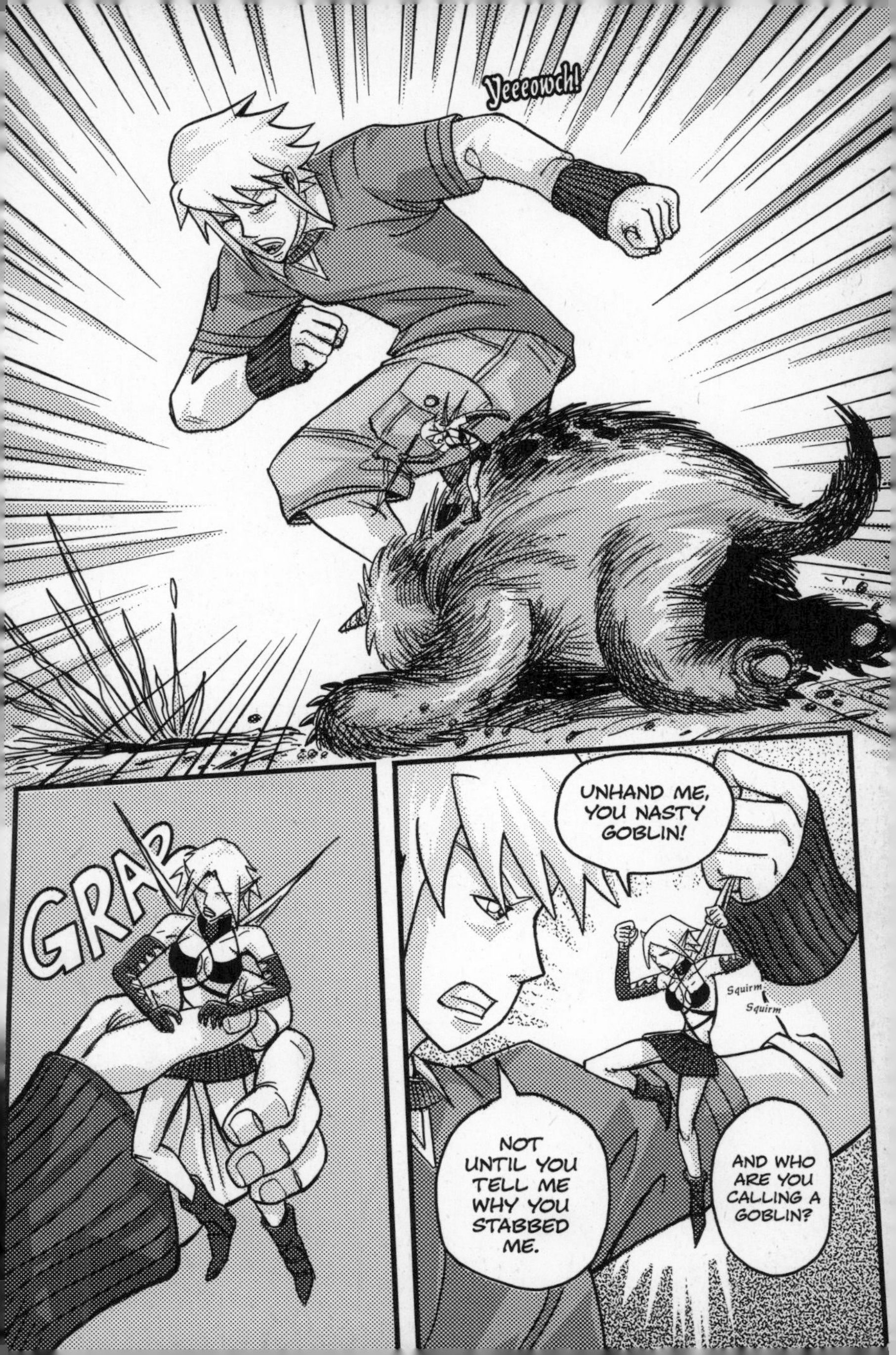
Yeeeowch!
GRAB
UNHAND ME, YOU NASTY GOBLIN!
Squirm
Squirm
NOT UNTIL YOU TELL ME WHY YOU STABBED ME.
AND WHO ARE YOU CALLING A GOBLIN?

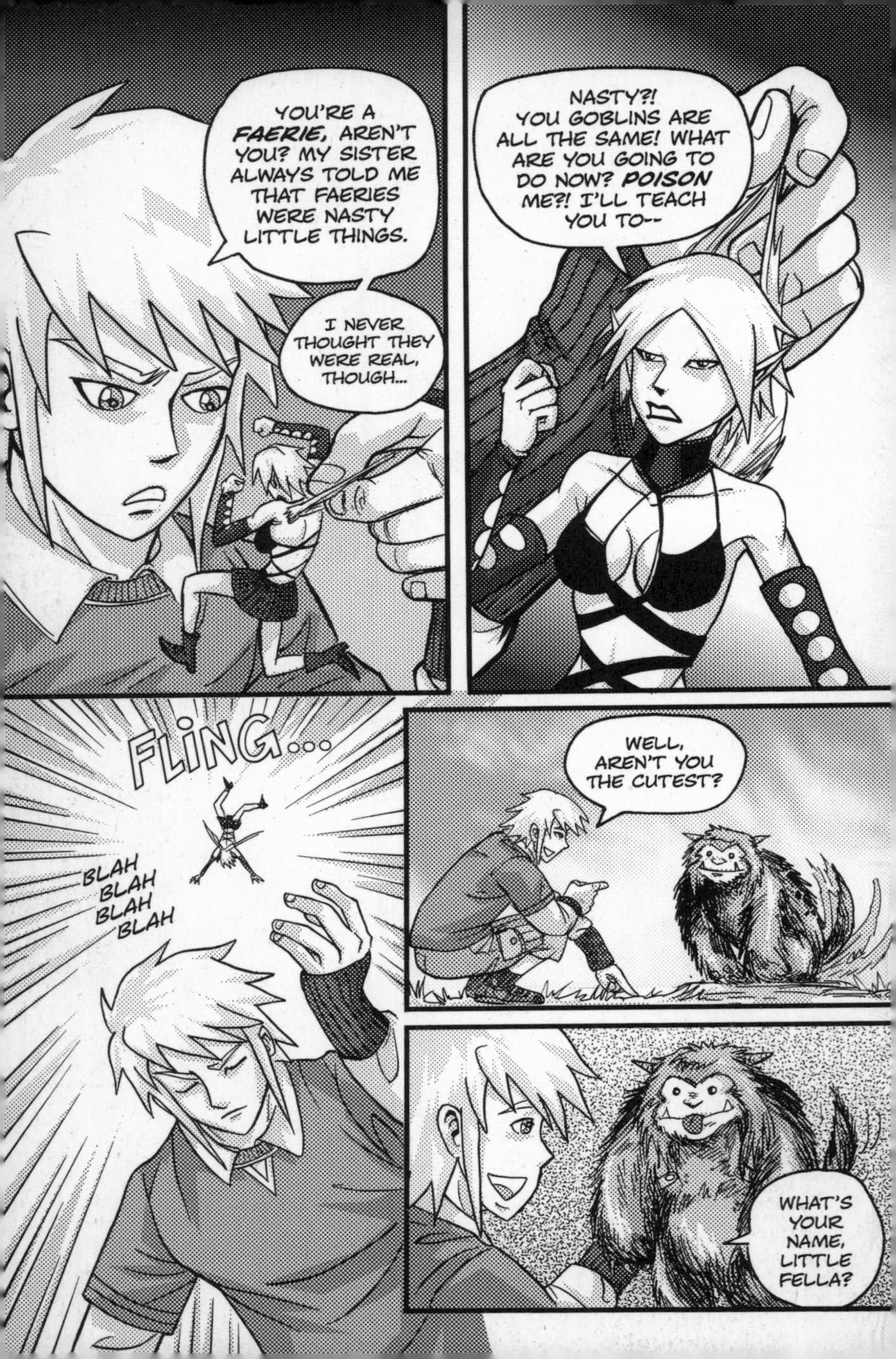
YOU'RE A **FAERIE,** AREN'T YOU? MY SISTER ALWAYS TOLD ME THAT FAERIES WERE NASTY LITTLE THINGS.
I NEVER THOUGHT THEY WERE REAL, THOUGH...
NASTY?! YOU GOBLINS ARE ALL THE SAME! WHAT ARE YOU GOING TO DO NOW? **POISON** ME?! I'LL TEACH YOU TO--
FLING...
BLAH BLAH BLAH BLAH
WELL, AREN'T YOU THE CUTEST?
WHAT'S YOUR NAME, LITTLE FELLA?

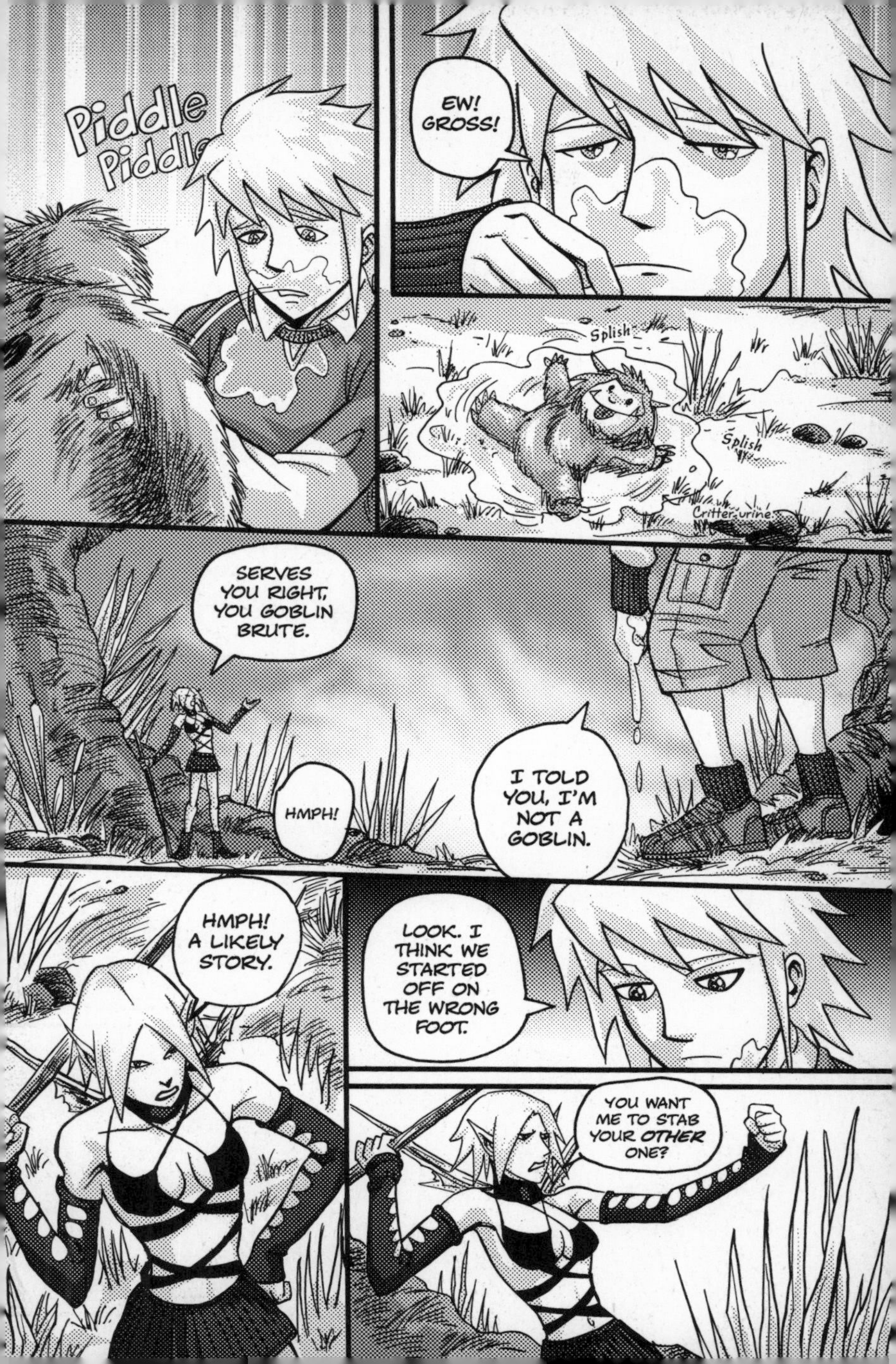
Piddle Piddle
EW! GROSS!
Splish
Splish
Critter urine
SERVES YOU RIGHT, YOU GOBLIN BRUTE.
HMPH!
I TOLD YOU, I'M NOT A GOBLIN.
HMPH! A LIKELY STORY.
LOOK. I THINK WE STARTED OFF ON THE WRONG FOOT.
YOU WANT ME TO STAB YOUR *OTHER* ONE?

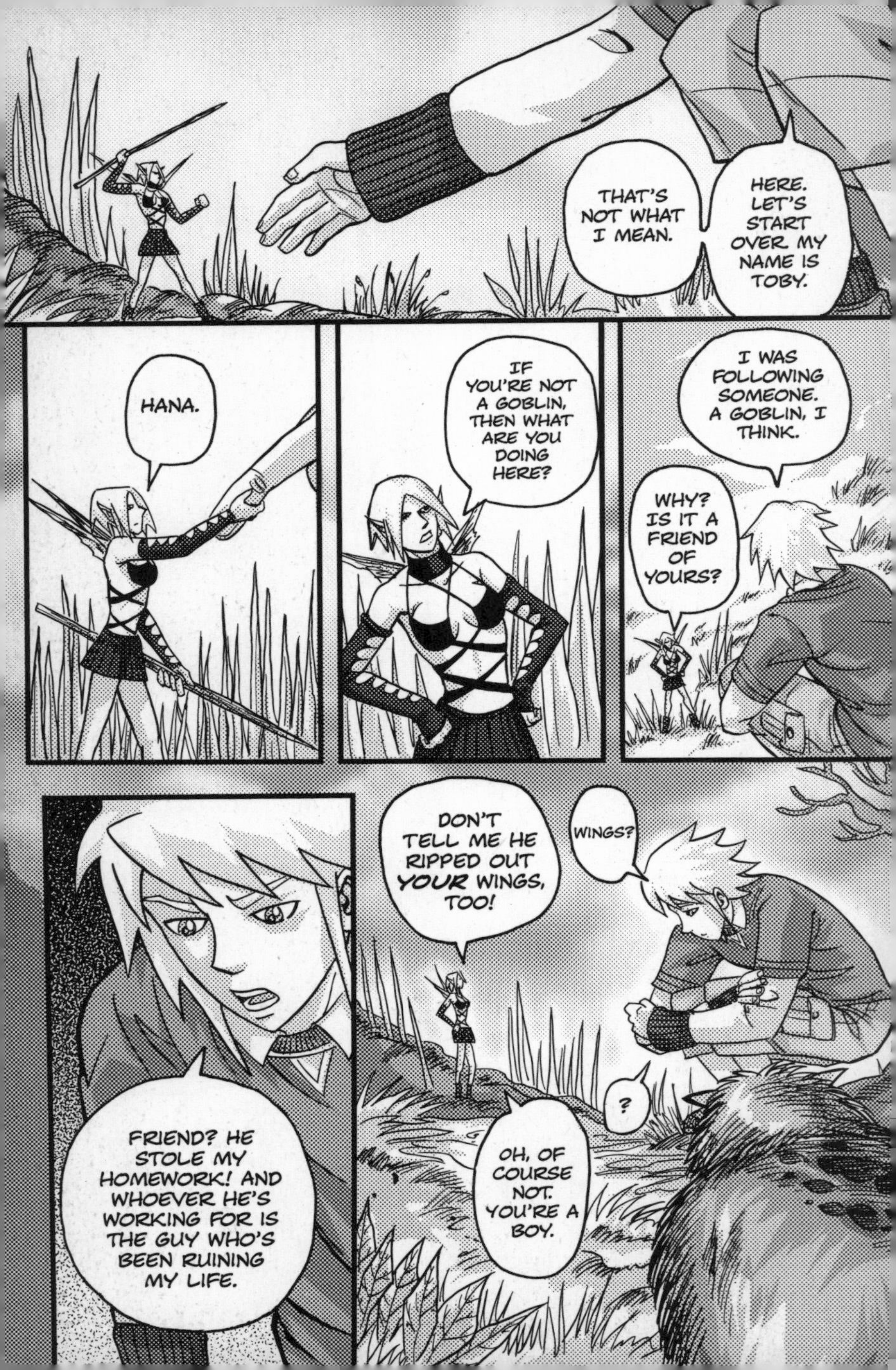
THAT'S NOT WHAT I MEAN.
HERE. LET'S START OVER MY NAME IS TOBY.
HANA.
IF YOU'RE NOT A GOBLIN, THEN WHAT ARE YOU DOING HERE?
I WAS FOLLOWING SOMEONE. A GOBLIN, I THINK.
WHY? IS IT A FRIEND OF YOURS?
FRIEND? HE STOLE MY HOMEWORK! AND WHOEVER HE'S WORKING FOR IS THE GUY WHO'S BEEN RUINING MY LIFE.
DON'T TELL ME HE RIPPED OUT *YOUR* WINGS, TOO!
WINGS?
?
OH, OF COURSE NOT. YOU'RE A BOY.

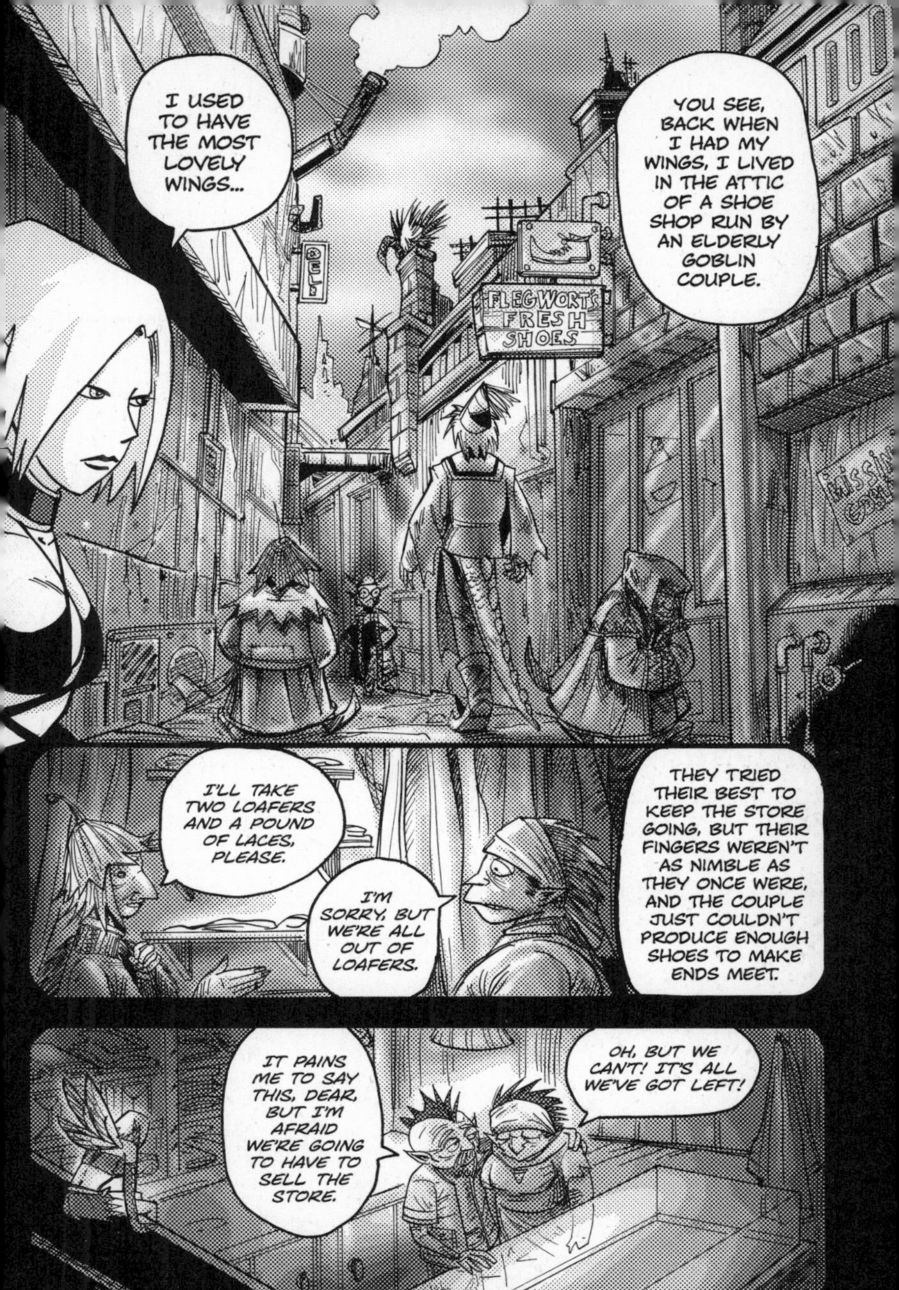
I USED TO HAVE THE MOST LOVELY WINGS...
DELI
FLEGWORT'S FRESH SHOES
YOU SEE, BACK WHEN I HAD MY WINGS, I LIVED IN THE ATTIC OF A SHOE SHOP RUN BY AN ELDERLY GOBLIN COUPLE.
I'LL TAKE TWO LOAFERS AND A POUND OF LACES, PLEASE.
I'M SORRY, BUT WE'RE ALL OUT OF LOAFERS.
THEY TRIED THEIR BEST TO KEEP THE STORE GOING, BUT THEIR FINGERS WEREN'T AS NIMBLE AS THEY ONCE WERE, AND THE COUPLE JUST COULDN'T PRODUCE ENOUGH SHOES TO MAKE ENDS MEET.
IT PAINS ME TO SAY THIS, DEAR, BUT I'M AFRAID WE'RE GOING TO HAVE TO SELL THE STORE.
OH, BUT WE CAN'T! IT'S ALL WE'VE GOT LEFT!

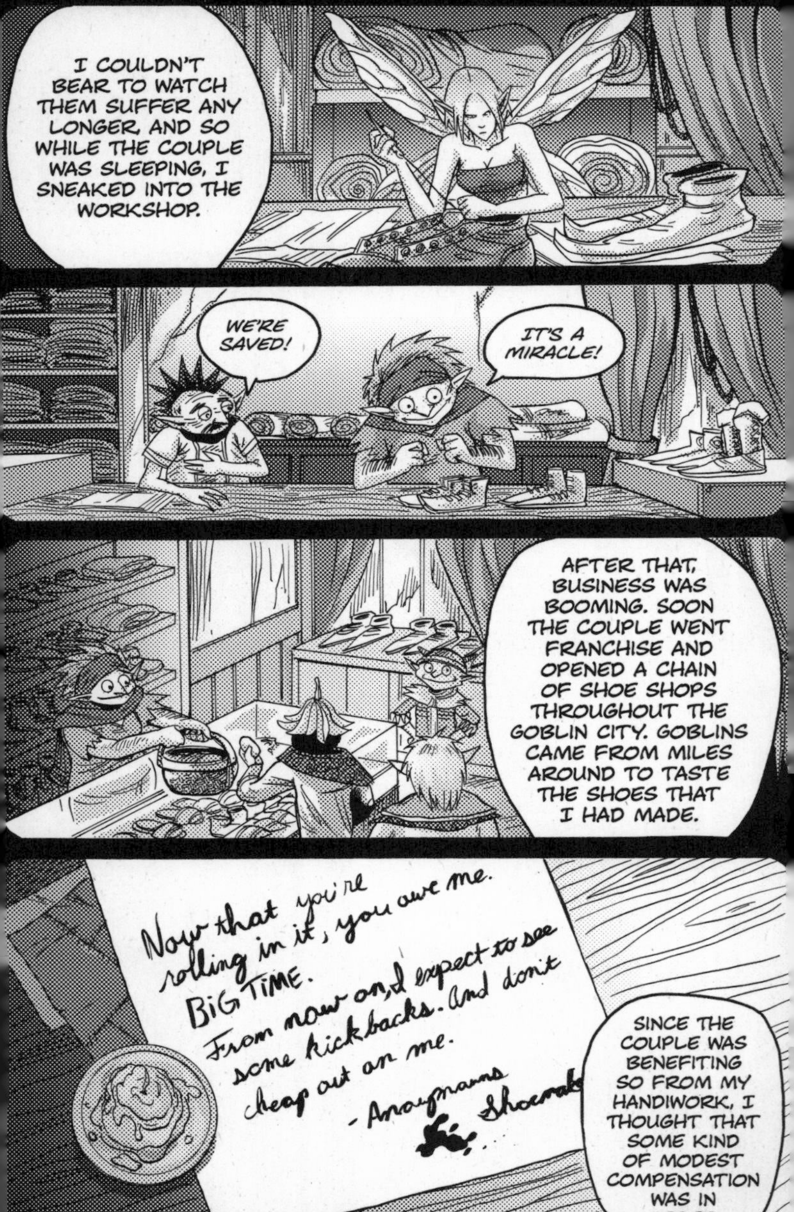
I COULDN'T BEAR TO WATCH THEM SUFFER ANY LONGER, AND SO WHILE THE COUPLE WAS SLEEPING, I SNEAKED INTO THE WORKSHOP.
WE'RE SAVED!
IT'S A MIRACLE!
AFTER THAT, BUSINESS WAS BOOMING. SOON THE COUPLE WENT FRANCHISE AND OPENED A CHAIN OF SHOE SHOPS THROUGHOUT THE GOBLIN CITY. GOBLINS CAME FROM MILES AROUND TO TASTE THE SHOES THAT I HAD MADE.
Now that you're rolling in it, you owe me. BIG TIME.
From now on, I expect to see some kickbacks. And don't cheap out on me.
- Anonymous
Shoemak
SINCE THE COUPLE WAS BENEFITING SO FROM MY HANDIWORK, I THOUGHT THAT SOME KIND OF MODEST COMPENSATION WAS IN ORDER

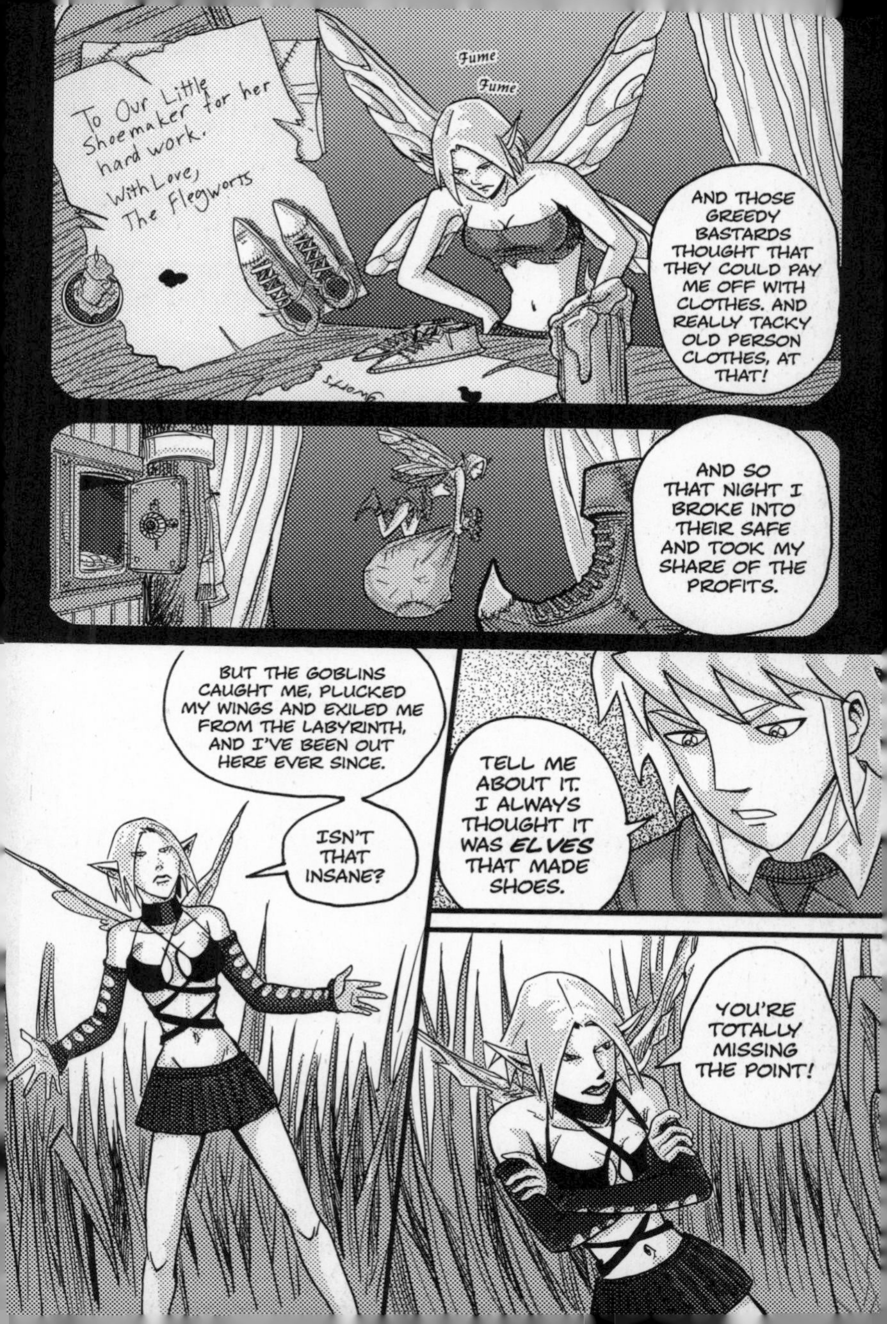
To Our Little Shoemaker for her hard work.
With Love, The Flegworts
Fume
Fume
AND THOSE GREEDY BASTARDS THOUGHT THAT THEY COULD PAY ME OFF WITH CLOTHES. AND REALLY TACKY OLD PERSON CLOTHES, AT THAT!
AND SO THAT NIGHT I BROKE INTO THEIR SAFE AND TOOK MY SHARE OF THE PROFITS.
BUT THE GOBLINS CAUGHT ME, PLUCKED MY WINGS AND EXILED ME FROM THE LABYRINTH, AND I'VE BEEN OUT HERE EVER SINCE.
ISN'T THAT INSANE?
TELL ME ABOUT IT. I ALWAYS THOUGHT IT WAS *ELVES* THAT MADE SHOES.
YOU'RE TOTALLY MISSING THE POINT!

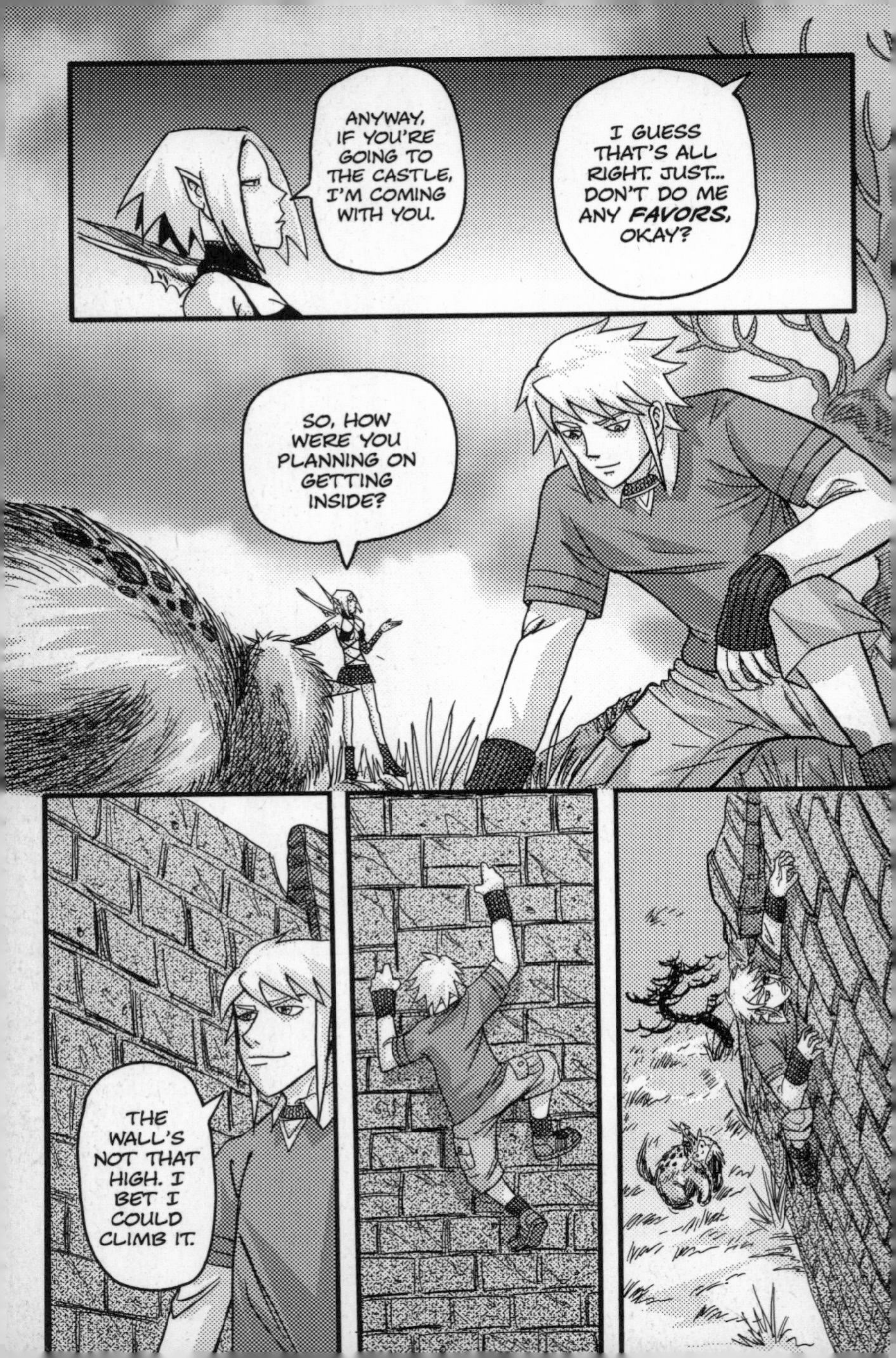
ANYWAY, IF YOU'RE GOING TO THE CASTLE, I'M COMING WITH YOU.
I GUESS THAT'S ALL RIGHT. JUST... DON'T DO ME ANY *FAVORS,* OKAY?
SO, HOW WERE YOU PLANNING ON GETTING INSIDE?
THE WALL'S NOT THAT HIGH. I BET I COULD CLIMB IT.

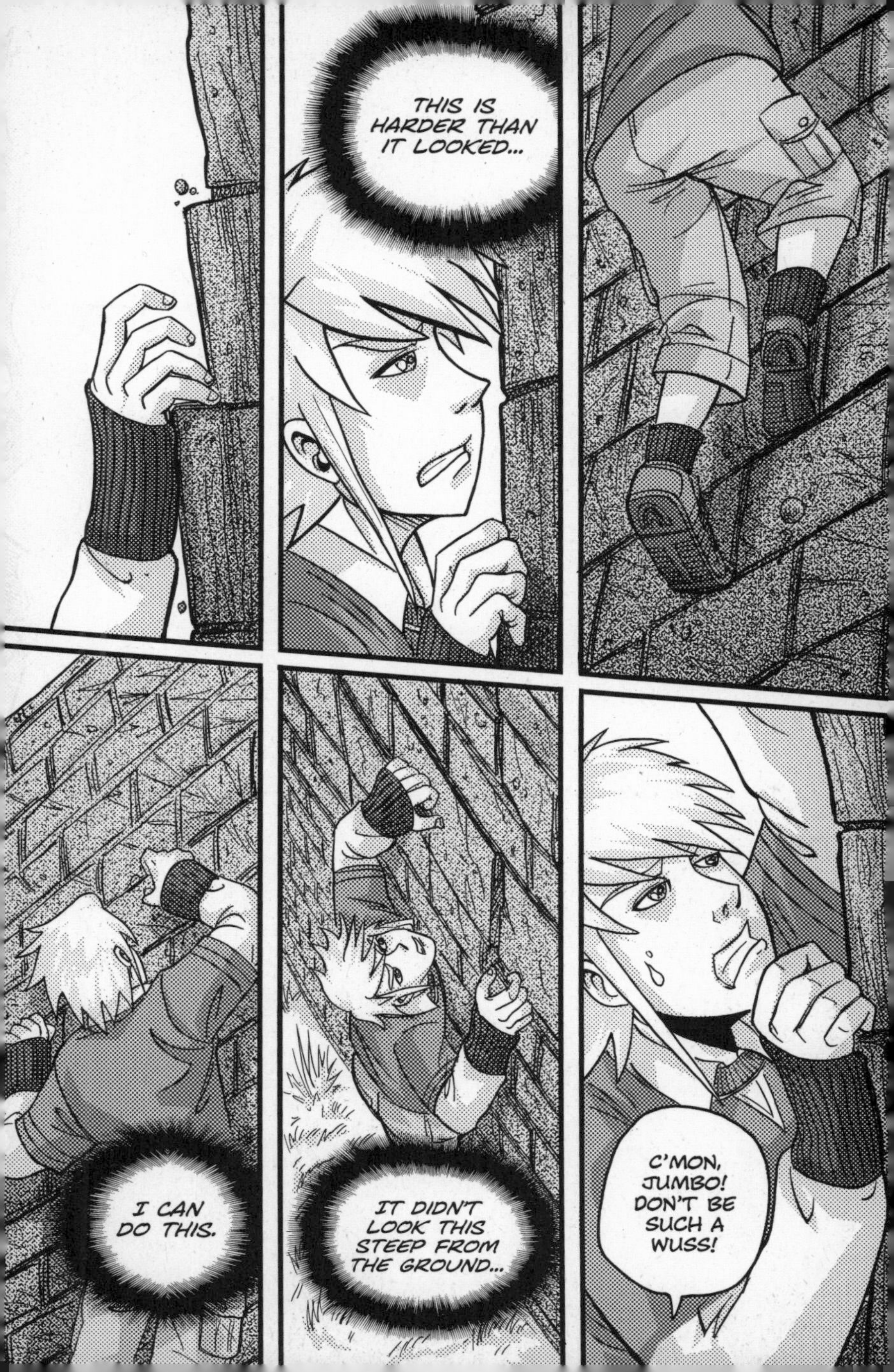
THIS IS HARDER THAN IT LOOKED...
I CAN DO THIS.
IT DIDN'T LOOK THIS STEEP FROM THE GROUND...
C'MON, JUMBO! DON'T BE SUCH A WUSS!

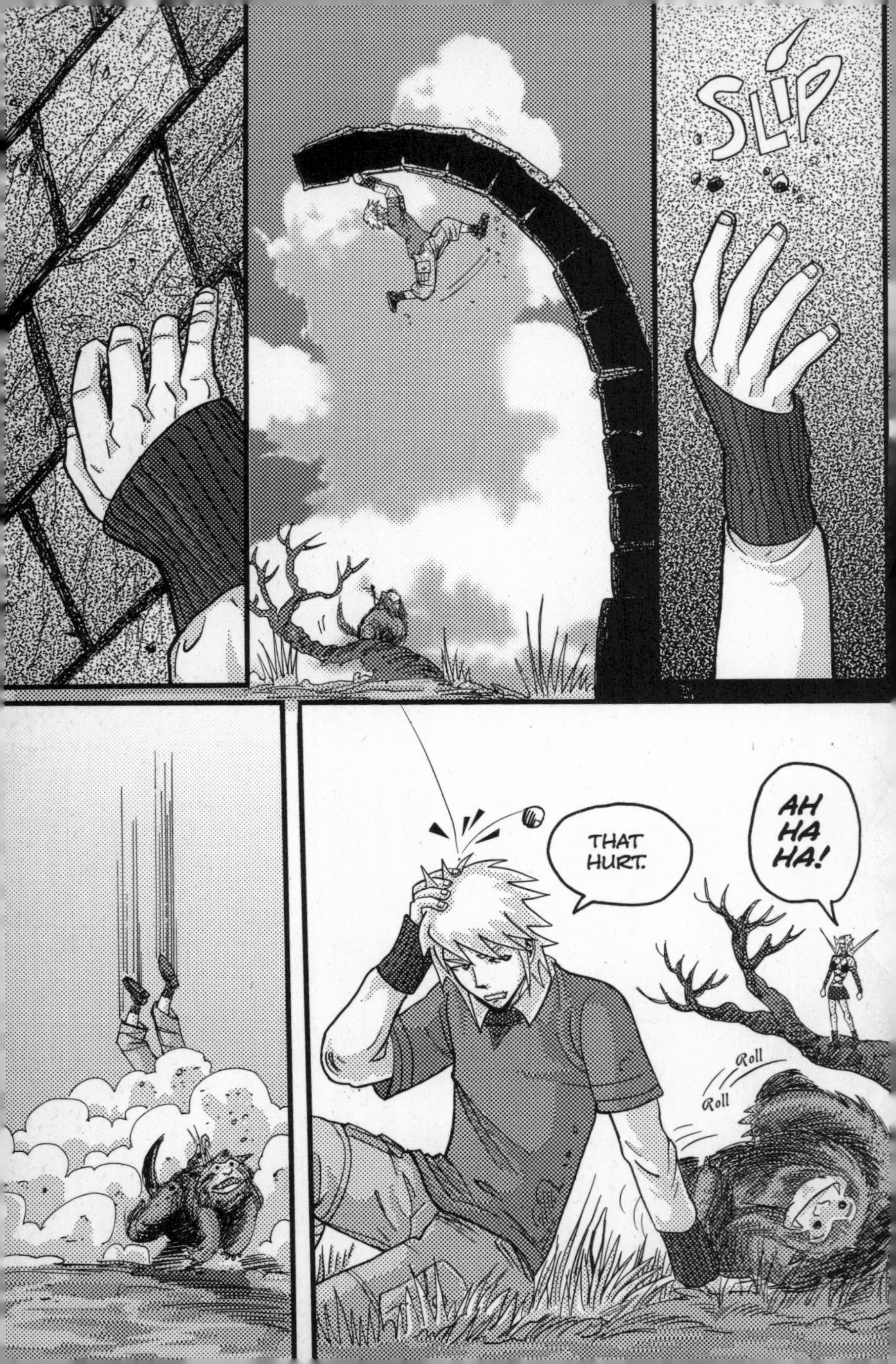
SLIP
THAT HURT.
AH HA HA!
Roll
Roll

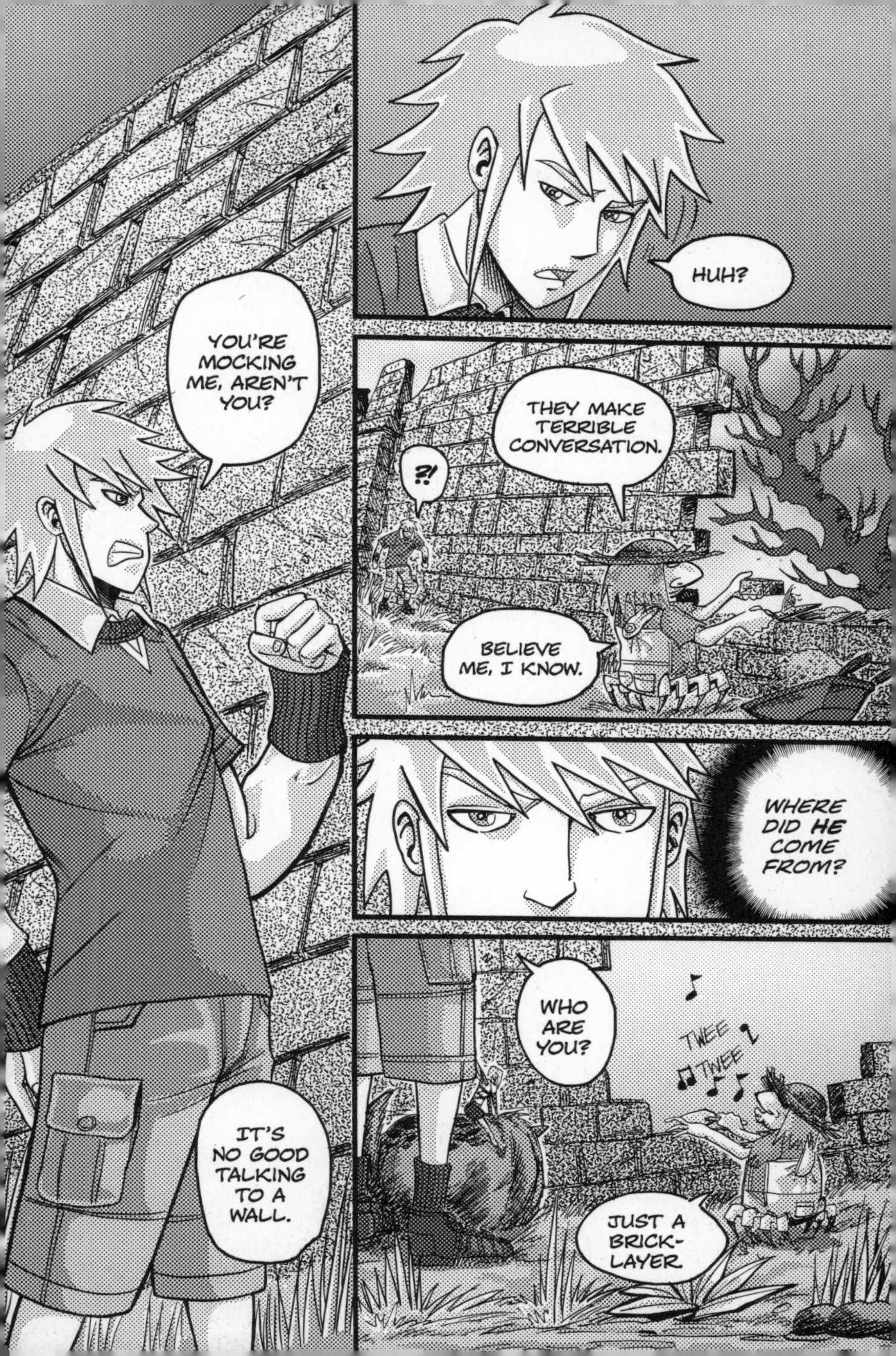
YOU'RE MOCKING ME, AREN'T YOU?
IT'S NO GOOD TALKING TO A WALL.
HUH?
THEY MAKE TERRIBLE CONVERSATION.
?!
BELIEVE ME, I KNOW.
WHERE DID HE COME FROM?
WHO ARE YOU?
TWEE TWEE
JUST A BRICK-LAYER

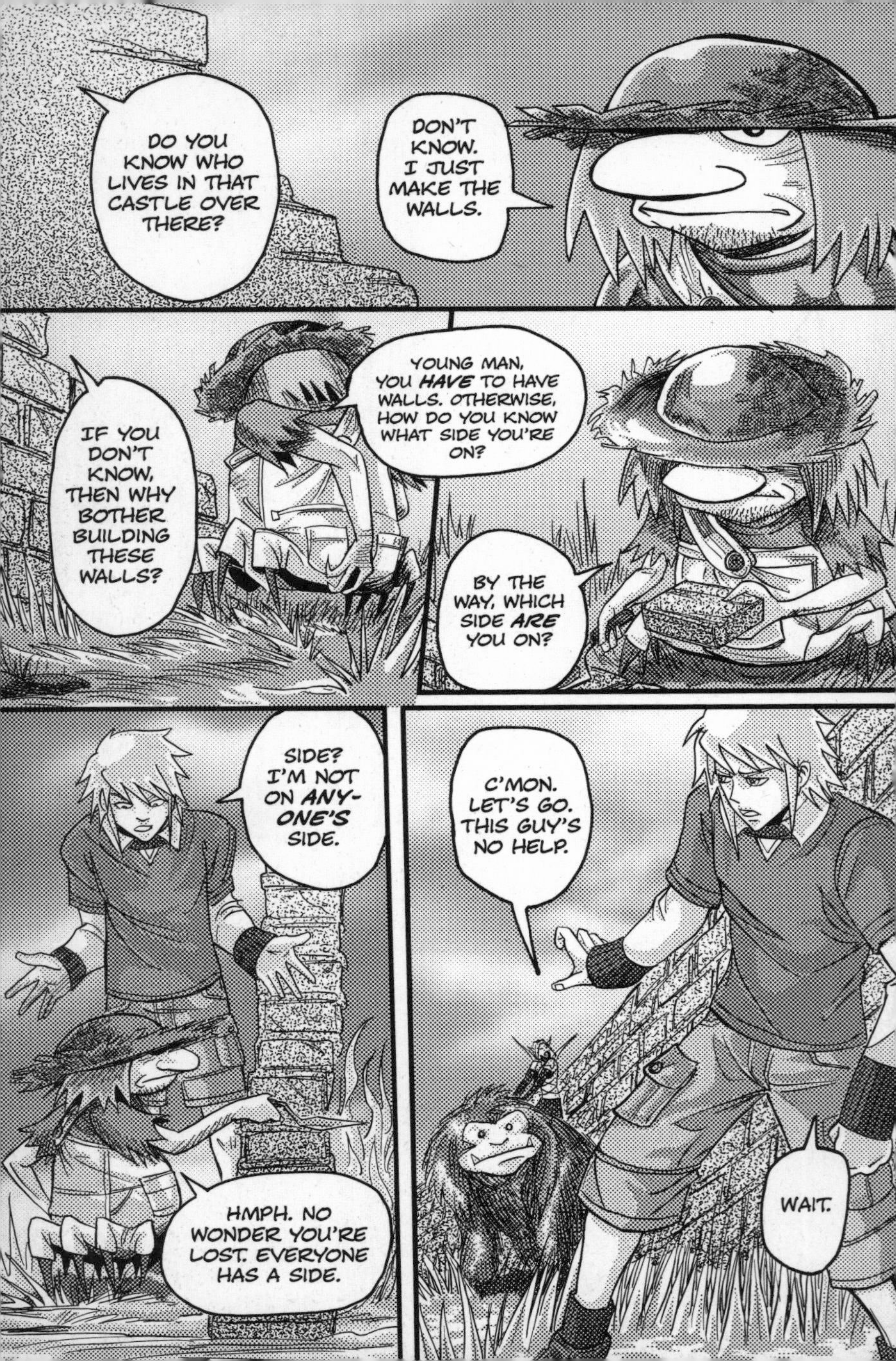
DO YOU KNOW WHO LIVES IN THAT CASTLE OVER THERE?
DON'T KNOW. I JUST MAKE THE WALLS.
IF YOU DON'T KNOW, THEN WHY BOTHER BUILDING THESE WALLS?
YOUNG MAN, YOU *HAVE* TO HAVE WALLS. OTHERWISE, HOW DO YOU KNOW WHAT SIDE YOU'RE ON?
BY THE WAY, WHICH SIDE *ARE* YOU ON?
SIDE? I'M NOT ON *ANY-ONE'S* SIDE.
HMPH. NO WONDER YOU'RE LOST. EVERYONE HAS A SIDE.
C'MON. LET'S GO. THIS GUY'S NO HELP.
WAIT.

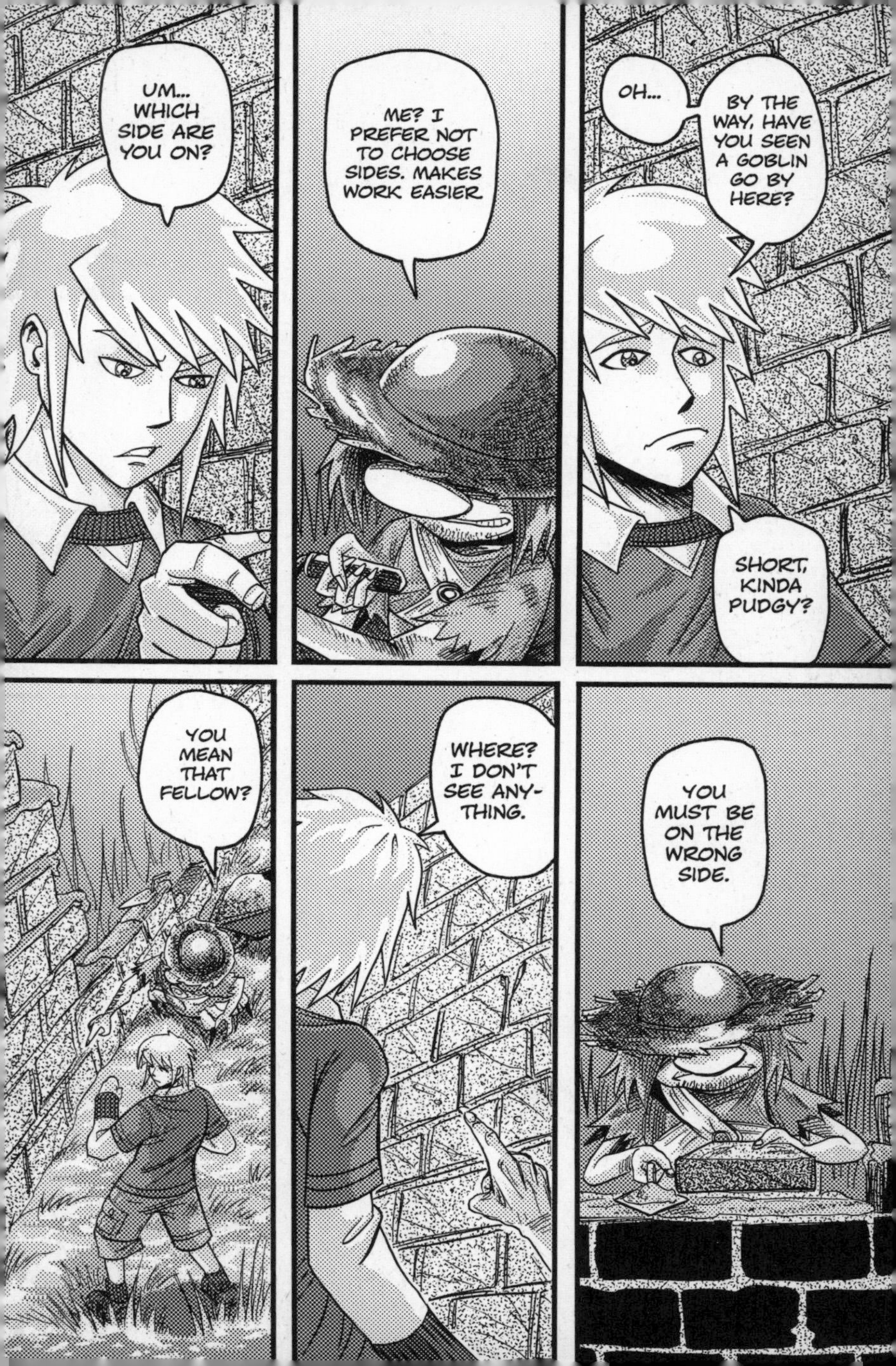
UM... WHICH SIDE ARE YOU ON?
ME? I PREFER NOT TO CHOOSE SIDES. MAKES WORK EASIER
OH...
BY THE WAY, HAVE YOU SEEN A GOBLIN GO BY HERE?
SHORT, KINDA PUDGY?
YOU MEAN THAT FELLOW?
WHERE? I DON'T SEE ANY-THING.
YOU MUST BE ON THE WRONG SIDE.

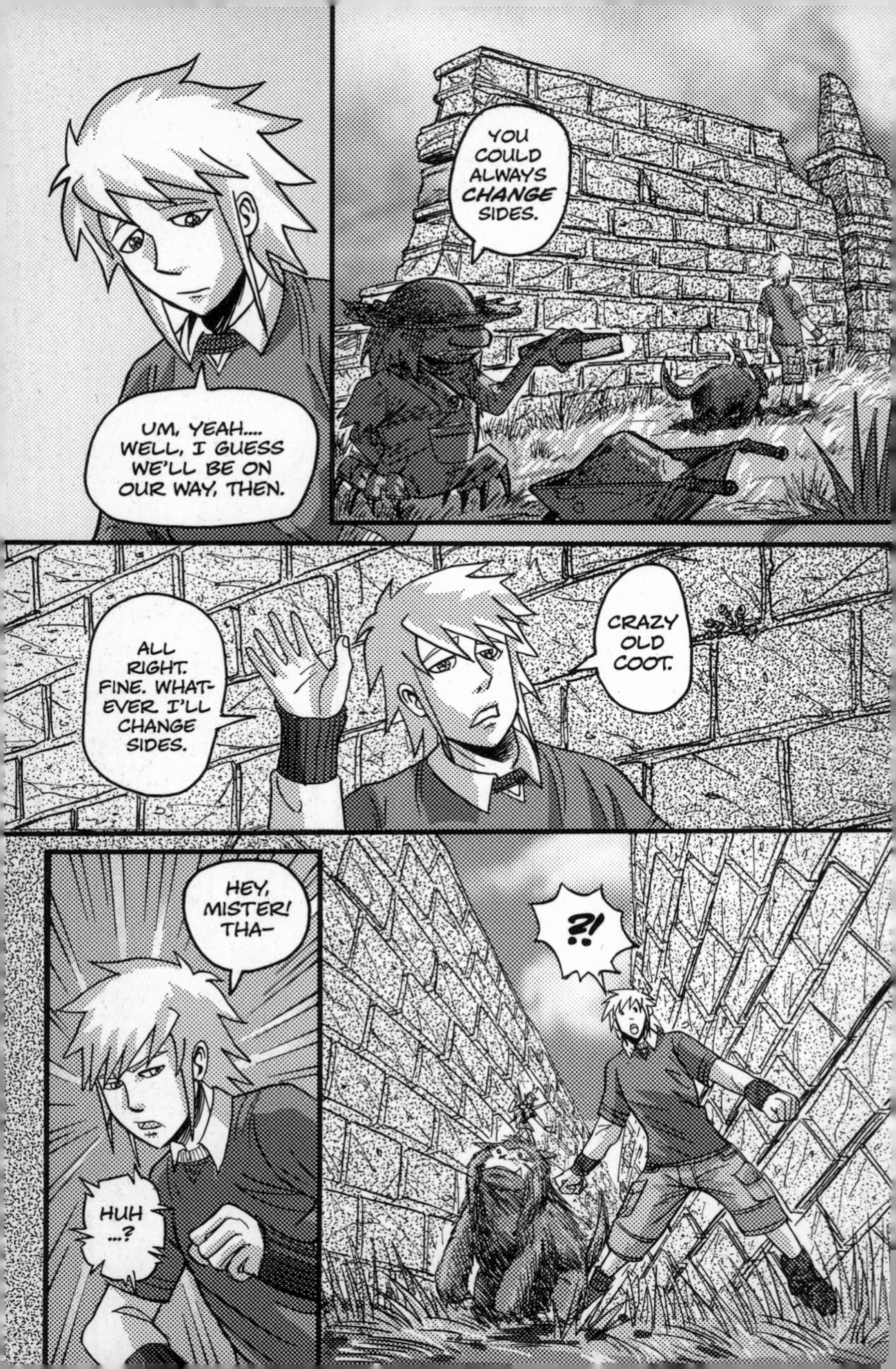
UM, YEAH.... WELL, I GUESS WE'LL BE ON OUR WAY, THEN.
YOU COULD ALWAYS *CHANGE* SIDES.
ALL RIGHT. FINE. WHAT-EVER. I'LL CHANGE SIDES.
CRAZY OLD COOT.
HEY, MISTER! THA-
HUH ...?
?!

JARETH...

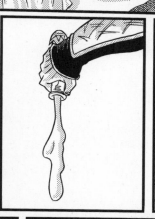

FIND THE BOY. DO NOT LET HIM REACH THE GOBLIN CASTLE!

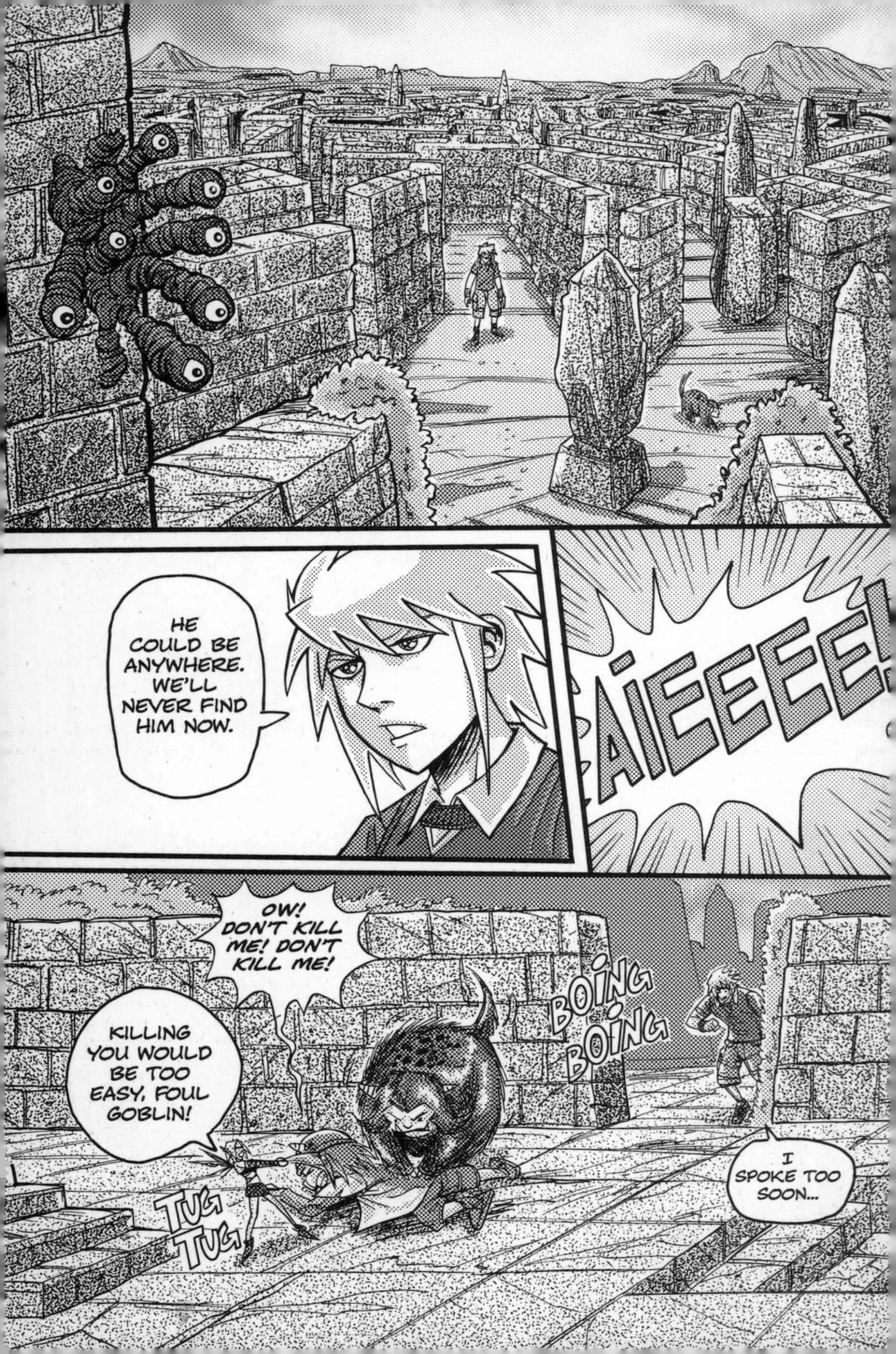
HE COULD BE ANYWHERE. WE'LL NEVER FIND HIM NOW.
AIEEEEE!
OW! DON'T KILL ME! DON'T KILL ME!
KILLING YOU WOULD BE TOO EASY, FOUL GOBLIN!
BOING BOING
TUG TUG
I SPOKE TOO SOON...

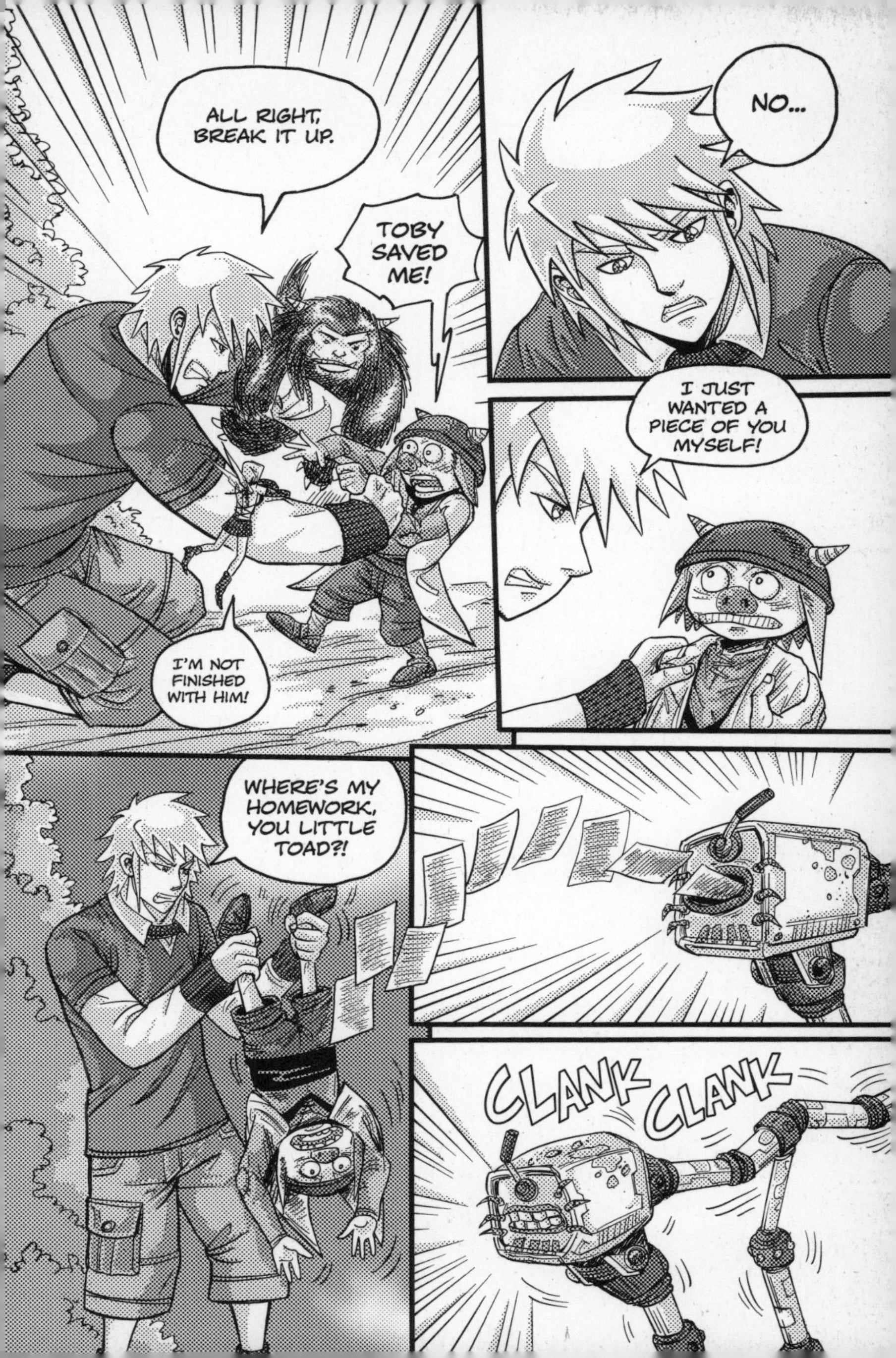
ALL RIGHT, BREAK IT UP.
TOBY SAVED ME!
I'M NOT FINISHED WITH HIM!
NO...
I JUST WANTED A PIECE OF YOU MYSELF!
WHERE'S MY HOMEWORK, YOU LITTLE TOAD?!
CLANK CLANK

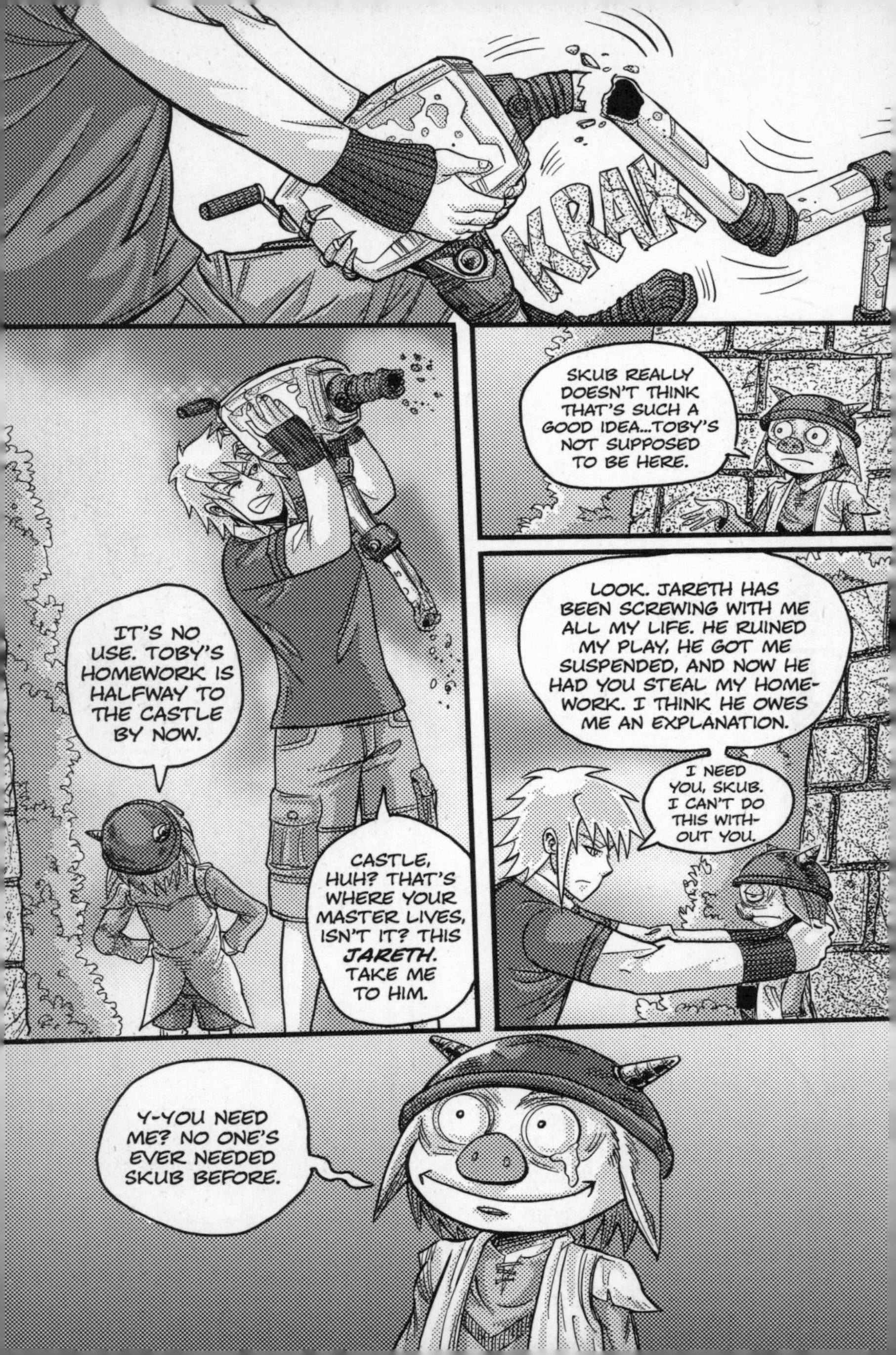
KRAK
IT'S NO USE. TOBY'S HOMEWORK IS HALFWAY TO THE CASTLE BY NOW.
CASTLE, HUH? THAT'S WHERE YOUR MASTER LIVES, ISN'T IT? THIS *JARETH*. TAKE ME TO HIM.
SKUB REALLY DOESN'T THINK THAT'S SUCH A GOOD IDEA...TOBY'S NOT SUPPOSED TO BE HERE.
LOOK. JARETH HAS BEEN SCREWING WITH ME ALL MY LIFE. HE RUINED MY PLAY, HE GOT ME SUSPENDED, AND NOW HE HAD YOU STEAL MY HOMEWORK. I THINK HE OWES ME AN EXPLANATION.
I NEED YOU, SKUB. I CAN'T DO THIS WITHOUT YOU.
Y-YOU NEED ME? NO ONE'S EVER NEEDED SKUB BEFORE.

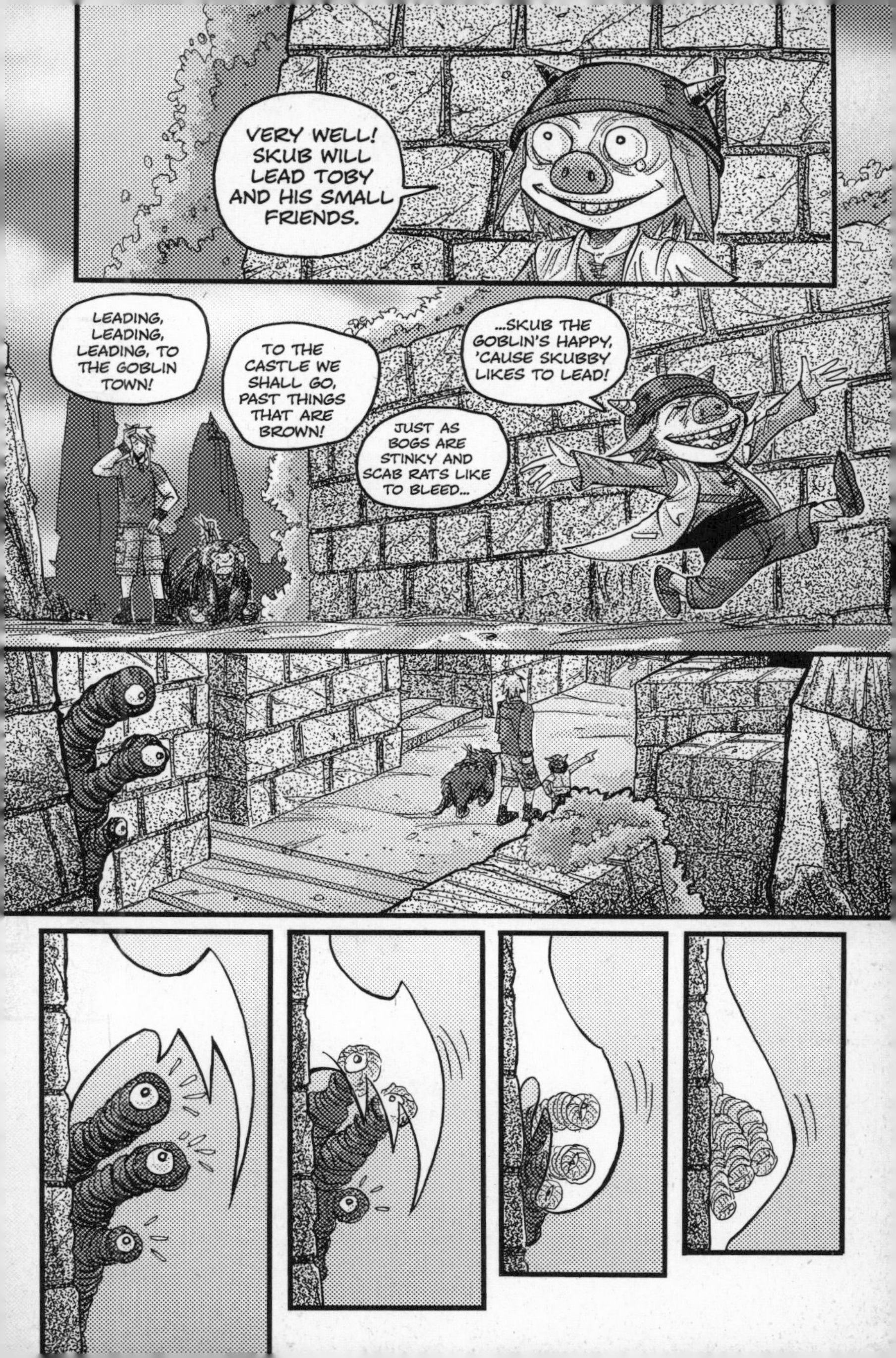
VERY WELL! SKUB WILL LEAD TOBY AND HIS SMALL FRIENDS.
LEADING, LEADING, LEADING, TO THE GOBLIN TOWN!
TO THE CASTLE WE SHALL GO, PAST THINGS THAT ARE BROWN!
JUST AS BOGS ARE STINKY AND SCAB RATS LIKE TO BLEED...
...SKUB THE GOBLIN'S HAPPY, 'CAUSE SKUBBY LIKES TO LEAD!

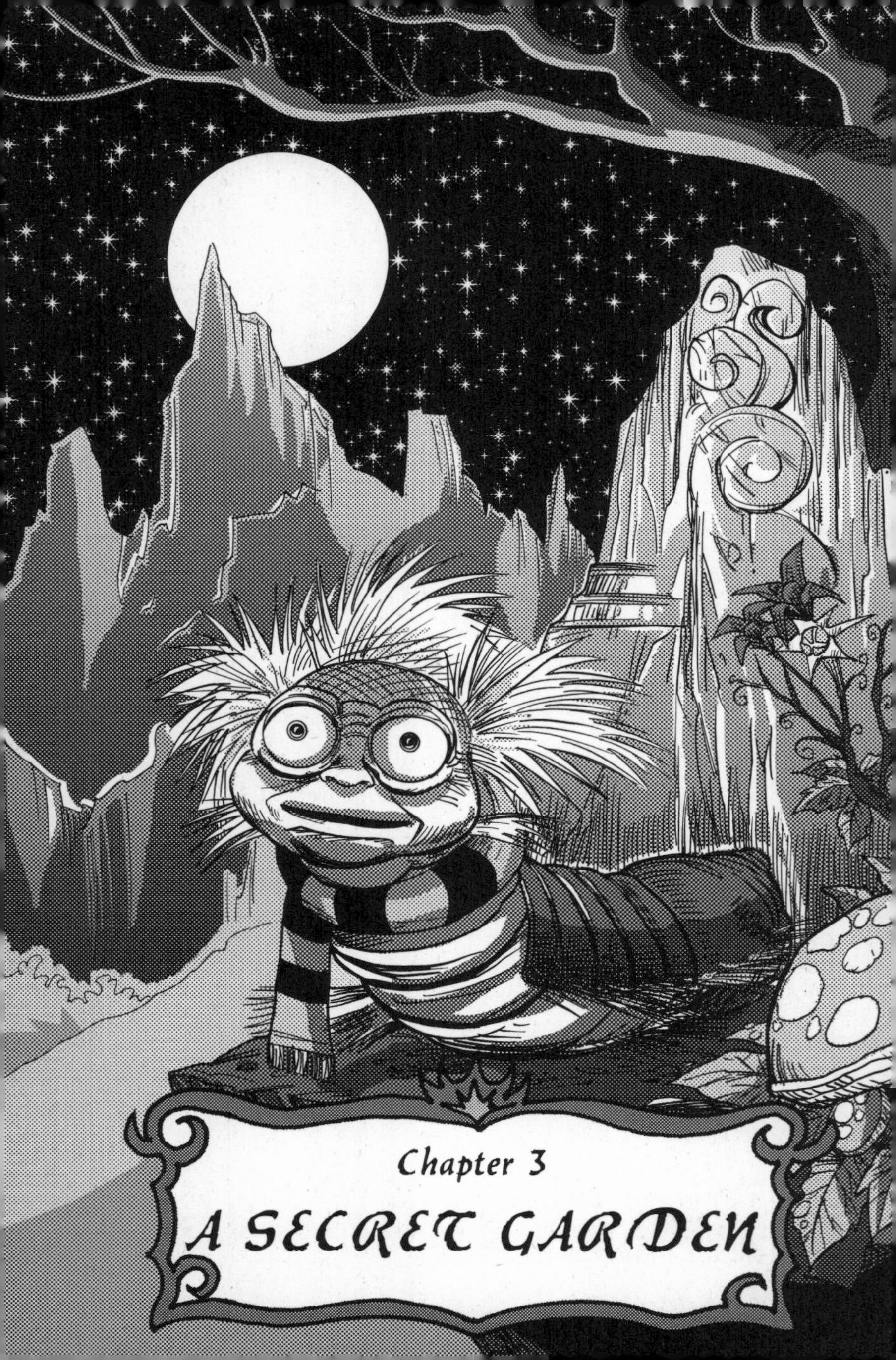

Chapter 3

A SECRET GARDEN

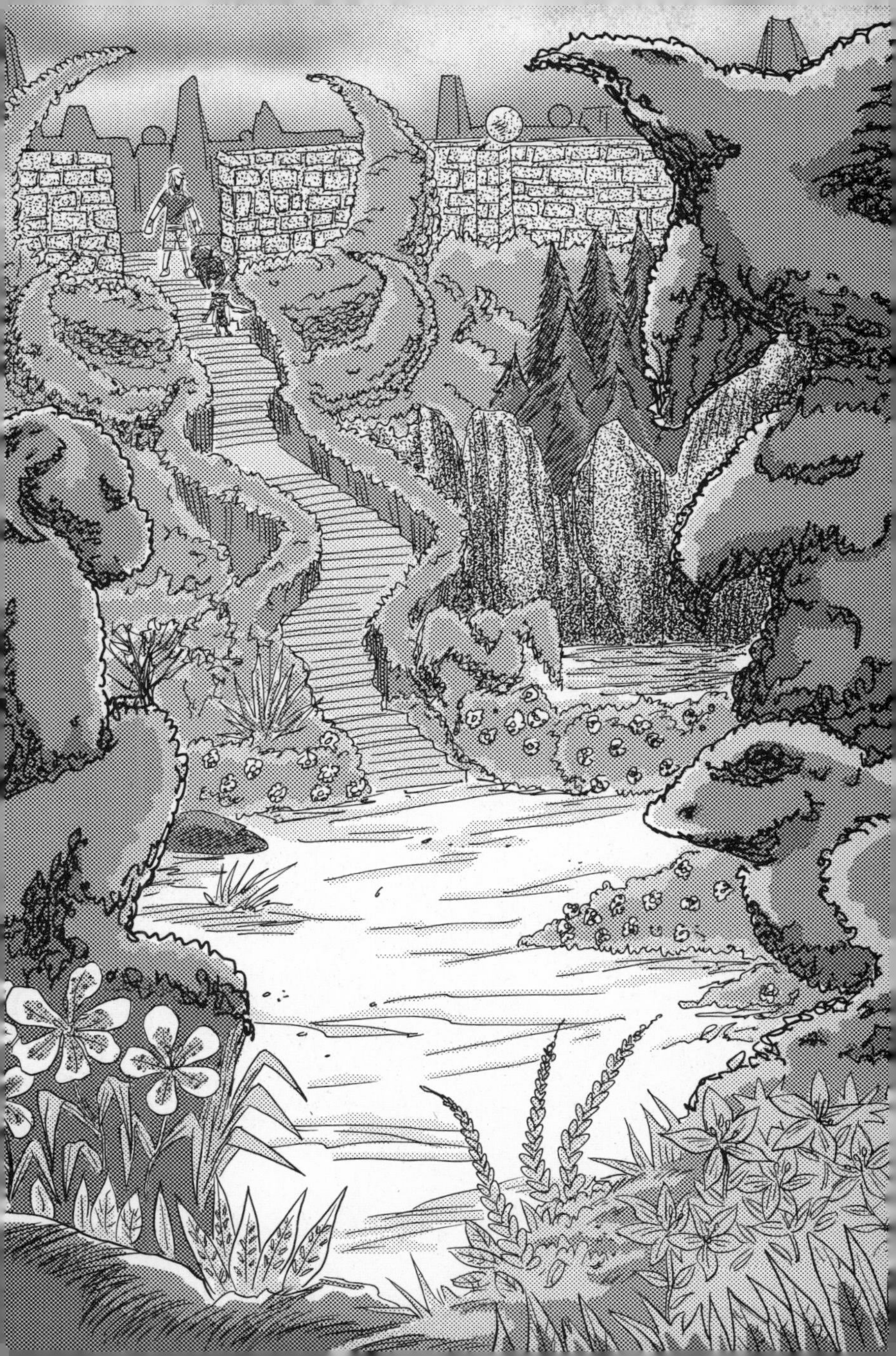

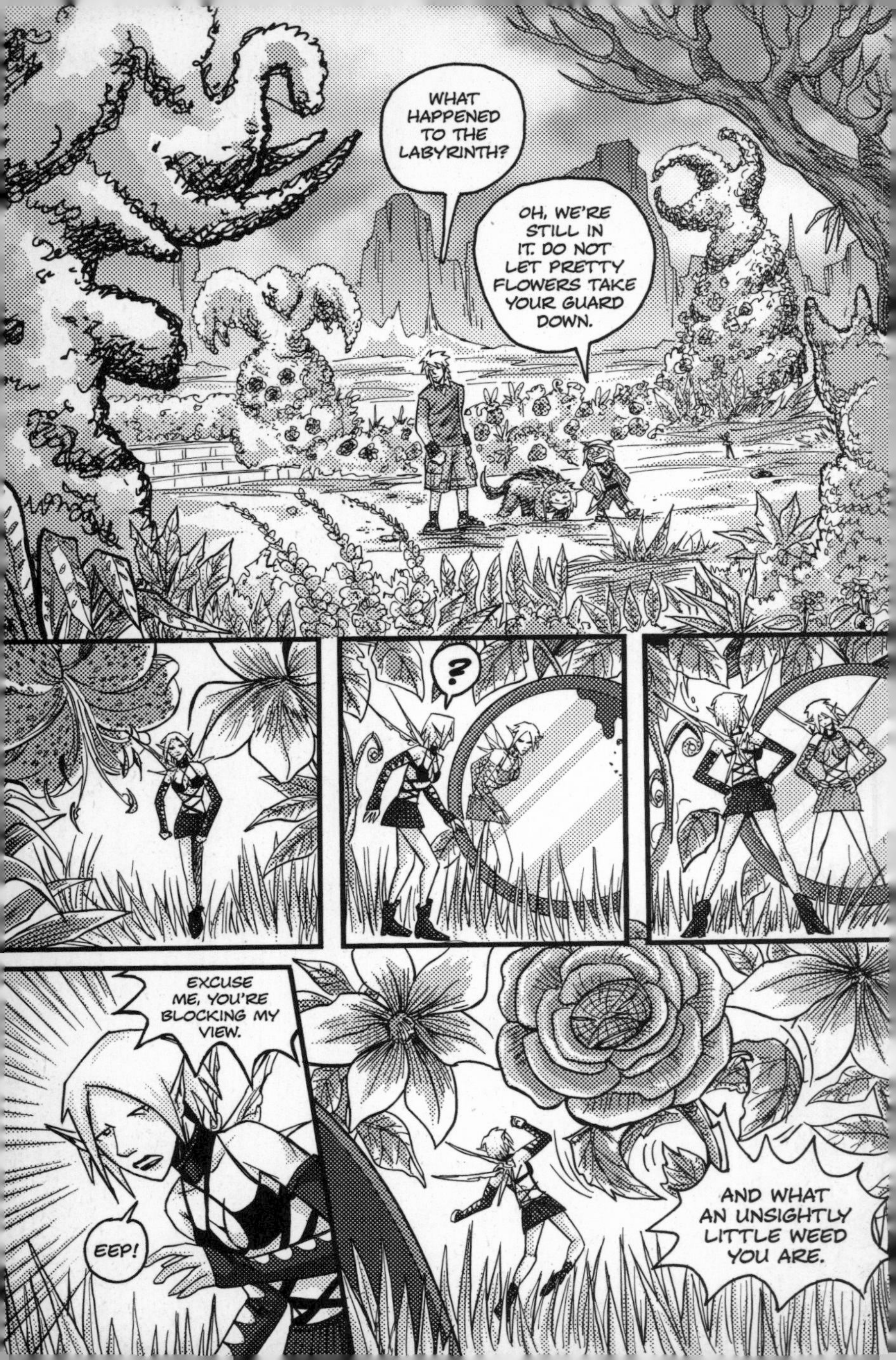

WHAT HAPPENED TO THE LABYRINTH?
OH, WE'RE STILL IN IT. DO NOT LET PRETTY FLOWERS TAKE YOUR GUARD DOWN.
?
EXCUSE ME, YOU'RE BLOCKING MY VIEW.
EEP!
AND WHAT AN UNSIGHTLY LITTLE WEED YOU ARE.

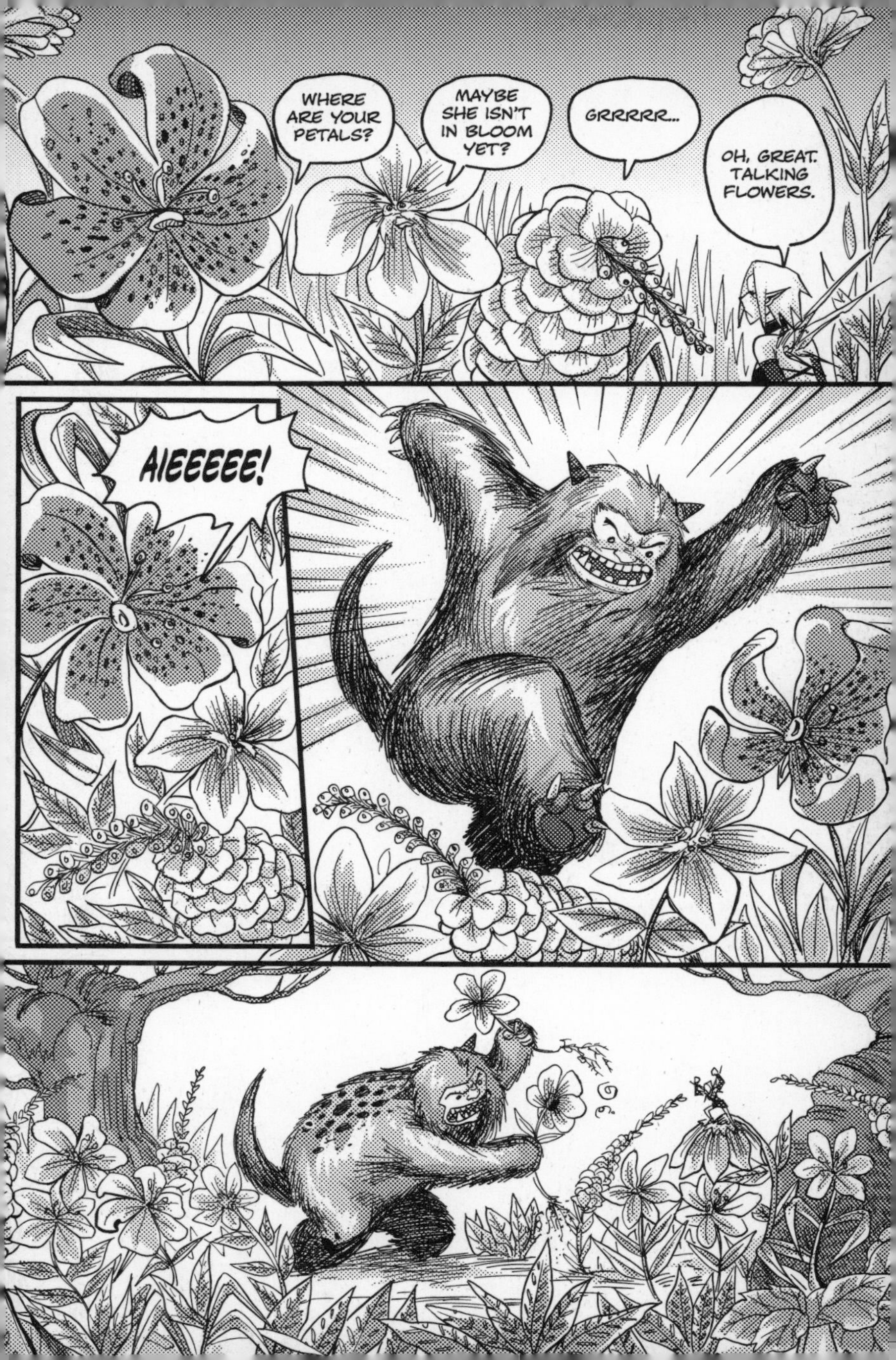
WHERE ARE YOUR PETALS?
MAYBE SHE ISN'T IN BLOOM YET?
GRRRRRR...
OH, GREAT. TALKING FLOWERS.
AIEEEEEE!

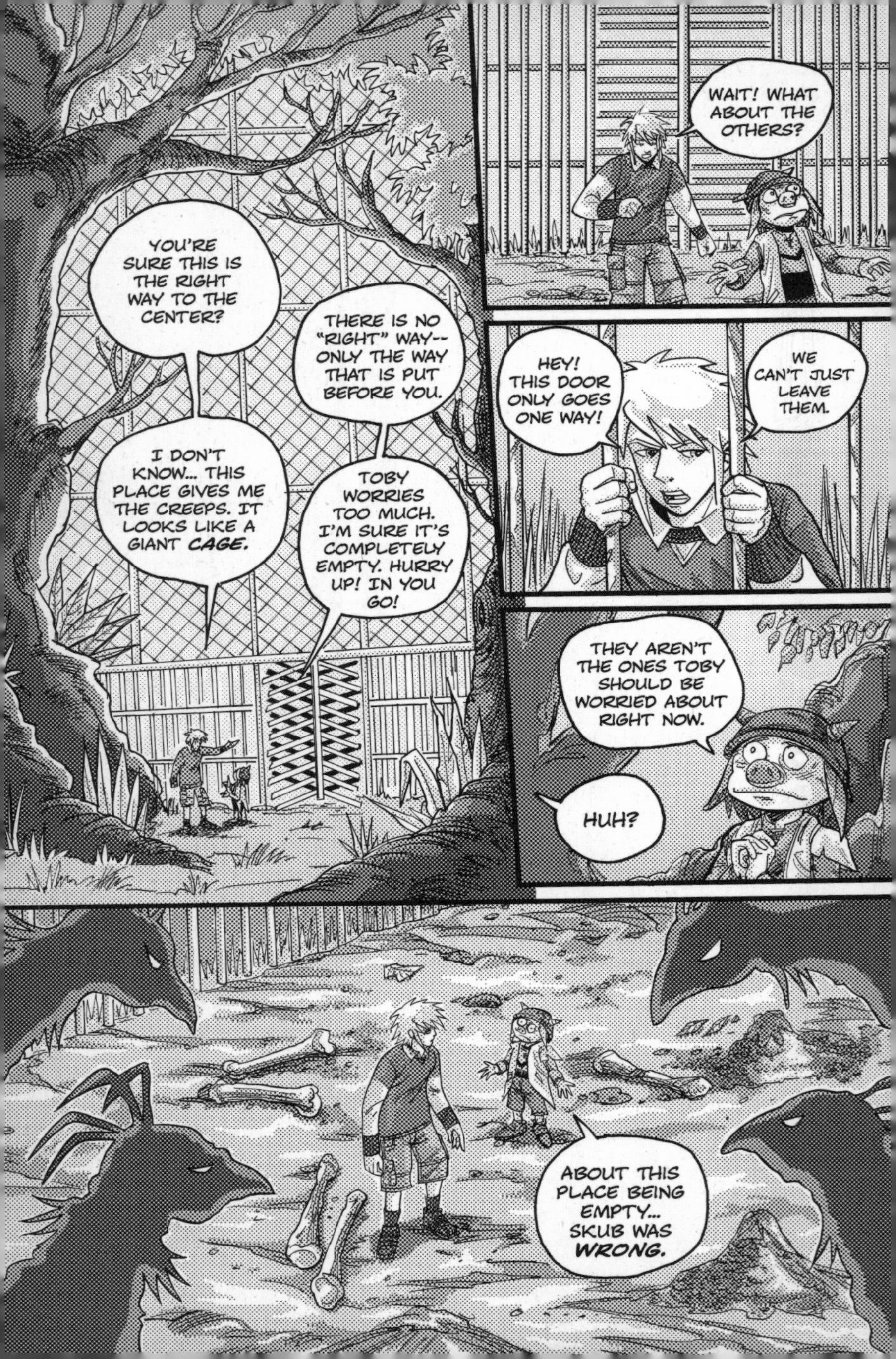
YOU'RE SURE THIS IS THE RIGHT WAY TO THE CENTER?
I DON'T KNOW... THIS PLACE GIVES ME THE CREEPS. IT LOOKS LIKE A GIANT ***CAGE.***
THERE IS NO "RIGHT" WAY--ONLY THE WAY THAT IS PUT BEFORE YOU.
TOBY WORRIES TOO MUCH. I'M SURE IT'S COMPLETELY EMPTY. HURRY UP! IN YOU GO!
WAIT! WHAT ABOUT THE OTHERS?
HEY! THIS DOOR ONLY GOES ONE WAY!
WE CAN'T JUST LEAVE THEM.
THEY AREN'T THE ONES TOBY SHOULD BE WORRIED ABOUT RIGHT NOW.
HUH?
ABOUT THIS PLACE BEING EMPTY... SKUB WAS ***WRONG.***

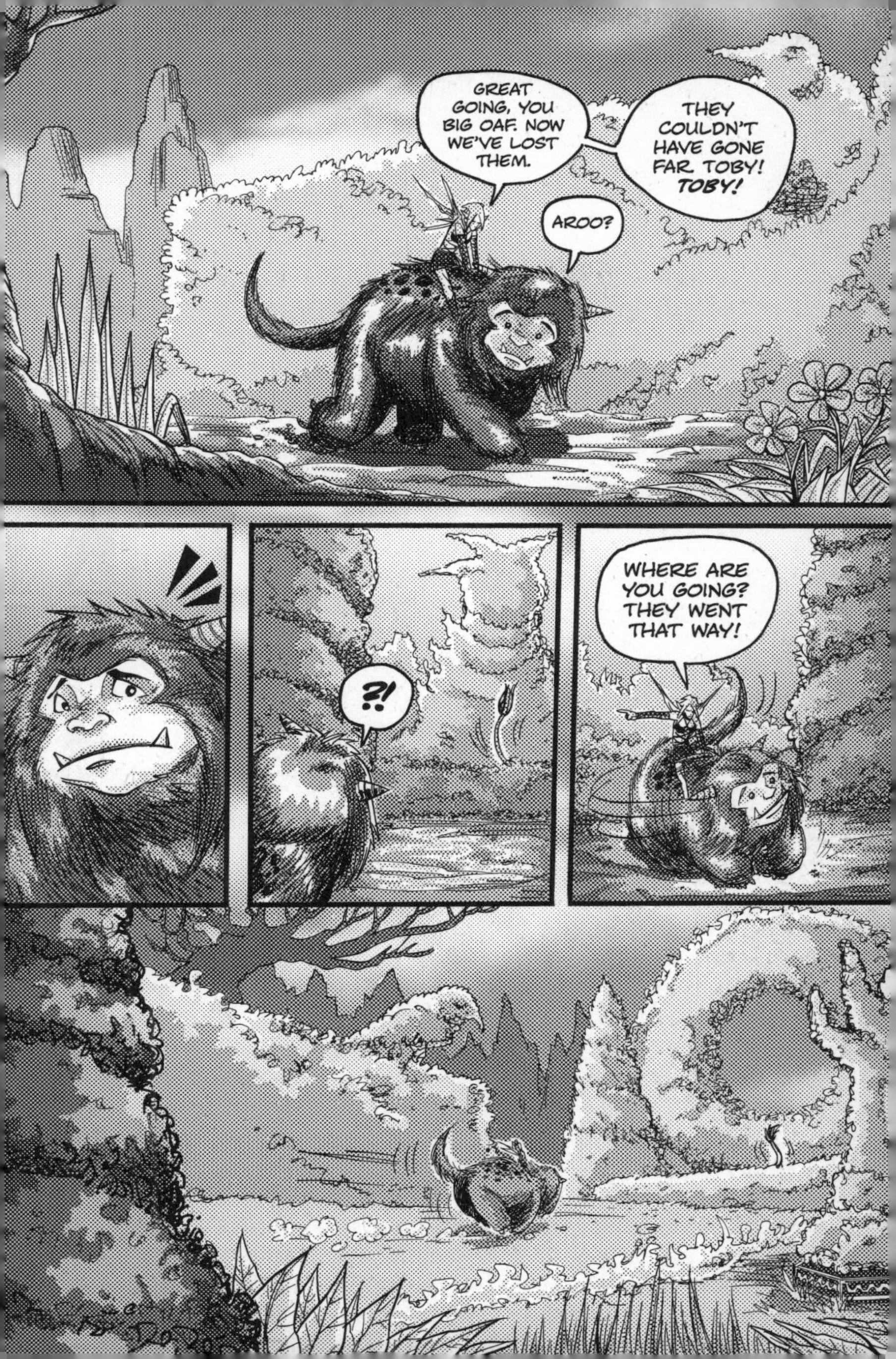
GREAT GOING, YOU BIG OAF. NOW WE'VE LOST THEM.
THEY COULDN'T HAVE GONE FAR TOBY! TOBY!
AROO?
?!
WHERE ARE YOU GOING? THEY WENT THAT WAY!

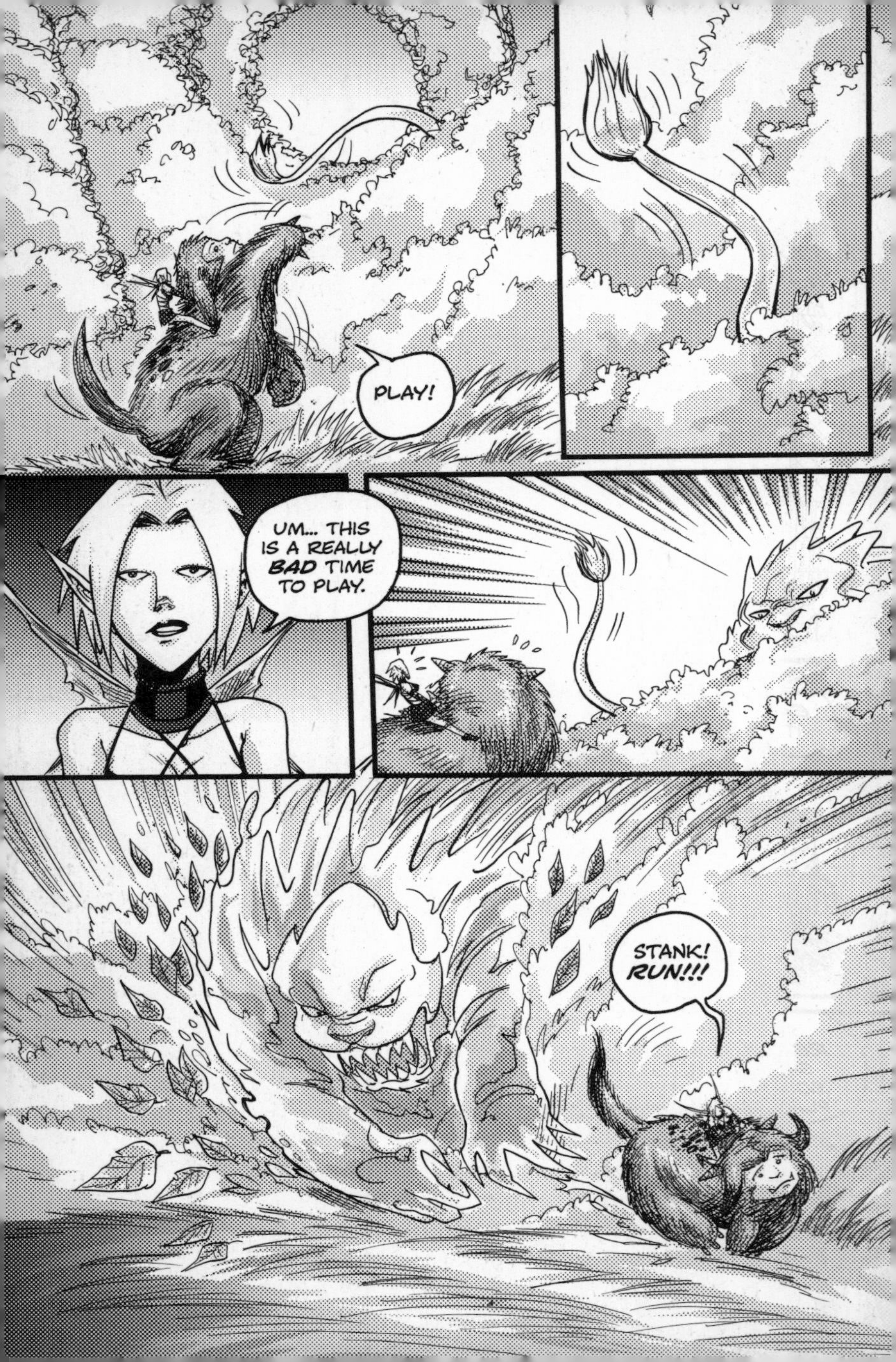
PLAY!
UM... THIS IS A REALLY **BAD** TIME TO PLAY.
STANK! **RUN!!!**

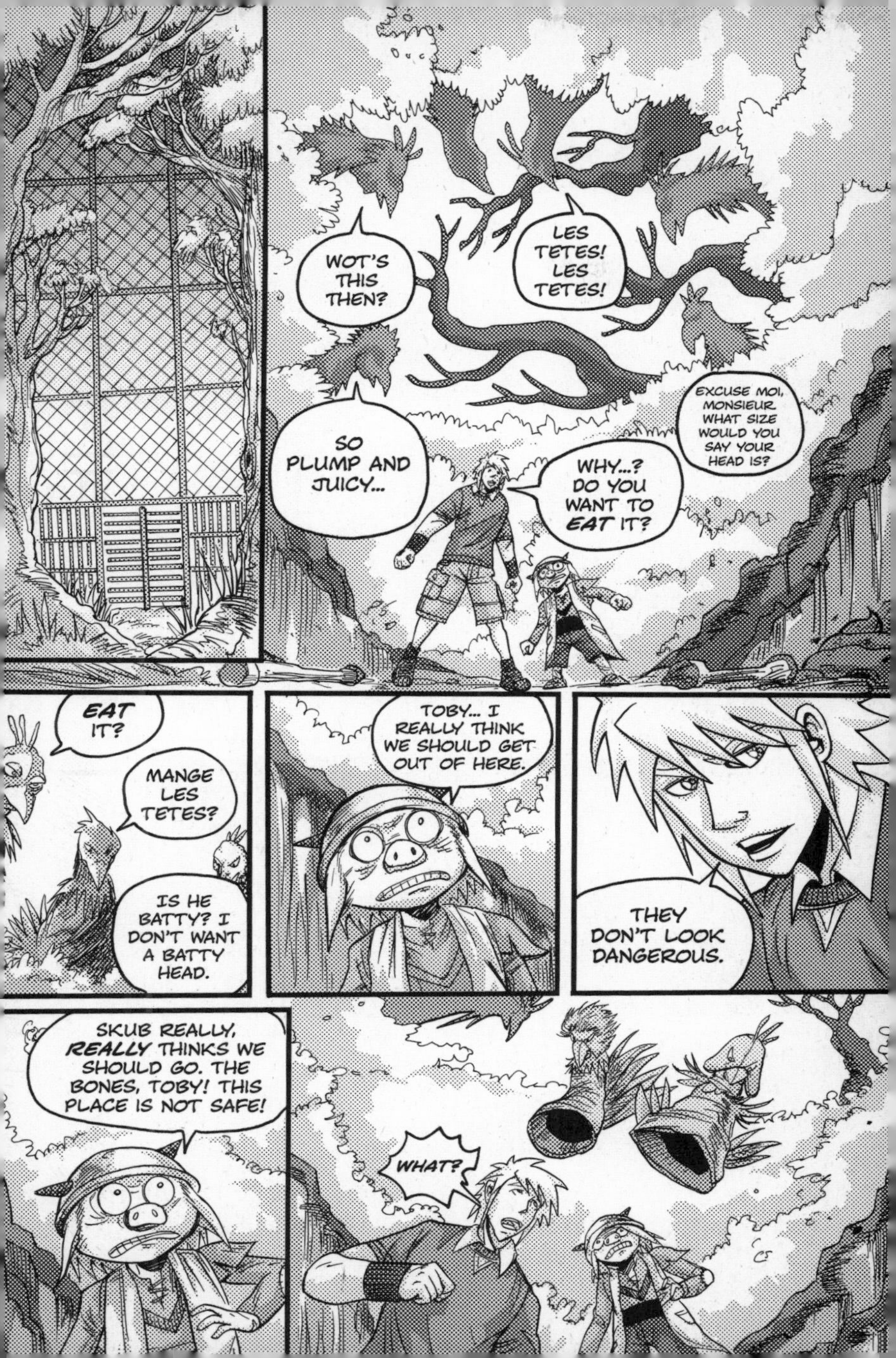
WOT'S THIS THEN?
LES TETES! LES TETES!
SO PLUMP AND JUICY...
EXCUSE MOI, MONSIEUR WHAT SIZE WOULD YOU SAY YOUR HEAD IS?
WHY...? DO YOU WANT TO *EAT* IT?
EAT IT?
MANGE LES TETES?
IS HE BATTY? I DON'T WANT A BATTY HEAD.
TOBY... I REALLY THINK WE SHOULD GET OUT OF HERE.
THEY DON'T LOOK DANGEROUS.
SKUB REALLY, *REALLY* THINKS WE SHOULD GO. THE BONES, TOBY! THIS PLACE IS NOT SAFE!
WHAT?

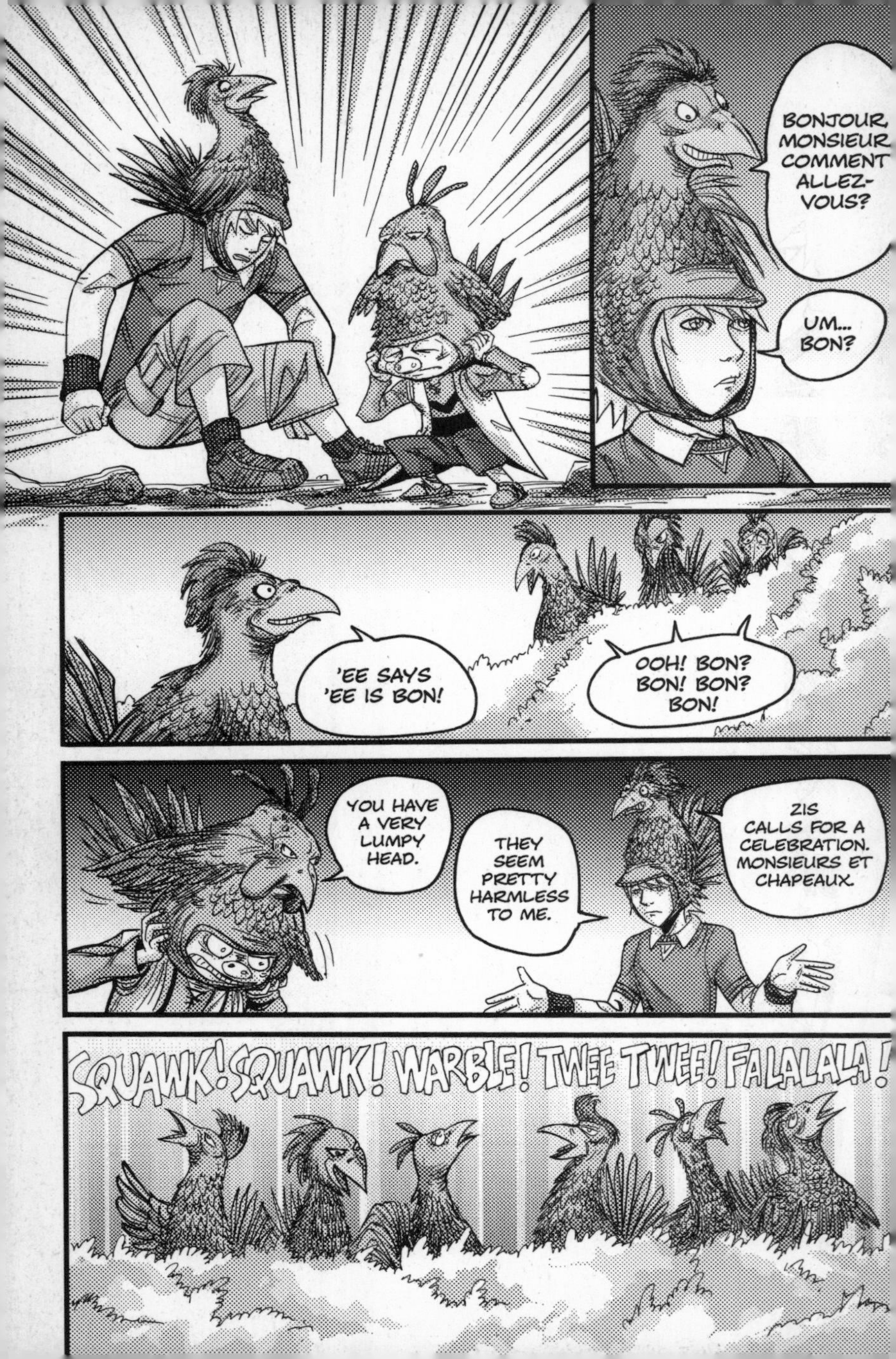
BONJOUR, MONSIEUR. COMMENT ALLEZ-VOUS?
UM... BON?
'EE SAYS 'EE IS BON!
OOH! BON? BON! BON? BON!
YOU HAVE A VERY LUMPY HEAD.
THEY SEEM PRETTY HARMLESS TO ME.
ZIS CALLS FOR A CELEBRATION. MONSIEURS ET CHAPEAUX.
SQUAWK! SQUAWK! WARBLE! TWEE TWEE! FALALALA!

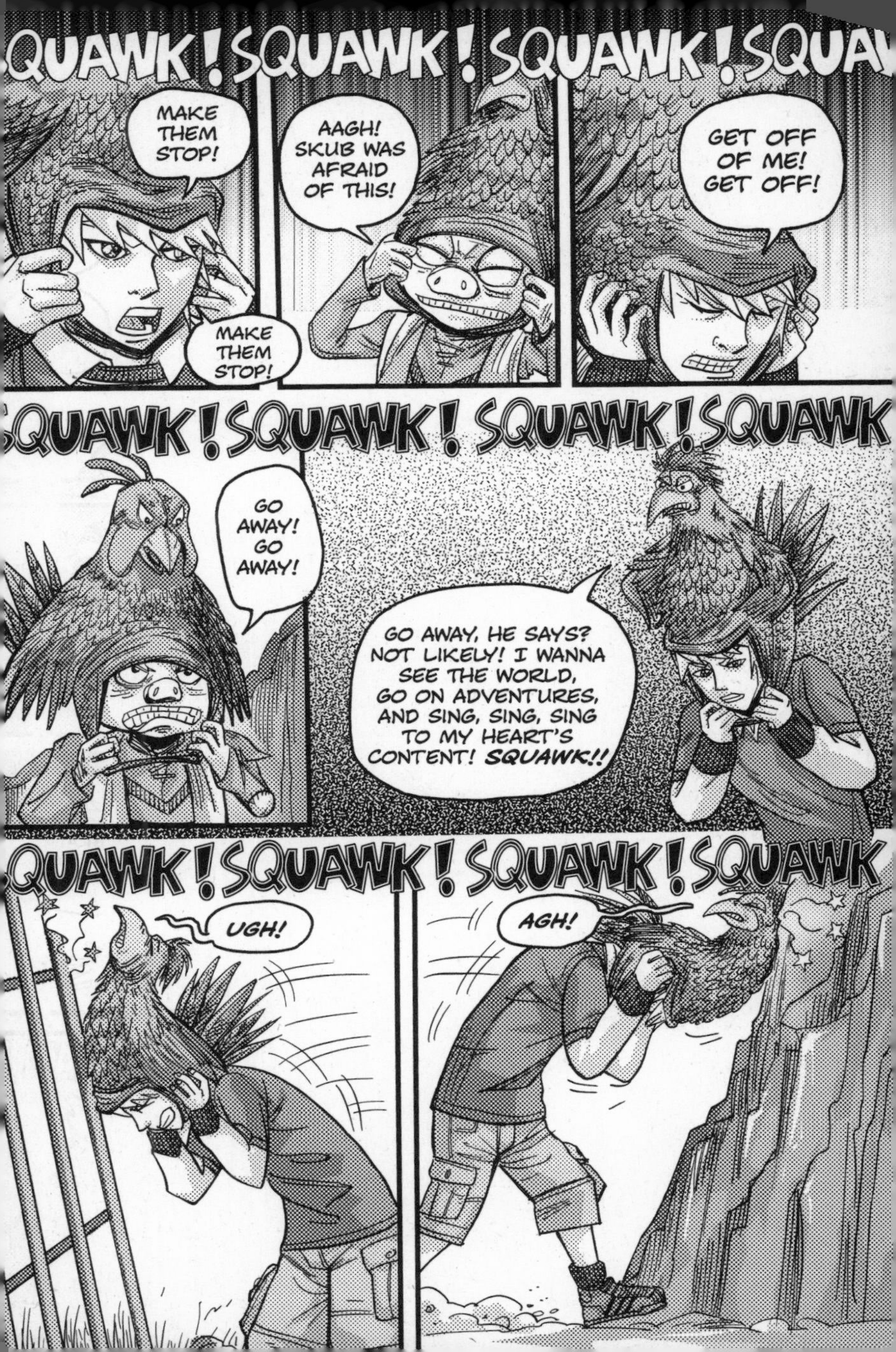
SQUAWK! SQUAWK! SQUAWK! SQUAW
MAKE THEM STOP!
MAKE THEM STOP!
AAGH! SKUB WAS AFRAID OF THIS!
GET OFF OF ME! GET OFF!
SQUAWK! SQUAWK! SQUAWK! SQUAWK
GO AWAY! GO AWAY!
GO AWAY, HE SAYS? NOT LIKELY! I WANNA SEE THE WORLD, GO ON ADVENTURES, AND SING, SING, SING TO MY HEART'S CONTENT! **SQUAWK!!**
QUAWK! SQUAWK! SQUAWK! SQUAWK
UGH!
AGH!

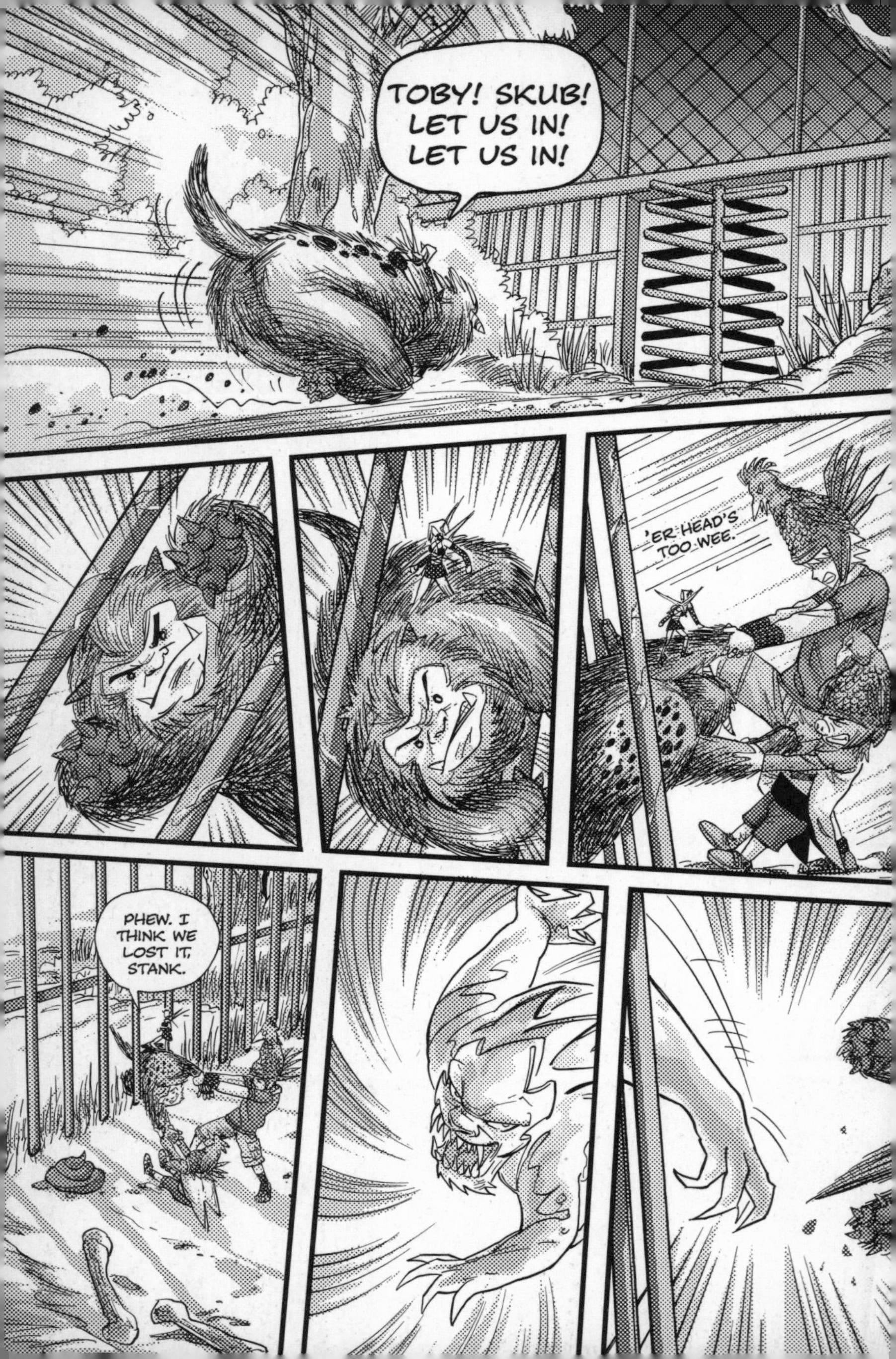
TOBY! SKUB! LET US IN! LET US IN!
'ER HEAD'S TOO WEE.
PHEW. I THINK WE LOST IT, STANK.

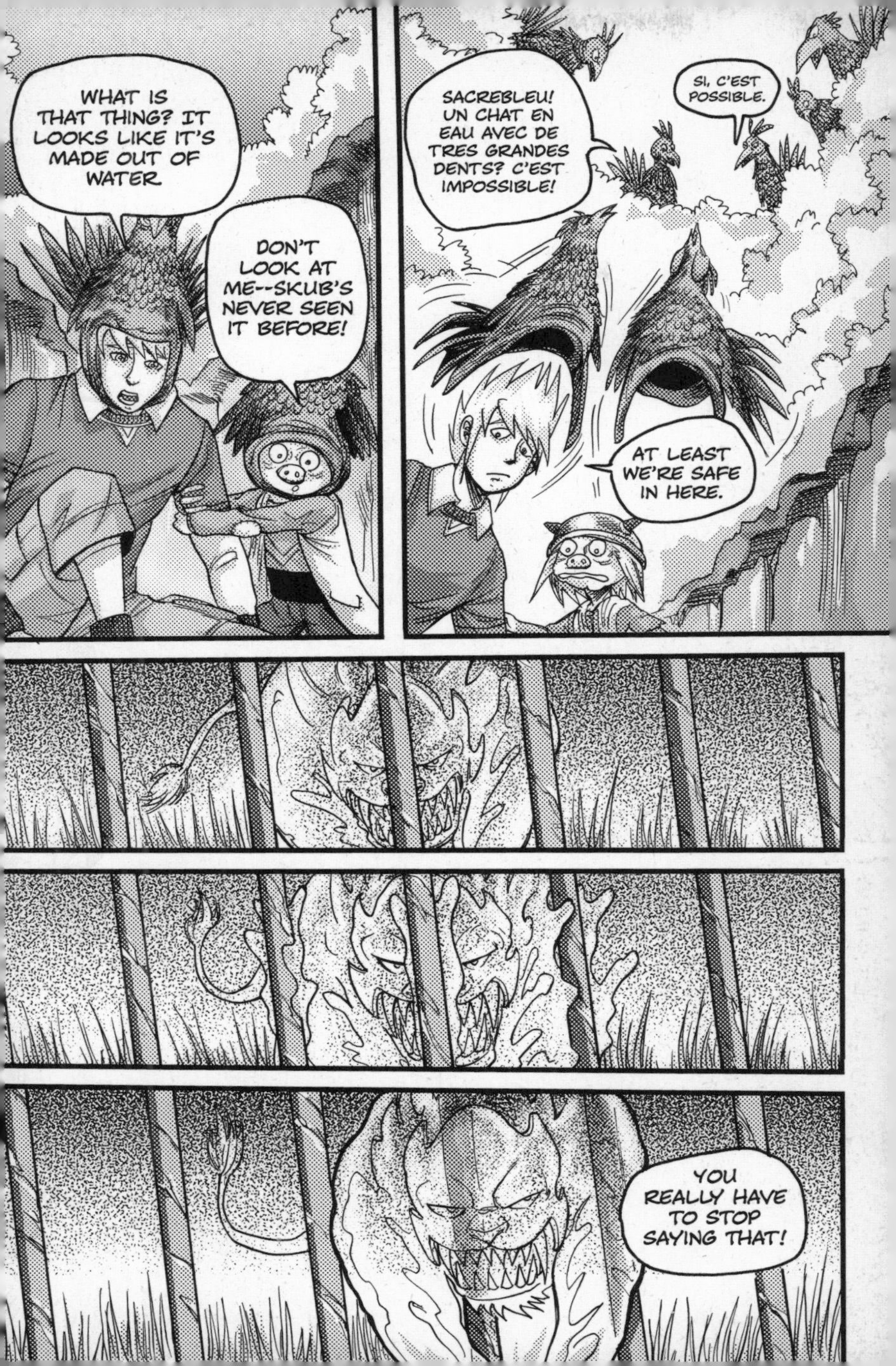
WHAT IS THAT THING? IT LOOKS LIKE IT'S MADE OUT OF WATER
DON'T LOOK AT ME--SKUB'S NEVER SEEN IT BEFORE!
SACREBLEU! UN CHAT EN EAU AVEC DE TRES GRANDES DENTS? C'EST IMPOSSIBLE!
SI, C'EST POSSIBLE.
AT LEAST WE'RE SAFE IN HERE.
YOU REALLY HAVE TO STOP SAYING THAT!

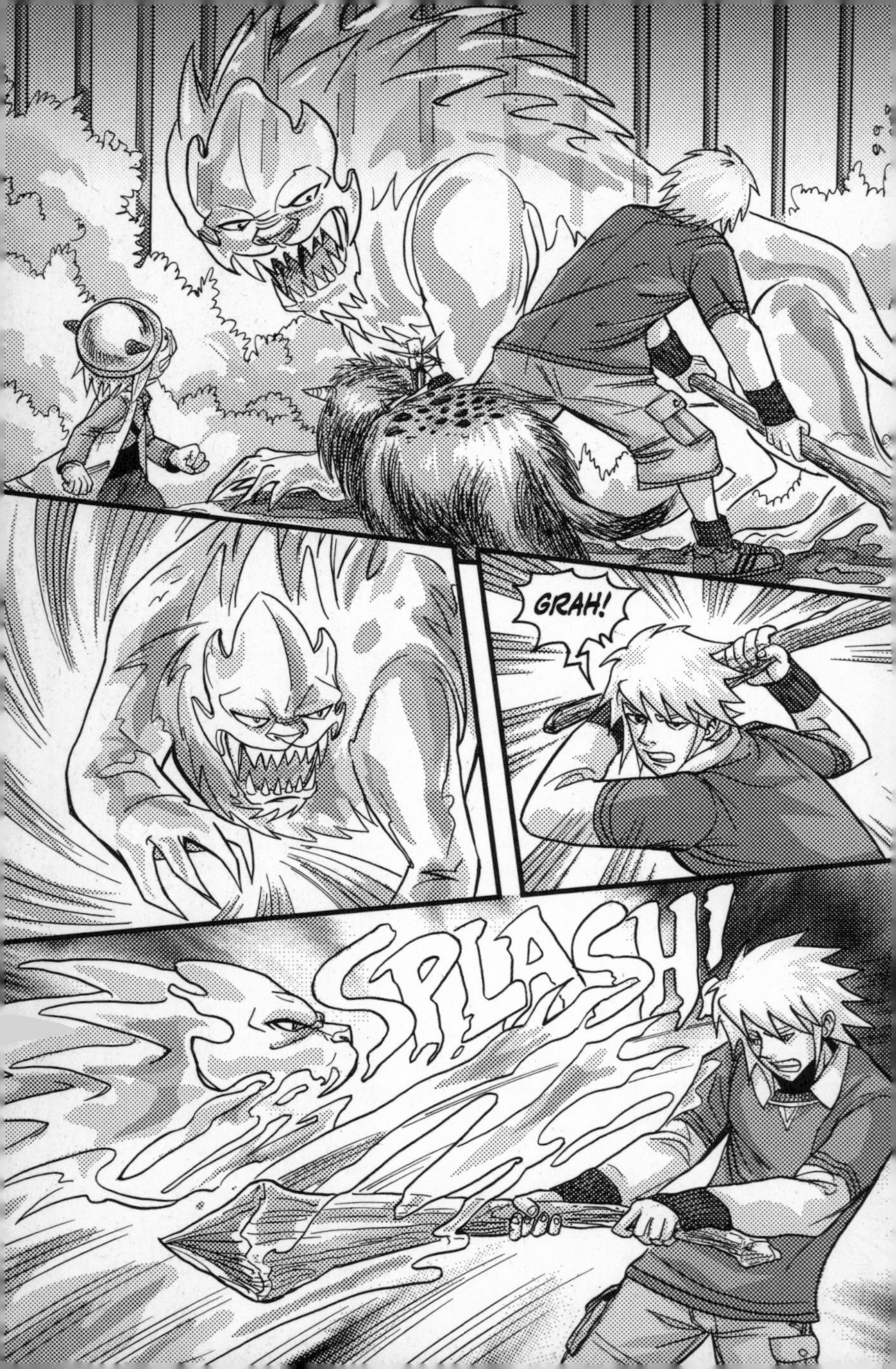
GRAH!
SPLASH!

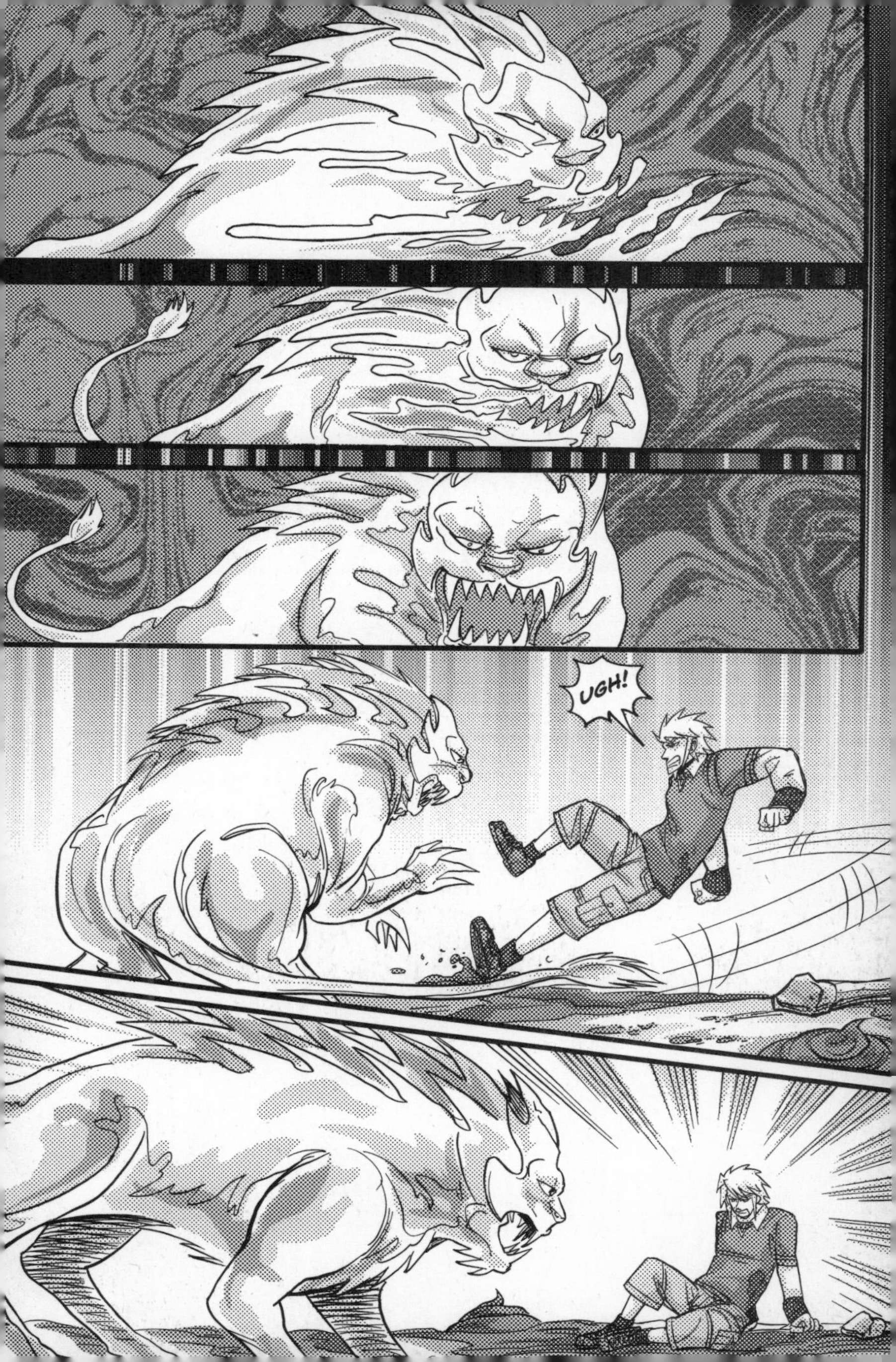
UGH!

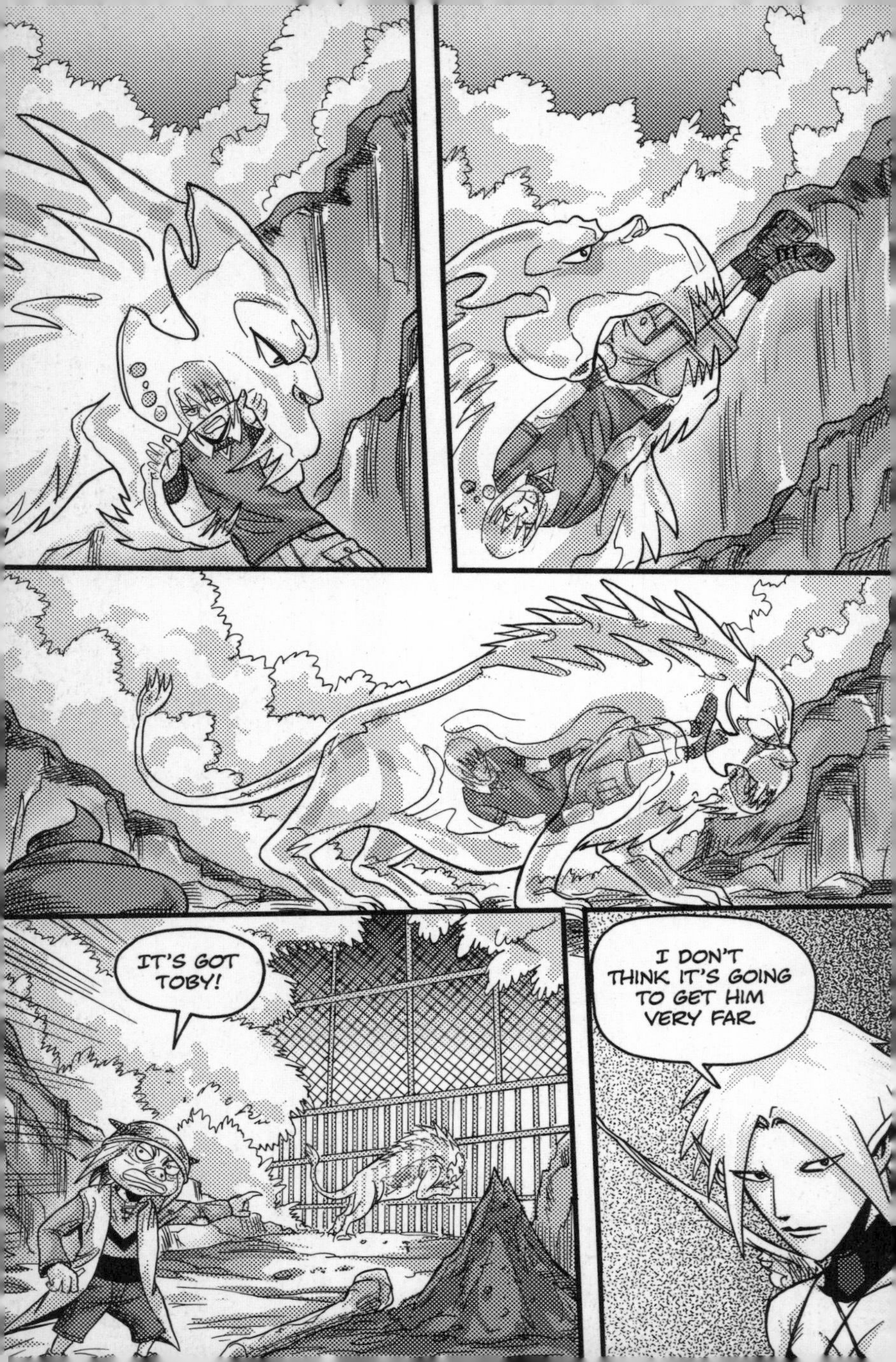
IT'S GOT TOBY!
I DON'T THINK IT'S GOING TO GET HIM VERY FAR

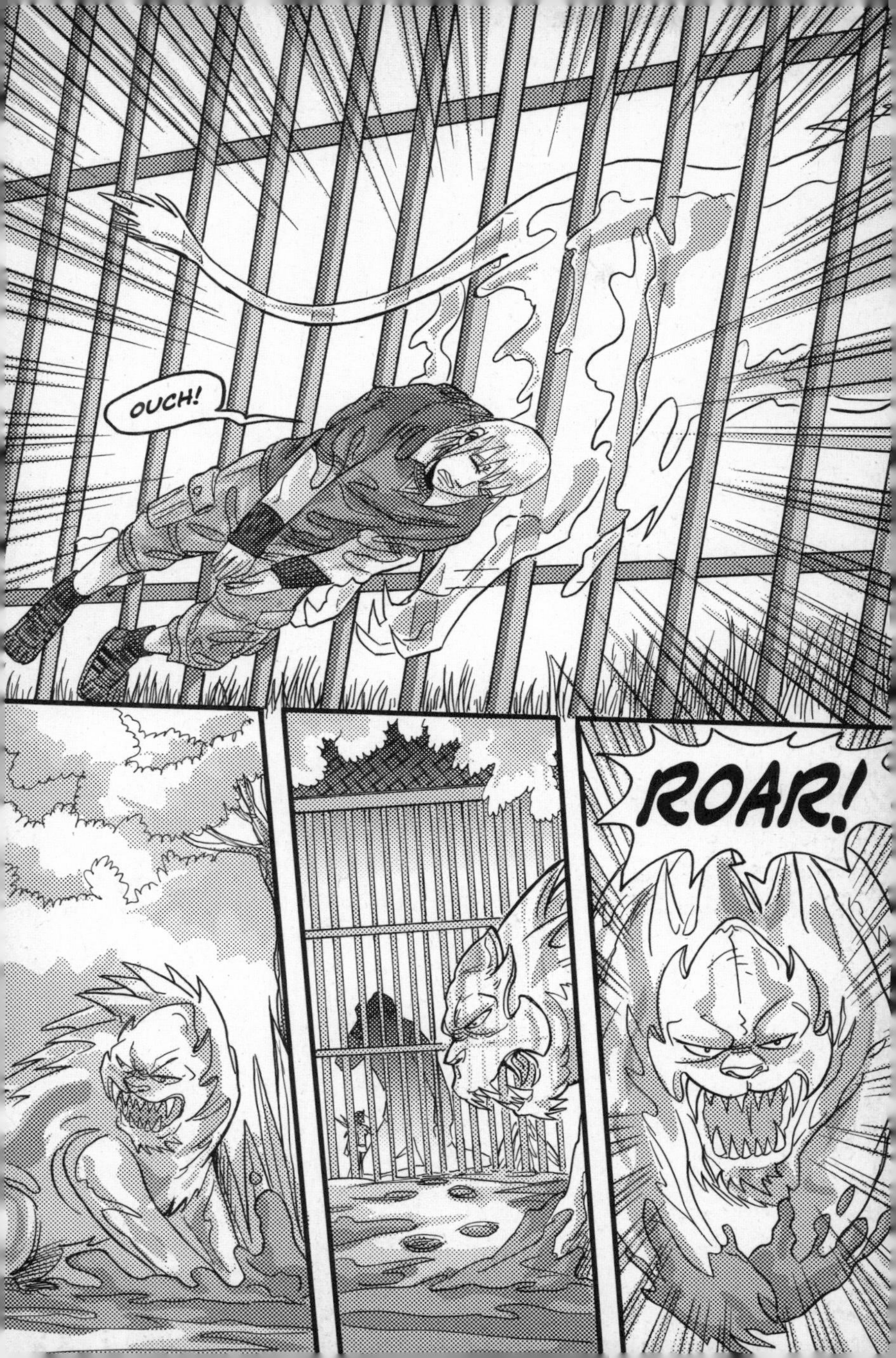
OUCH!
ROAR!

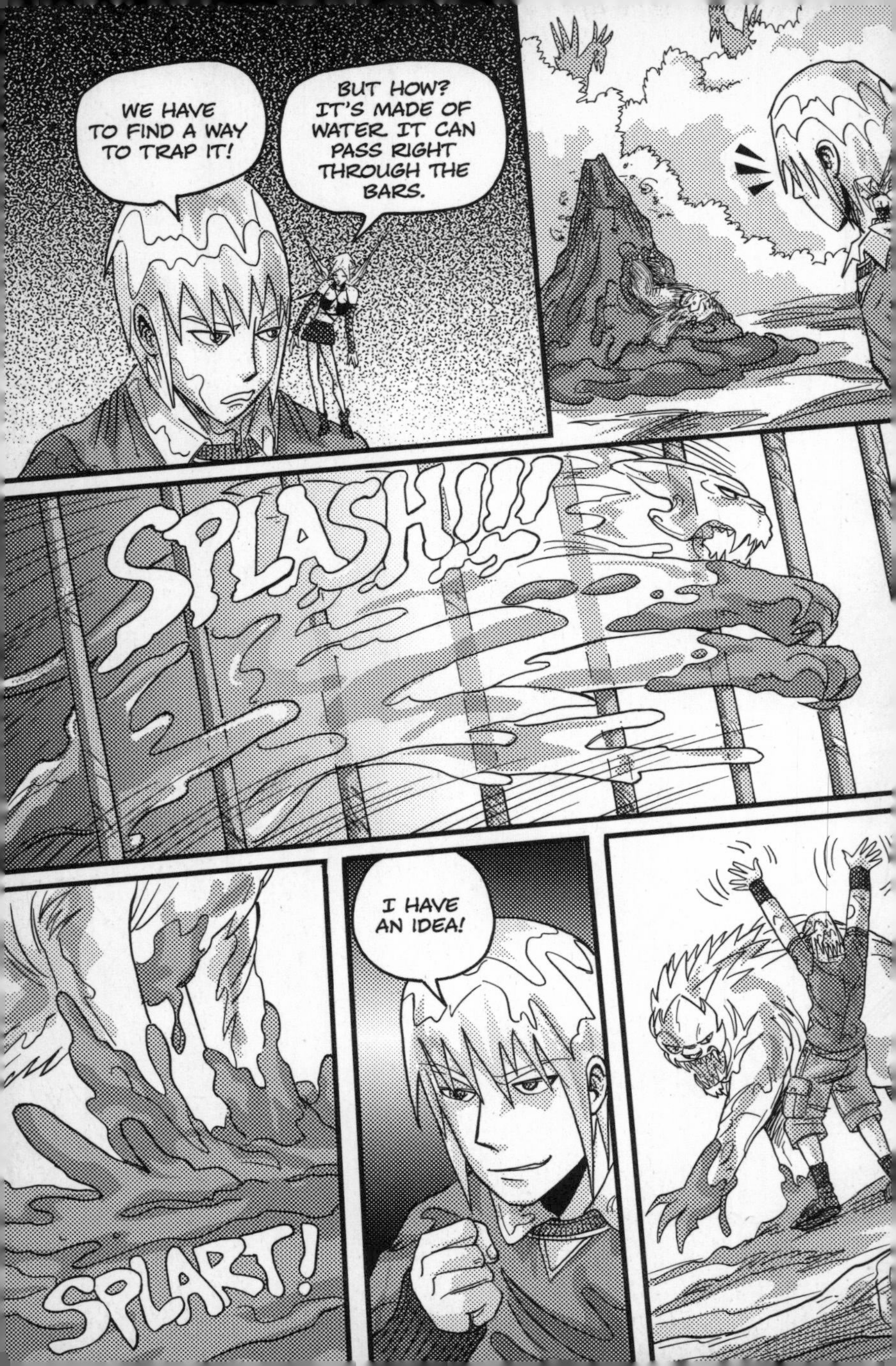
WE HAVE TO FIND A WAY TO TRAP IT!
BUT HOW? IT'S MADE OF WATER. IT CAN PASS RIGHT THROUGH THE BARS.
SPLASH!!!
SPLART!
I HAVE AN IDEA!

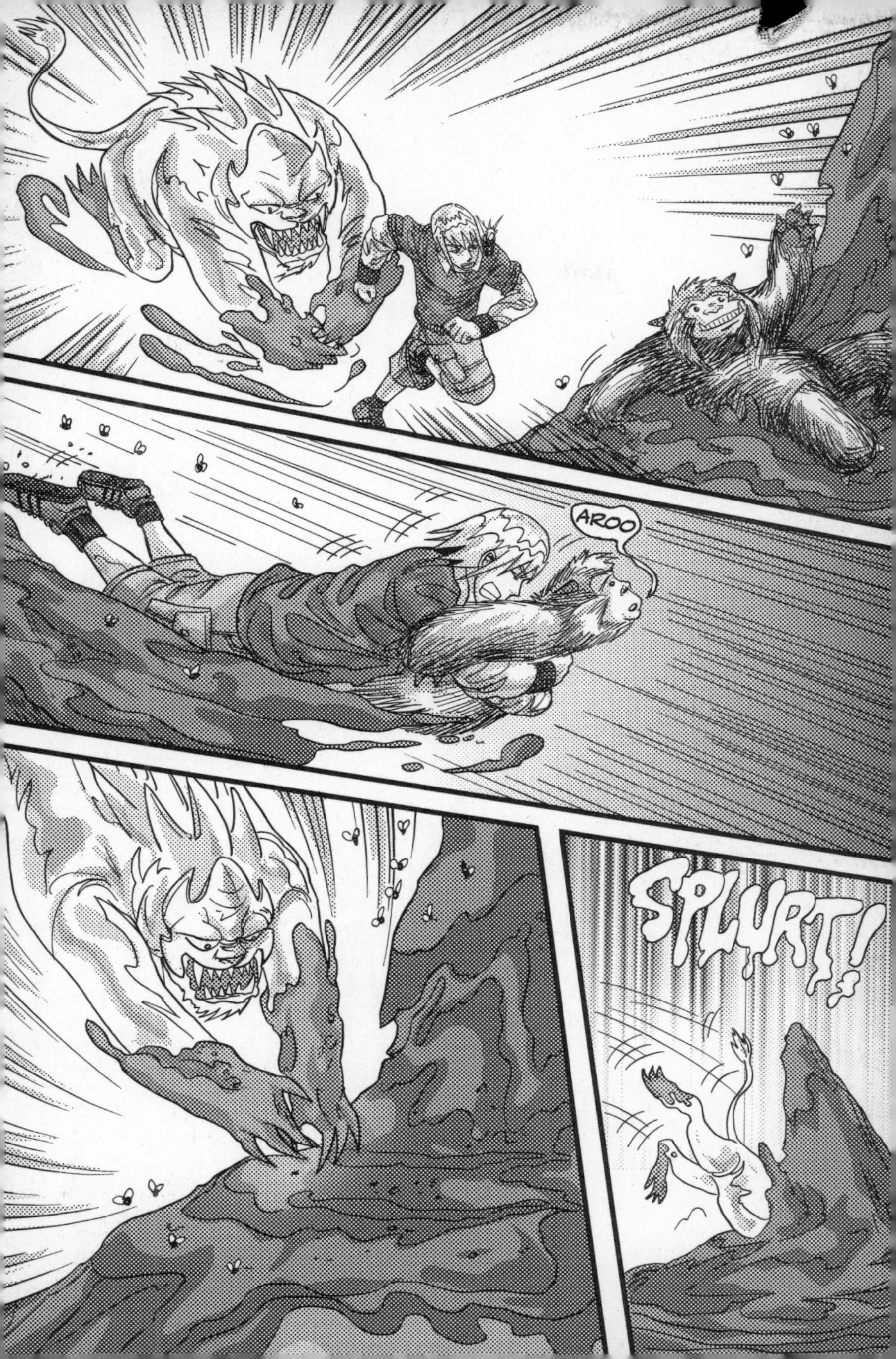
AROO
SPLURT!

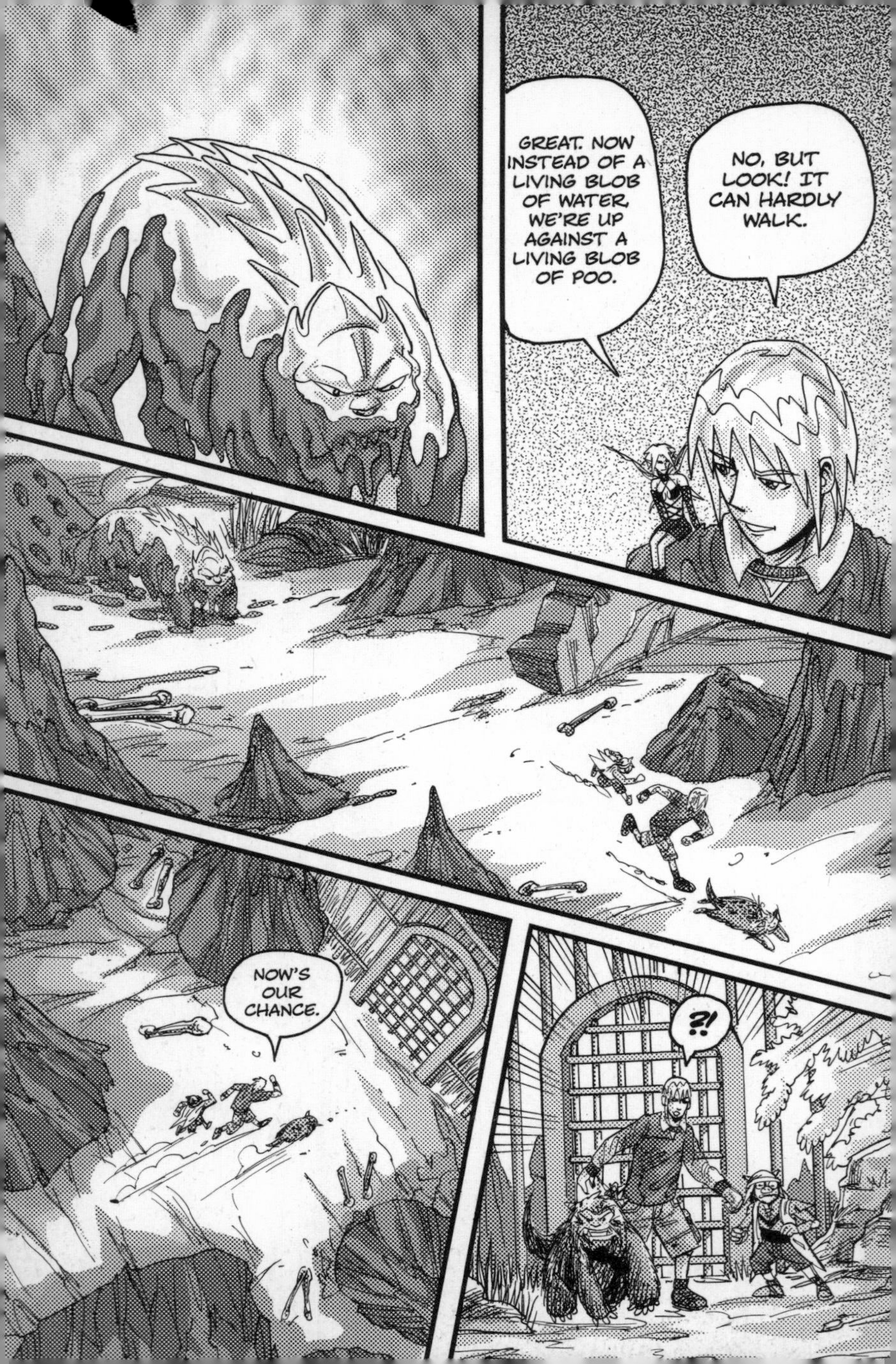
GREAT. NOW INSTEAD OF A LIVING BLOB OF WATER, WE'RE UP AGAINST A LIVING BLOB OF POO.
NO, BUT LOOK! IT CAN HARDLY WALK.
NOW'S OUR CHANCE.
?!

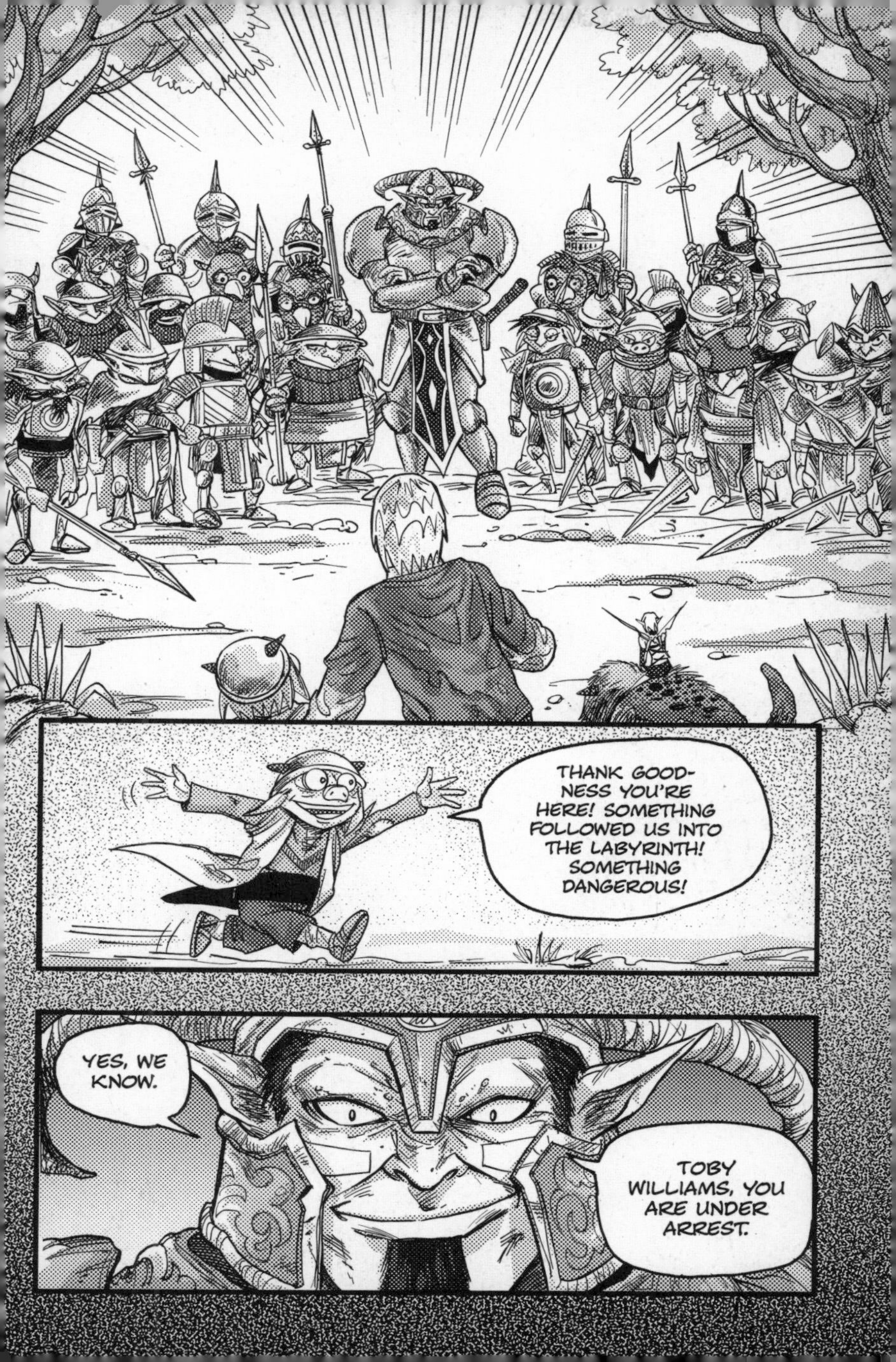
THANK GOODNESS YOU'RE HERE! SOMETHING FOLLOWED US INTO THE LABYRINTH! SOMETHING DANGEROUS!
YES, WE KNOW.
TOBY WILLIAMS, YOU ARE UNDER ARREST.

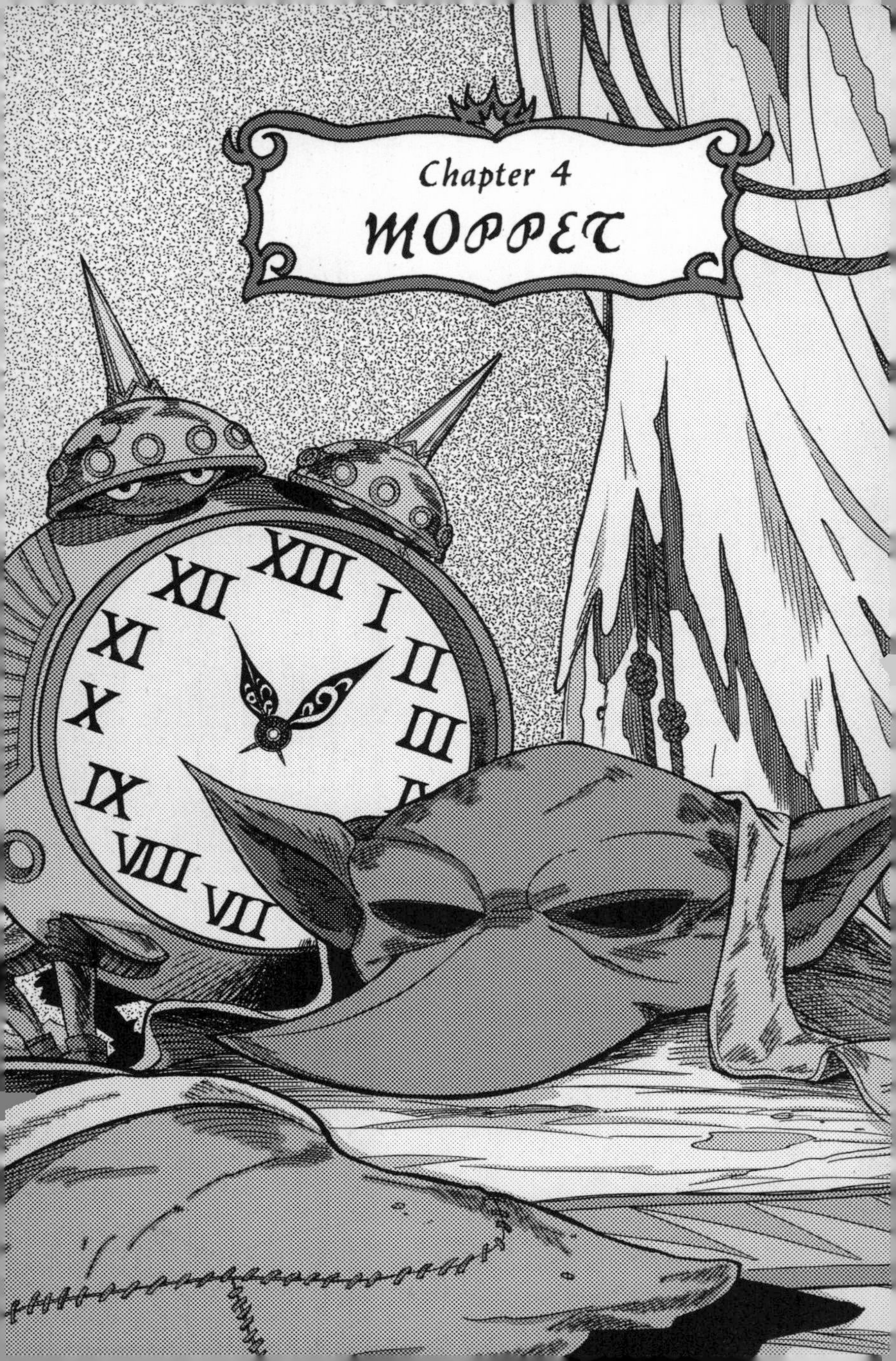
Chapter 4
MOPPET

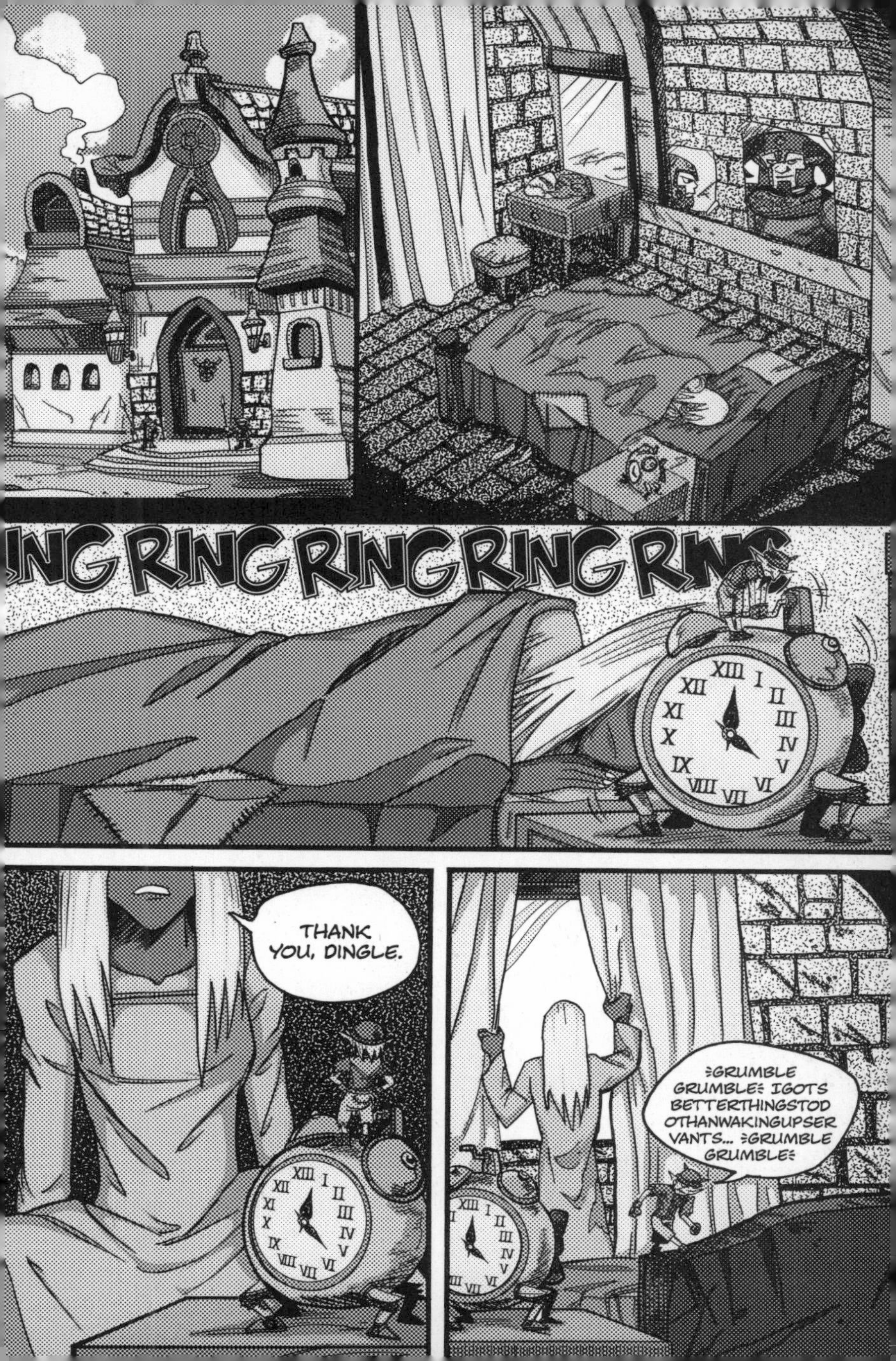
ING RING RING RING RIN
THANK YOU, DINGLE.
⚞GRUMBLE GRUMBLE⚟ IGOTS BETTERTHINGSTOD OTHANWAKINGUPSER VANTS... ⚞GRUMBLE GRUMBLE⚟

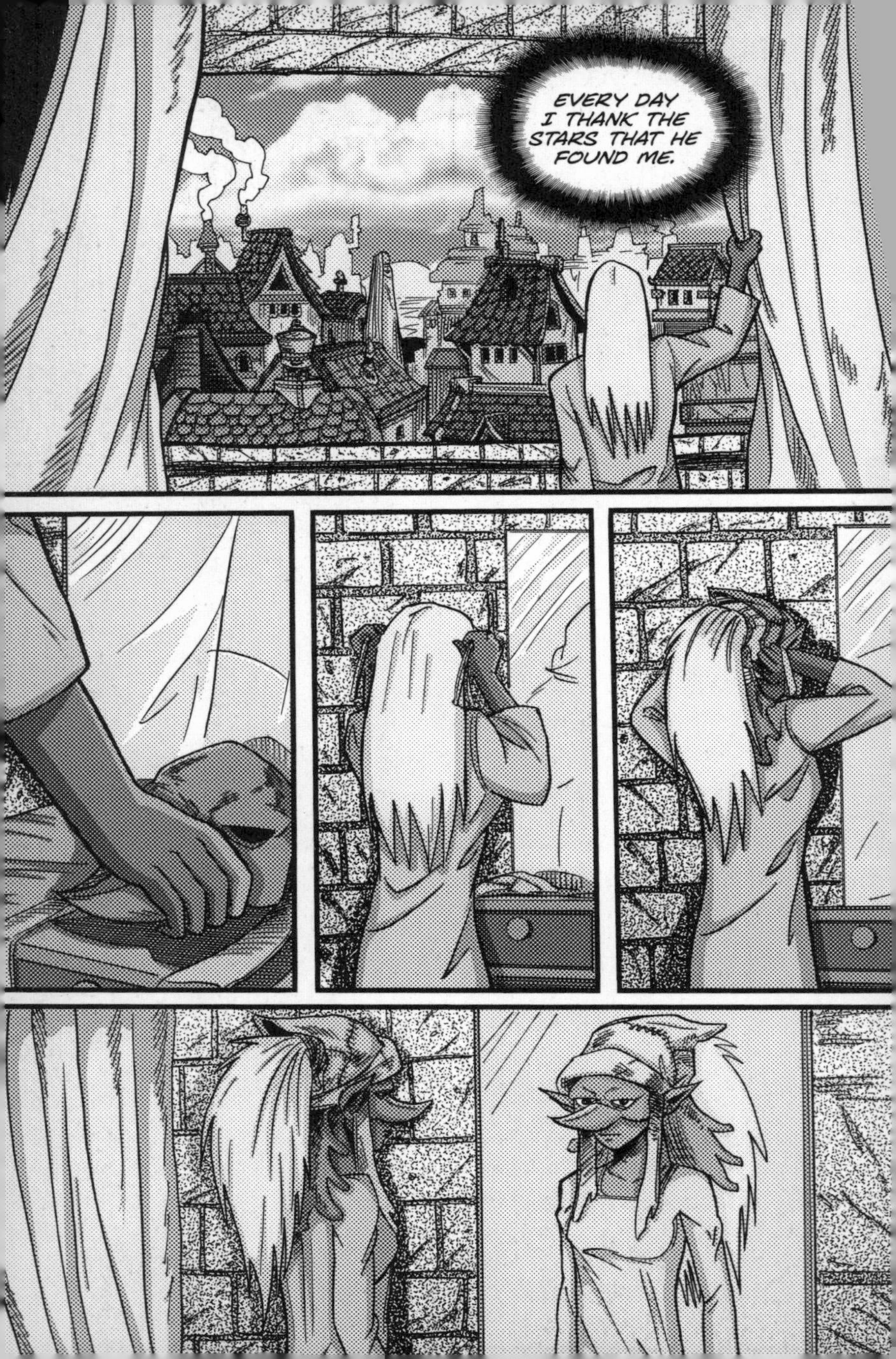
EVERY DAY I THANK THE STARS THAT HE FOUND ME.

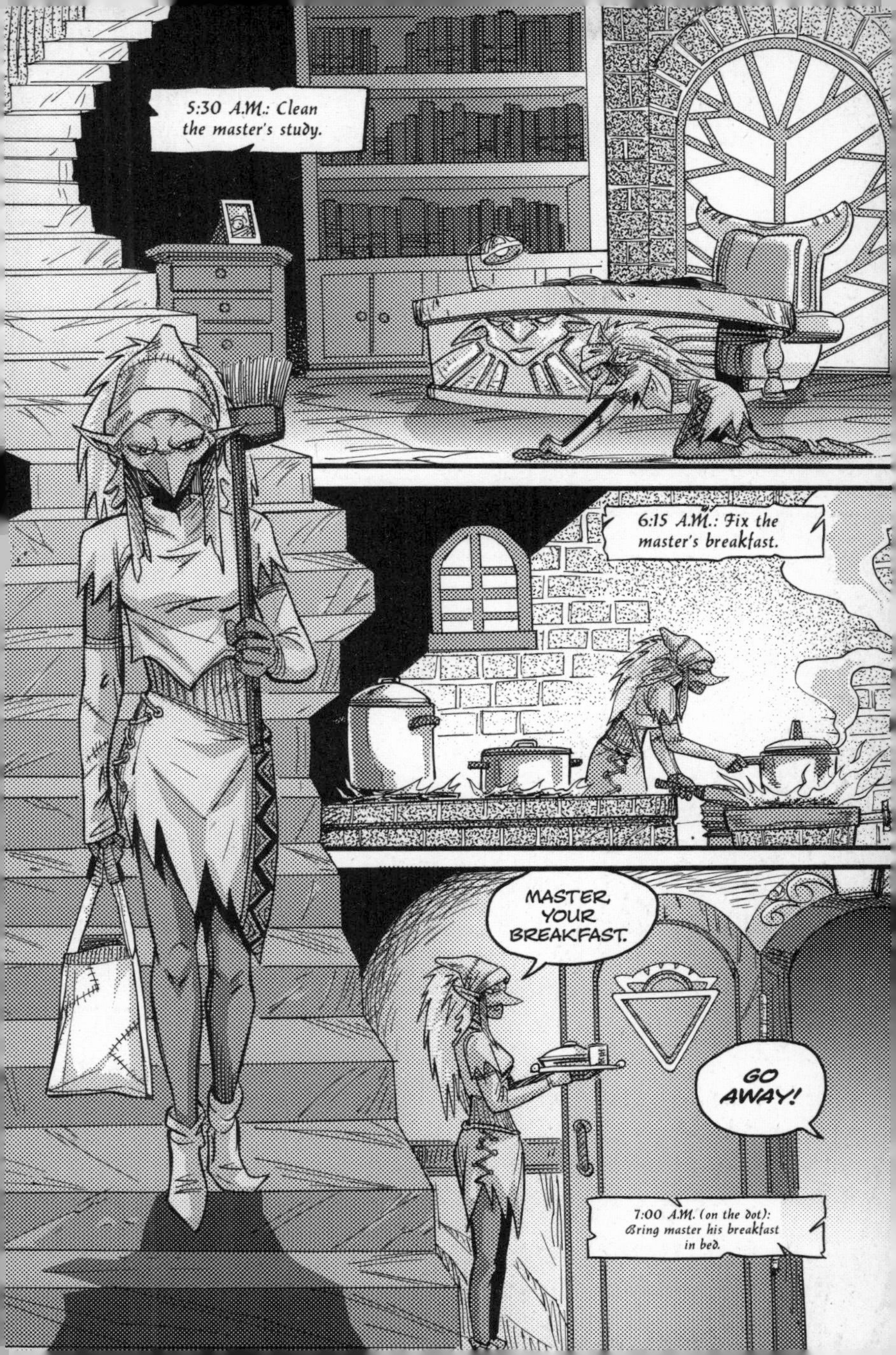
5:30 A.M.: Clean the master's study.
6:15 A.M.: Fix the master's breakfast.
MASTER, YOUR BREAKFAST.
GO AWAY!
7:00 A.M. (on the dot): Bring master his breakfast in bed.

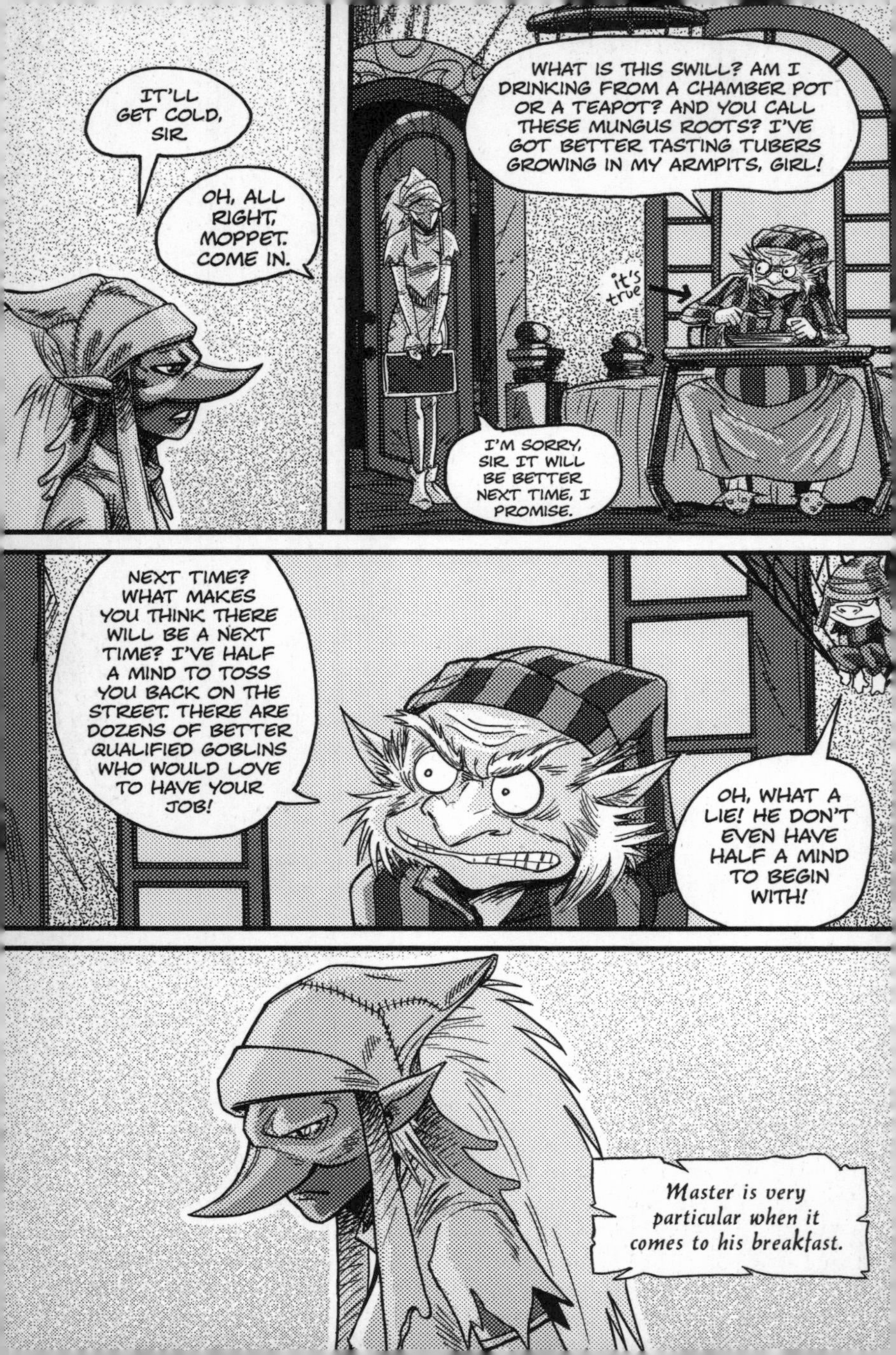
IT'LL GET COLD, SIR
OH, ALL RIGHT, MOPPET. COME IN.
WHAT IS THIS SWILL? AM I DRINKING FROM A CHAMBER POT OR A TEAPOT? AND YOU CALL THESE MUNGUS ROOTS? I'VE GOT BETTER TASTING TUBERS GROWING IN MY ARMPITS, GIRL!
it's true
I'M SORRY, SIR. IT WILL BE BETTER NEXT TIME, I PROMISE.
NEXT TIME? WHAT MAKES YOU THINK THERE WILL BE A NEXT TIME? I'VE HALF A MIND TO TOSS YOU BACK ON THE STREET. THERE ARE DOZENS OF BETTER QUALIFIED GOBLINS WHO WOULD LOVE TO HAVE YOUR JOB!
OH, WHAT A LIE! HE DON'T EVEN HAVE HALF A MIND TO BEGIN WITH!
Master is very particular when it comes to his breakfast.

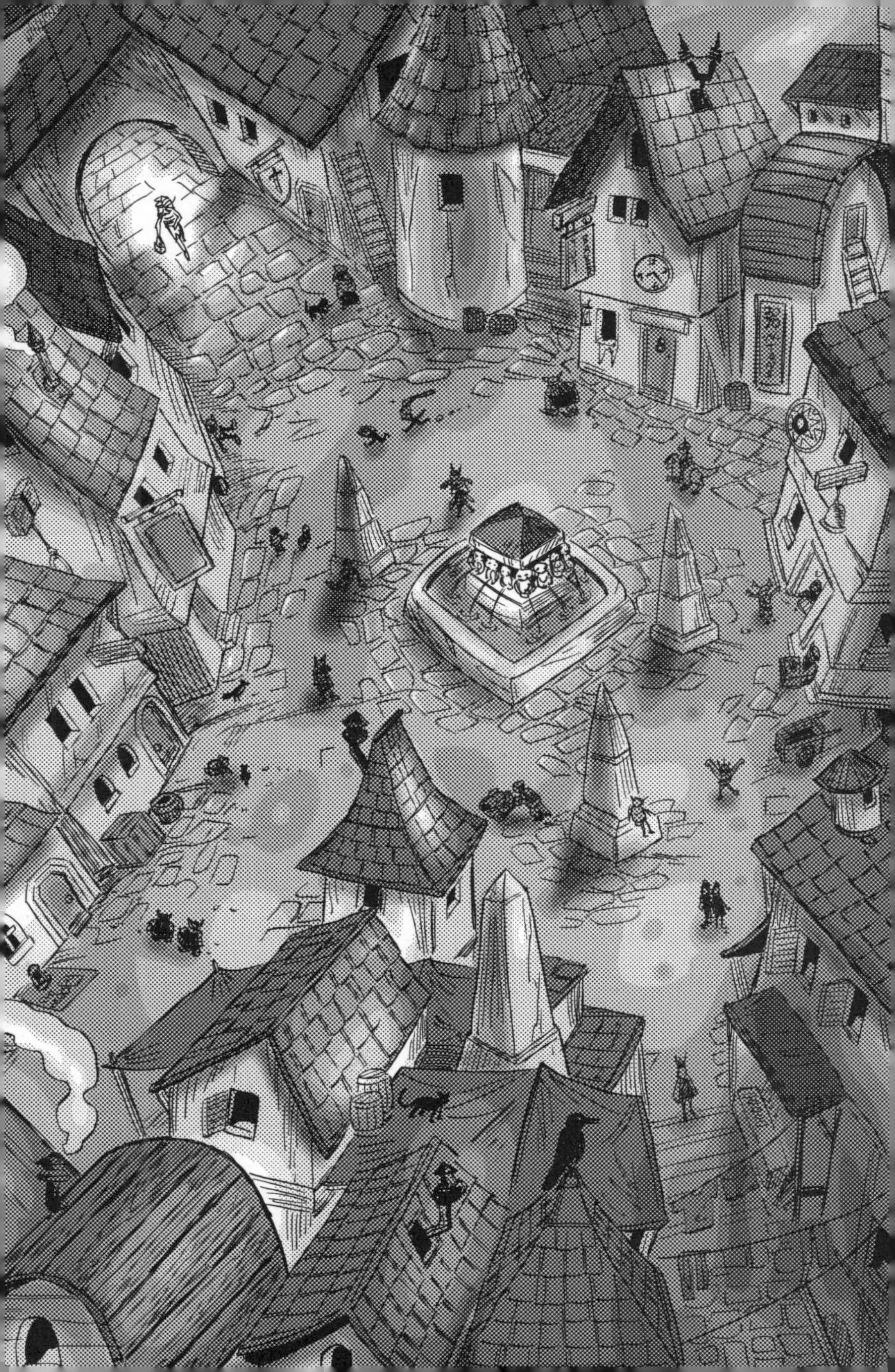

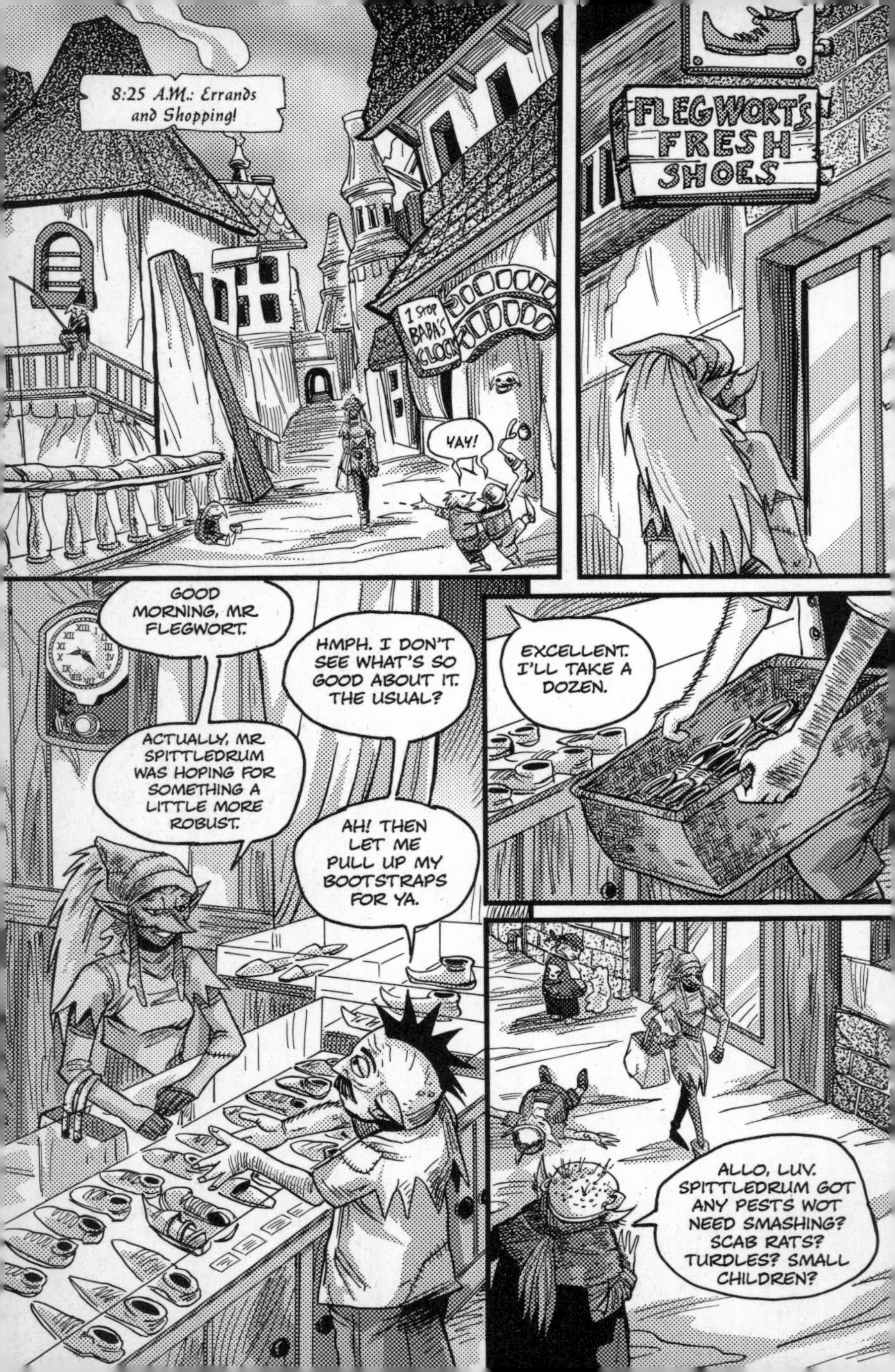
8:25 A.M.: Errands and Shopping!
1 STOP BABA'S CLOCK
YAY!
FLEGWORT'S FRESH SHOES
GOOD MORNING, MR FLEGWORT.
HMPH. I DON'T SEE WHAT'S SO GOOD ABOUT IT. THE USUAL?
ACTUALLY, MR SPITTLEDRUM WAS HOPING FOR SOMETHING A LITTLE MORE ROBUST.
AH! THEN LET ME PULL UP MY BOOTSTRAPS FOR YA.
EXCELLENT. I'LL TAKE A DOZEN.
ALLO, LUV. SPITTLEDRUM GOT ANY PESTS WOT NEED SMASHING? SCAB RATS? TURDLES? SMALL CHILDREN?

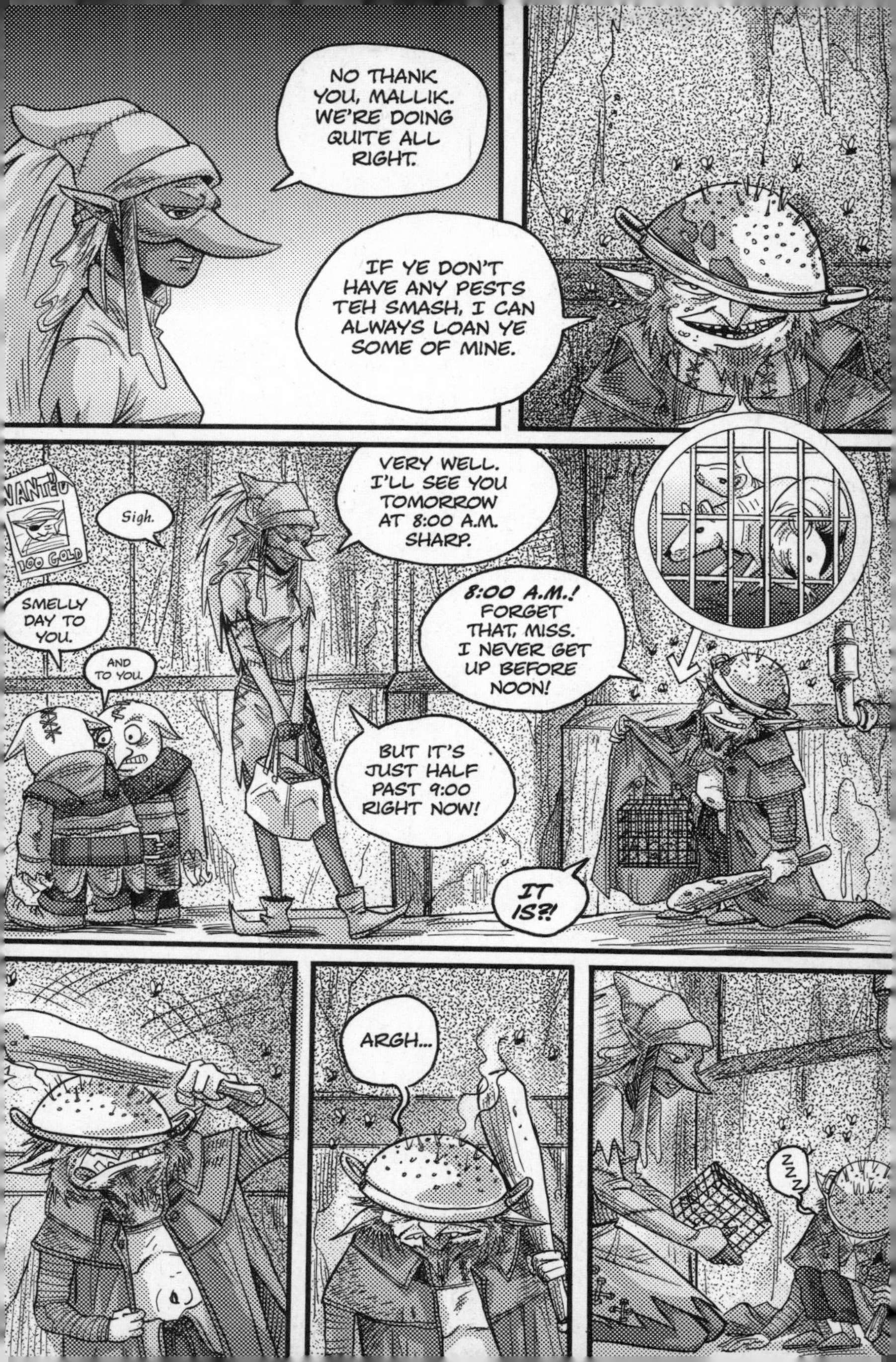

NO THANK YOU, MALLIK. WE'RE DOING QUITE ALL RIGHT.
IF YE DON'T HAVE ANY PESTS TEH SMASH, I CAN ALWAYS LOAN YE SOME OF MINE.
100 GOLD
Sigh.
SMELLY DAY TO YOU.
AND TO YOU.
VERY WELL. I'LL SEE YOU TOMORROW AT 8:00 A.M. SHARP.
8:00 A.M.! FORGET THAT, MISS. I NEVER GET UP BEFORE NOON!
BUT IT'S JUST HALF PAST 9:00 RIGHT NOW!
IT IS?!
ARGH...
ZZZ

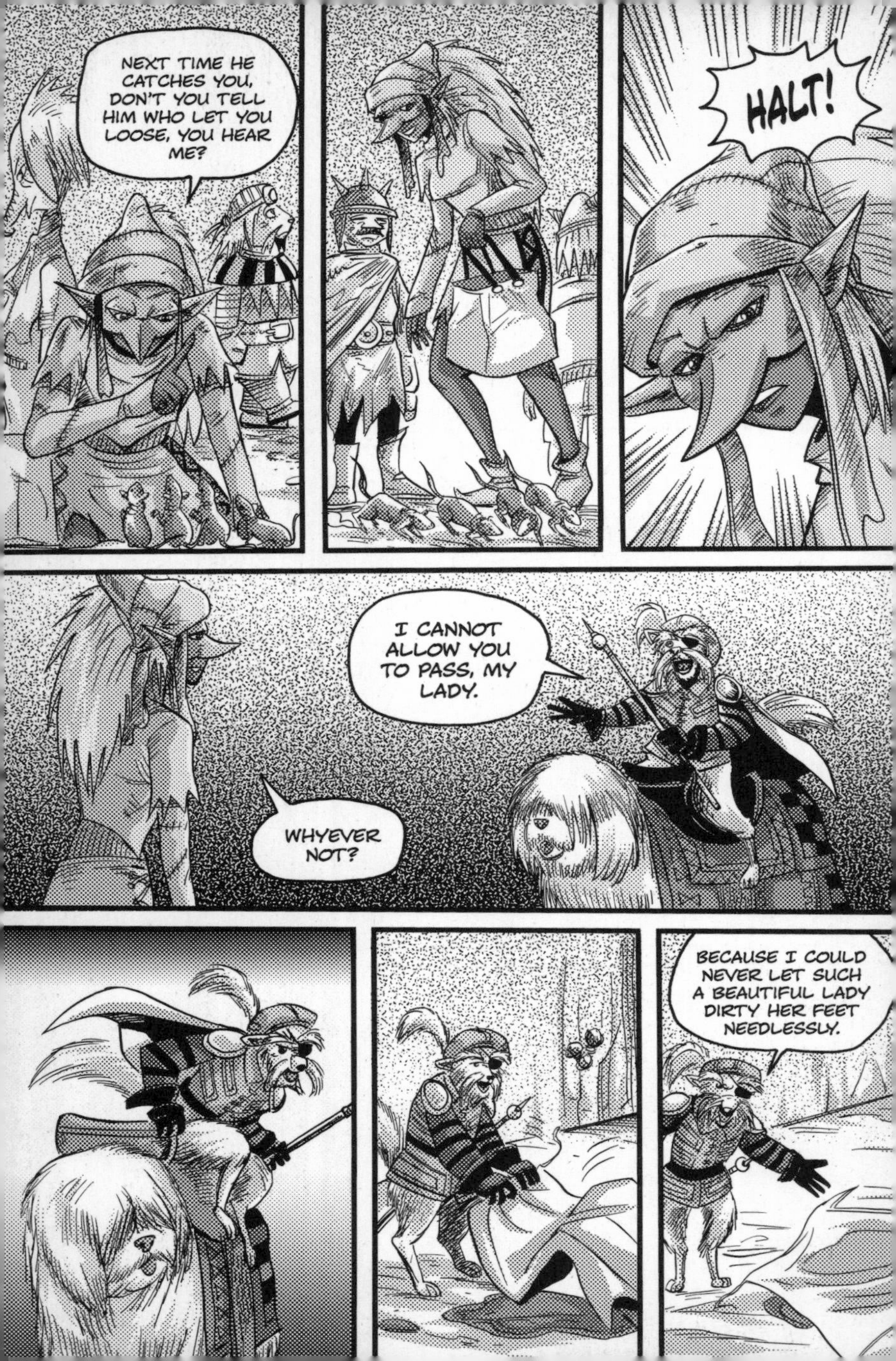
NEXT TIME HE CATCHES YOU, DON'T YOU TELL HIM WHO LET YOU LOOSE, YOU HEAR ME?
HALT!
I CANNOT ALLOW YOU TO PASS, MY LADY.
WHYEVER NOT?
BECAUSE I COULD NEVER LET SUCH A BEAUTIFUL LADY DIRTY HER FEET NEEDLESSLY.

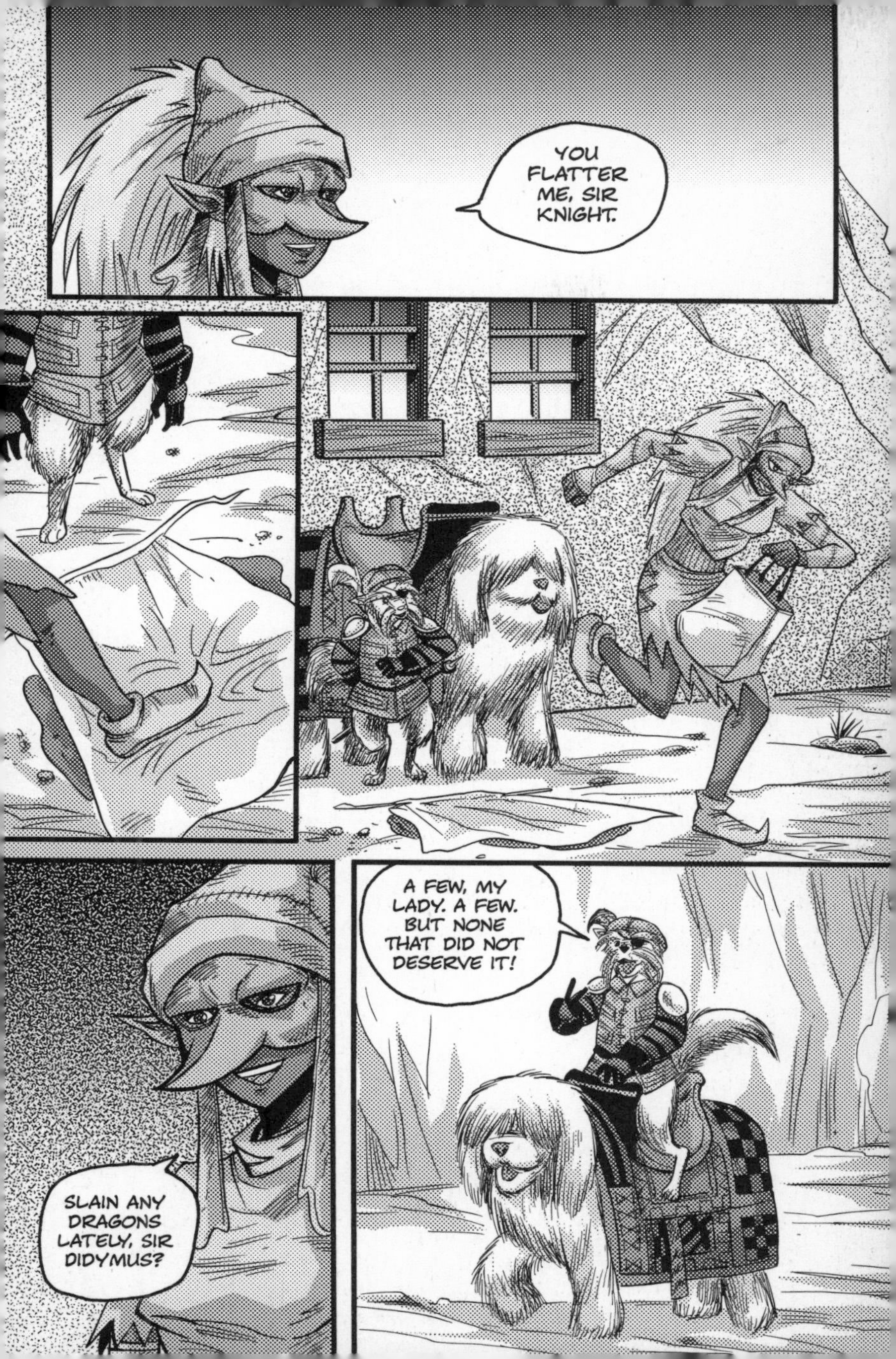
YOU FLATTER ME, SIR KNIGHT.
SLAIN ANY DRAGONS LATELY, SIR DIDYMUS?
A FEW, MY LADY. A FEW. BUT NONE THAT DID NOT DESERVE IT!

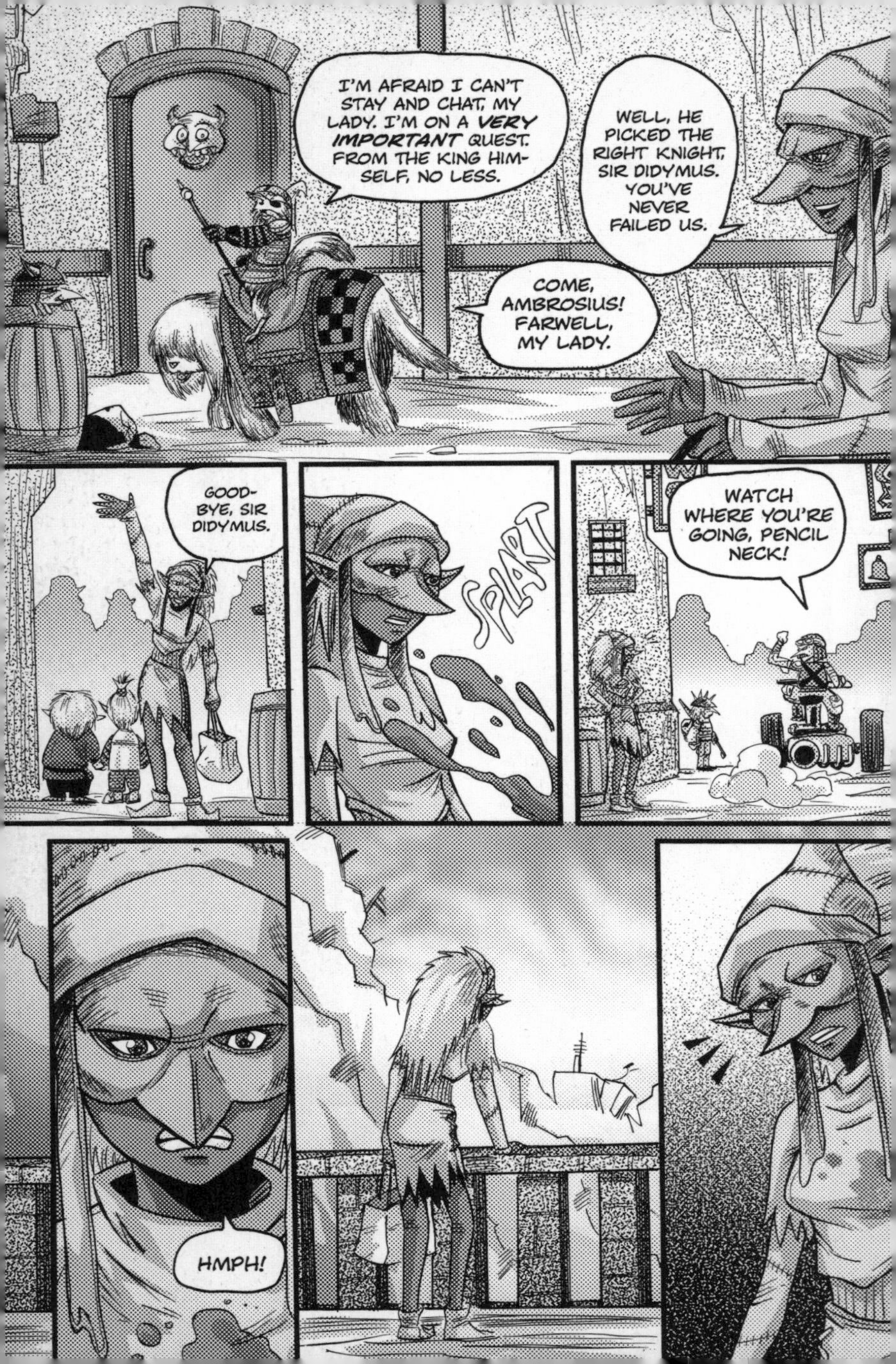
I'M AFRAID I CAN'T STAY AND CHAT, MY LADY. I'M ON A *VERY IMPORTANT* QUEST. FROM THE KING HIM-SELF, NO LESS.
WELL, HE PICKED THE RIGHT KNIGHT, SIR DIDYMUS. YOU'VE NEVER FAILED US.
COME, AMBROSIUS! FARWELL, MY LADY.
GOOD-BYE, SIR DIDYMUS.
SPLAT
WATCH WHERE YOU'RE GOING, PENCIL NECK!
HMPH!

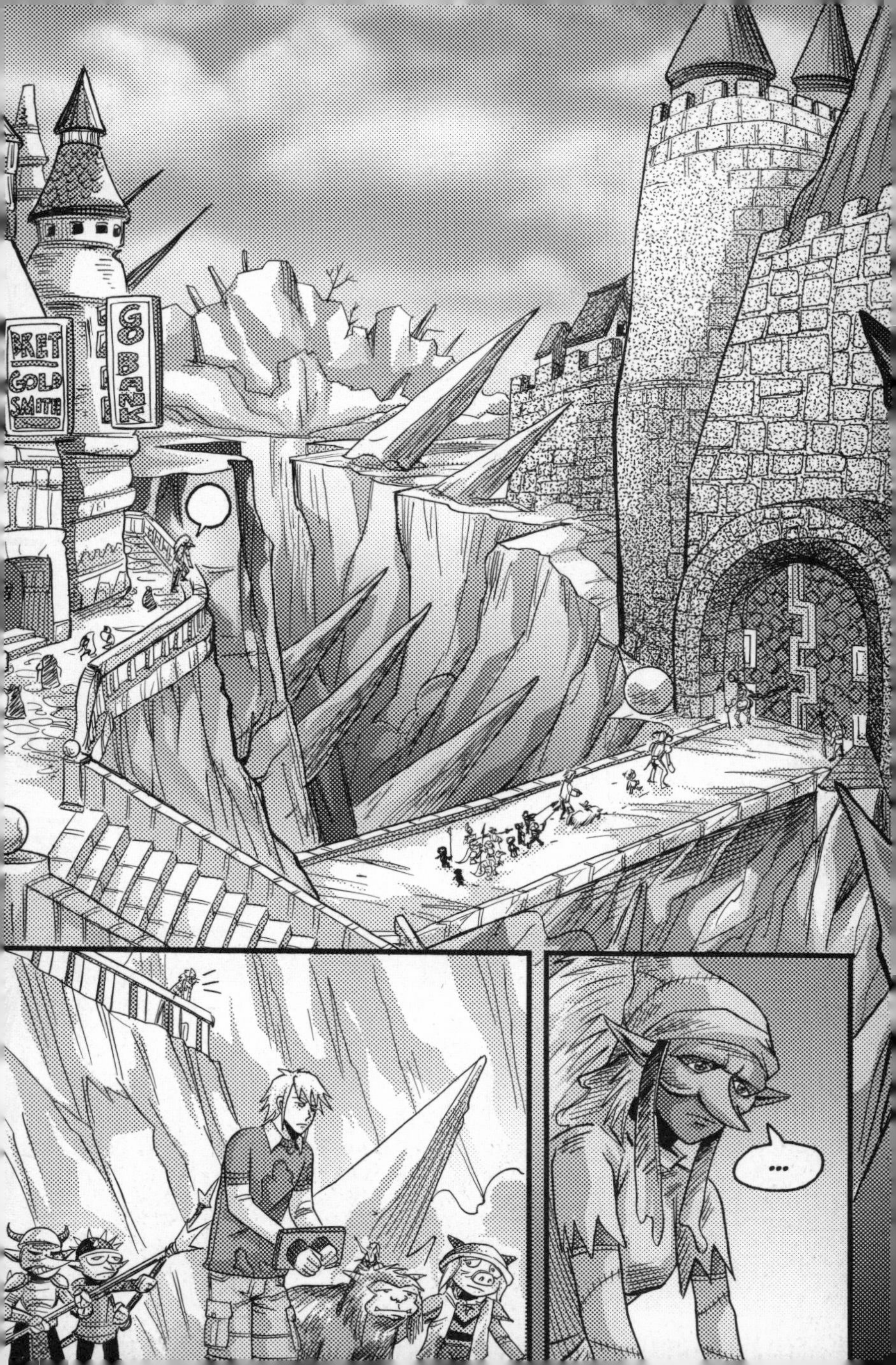
BRET GOLD SMITH
GO BANK
...

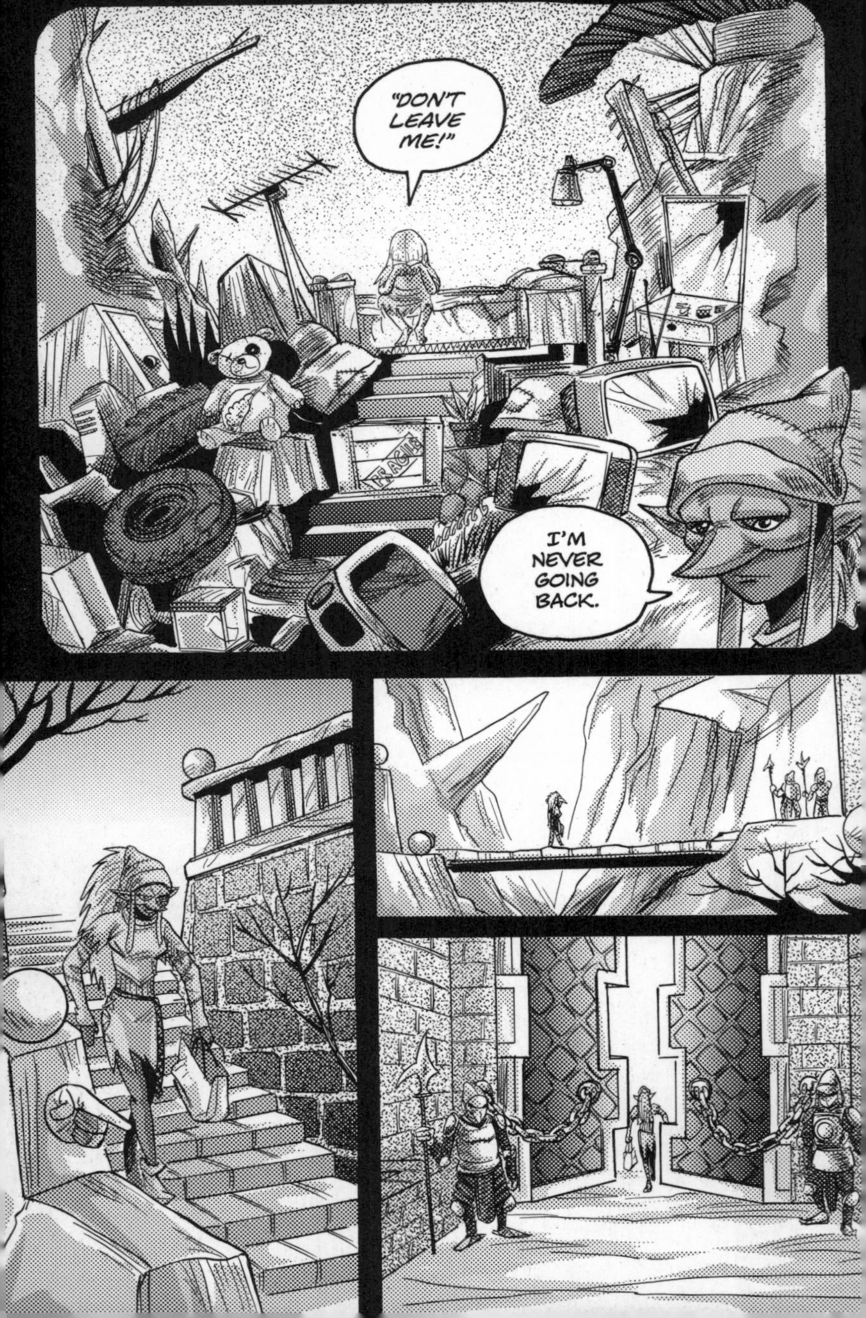
"DON'T LEAVE ME!"
I'M NEVER GOING BACK.

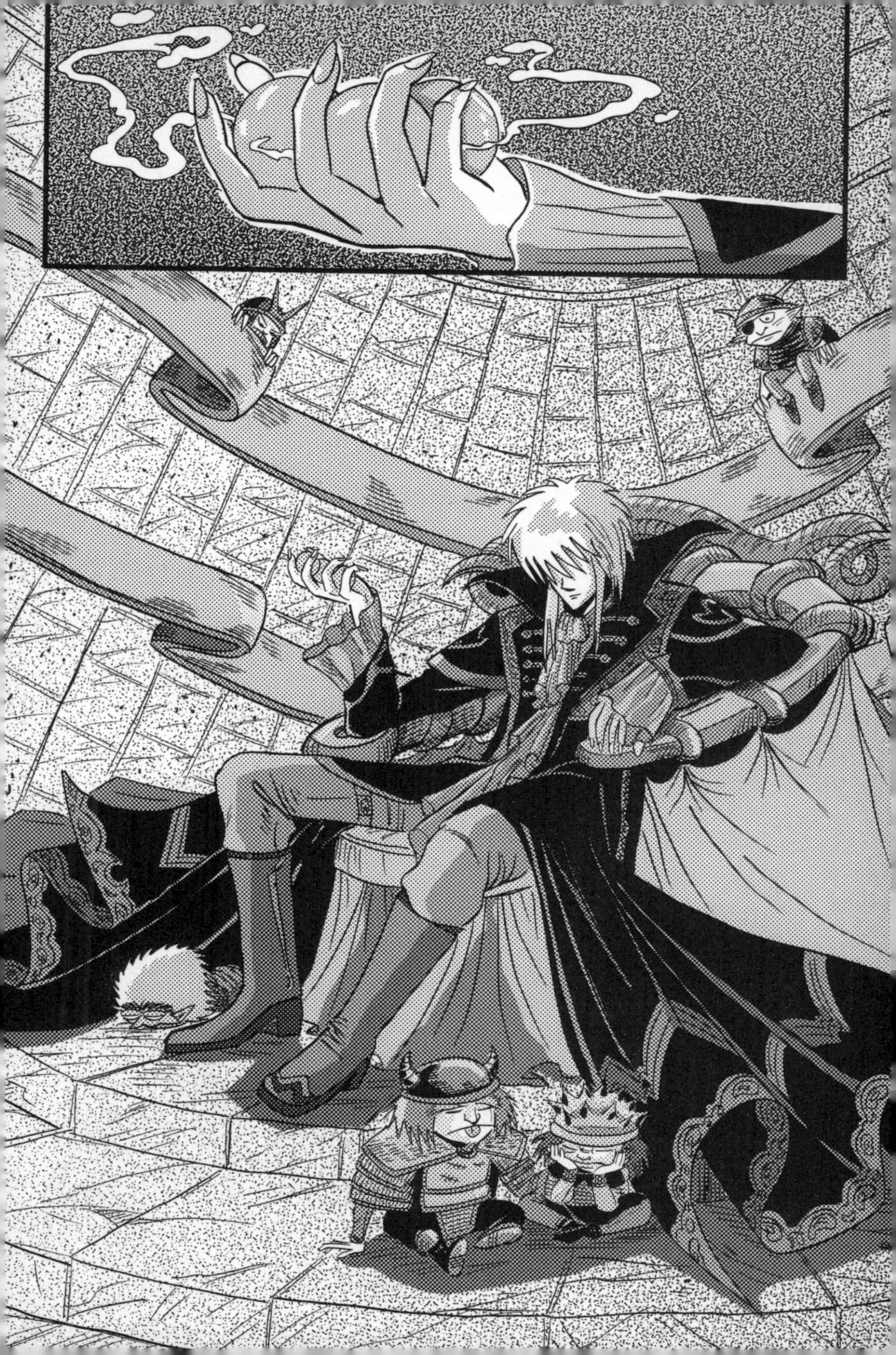

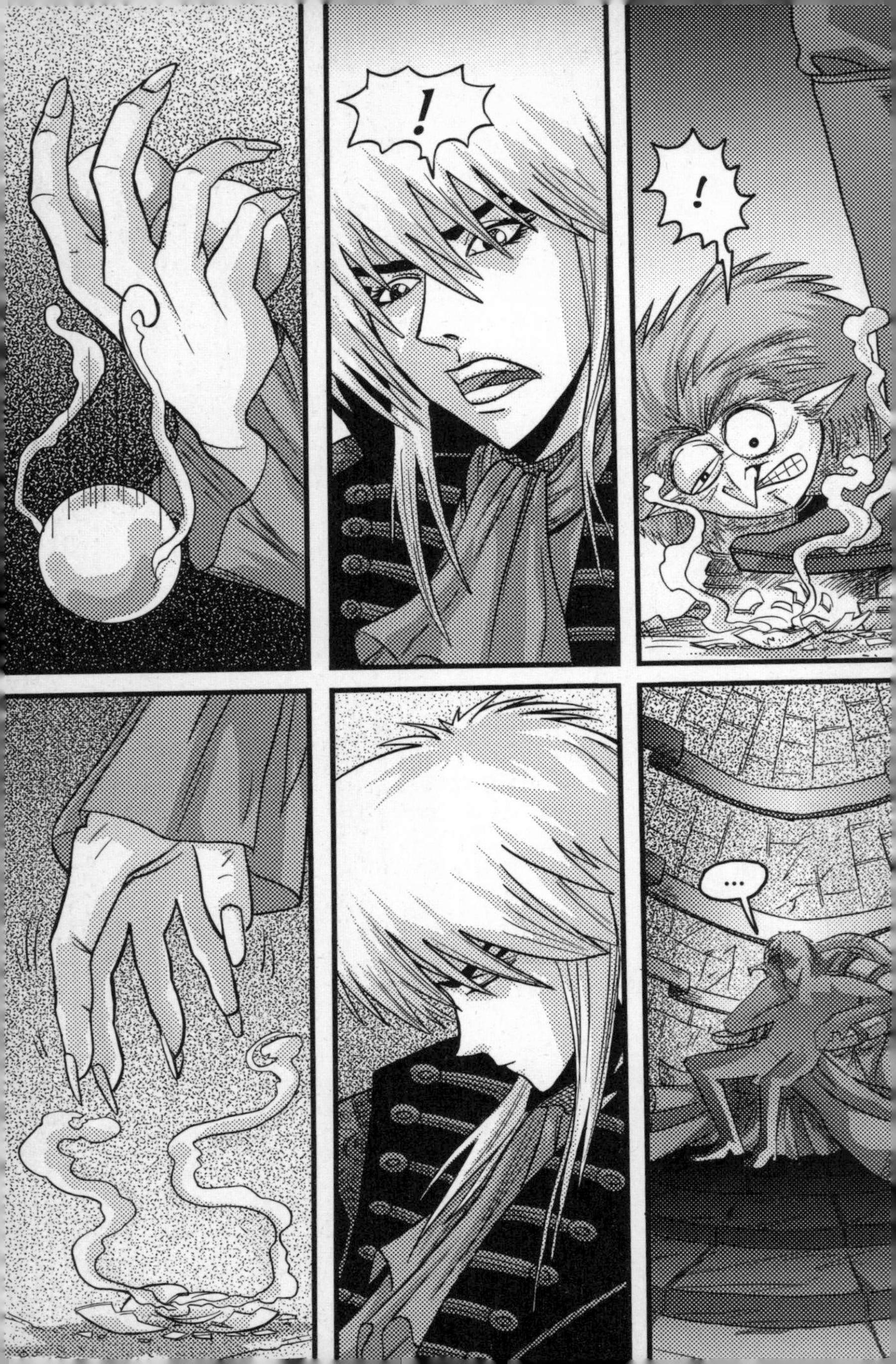
!
!
...

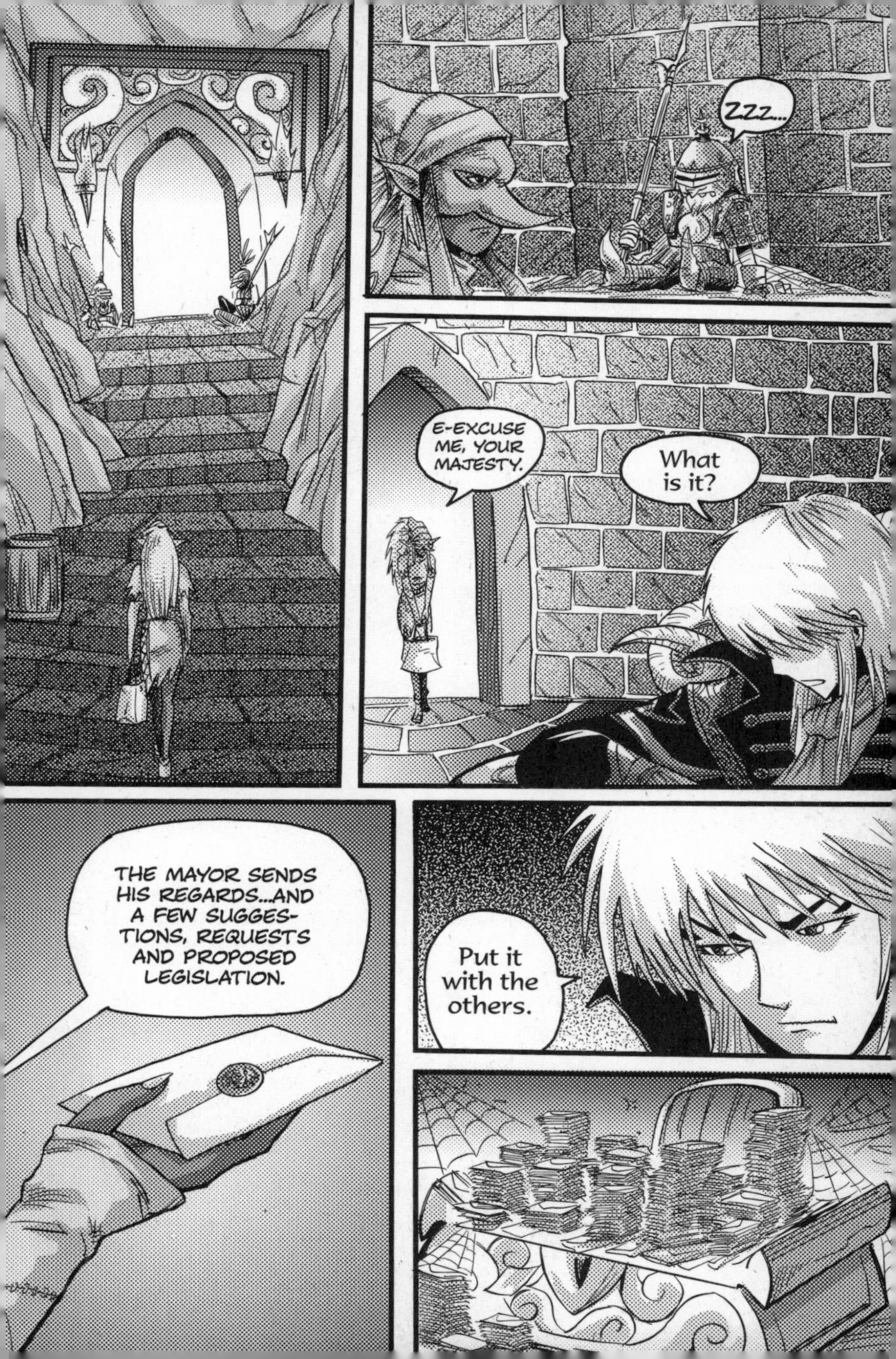
ZZZ...
E-EXCUSE ME, YOUR MAJESTY.
What is it?
THE MAYOR SENDS HIS REGARDS...AND A FEW SUGGES-TIONS, REQUESTS AND PROPOSED LEGISLATION.
Put it with the others.

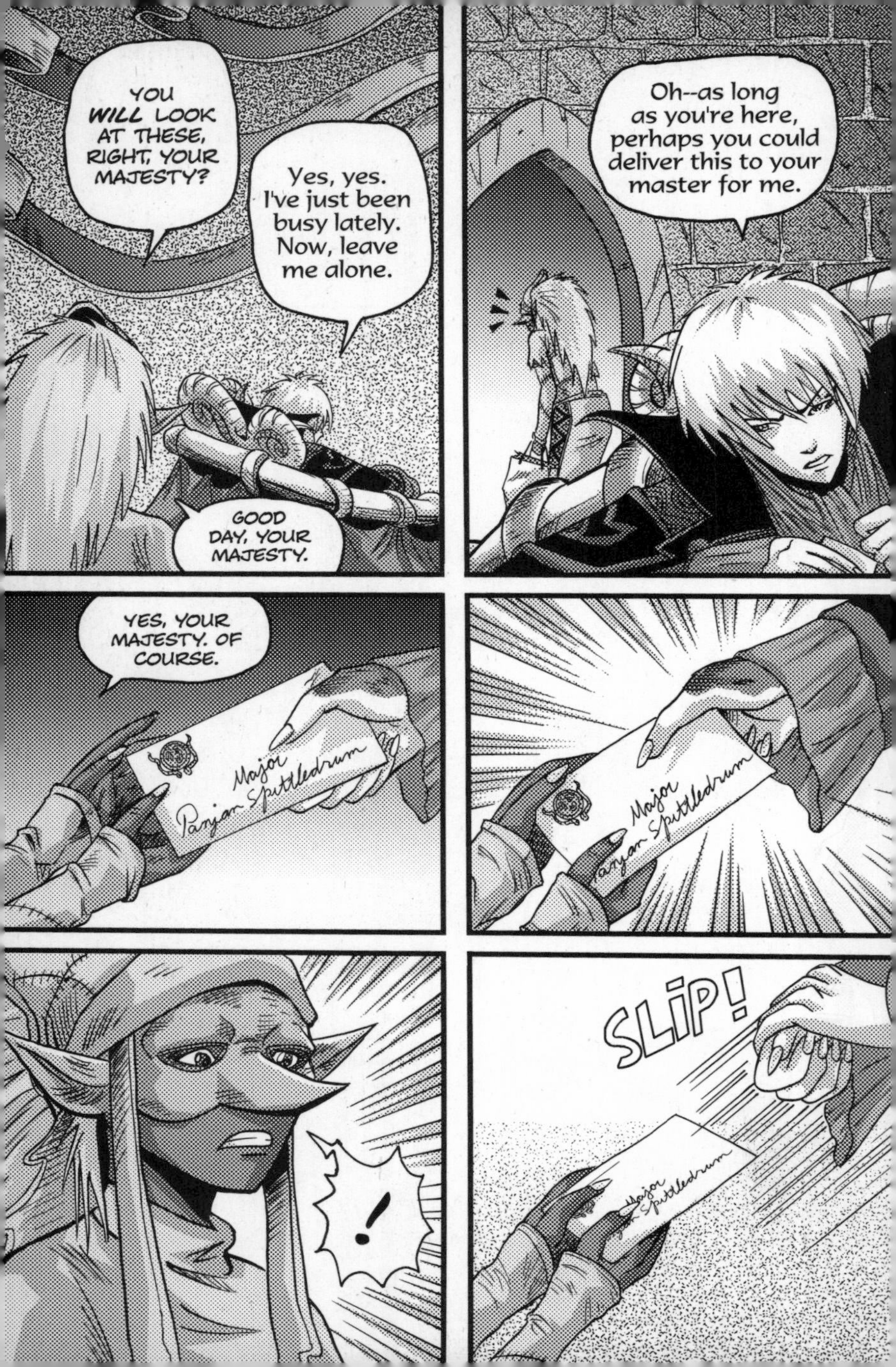
YOU **WILL** LOOK AT THESE, RIGHT, YOUR MAJESTY?
Yes, yes. I've just been busy lately. Now, leave me alone.
GOOD DAY, YOUR MAJESTY.
Oh--as long as you're here, perhaps you could deliver this to your master for me.
YES, YOUR MAJESTY. OF COURSE.
Major Panjan Spittledrum
Major Panjan Spittledrum
!
SLIP!

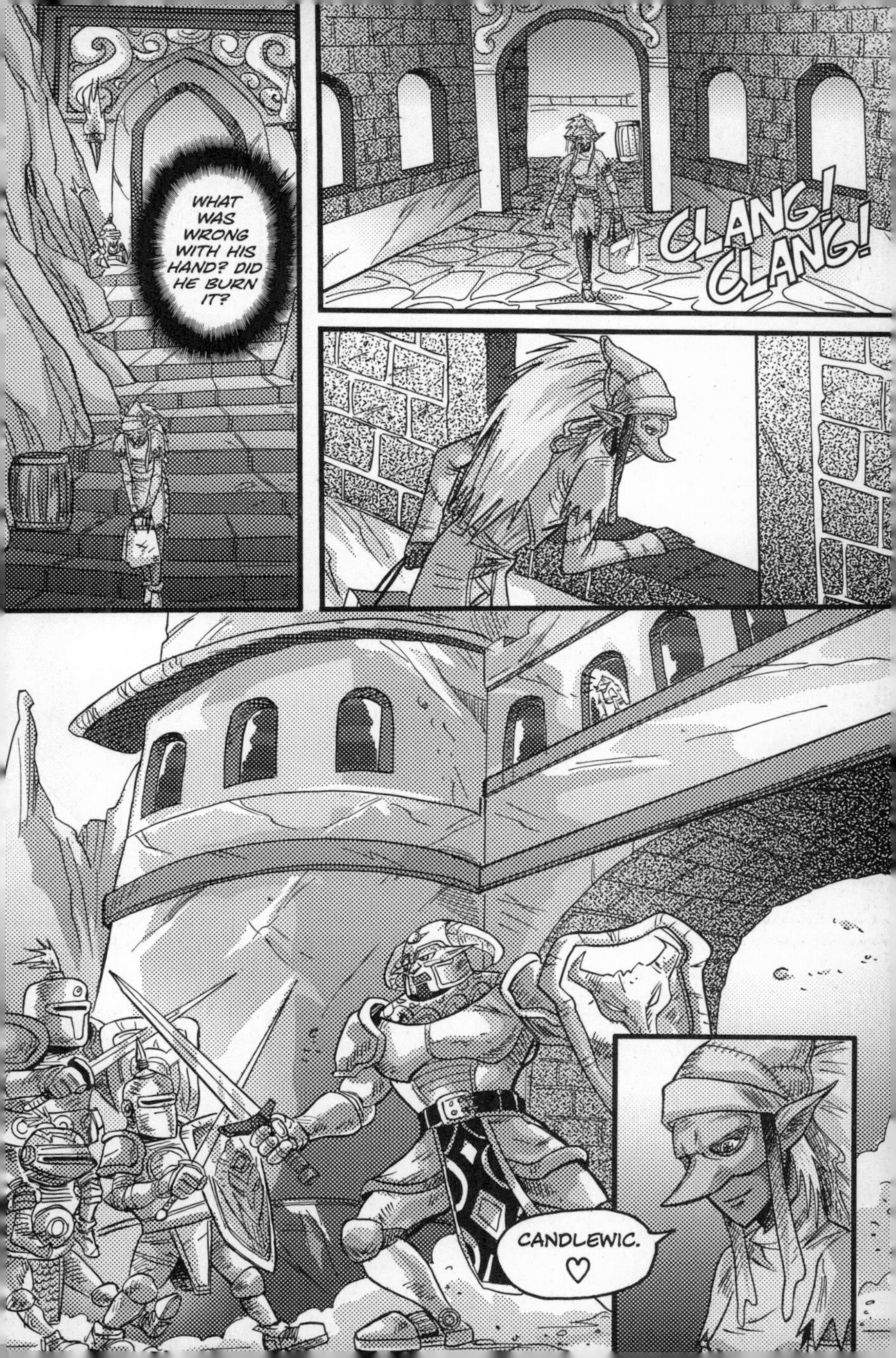
WHAT WAS WRONG WITH HIS HAND? DID HE BURN IT?
CLANG! CLANG!
CANDLEWIC. ♡

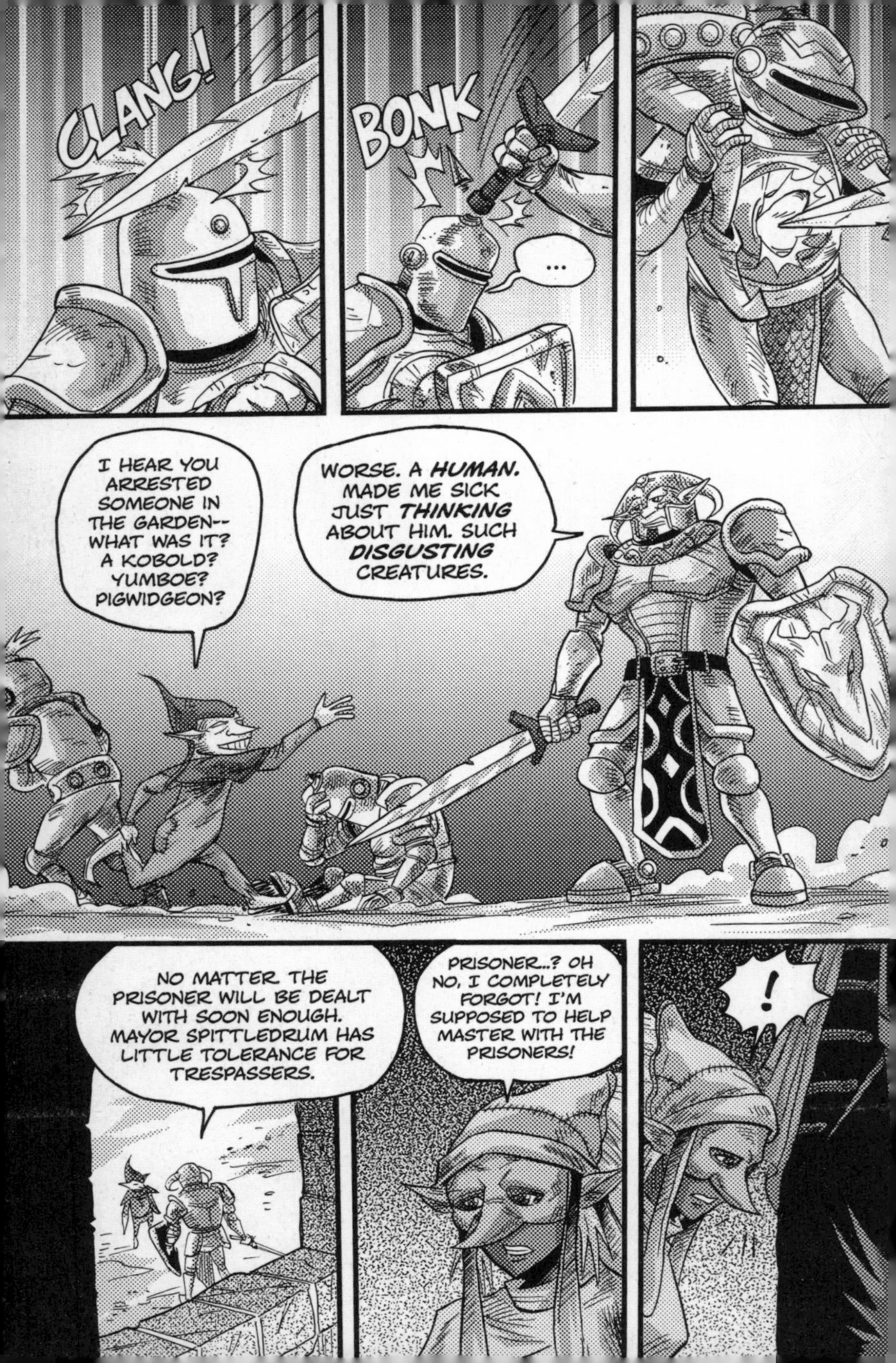
CLANG!
BONK
...
I HEAR YOU ARRESTED SOMEONE IN THE GARDEN--WHAT WAS IT? A KOBOLD? YUMBOE? PIGWIDGEON?
WORSE. A **HUMAN.** MADE ME SICK JUST **THINKING** ABOUT HIM. SUCH **DISGUSTING** CREATURES.
NO MATTER. THE PRISONER WILL BE DEALT WITH SOON ENOUGH. MAYOR SPITTLEDRUM HAS LITTLE TOLERANCE FOR TRESPASSERS.
PRISONER...? OH NO, I COMPLETELY FORGOT! I'M SUPPOSED TO HELP MASTER WITH THE PRISONERS!
!

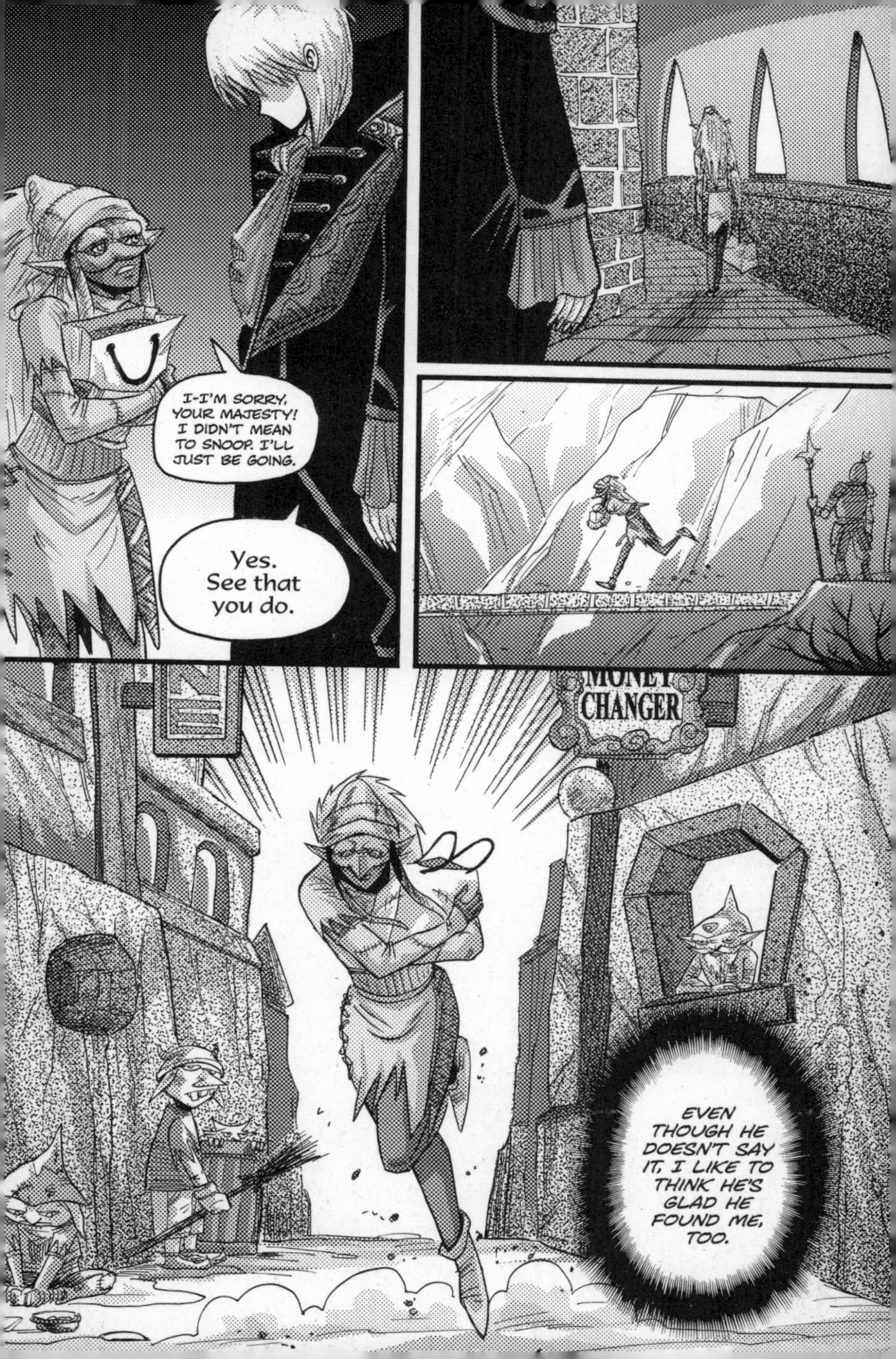
I-I'M SORRY, YOUR MAJESTY! I DIDN'T MEAN TO SNOOP. I'LL JUST BE GOING.
Yes. See that you do.
MONEY CHANGER
EVEN THOUGH HE DOESN'T SAY IT, I LIKE TO THINK HE'S GLAD HE FOUND ME, TOO.

Chapter 5
WHERE'S THE BARRISTER?!

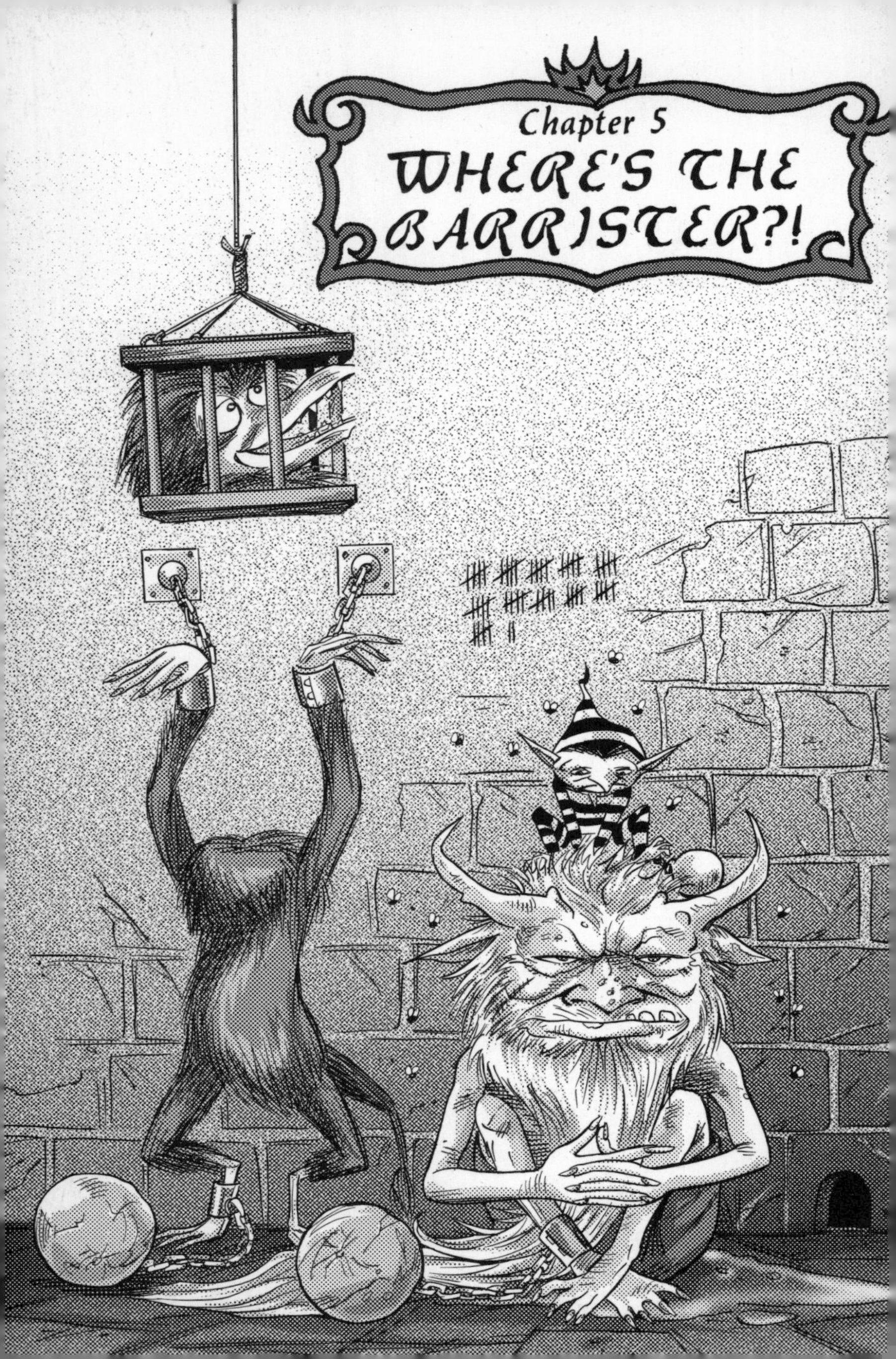

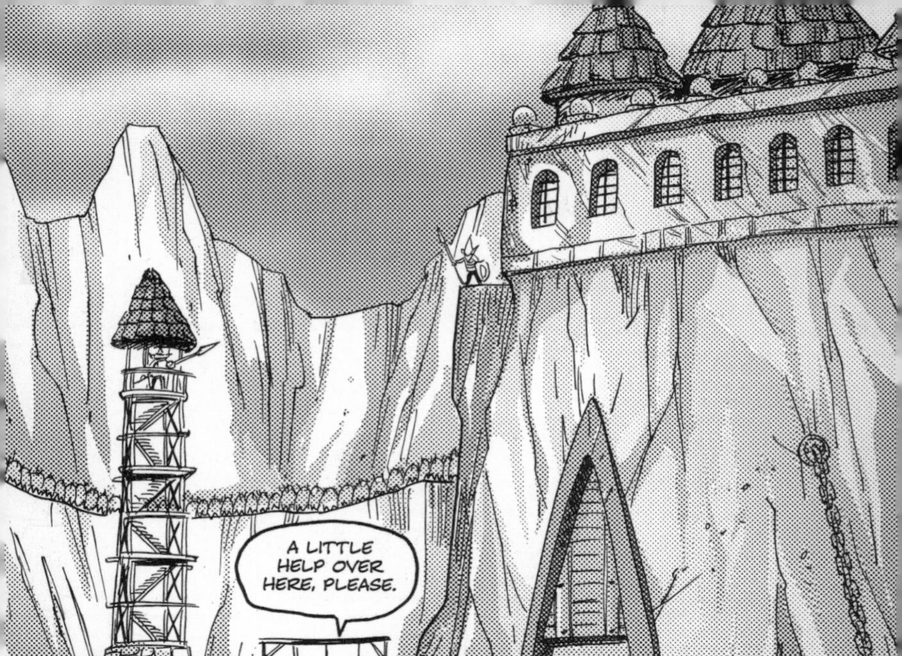
A LITTLE HELP OVER HERE, PLEASE.
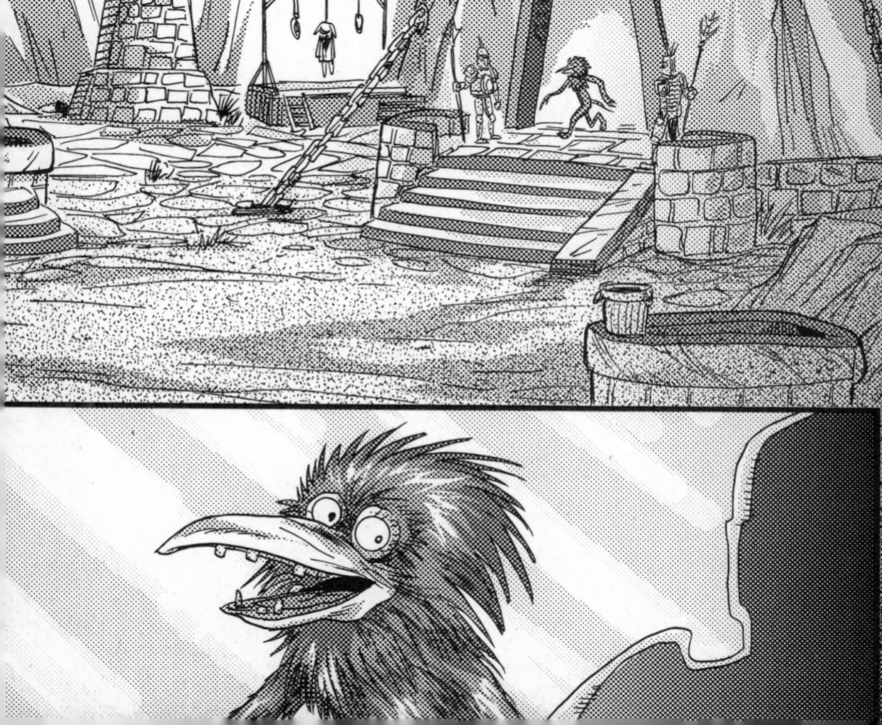

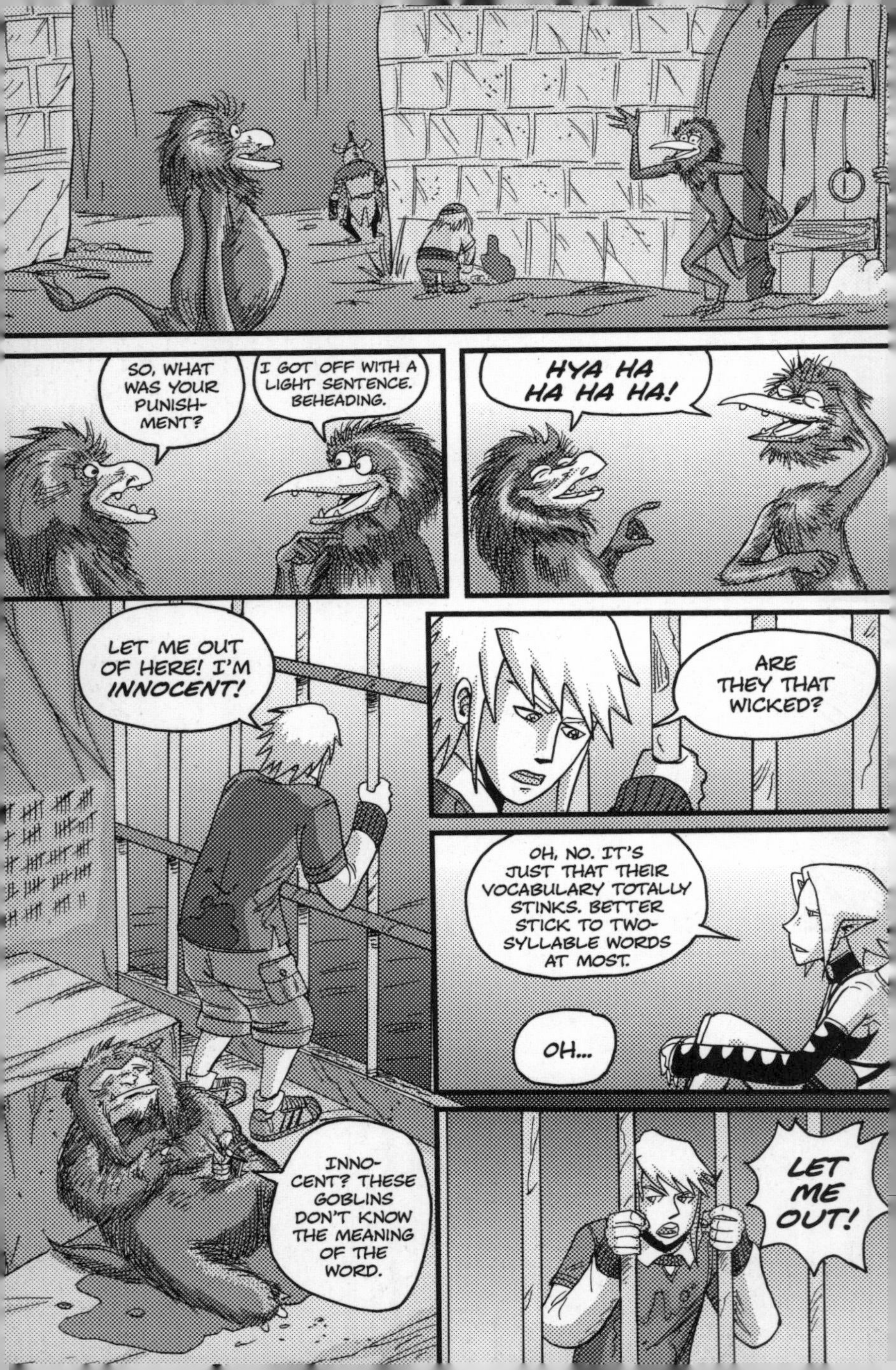
SO, WHAT WAS YOUR PUNISH-MENT?
I GOT OFF WITH A LIGHT SENTENCE. BEHEADING.
HYA HA HA HA HA!
LET ME OUT OF HERE! I'M INNOCENT!
INNO-CENT? THESE GOBLINS DON'T KNOW THE MEANING OF THE WORD.
ARE THEY THAT WICKED?
OH, NO. IT'S JUST THAT THEIR VOCABULARY TOTALLY STINKS. BETTER STICK TO TWO-SYLLABLE WORDS AT MOST.
OH...
LET ME OUT!

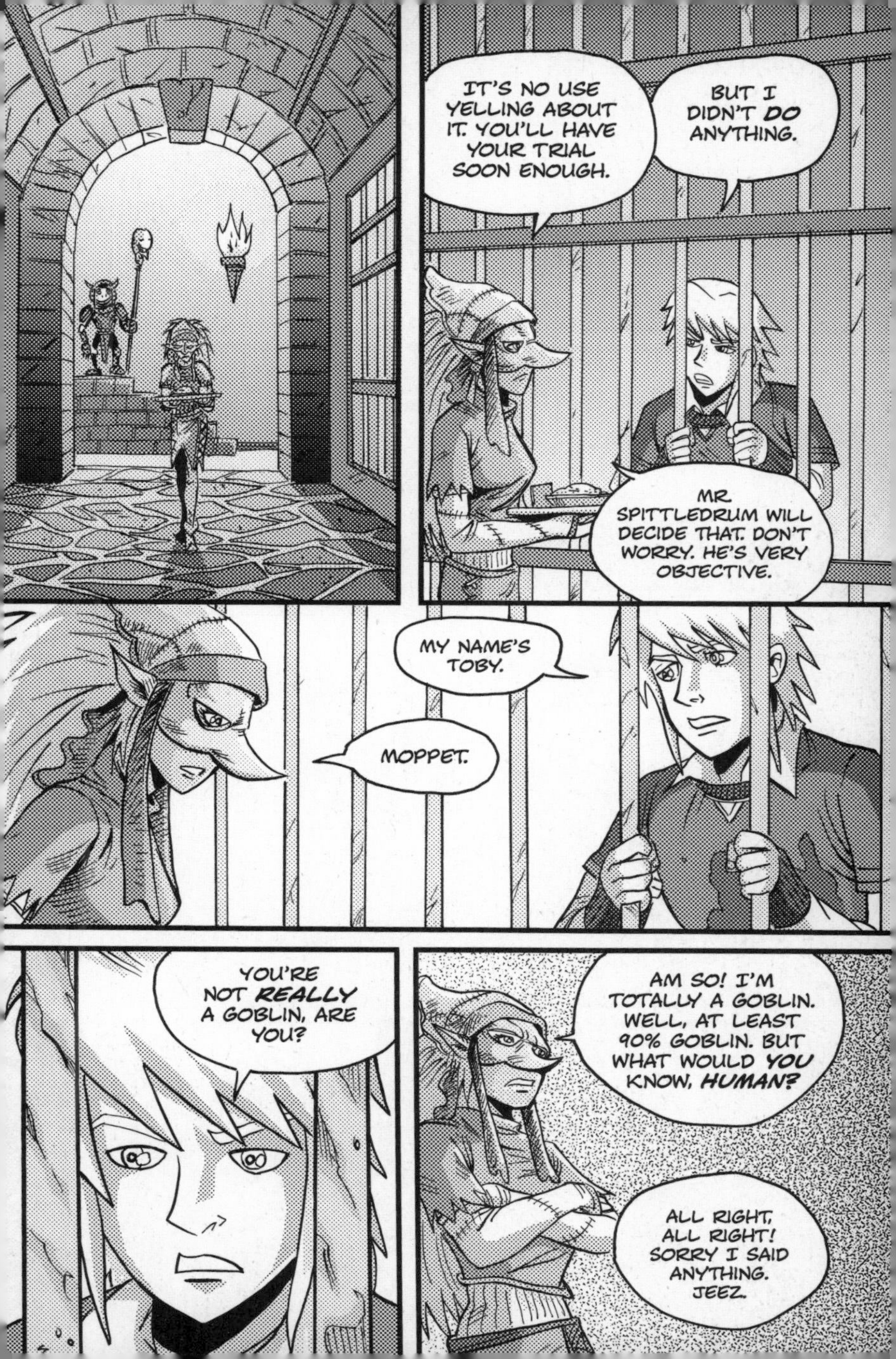
IT'S NO USE YELLING ABOUT IT. YOU'LL HAVE YOUR TRIAL SOON ENOUGH.
BUT I DIDN'T DO ANYTHING.
MR SPITTLEDRUM WILL DECIDE THAT. DON'T WORRY. HE'S VERY OBJECTIVE.
MY NAME'S TOBY.
MOPPET.
YOU'RE NOT REALLY A GOBLIN, ARE YOU?
AM SO! I'M TOTALLY A GOBLIN. WELL, AT LEAST 90% GOBLIN. BUT WHAT WOULD YOU KNOW, HUMAN?
ALL RIGHT, ALL RIGHT! SORRY I SAID ANYTHING. JEEZ.

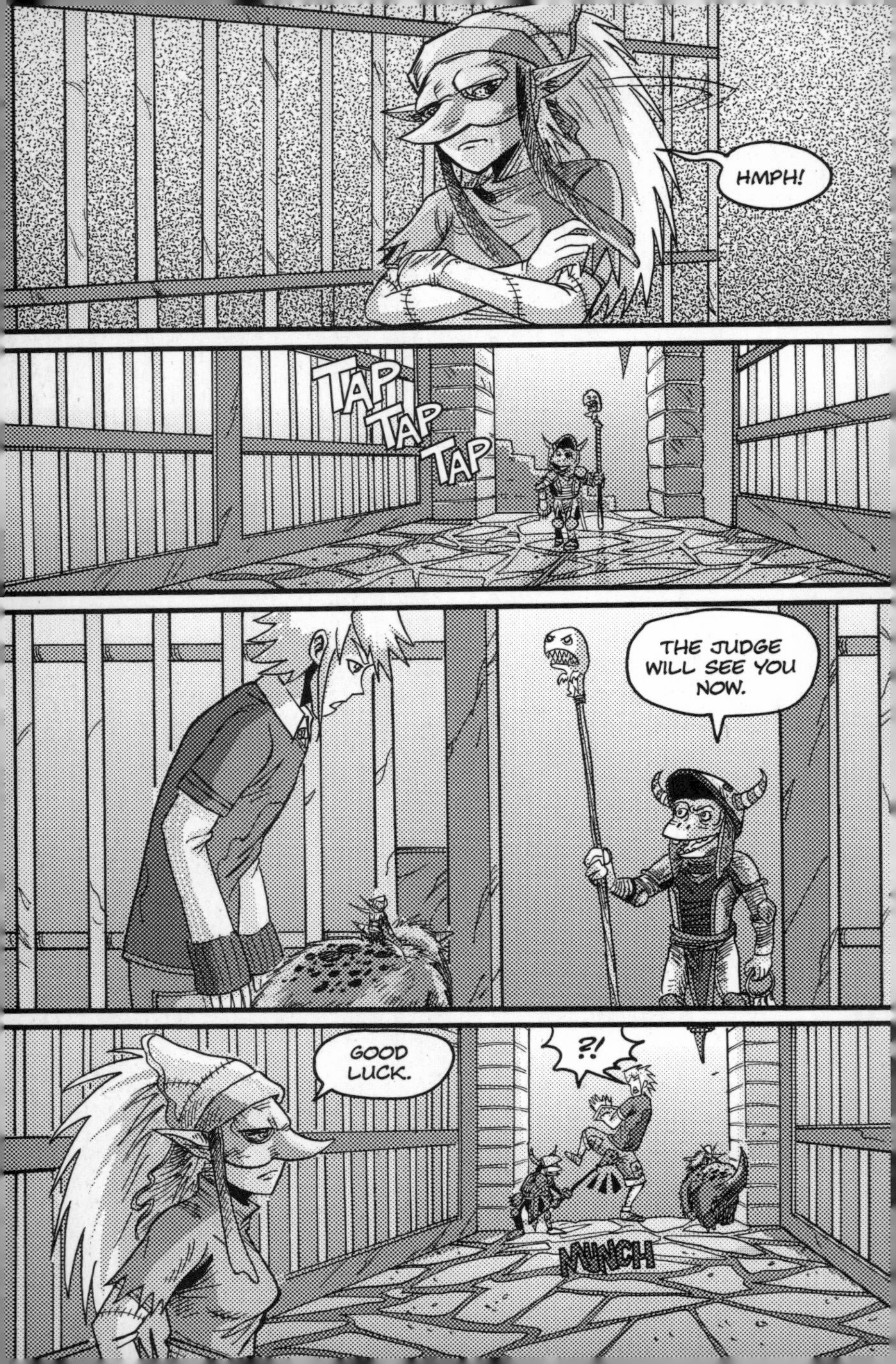
HMPH!
TAP TAP TAP
THE JUDGE WILL SEE YOU NOW.
GOOD LUCK.
?!
MUNCH

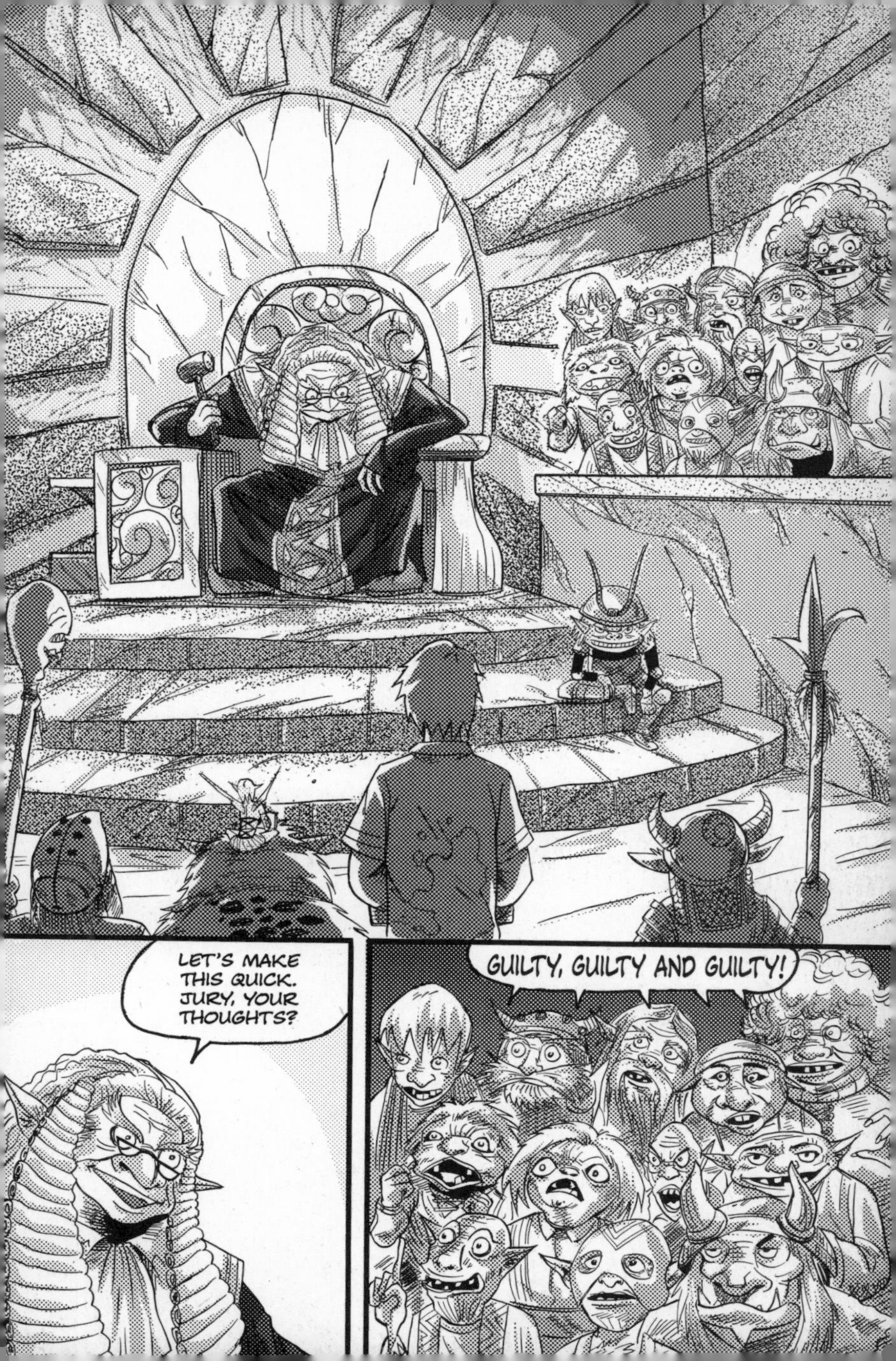
LET'S MAKE THIS QUICK. JURY, YOUR THOUGHTS?
GUILTY, GUILTY AND GUILTY!

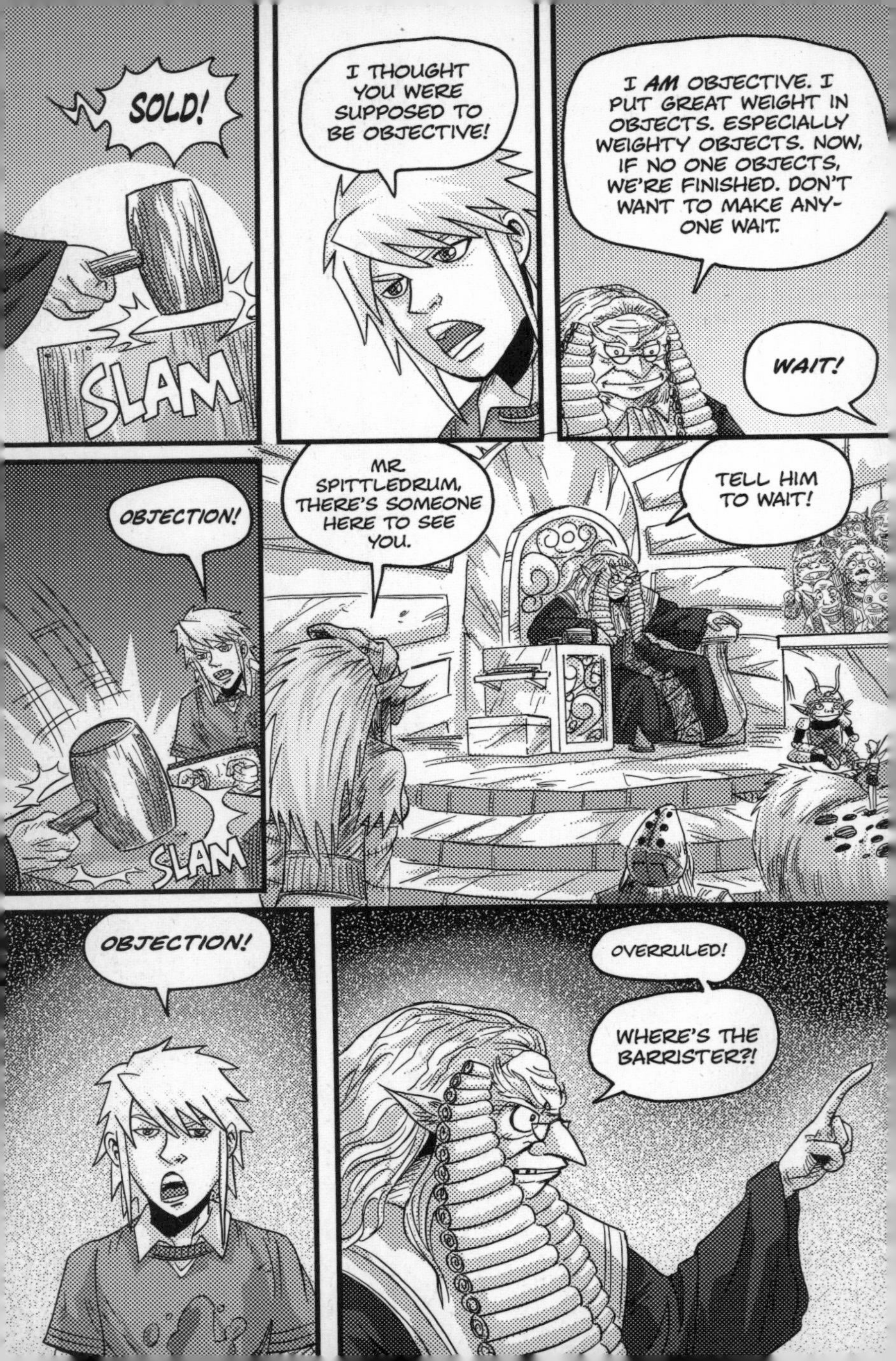
SOLD!
SLAM
I THOUGHT YOU WERE SUPPOSED TO BE OBJECTIVE!
I AM OBJECTIVE. I PUT GREAT WEIGHT IN OBJECTS. ESPECIALLY WEIGHTY OBJECTS. NOW, IF NO ONE OBJECTS, WE'RE FINISHED. DON'T WANT TO MAKE ANY-ONE WAIT.
WAIT!
OBJECTION!
SLAM
MR. SPITTLEDRUM, THERE'S SOMEONE HERE TO SEE YOU.
TELL HIM TO WAIT!
OBJECTION!
OVERRULED!
WHERE'S THE BARRISTER?!

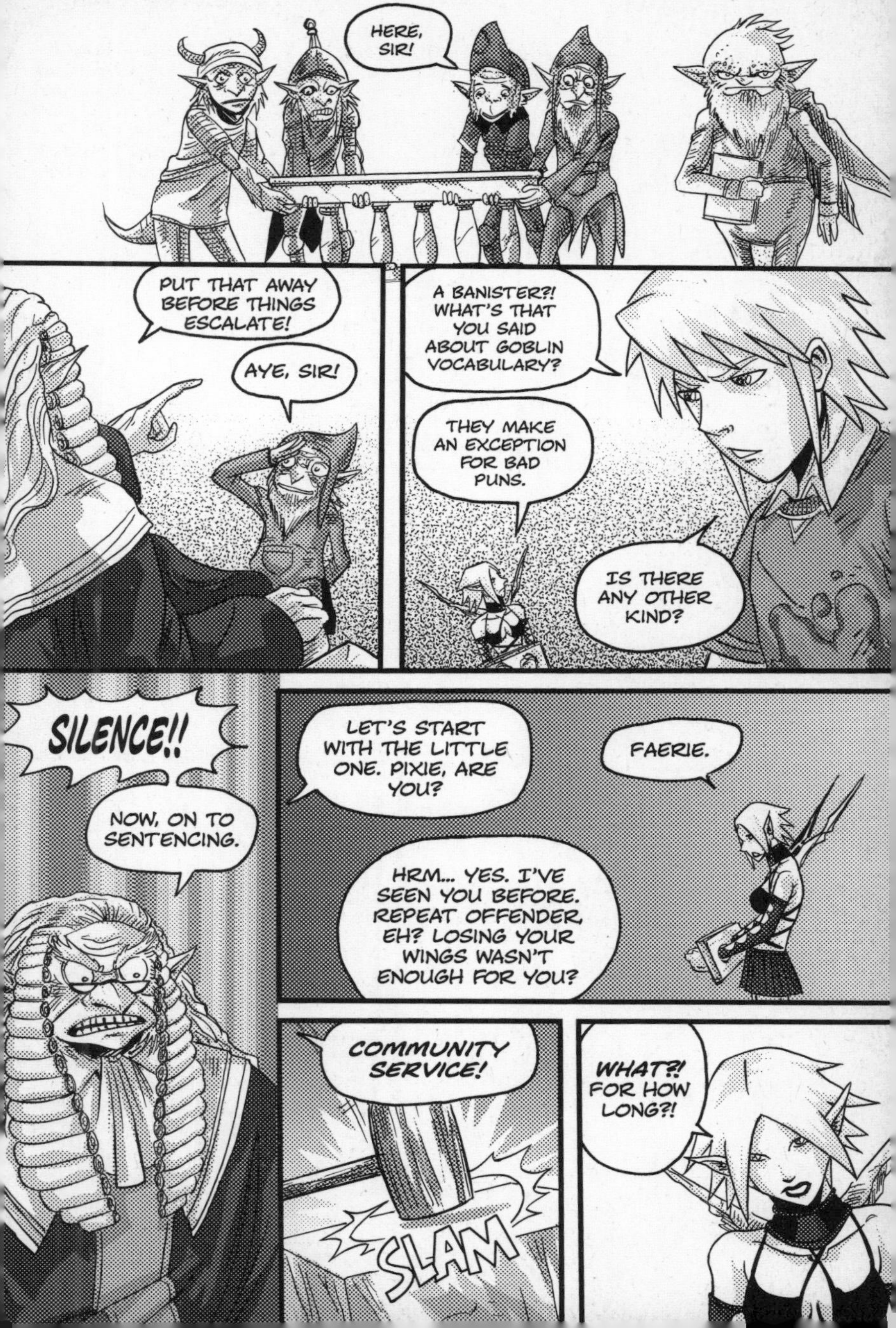
HERE, SIR!
PUT THAT AWAY BEFORE THINGS ESCALATE!
AYE, SIR!
A BANISTER?! WHAT'S THAT YOU SAID ABOUT GOBLIN VOCABULARY?
THEY MAKE AN EXCEPTION FOR BAD PUNS.
IS THERE ANY OTHER KIND?
SILENCE!!
NOW, ON TO SENTENCING.
LET'S START WITH THE LITTLE ONE. PIXIE, ARE YOU?
FAERIE.
HRM... YES. I'VE SEEN YOU BEFORE. REPEAT OFFENDER, EH? LOSING YOUR WINGS WASN'T ENOUGH FOR YOU?
COMMUNITY SERVICE!
SLAM
WHAT?! FOR HOW LONG?!

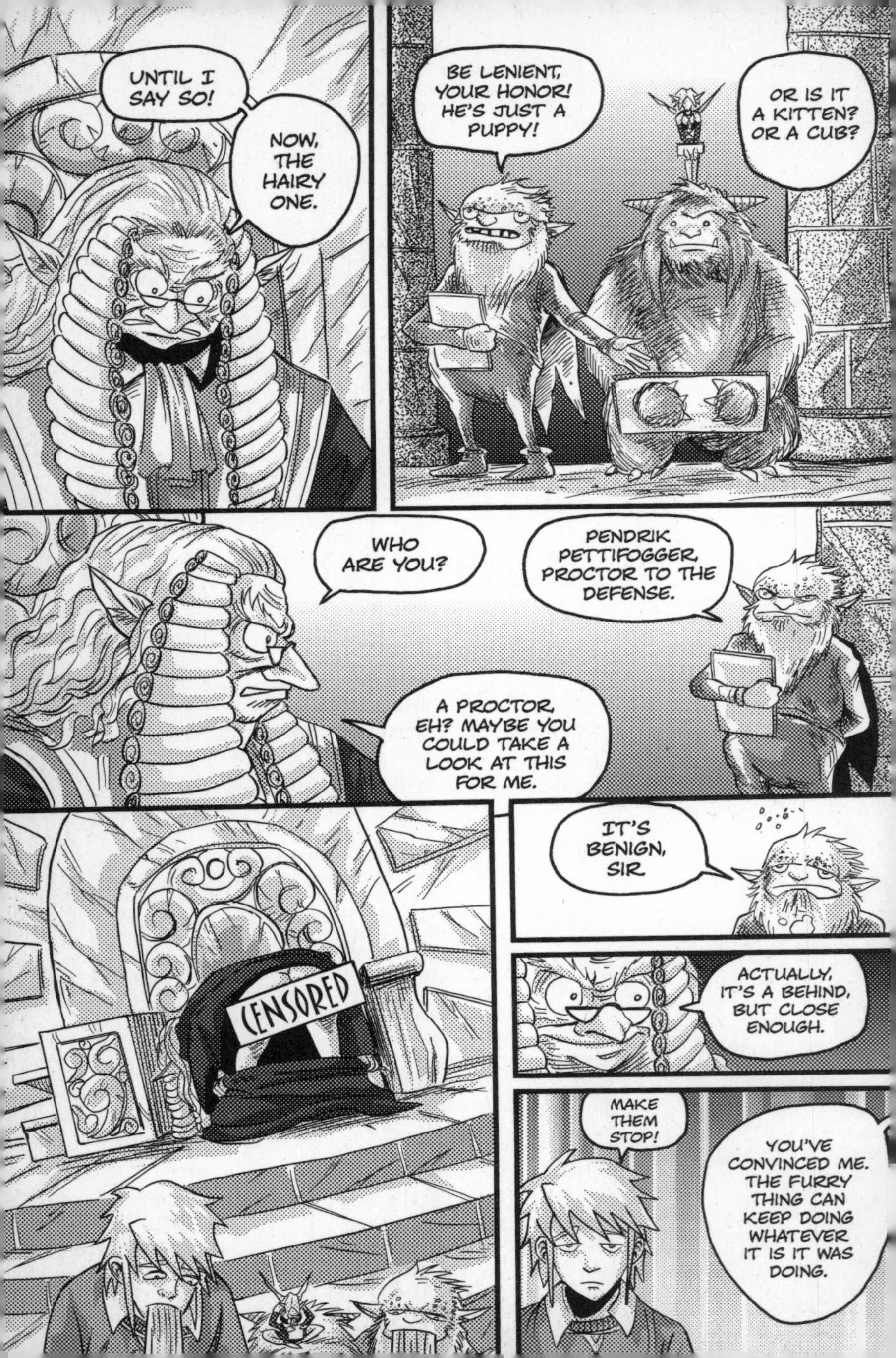
UNTIL I SAY SO!
NOW, THE HAIRY ONE.
BE LENIENT, YOUR HONOR! HE'S JUST A PUPPY!
OR IS IT A KITTEN? OR A CUB?
WHO ARE YOU?
PENDRIK PETTIFOGGER, PROCTOR TO THE DEFENSE.
A PROCTOR, EH? MAYBE YOU COULD TAKE A LOOK AT THIS FOR ME.
CENSORED
IT'S BENIGN, SIR
ACTUALLY, IT'S A BEHIND, BUT CLOSE ENOUGH.
MAKE THEM STOP!
YOU'VE CONVINCED ME. THE FURRY THING CAN KEEP DOING WHATEVER IT IS IT WAS DOING.

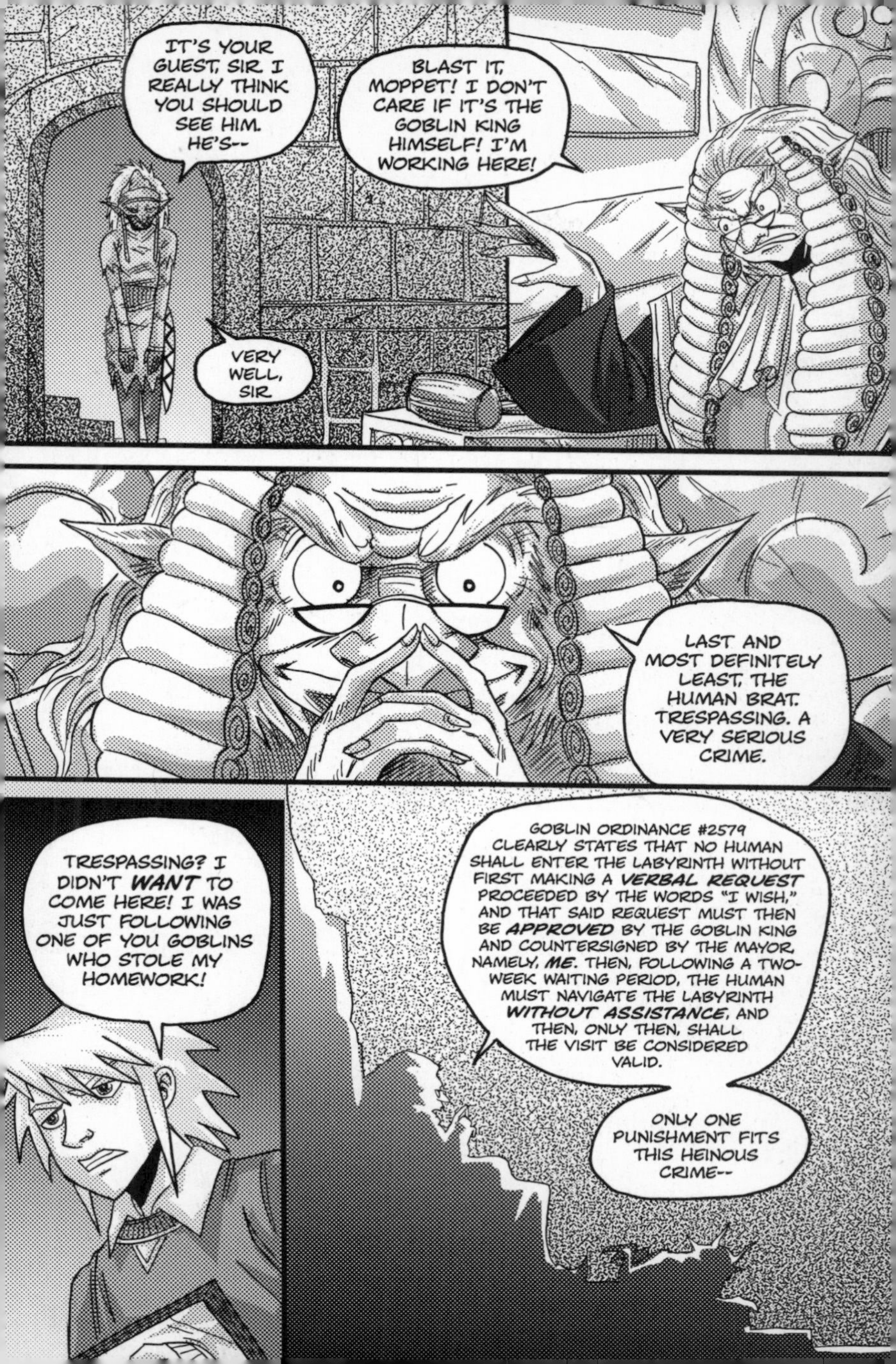
IT'S YOUR GUEST, SIR. I REALLY THINK YOU SHOULD SEE HIM. HE'S--
BLAST IT, MOPPET! I DON'T CARE IF IT'S THE GOBLIN KING HIMSELF! I'M WORKING HERE!
VERY WELL, SIR
LAST AND MOST DEFINITELY LEAST, THE HUMAN BRAT. TRESPASSING. A VERY SERIOUS CRIME.
TRESPASSING? I DIDN'T *WANT* TO COME HERE! I WAS JUST FOLLOWING ONE OF YOU GOBLINS WHO STOLE MY HOMEWORK!
GOBLIN ORDINANCE #2579 CLEARLY STATES THAT NO HUMAN SHALL ENTER THE LABYRINTH WITHOUT FIRST MAKING A *VERBAL REQUEST* PROCEEDED BY THE WORDS "I WISH," AND THAT SAID REQUEST MUST THEN BE *APPROVED* BY THE GOBLIN KING AND COUNTERSIGNED BY THE MAYOR, NAMELY, *ME*. THEN, FOLLOWING A TWO-WEEK WAITING PERIOD, THE HUMAN MUST NAVIGATE THE LABYRINTH *WITHOUT ASSISTANCE*, AND THEN, ONLY THEN, SHALL THE VISIT BE CONSIDERED VALID.
ONLY ONE PUNISHMENT FITS THIS HEINOUS CRIME--

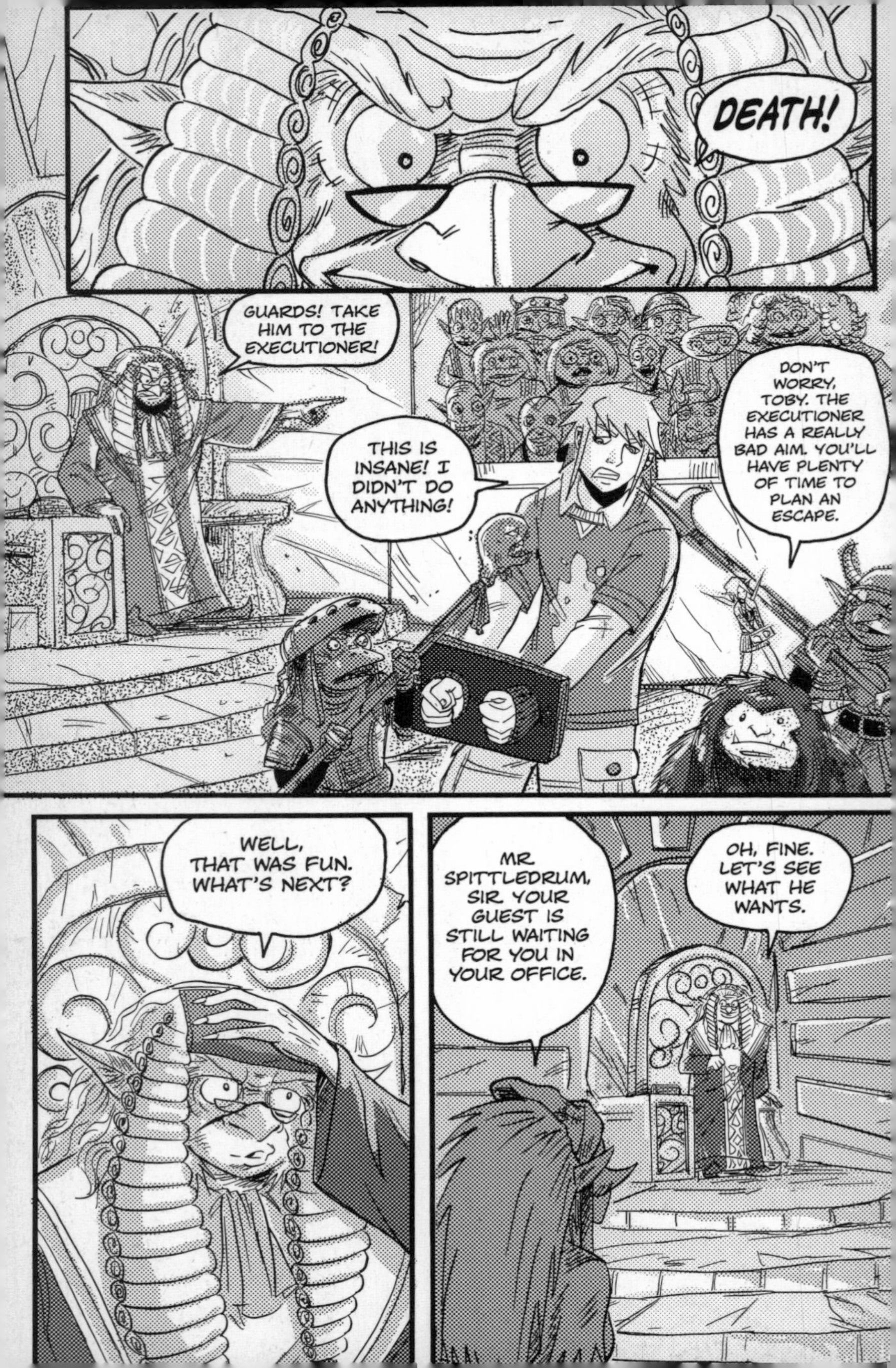
DEATH!
GUARDS! TAKE HIM TO THE EXECUTIONER!
THIS IS INSANE! I DIDN'T DO ANYTHING!
DON'T WORRY, TOBY. THE EXECUTIONER HAS A REALLY BAD AIM. YOU'LL HAVE PLENTY OF TIME TO PLAN AN ESCAPE.
WELL, THAT WAS FUN. WHAT'S NEXT?
MR SPITTLEDRUM, SIR YOUR GUEST IS STILL WAITING FOR YOU IN YOUR OFFICE.
OH, FINE. LET'S SEE WHAT HE WANTS.

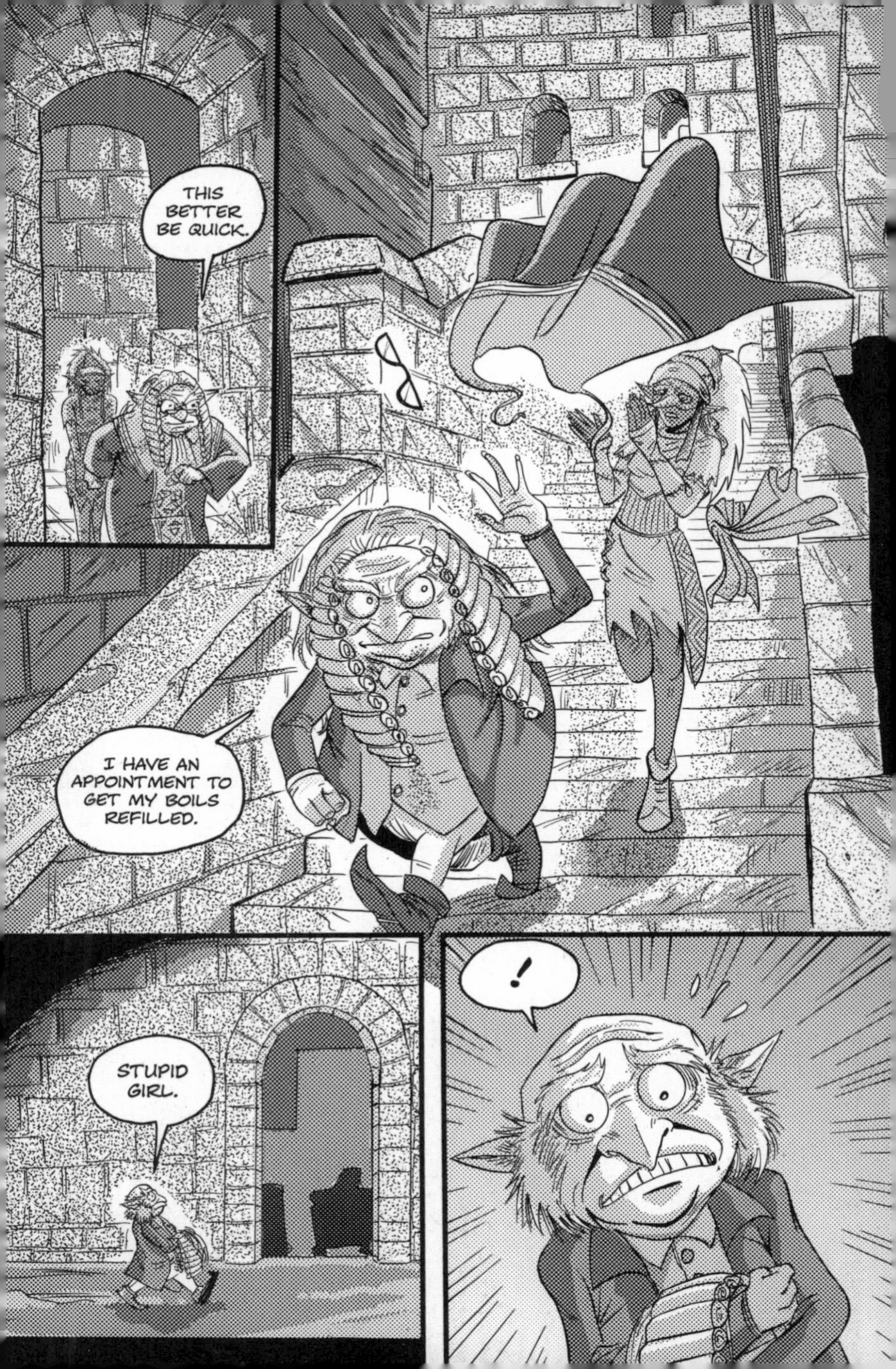
THIS BETTER BE QUICK.
I HAVE AN APPOINTMENT TO GET MY BOILS REFILLED.
STUPID GIRL.
!

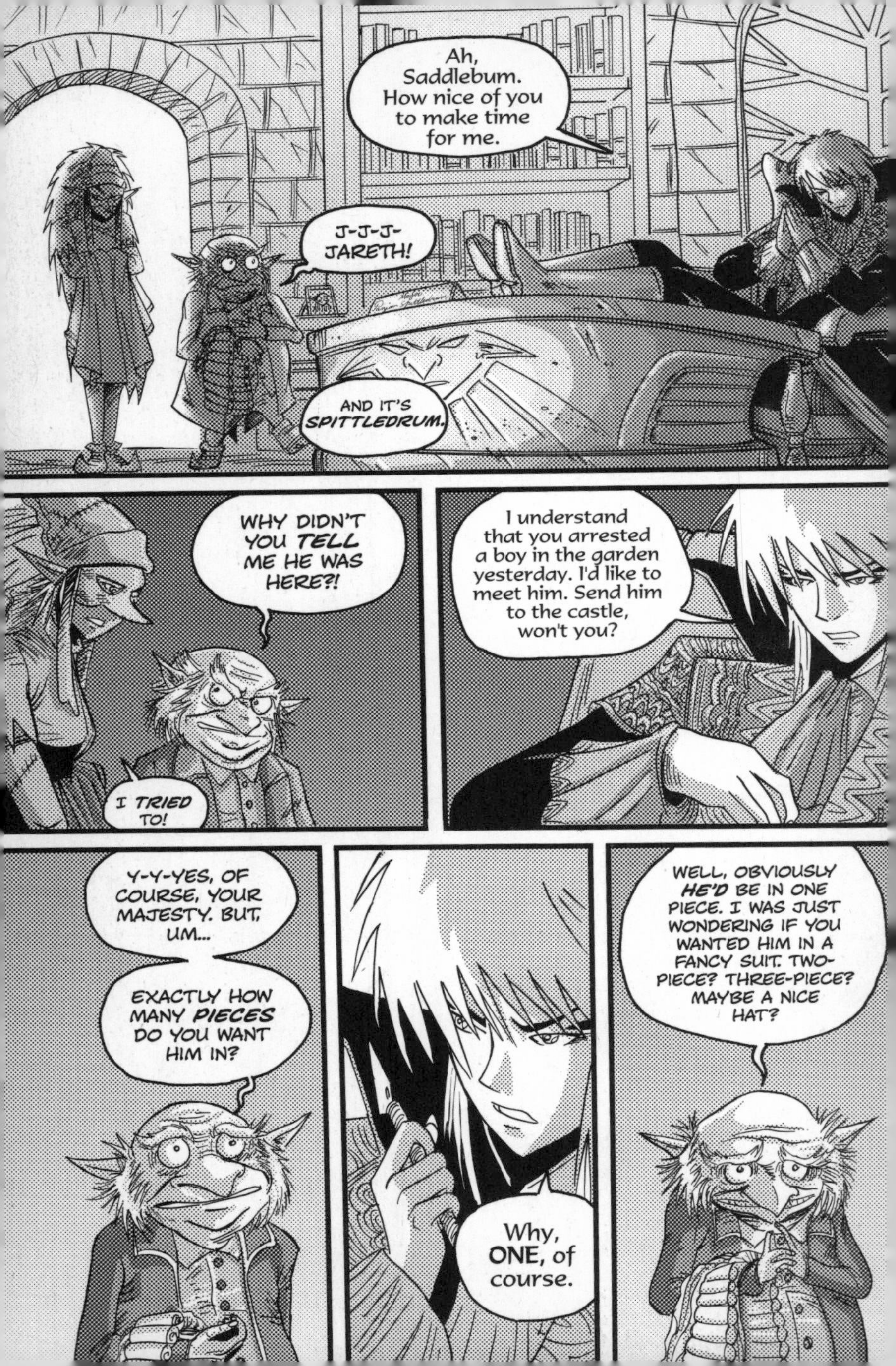

Ah, Saddlebum. How nice of you to make time for me.
J-J-J-JARETH!
AND IT'S SPITTLEDRUM.
WHY DIDN'T YOU TELL ME HE WAS HERE?!
I TRIED TO!
I understand that you arrested a boy in the garden yesterday. I'd like to meet him. Send him to the castle, won't you?
Y-Y-YES, OF COURSE, YOUR MAJESTY. BUT, UM...
EXACTLY HOW MANY PIECES DO YOU WANT HIM IN?
Why, ONE, of course.
WELL, OBVIOUSLY HE'D BE IN ONE PIECE. I WAS JUST WONDERING IF YOU WANTED HIM IN A FANCY SUIT. TWO-PIECE? THREE-PIECE? MAYBE A NICE HAT?

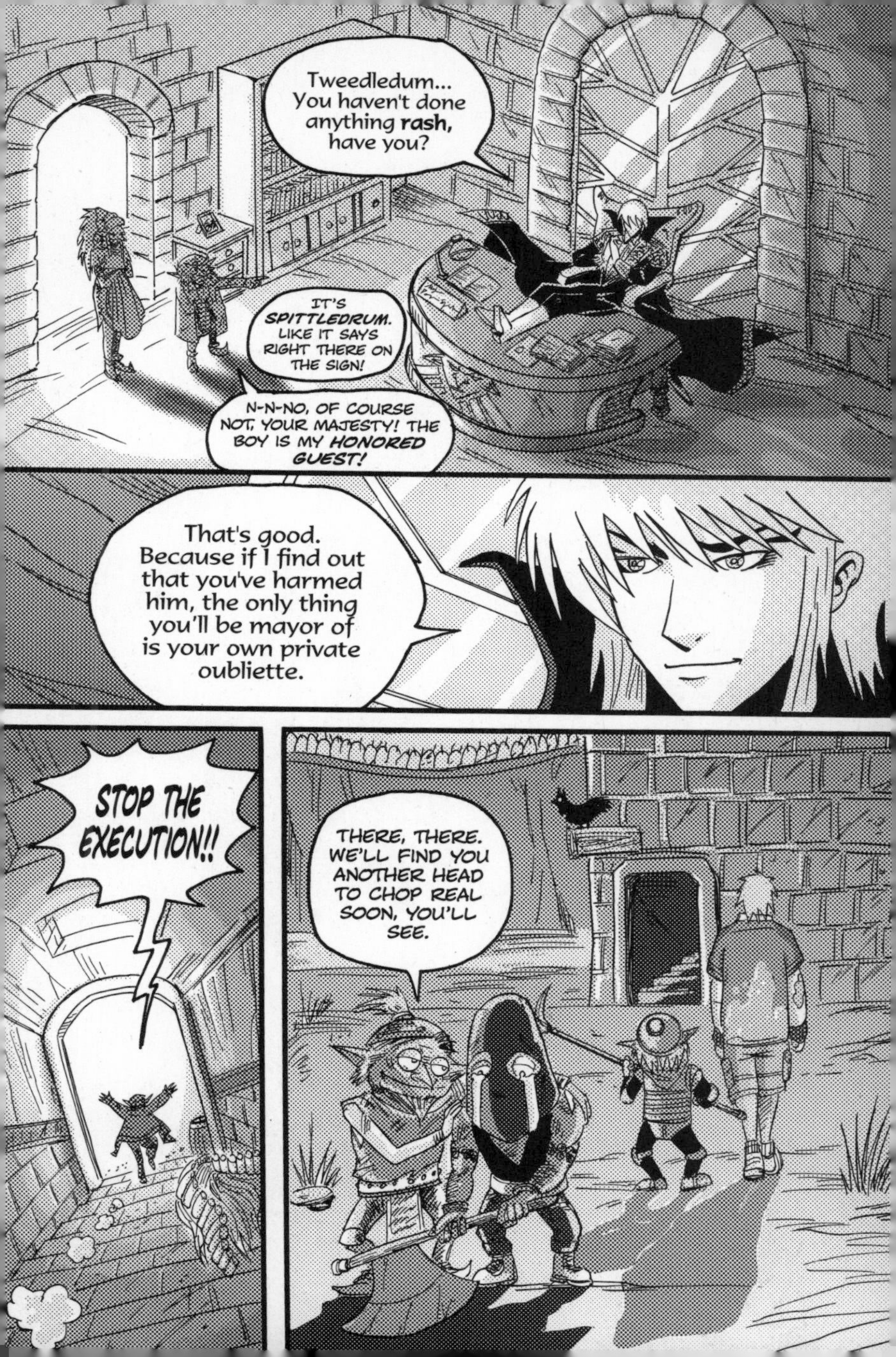
Tweedledum... You haven't done anything **rash,** have you?
IT'S *SPITTLEDRUM.* LIKE IT SAYS RIGHT THERE ON THE SIGN!
N-N-NO, OF COURSE NOT, YOUR MAJESTY! THE BOY IS MY *HONORED GUEST!*
That's good. Because if I find out that you've harmed him, the only thing you'll be mayor of is your own private oubliette.
STOP THE EXECUTION!!
THERE, THERE. WE'LL FIND YOU ANOTHER HEAD TO CHOP REAL SOON, YOU'LL SEE.

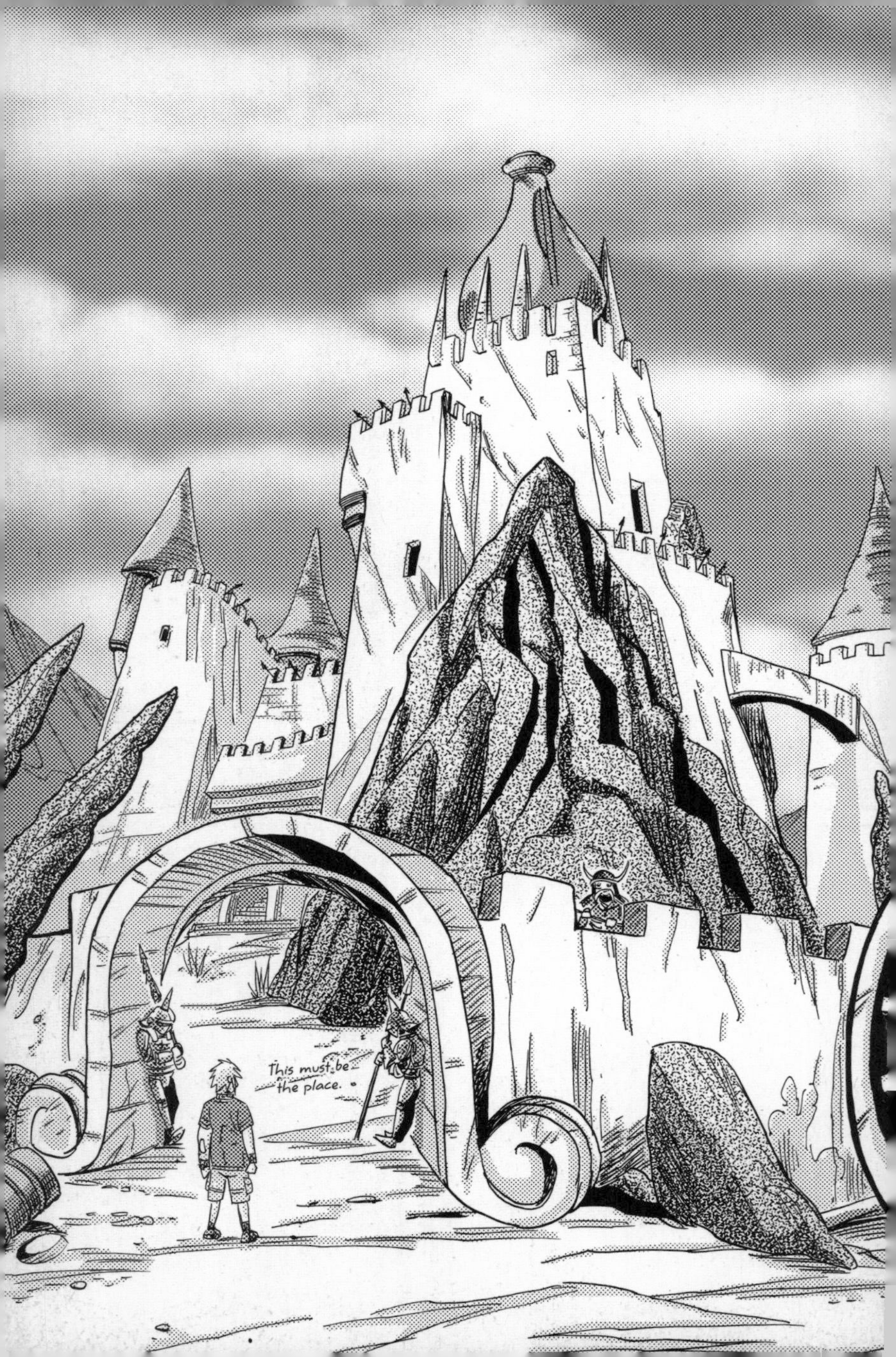
This must be the place.

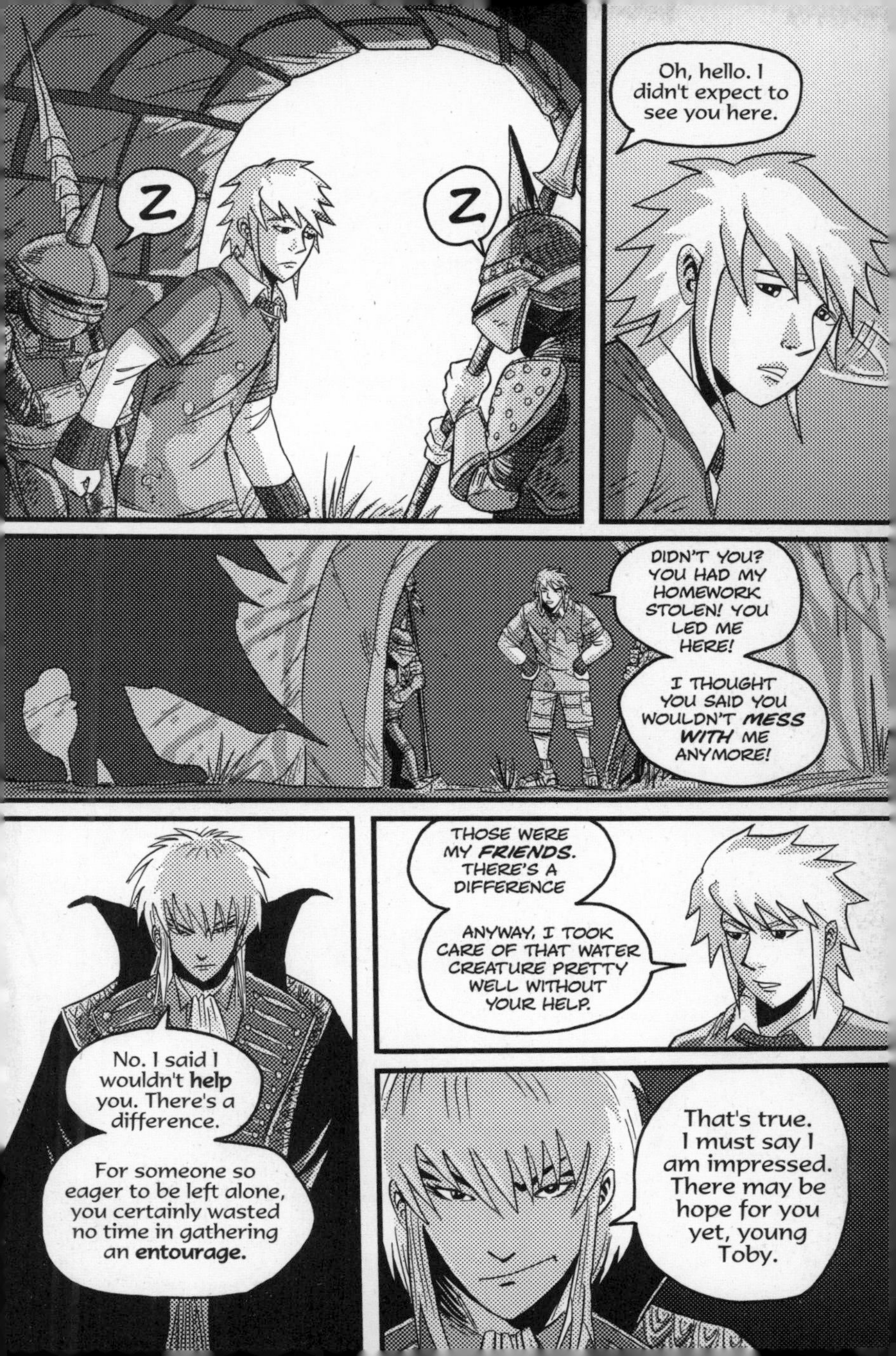
Z
Z
Oh, hello. I didn't expect to see you here.
DIDN'T YOU? YOU HAD MY HOMEWORK STOLEN! YOU LED ME HERE!
I THOUGHT YOU SAID YOU WOULDN'T MESS WITH ME ANYMORE!
No. I said I wouldn't help you. There's a difference.
For someone so eager to be left alone, you certainly wasted no time in gathering an entourage.
THOSE WERE MY FRIENDS. THERE'S A DIFFERENCE
ANYWAY, I TOOK CARE OF THAT WATER CREATURE PRETTY WELL WITHOUT YOUR HELP.
That's true. I must say I am impressed. There may be hope for you yet, young Toby.

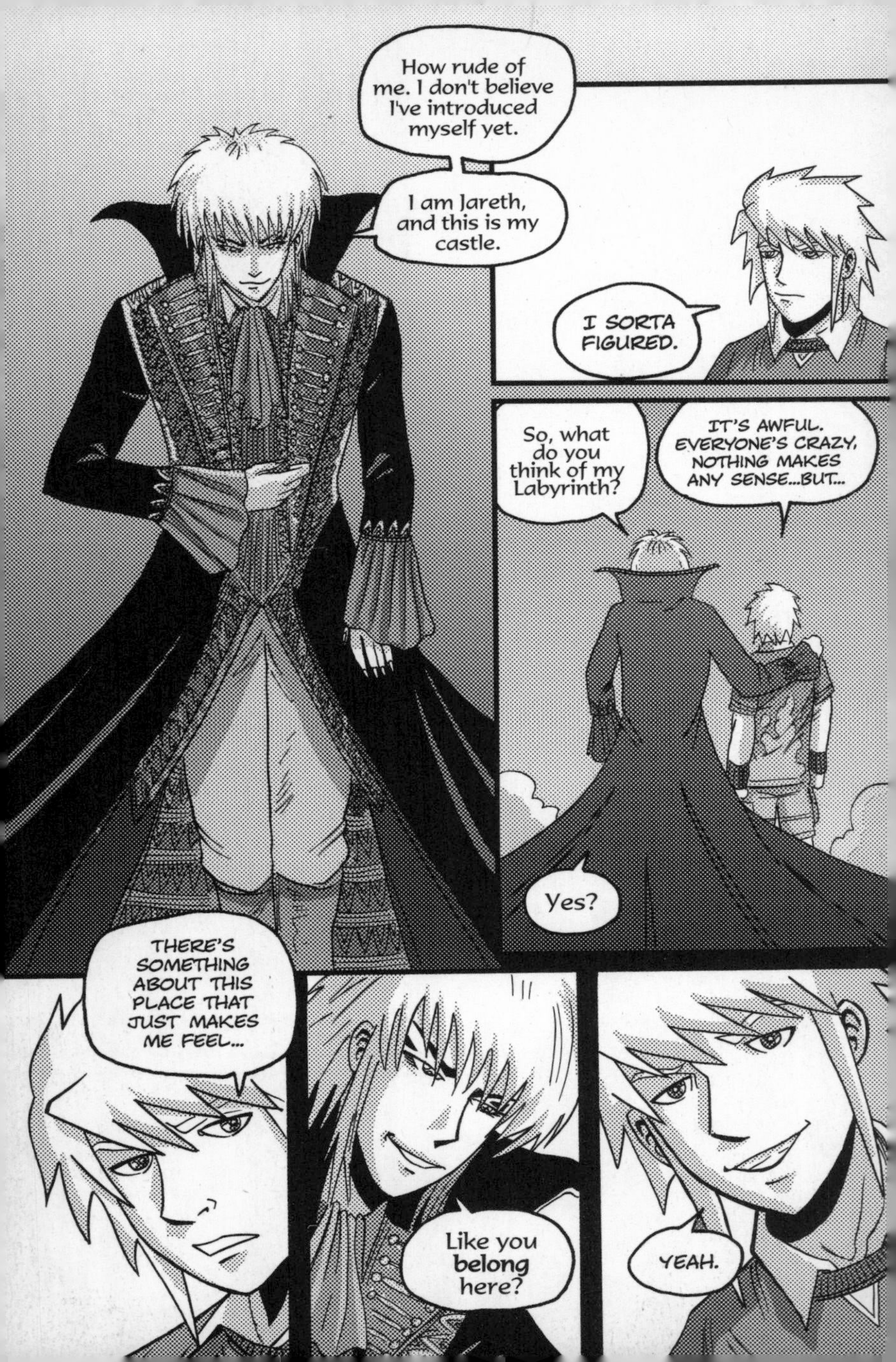
How rude of me. I don't believe I've introduced myself yet.
I am Jareth, and this is my castle.
I SORTA FIGURED.
So, what do you think of my Labyrinth?
IT'S AWFUL. EVERYONE'S CRAZY, NOTHING MAKES ANY SENSE...BUT...
Yes?
THERE'S SOMETHING ABOUT THIS PLACE THAT JUST MAKES ME FEEL...
Like you **belong** here?
YEAH.

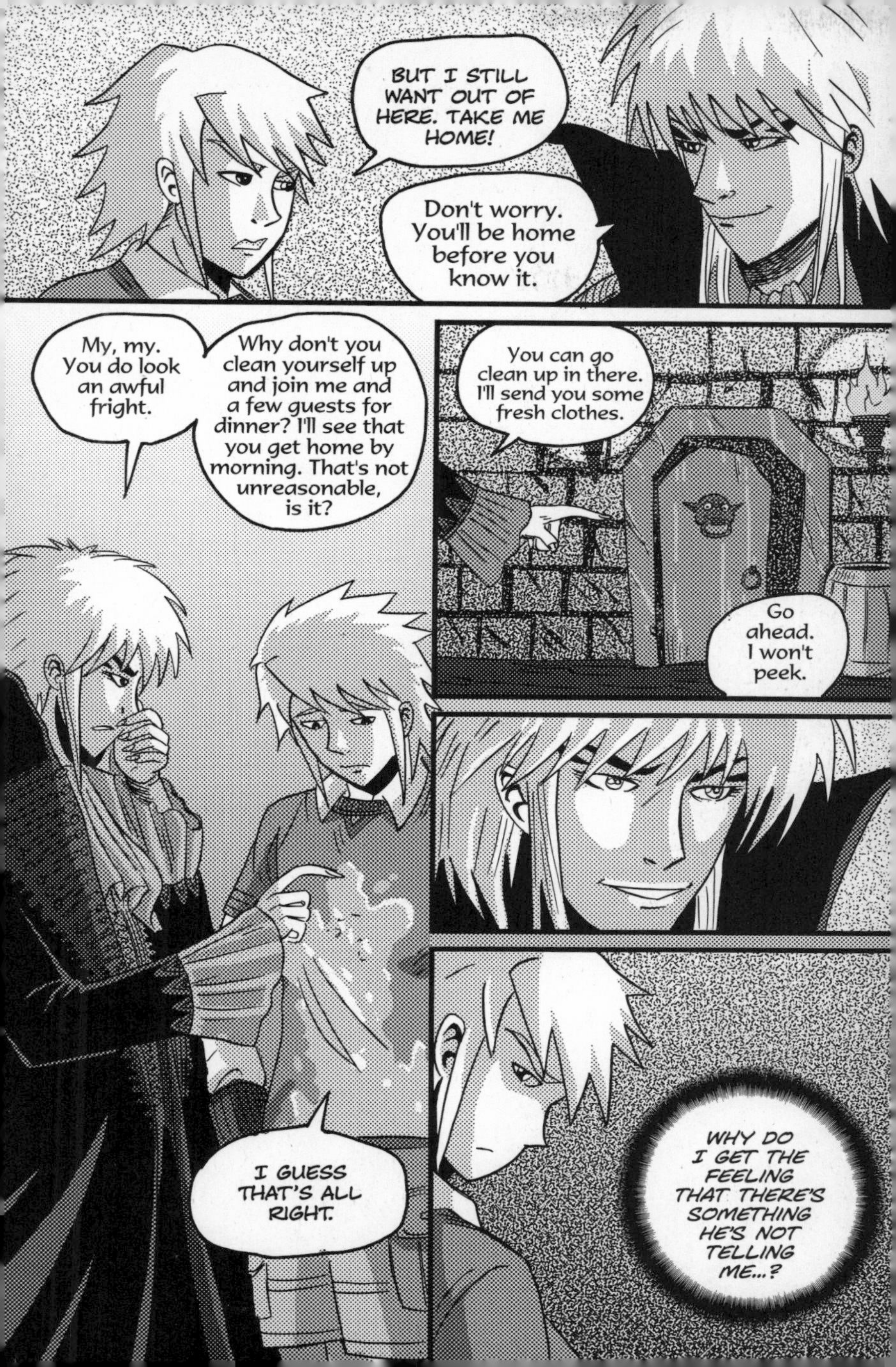
BUT I STILL WANT OUT OF HERE. TAKE ME HOME!
Don't worry. You'll be home before you know it.
My, my. You do look an awful fright.
Why don't you clean yourself up and join me and a few guests for dinner? I'll see that you get home by morning. That's not unreasonable, is it?
You can go clean up in there. I'll send you some fresh clothes.
Go ahead. I won't peek.
I GUESS THAT'S ALL RIGHT.
WHY DO I GET THE FEELING THAT THERE'S SOMETHING HE'S NOT TELLING ME...?

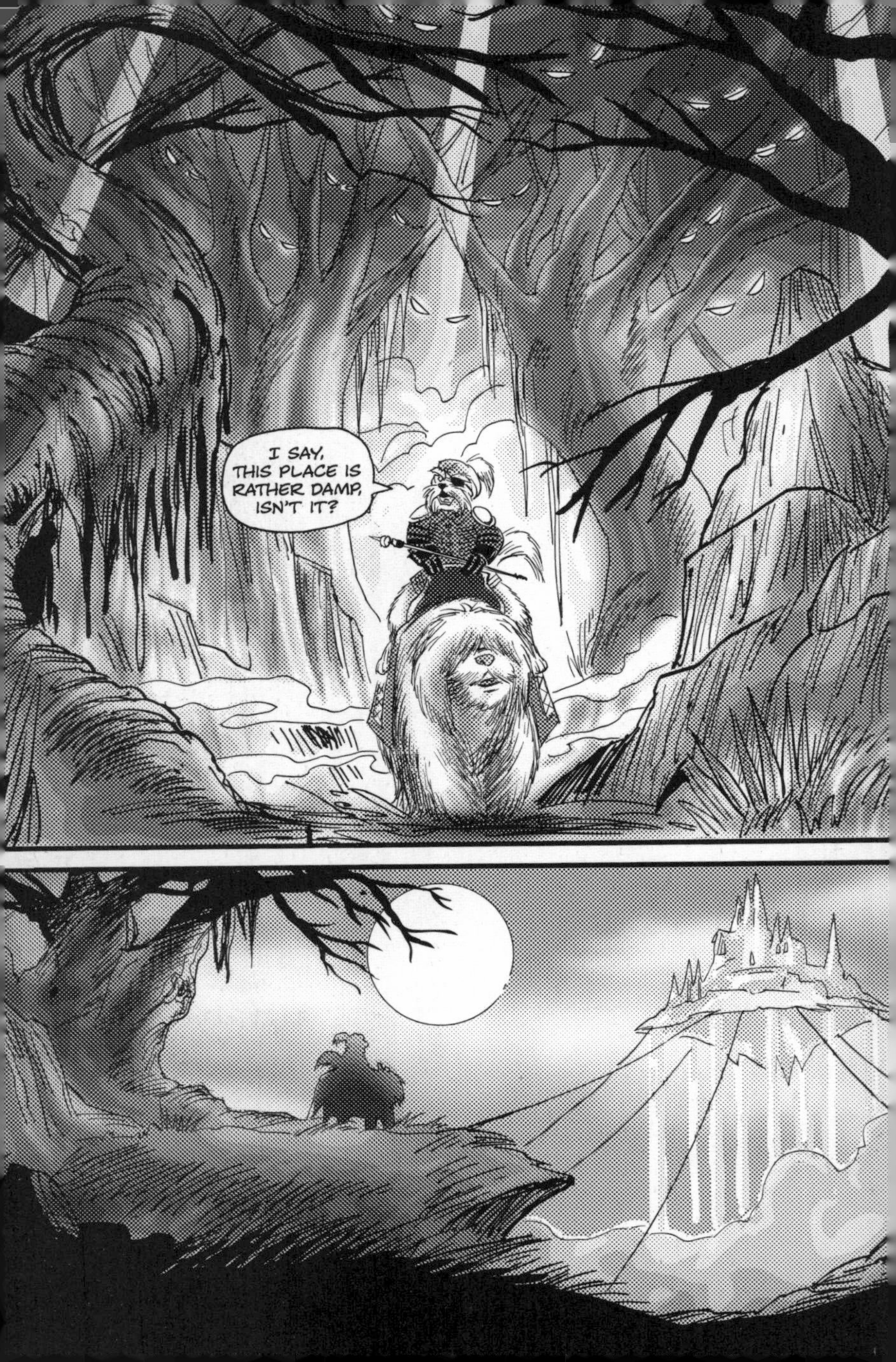
I SAY, THIS PLACE IS RATHER DAMP, ISN'T IT?

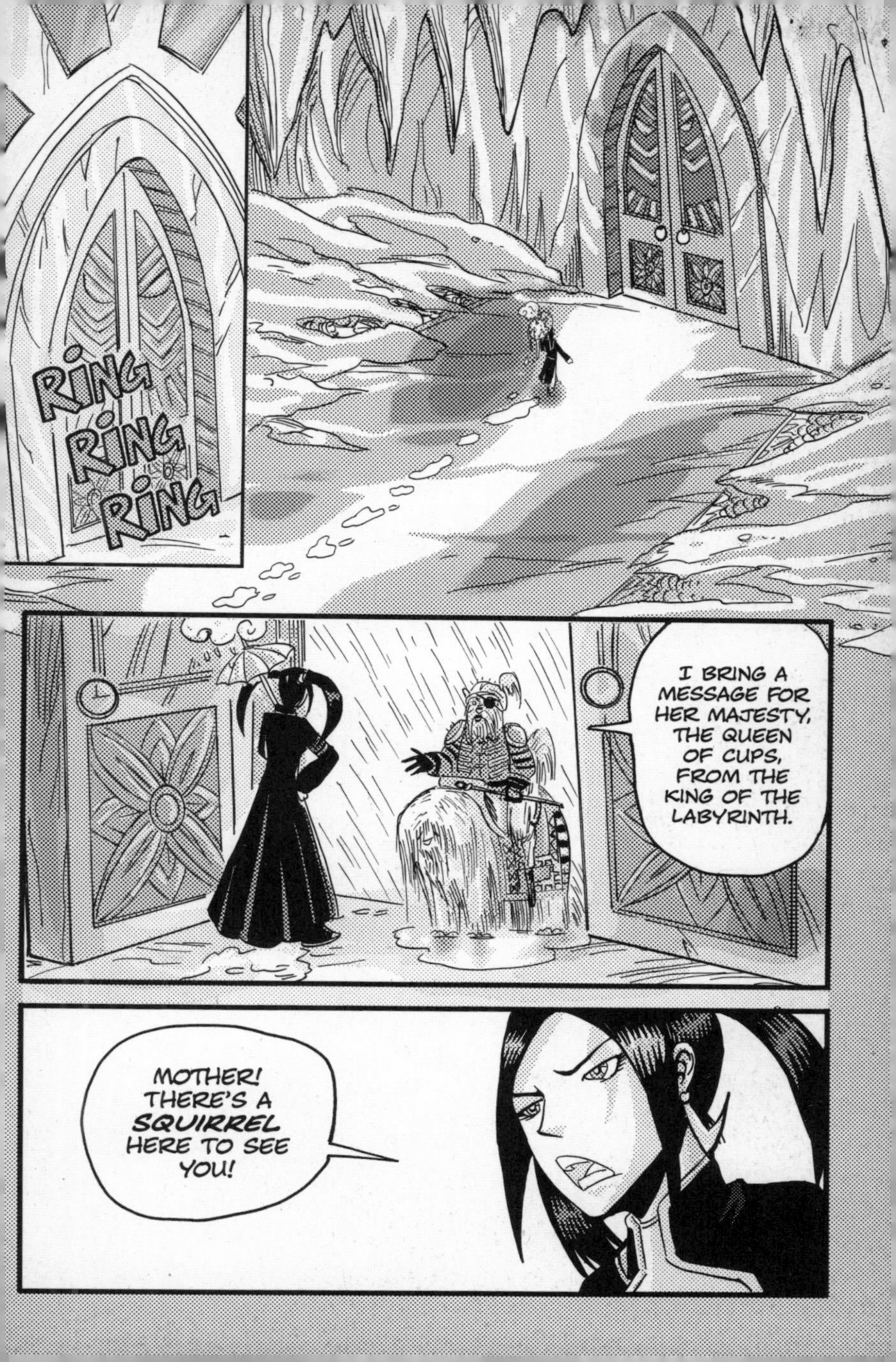
RING RING RING
I BRING A MESSAGE FOR HER MAJESTY, THE QUEEN OF CUPS, FROM THE KING OF THE LABYRINTH.
MOTHER! THERE'S A *SQUIRREL* HERE TO SEE YOU!

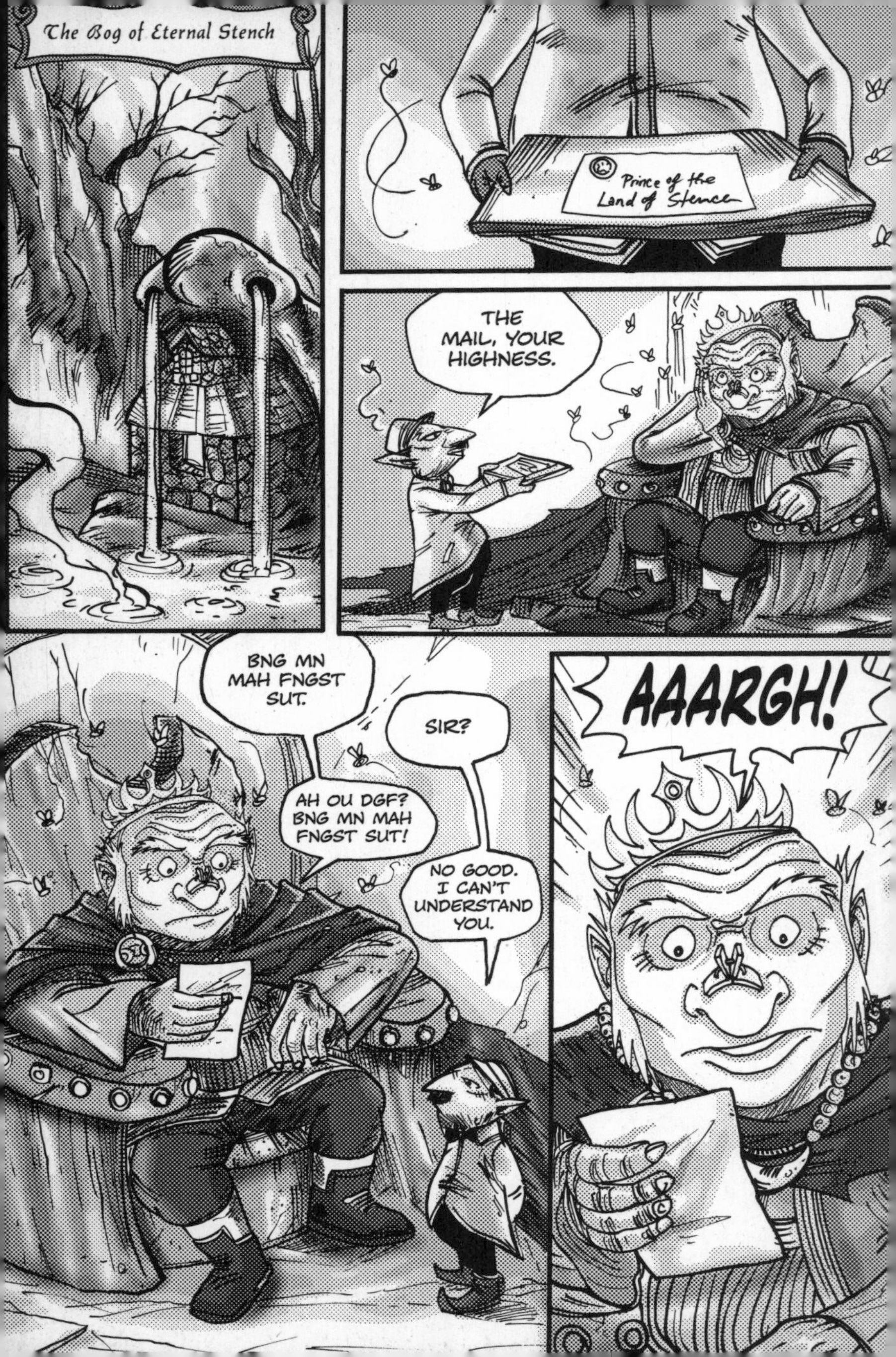

The Bog of Eternal Stench
Prince of the Land of Stence
THE MAIL, YOUR HIGHNESS.
BNG MN MAH FNGST SUT.
SIR?
AH OU DGF? BNG MN MAH FNGST SUT!
NO GOOD. I CAN'T UNDERSTAND YOU.
AAARGH!

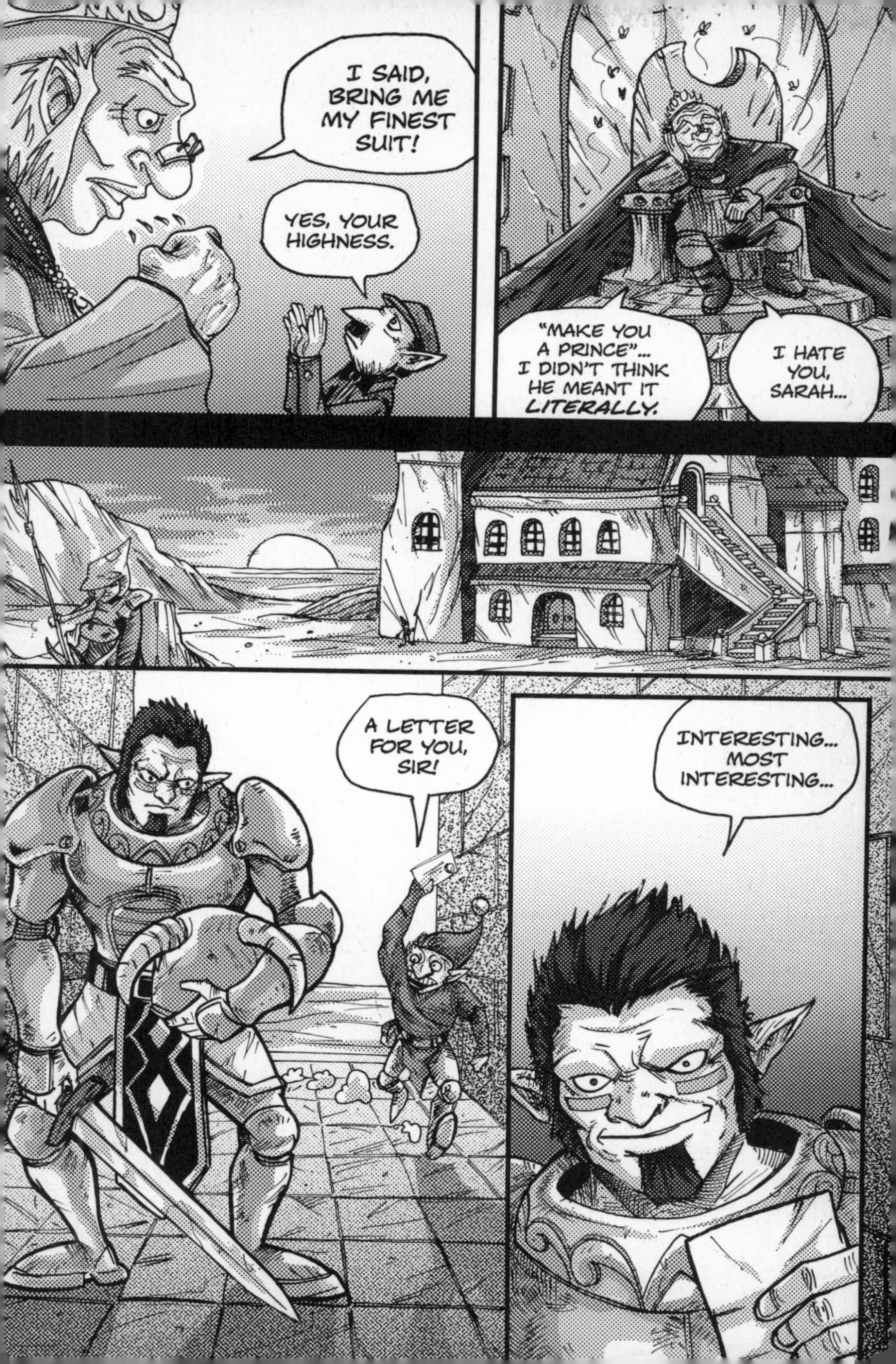
I SAID, BRING ME MY FINEST SUIT!
YES, YOUR HIGHNESS.
"MAKE YOU A PRINCE"... I DIDN'T THINK HE MEANT IT *LITERALLY.*
I HATE YOU, SARAH...
A LETTER FOR YOU, SIR!
INTERESTING... MOST INTERESTING...

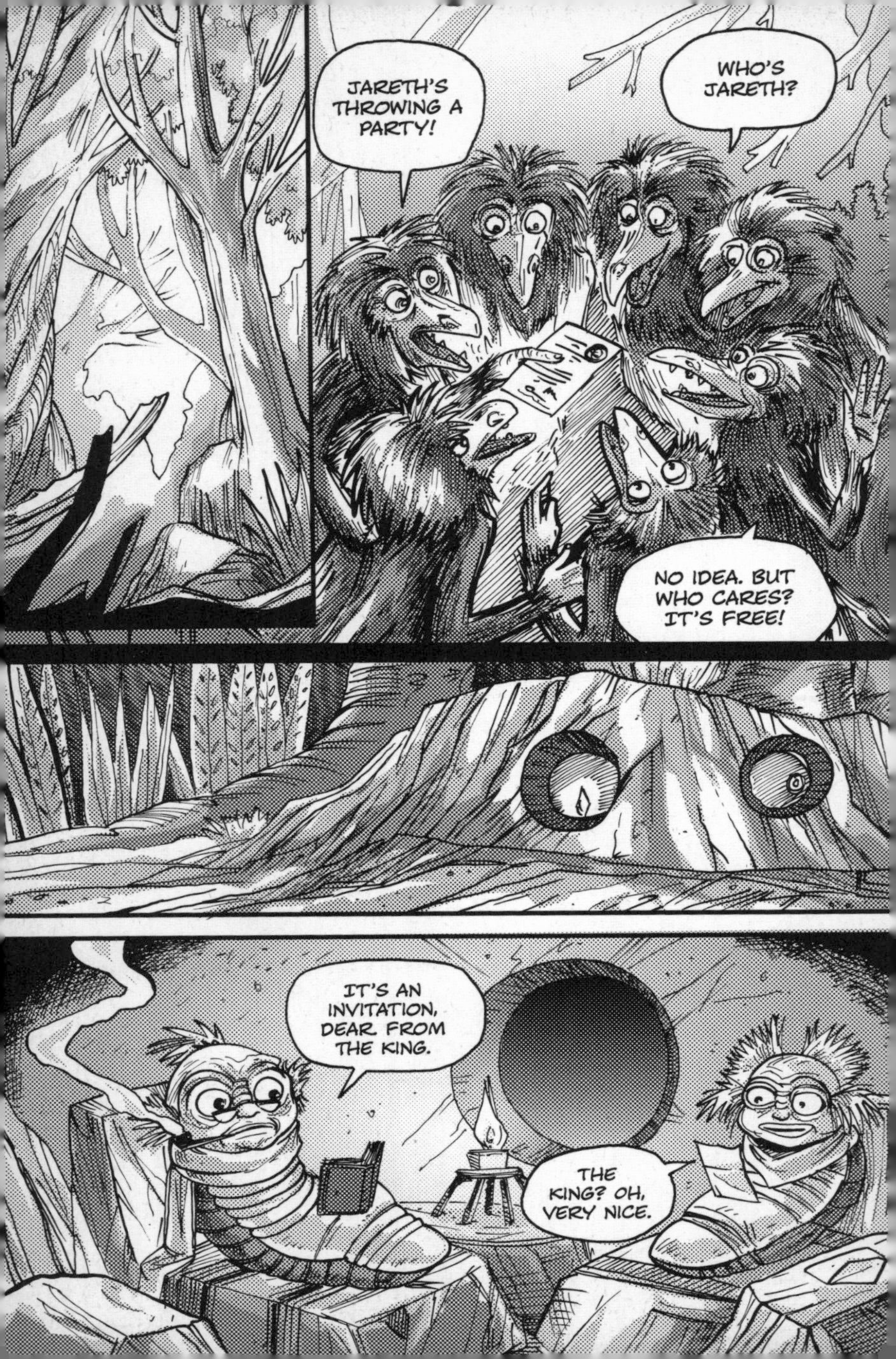
JARETH'S THROWING A PARTY!
WHO'S JARETH?
NO IDEA. BUT WHO CARES? IT'S FREE!
IT'S AN INVITATION, DEAR FROM THE KING.
THE KING? OH, VERY NICE.

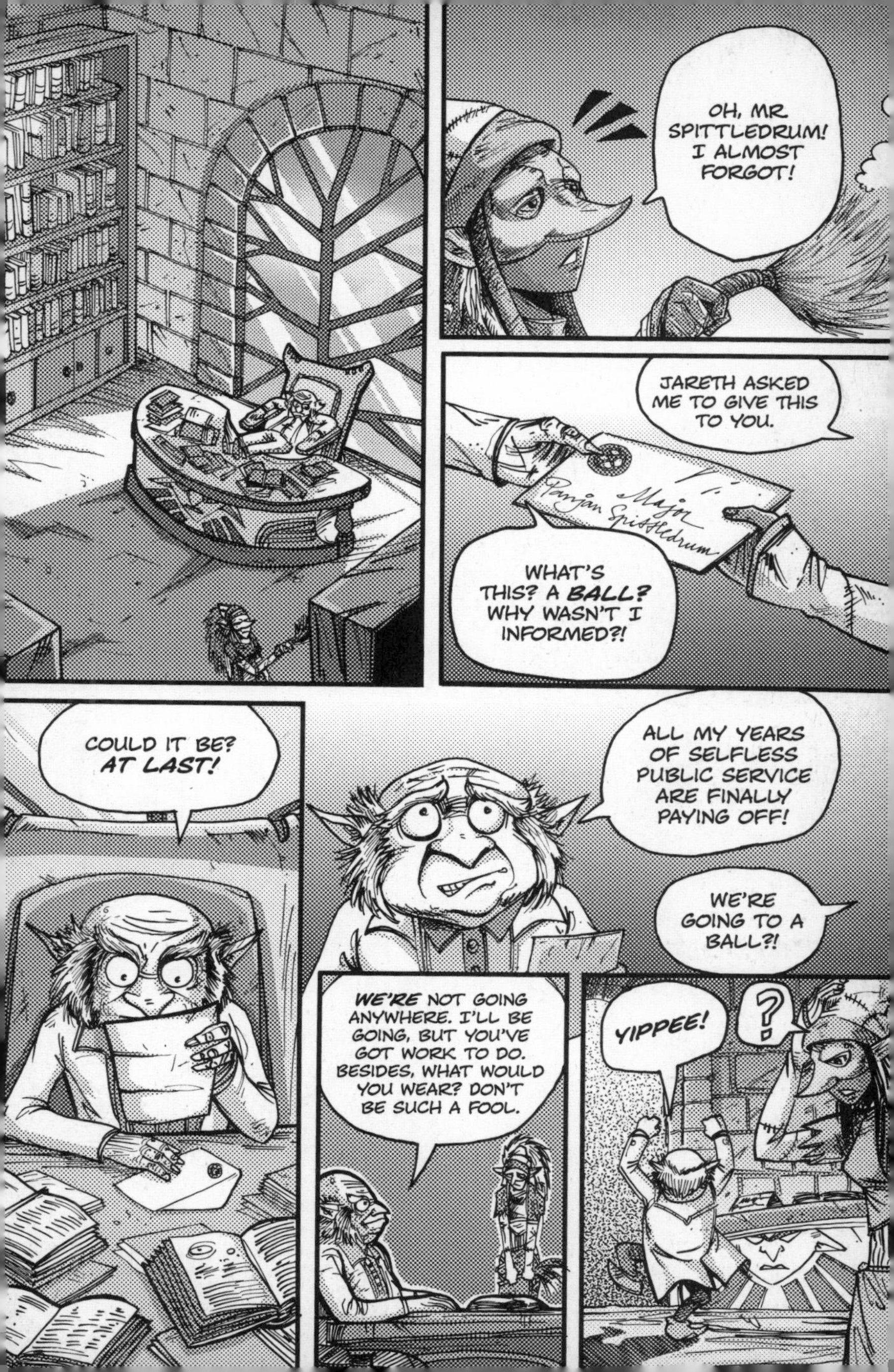

OH, MR SPITTLEDRUM! I ALMOST FORGOT!
JARETH ASKED ME TO GIVE THIS TO YOU.
Major Panjan Spittledrum
WHAT'S THIS? A BALL? WHY WASN'T I INFORMED?!
COULD IT BE? AT LAST!
ALL MY YEARS OF SELFLESS PUBLIC SERVICE ARE FINALLY PAYING OFF!
WE'RE GOING TO A BALL?!
WE'RE NOT GOING ANYWHERE. I'LL BE GOING, BUT YOU'VE GOT WORK TO DO. BESIDES, WHAT WOULD YOU WEAR? DON'T BE SUCH A FOOL.
YIPPEE!
?

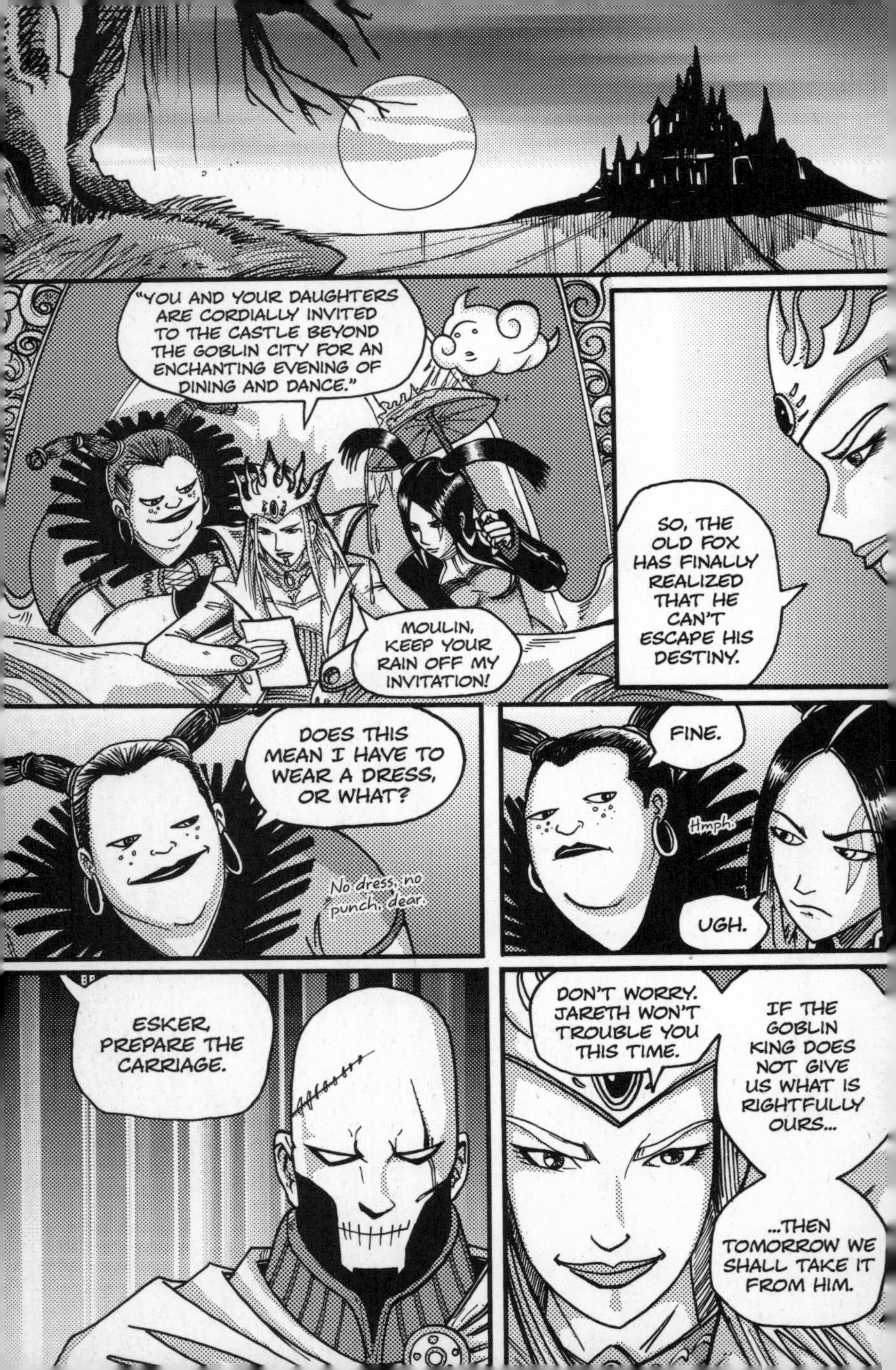

"YOU AND YOUR DAUGHTERS ARE CORDIALLY INVITED TO THE CASTLE BEYOND THE GOBLIN CITY FOR AN ENCHANTING EVENING OF DINING AND DANCE."
MOULIN, KEEP YOUR RAIN OFF MY INVITATION!
SO, THE OLD FOX HAS FINALLY REALIZED THAT HE CAN'T ESCAPE HIS DESTINY.
DOES THIS MEAN I HAVE TO WEAR A DRESS, OR WHAT?
No dress, no punch, dear.
FINE.
Hmph.
UGH.
ESKER, PREPARE THE CARRIAGE.
DON'T WORRY. JARETH WON'T TROUBLE YOU THIS TIME.
IF THE GOBLIN KING DOES NOT GIVE US WHAT IS RIGHTFULLY OURS...
...THEN TOMORROW WE SHALL TAKE IT FROM HIM.

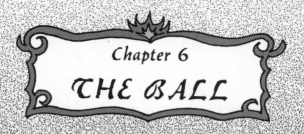

Chapter 6

THE BALL

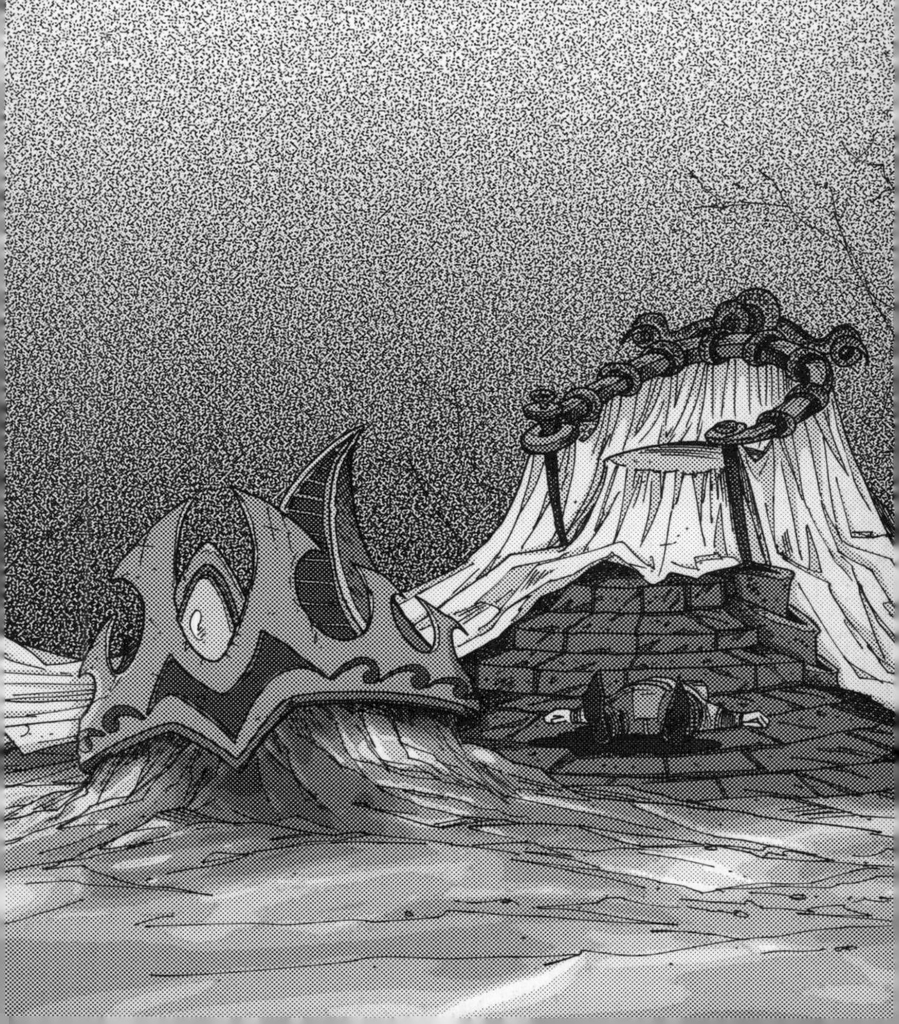

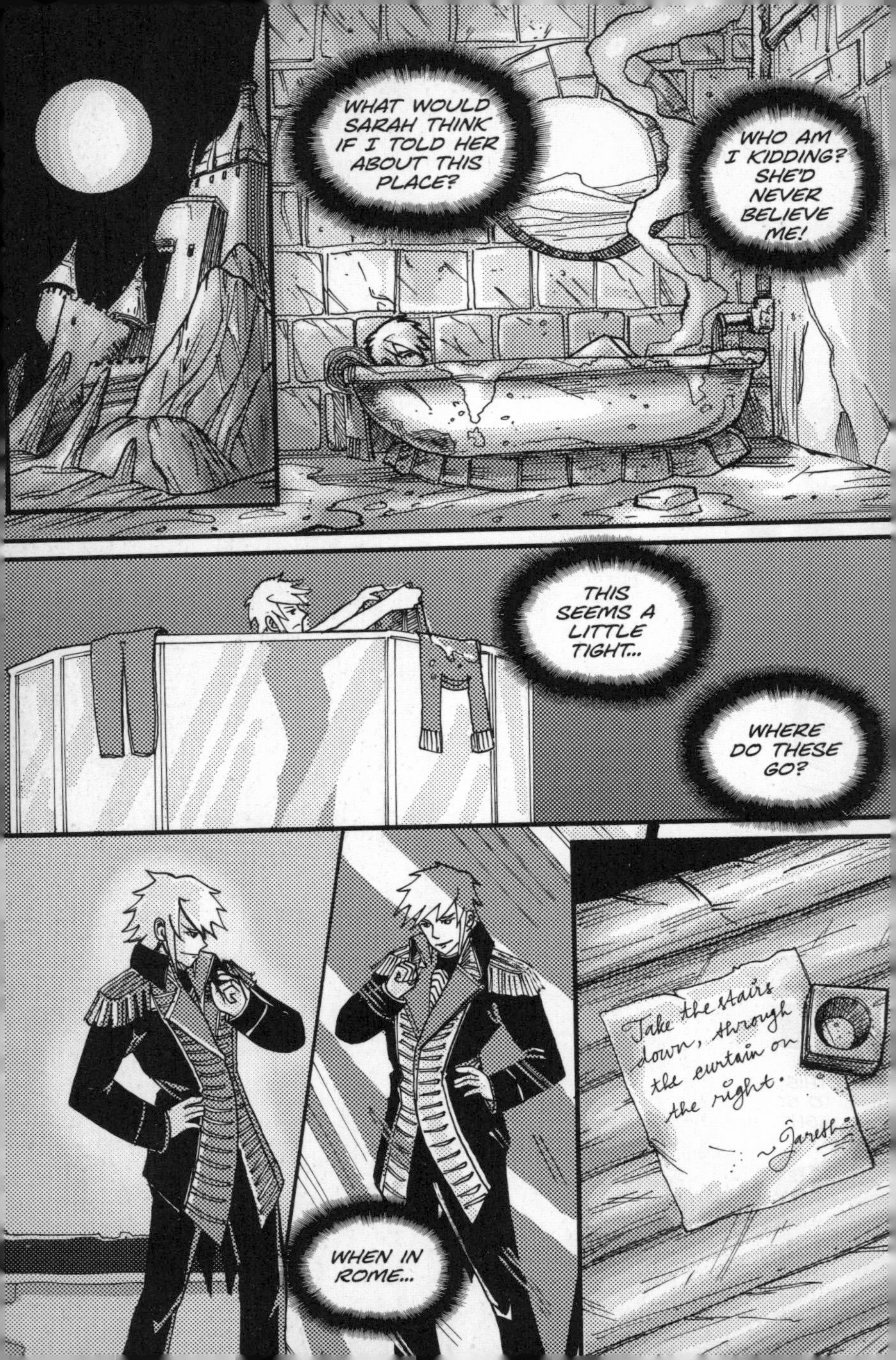
WHAT WOULD SARAH THINK IF I TOLD HER ABOUT THIS PLACE?
WHO AM I KIDDING? SHE'D NEVER BELIEVE ME!
THIS SEEMS A LITTLE TIGHT...
WHERE DO THESE GO?
WHEN IN ROME...
Take the stairs down, through the curtain on the right.
~ Jareth

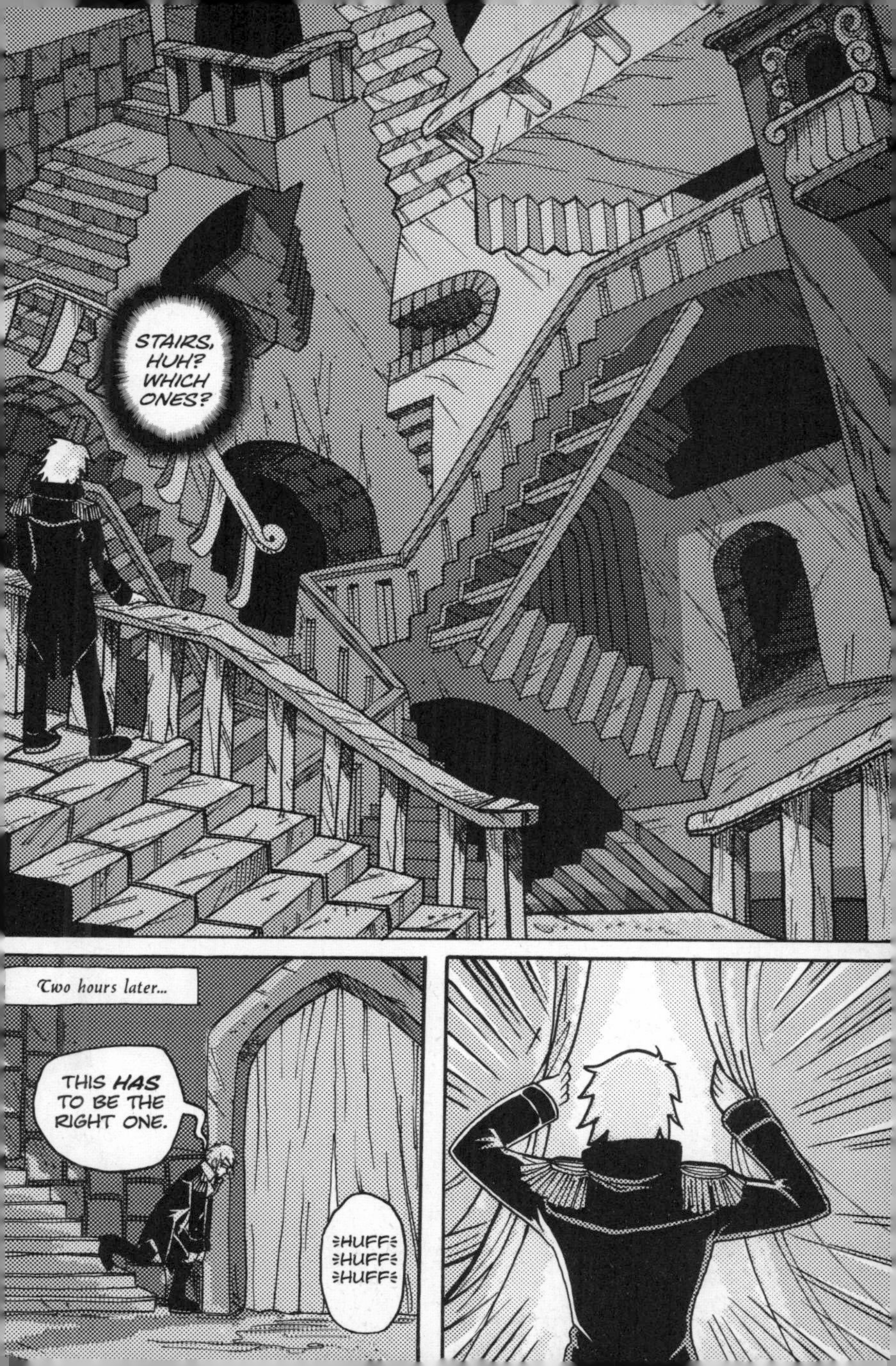
STAIRS, HUH? WHICH ONES?
Two hours later...
THIS HAS TO BE THE RIGHT ONE.
HUFF HUFF HUFF

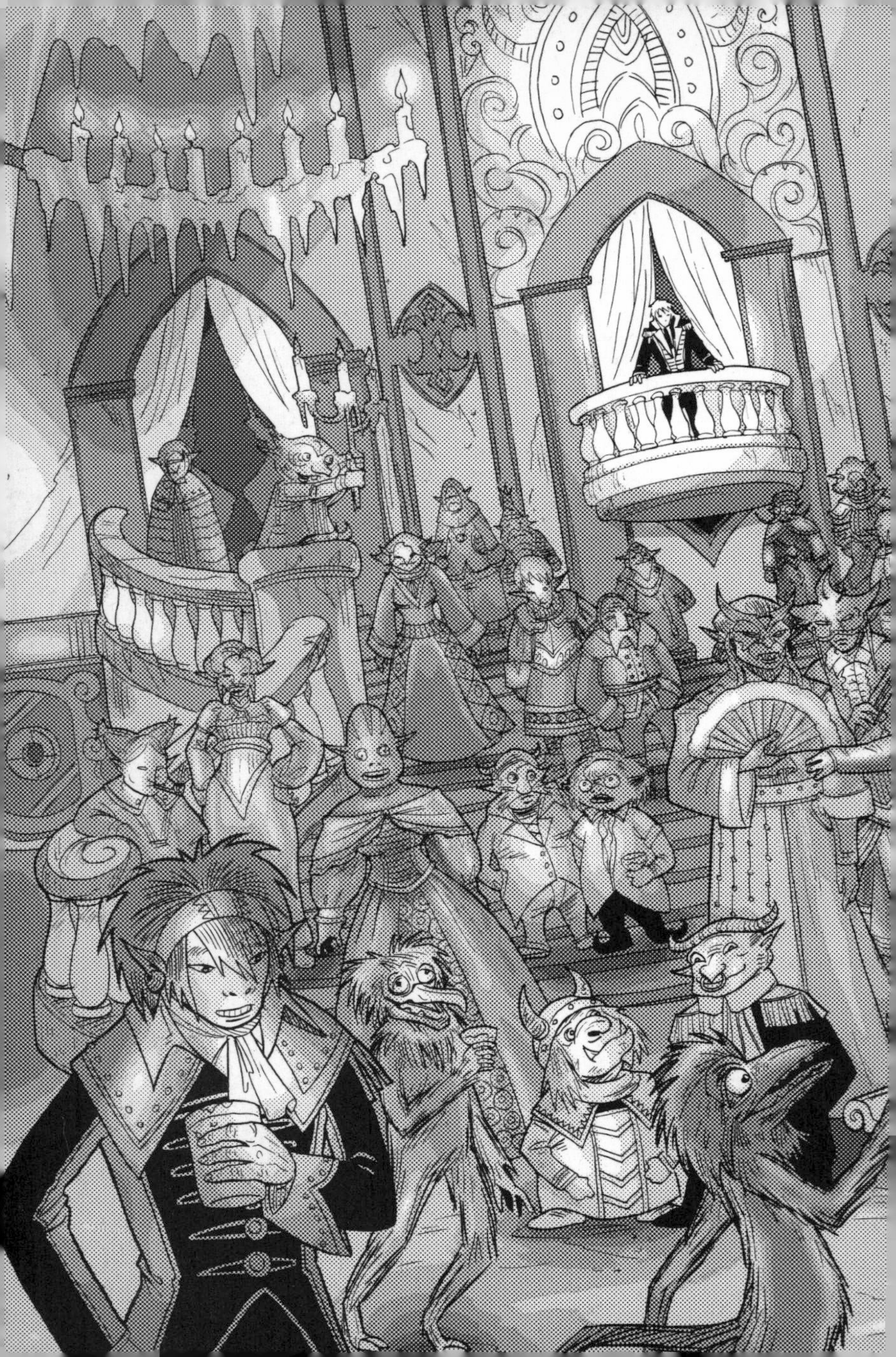

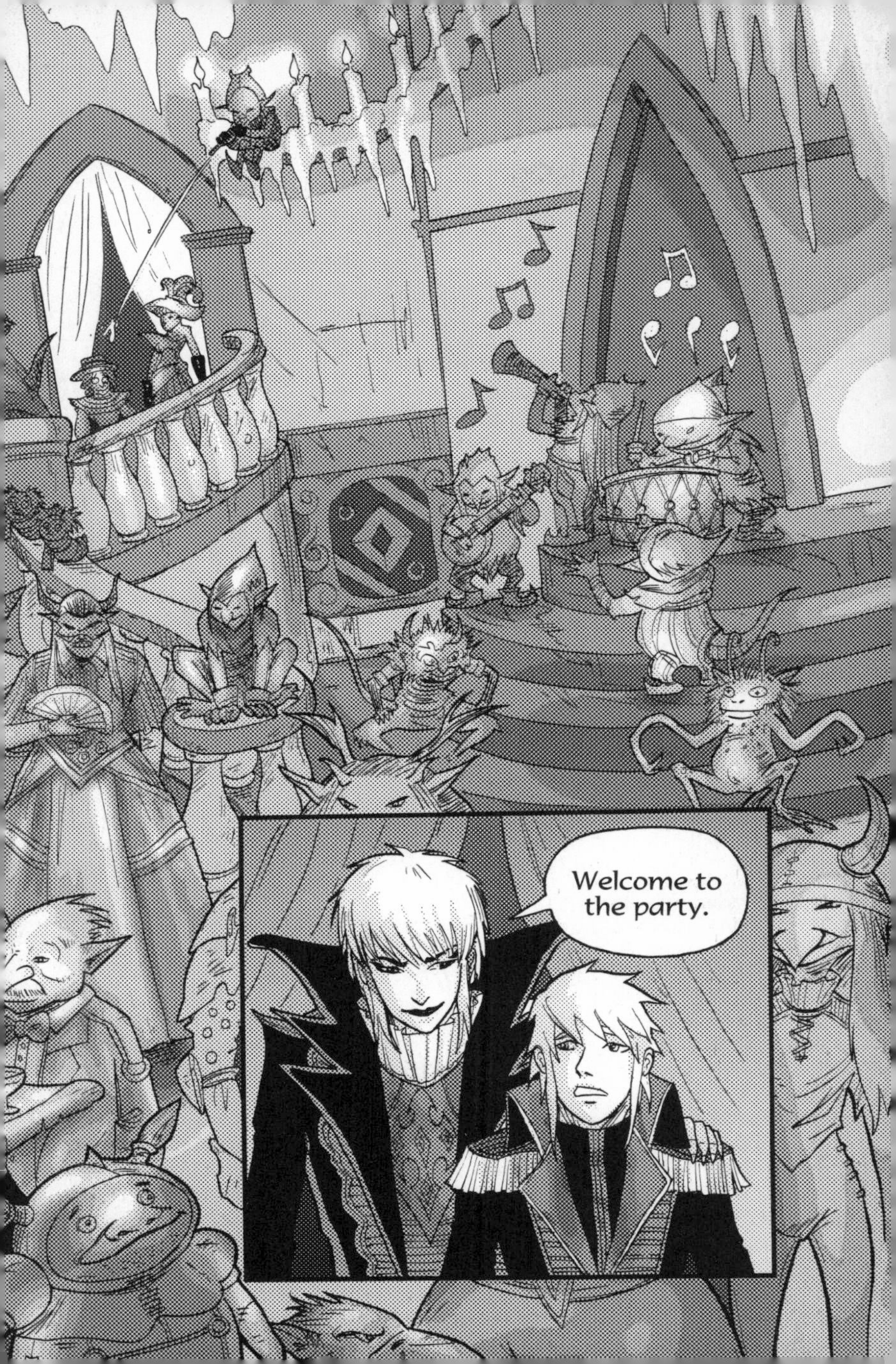
Welcome to the party.

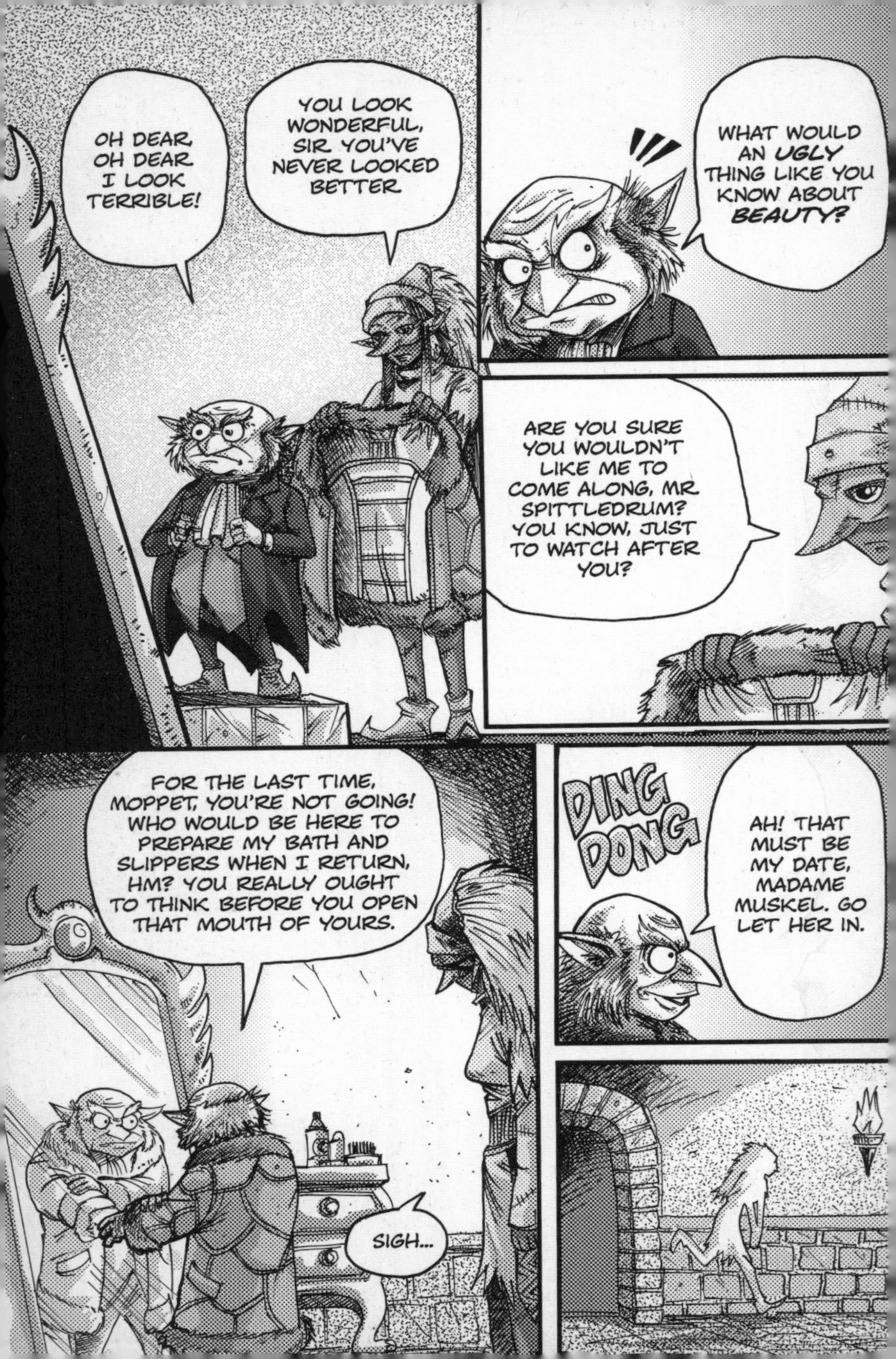
OH DEAR, OH DEAR I LOOK TERRIBLE!
YOU LOOK WONDERFUL, SIR. YOU'VE NEVER LOOKED BETTER.
WHAT WOULD AN UGLY THING LIKE YOU KNOW ABOUT BEAUTY?
ARE YOU SURE YOU WOULDN'T LIKE ME TO COME ALONG, MR SPITTLEDRUM? YOU KNOW, JUST TO WATCH AFTER YOU?
FOR THE LAST TIME, MOPPET, YOU'RE NOT GOING! WHO WOULD BE HERE TO PREPARE MY BATH AND SLIPPERS WHEN I RETURN, HM? YOU REALLY OUGHT TO THINK BEFORE YOU OPEN THAT MOUTH OF YOURS.
SIGH...
DING DONG
AH! THAT MUST BE MY DATE, MADAME MUSKEL. GO LET HER IN.

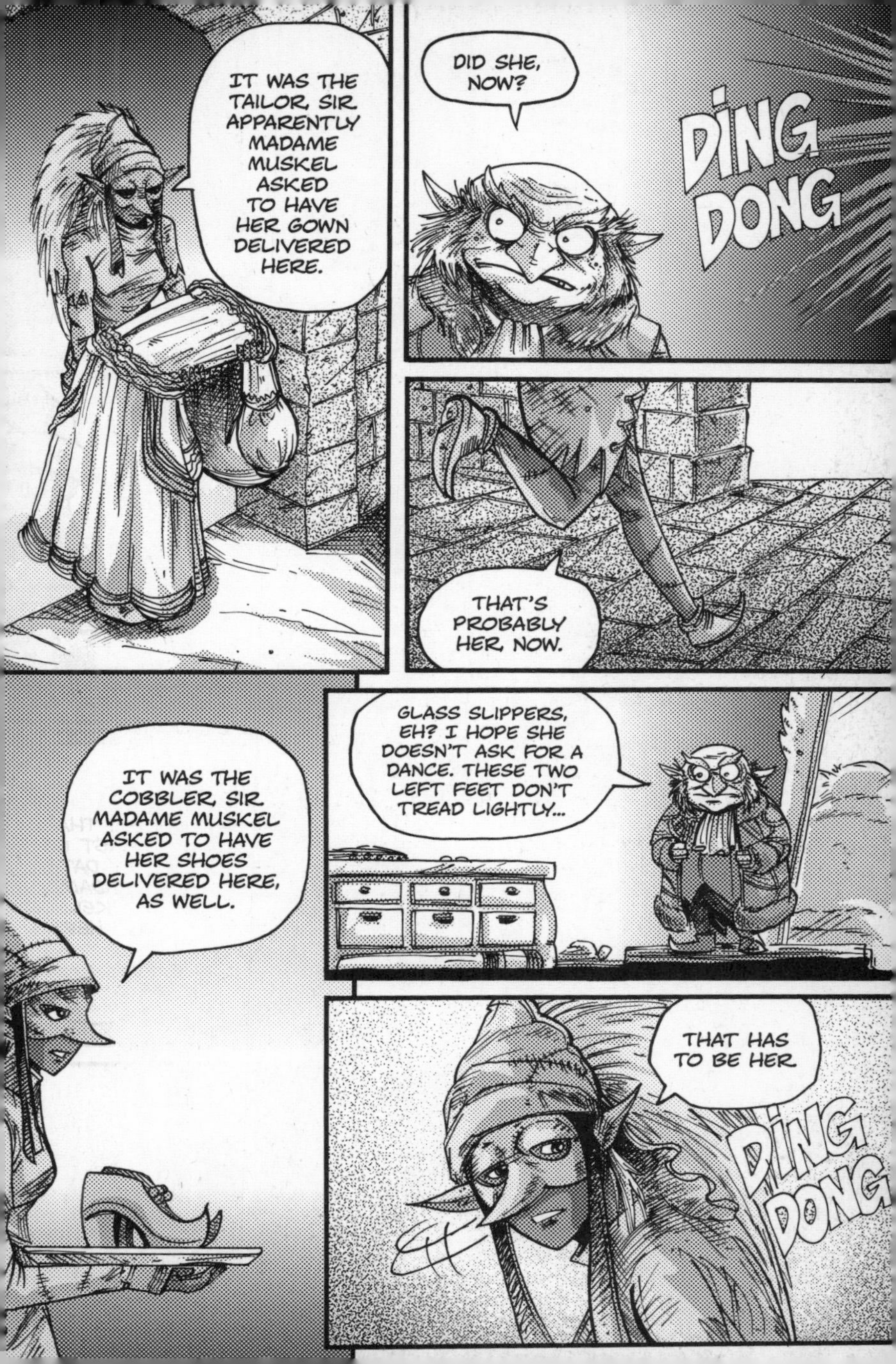
IT WAS THE TAILOR, SIR. APPARENTLY MADAME MUSKEL ASKED TO HAVE HER GOWN DELIVERED HERE.
DID SHE, NOW?
DING DONG
THAT'S PROBABLY HER, NOW.
IT WAS THE COBBLER, SIR. MADAME MUSKEL ASKED TO HAVE HER SHOES DELIVERED HERE, AS WELL.
GLASS SLIPPERS, EH? I HOPE SHE DOESN'T ASK FOR A DANCE. THESE TWO LEFT FEET DON'T TREAD LIGHTLY...
THAT HAS TO BE HER
DING DONG

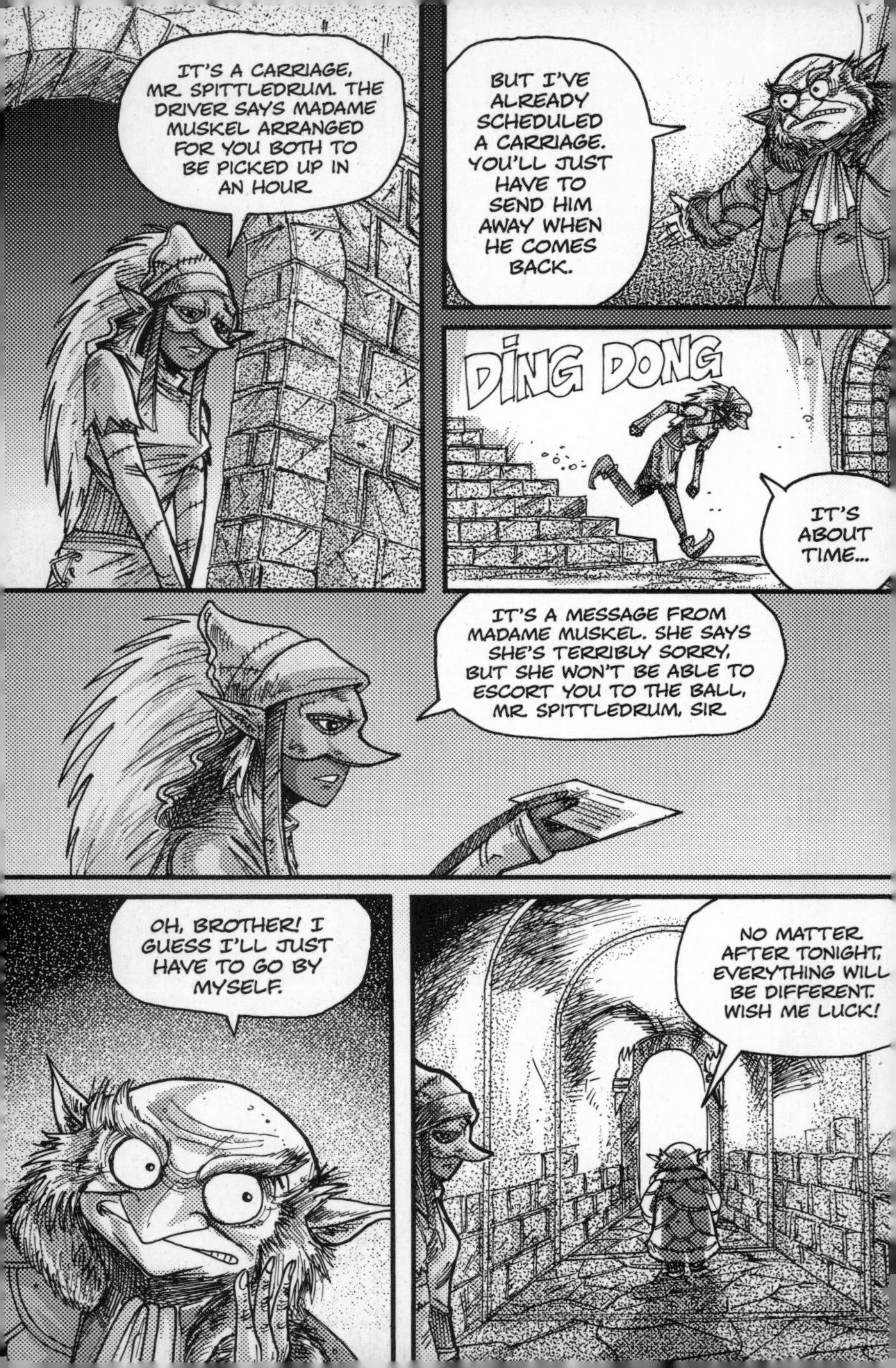
IT'S A CARRIAGE, MR. SPITTLEDRUM. THE DRIVER SAYS MADAME MUSKEL ARRANGED FOR YOU BOTH TO BE PICKED UP IN AN HOUR
BUT I'VE ALREADY SCHEDULED A CARRIAGE. YOU'LL JUST HAVE TO SEND HIM AWAY WHEN HE COMES BACK.
DING DONG
IT'S ABOUT TIME...
IT'S A MESSAGE FROM MADAME MUSKEL. SHE SAYS SHE'S TERRIBLY SORRY, BUT SHE WON'T BE ABLE TO ESCORT YOU TO THE BALL, MR. SPITTLEDRUM, SIR
OH, BROTHER! I GUESS I'LL JUST HAVE TO GO BY MYSELF.
NO MATTER AFTER TONIGHT, EVERYTHING WILL BE DIFFERENT. WISH ME LUCK!

OH, AND MOPPET--KEEP THE DRESS.
YOU COULD MAKE SOME NICE DISHRAGS FROM THAT, I THINK.
TA TA!
GOOD LUCK, SIR
FORGIVE ME, MASTER!

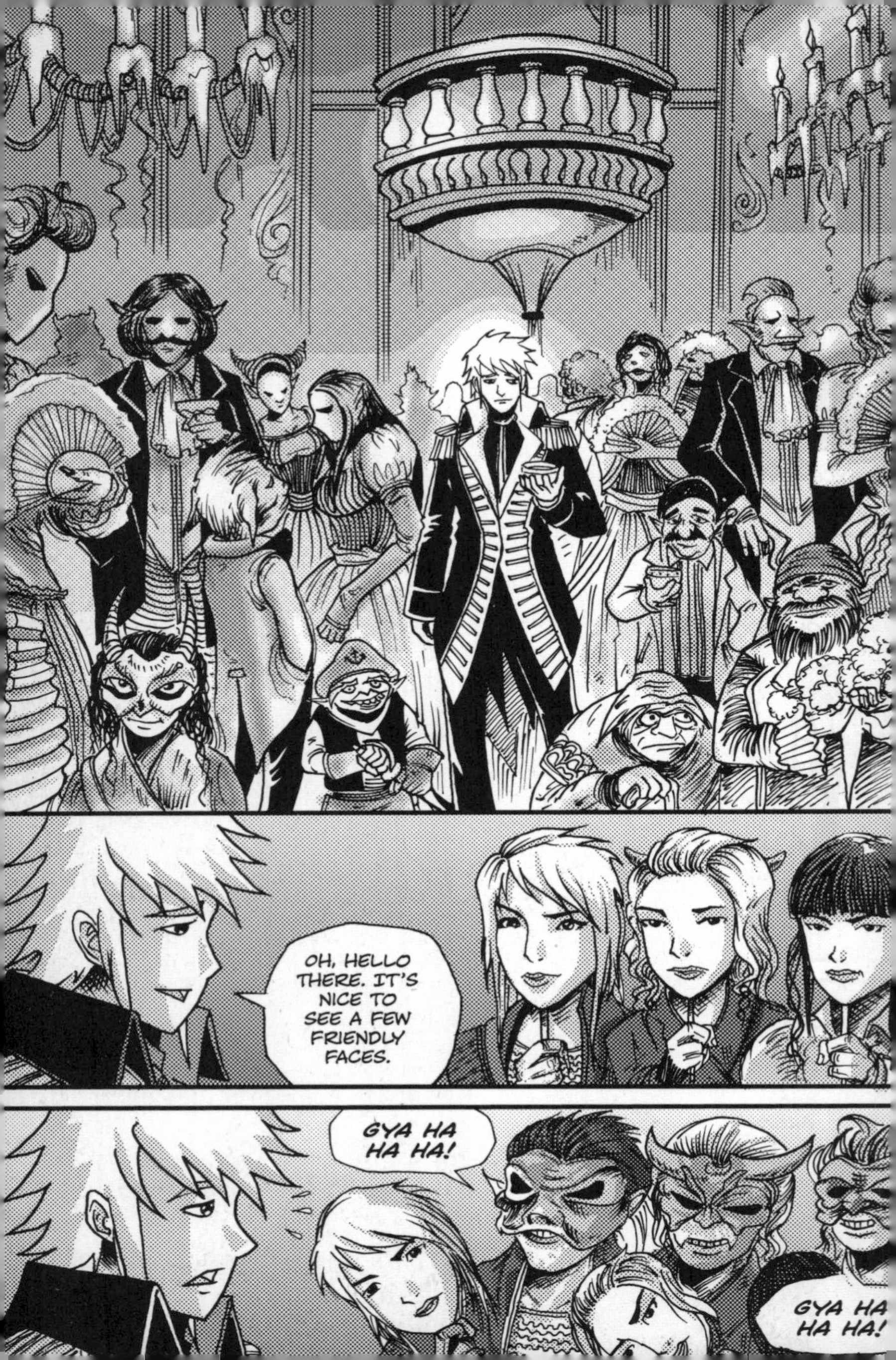
OH, HELLO THERE. IT'S NICE TO SEE A FEW FRIENDLY FACES.
GYA HA HA HA!
GYA HA HA HA!

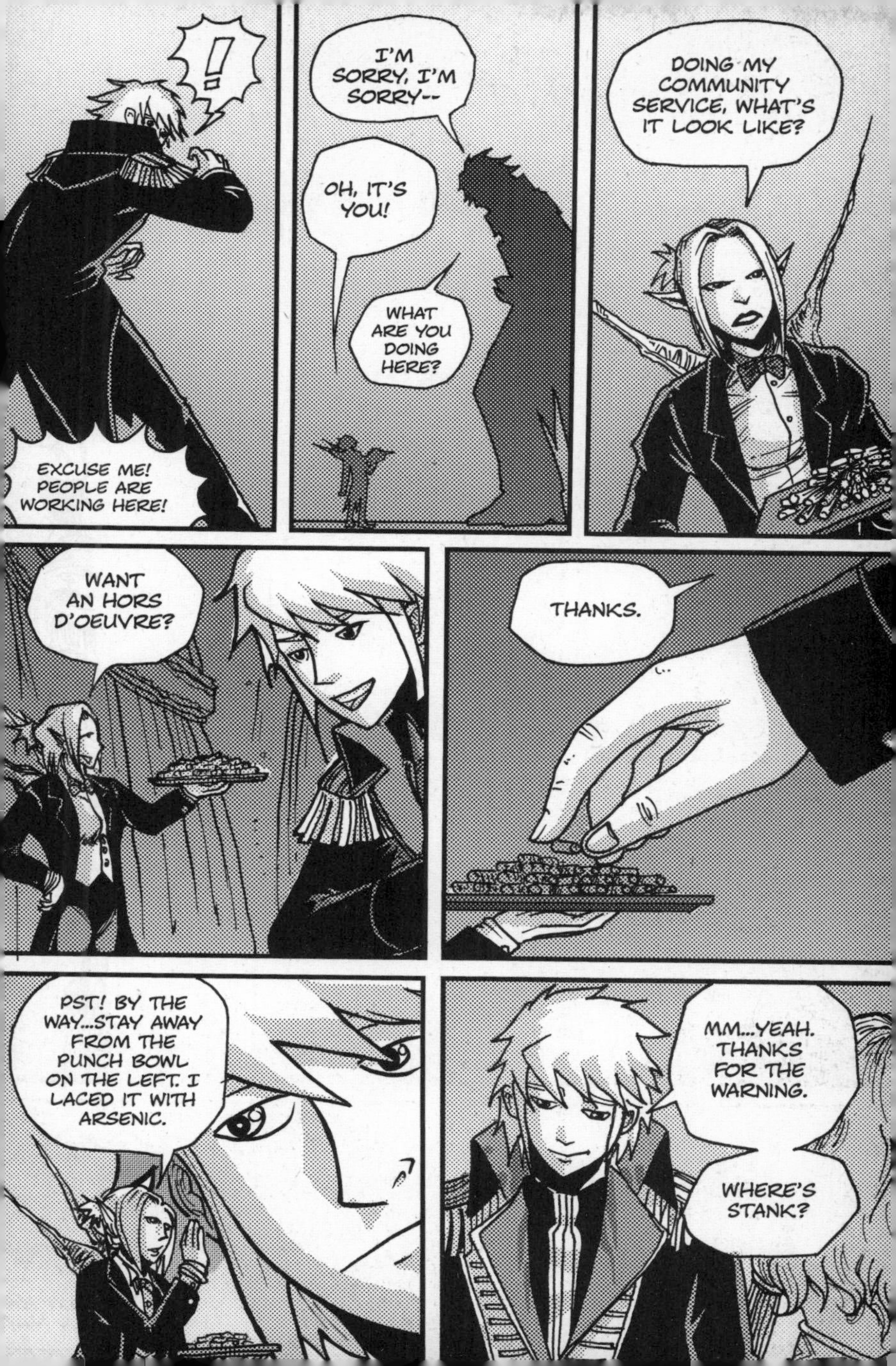
!
EXCUSE ME! PEOPLE ARE WORKING HERE!
I'M SORRY, I'M SORRY--
OH, IT'S YOU!
WHAT ARE YOU DOING HERE?
DOING MY COMMUNITY SERVICE, WHAT'S IT LOOK LIKE?
WANT AN HORS D'OEUVRE?
THANKS.
PST! BY THE WAY...STAY AWAY FROM THE PUNCH BOWL ON THE LEFT. I LACED IT WITH ARSENIC.
MM...YEAH. THANKS FOR THE WARNING.
WHERE'S STANK?

THEY PUT HIM TO WORK TOO.

SHREK

SHREK

SHREK

EXCUSE ME, TINY SILLY PERSON. DO YOU HAVE ANYTHING WITH RADISHES?

YOU'D BETTER REPLACE THE PUNCH. I THINK IT'S GONE BAD.

WELL...UH... SEE YOU AROUND, I GUESS. STAY OUT OF TROUBLE.

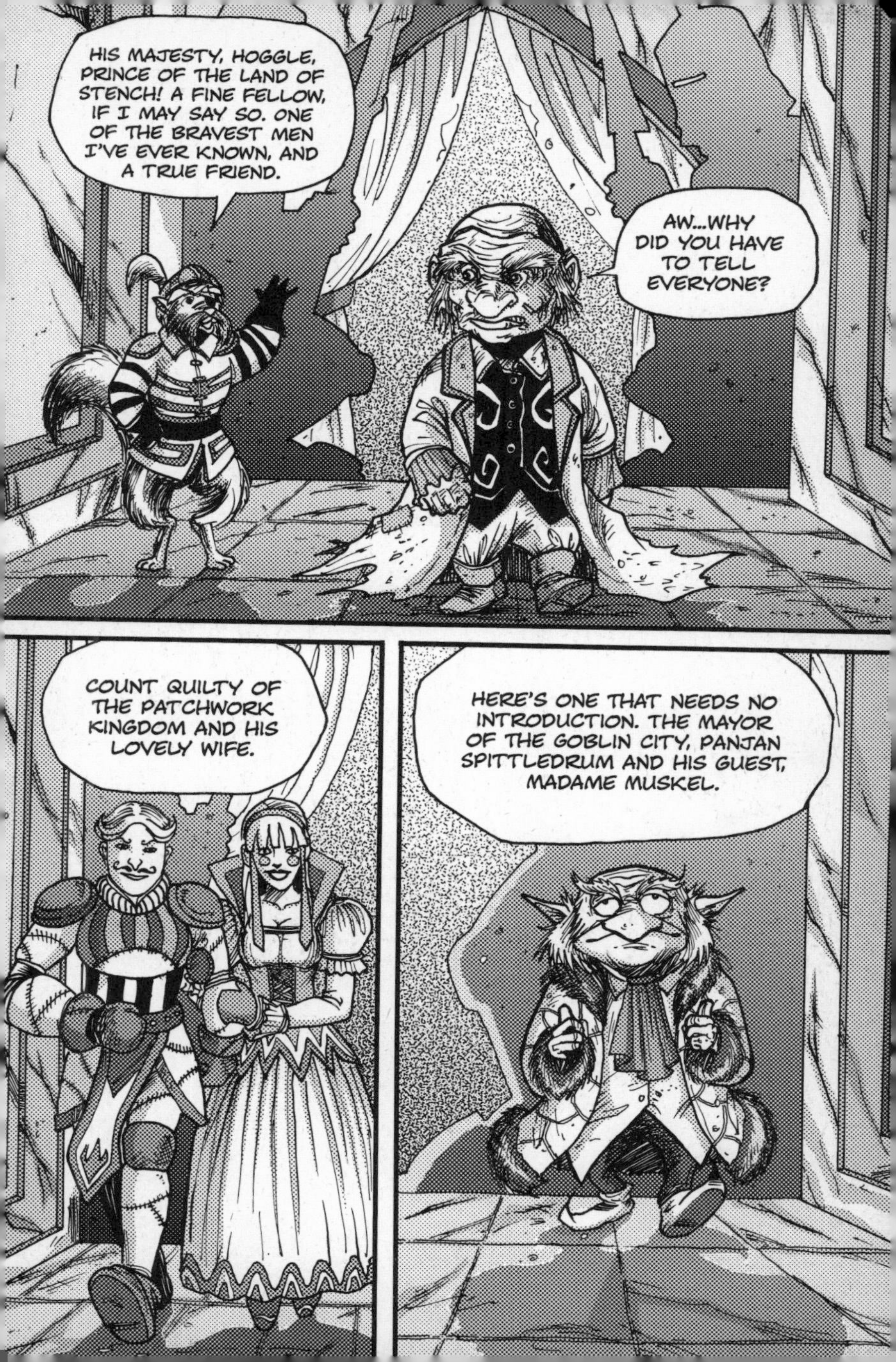
HIS MAJESTY, HOGGLE, PRINCE OF THE LAND OF STENCH! A FINE FELLOW, IF I MAY SAY SO. ONE OF THE BRAVEST MEN I'VE EVER KNOWN, AND A TRUE FRIEND.
AW...WHY DID YOU HAVE TO TELL EVERYONE?
COUNT QUILTY OF THE PATCHWORK KINGDOM AND HIS LOVELY WIFE.
HERE'S ONE THAT NEEDS NO INTRODUCTION. THE MAYOR OF THE GOBLIN CITY, PANJAN SPITTLEDRUM AND HIS GUEST, MADAME MUSKEL.

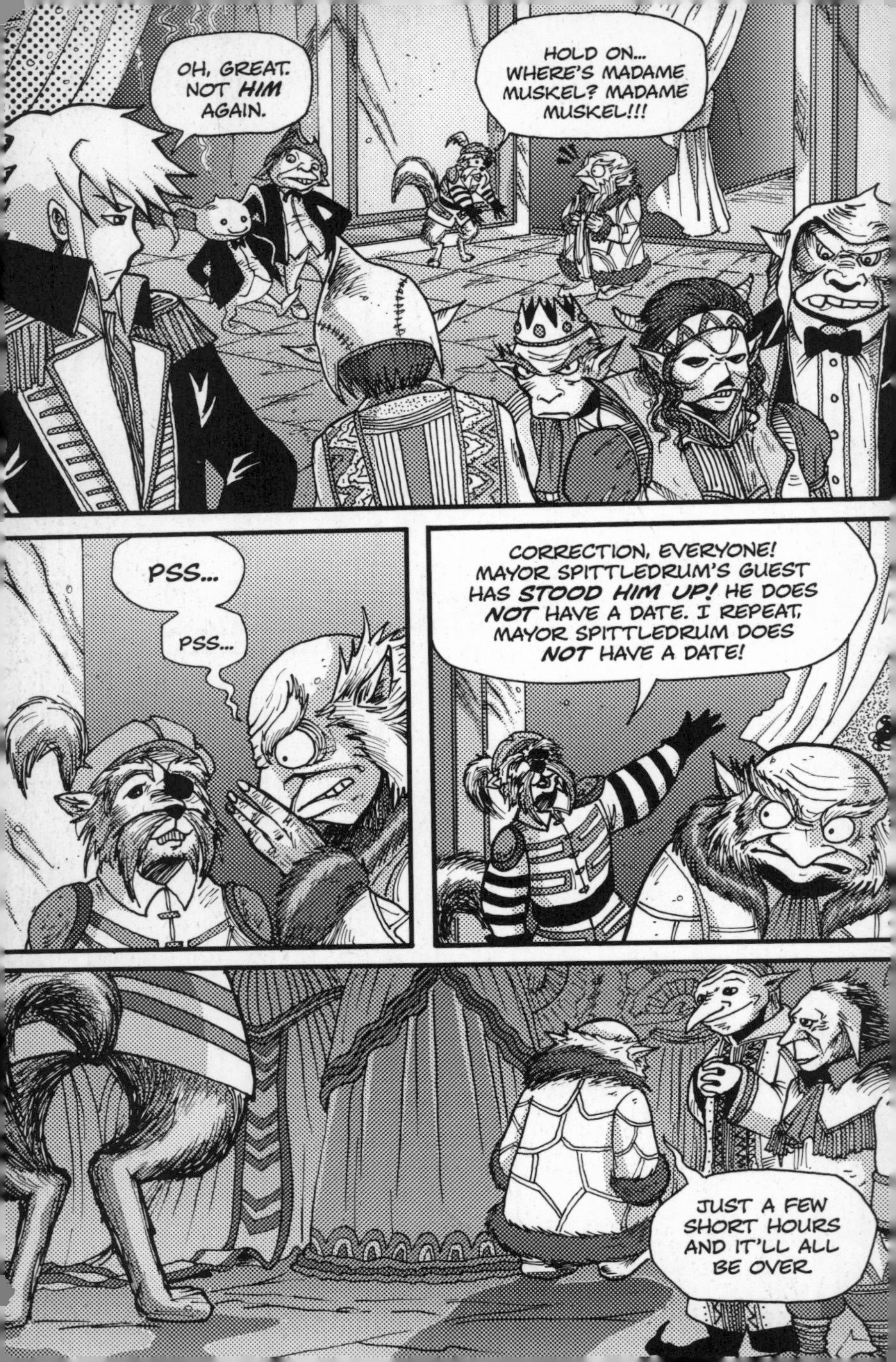
OH, GREAT. NOT **HIM** AGAIN.
HOLD ON... WHERE'S MADAME MUSKEL? MADAME MUSKEL!!!
PSS...
PSS...
CORRECTION, EVERYONE! MAYOR SPITTLEDRUM'S GUEST HAS **STOOD HIM UP!** HE DOES **NOT** HAVE A DATE. I REPEAT, MAYOR SPITTLEDRUM DOES **NOT** HAVE A DATE!
JUST A FEW SHORT HOURS AND IT'LL ALL BE OVER

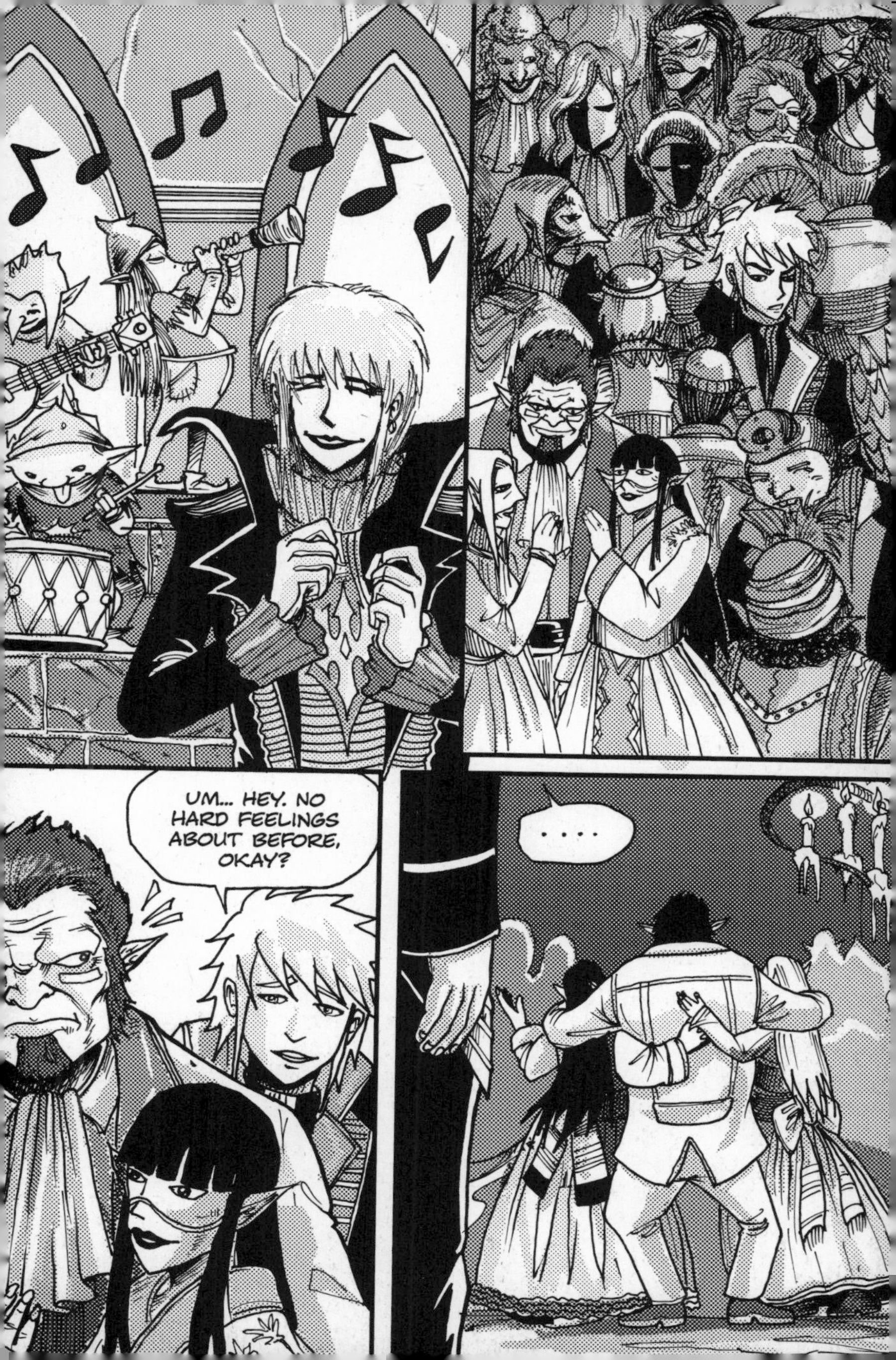

UM... HEY. NO HARD FEELINGS ABOUT BEFORE, OKAY?
. . . .

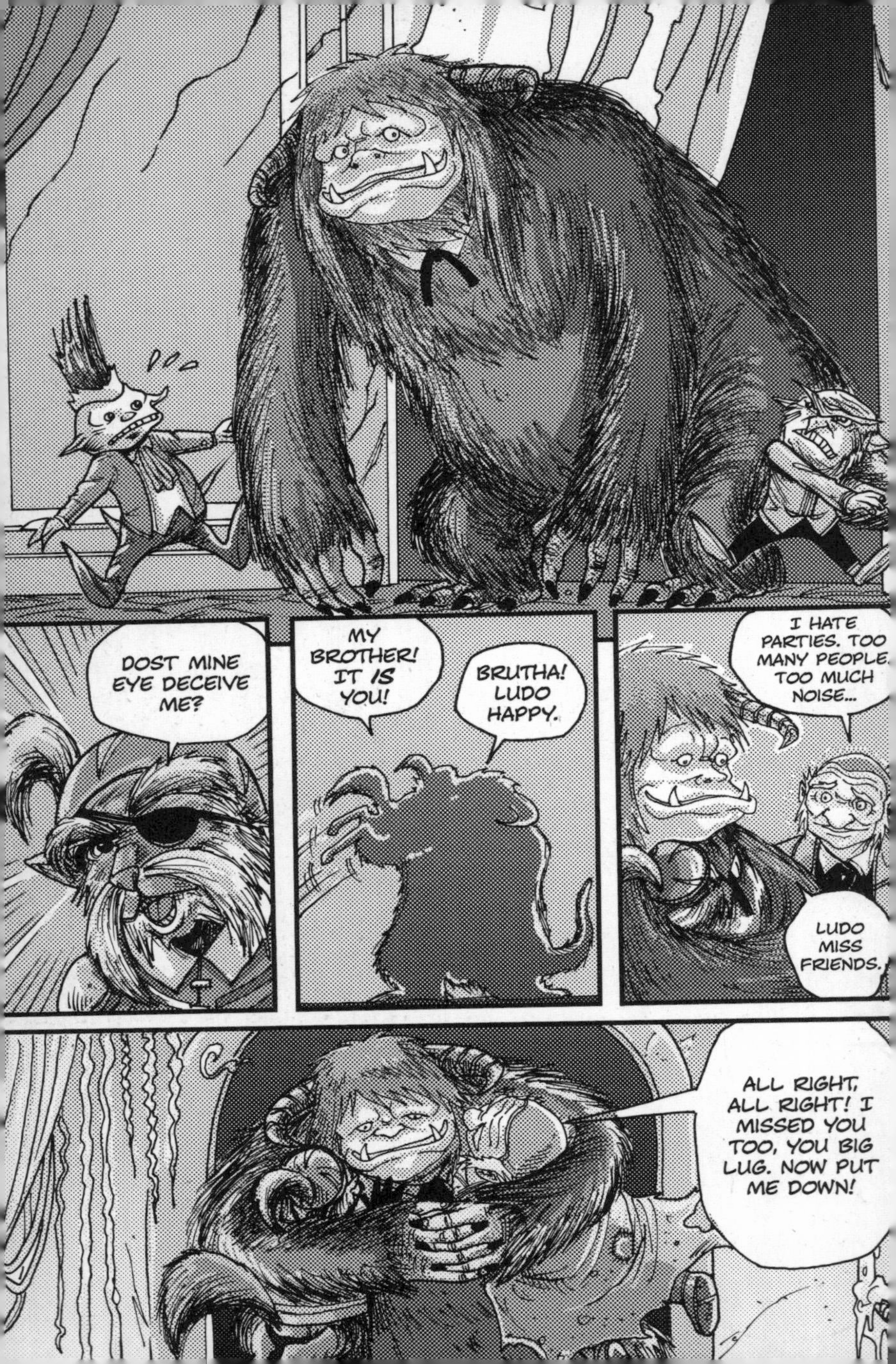
DOST MINE EYE DECEIVE ME?
MY BROTHER! IT IS YOU!
BRUTHA! LUDO HAPPY.
I HATE PARTIES. TOO MANY PEOPLE. TOO MUCH NOISE...
LUDO MISS FRIENDS.
ALL RIGHT, ALL RIGHT! I MISSED YOU TOO, YOU BIG LUG. NOW PUT ME DOWN!

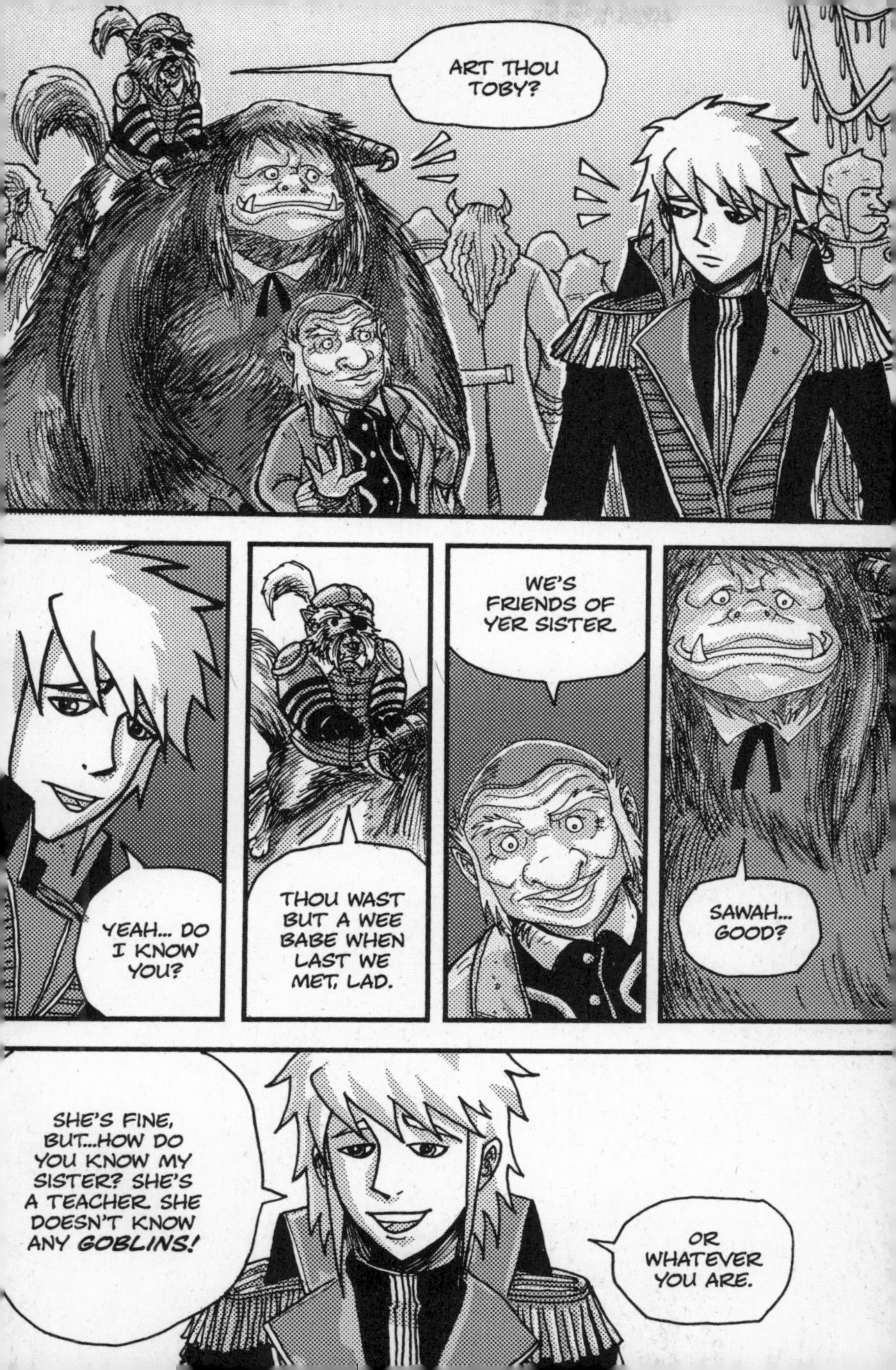
ART THOU TOBY?
YEAH... DO I KNOW YOU?
THOU WAST BUT A WEE BABE WHEN LAST WE MET, LAD.
WE'S FRIENDS OF YER SISTER
SAWAH... GOOD?
SHE'S FINE, BUT...HOW DO YOU KNOW MY SISTER? SHE'S A TEACHER. SHE DOESN'T KNOW ANY *GOBLINS!*
OR WHATEVER YOU ARE.

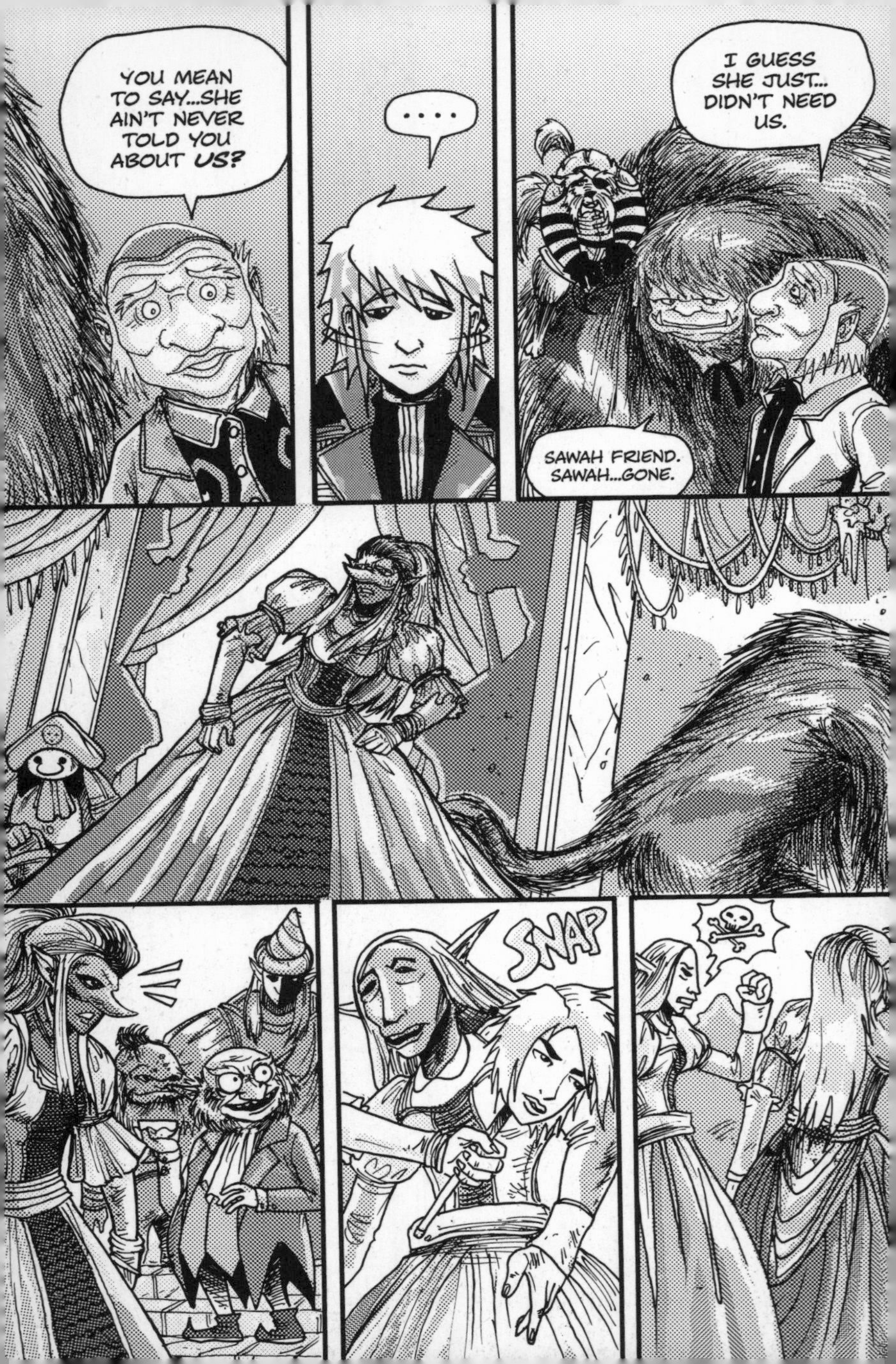

YOU MEAN TO SAY...SHE AIN'T NEVER TOLD YOU ABOUT US?
. . . .
I GUESS SHE JUST... DIDN'T NEED US.
SAWAH FRIEND. SAWAH...GONE.
SNAP

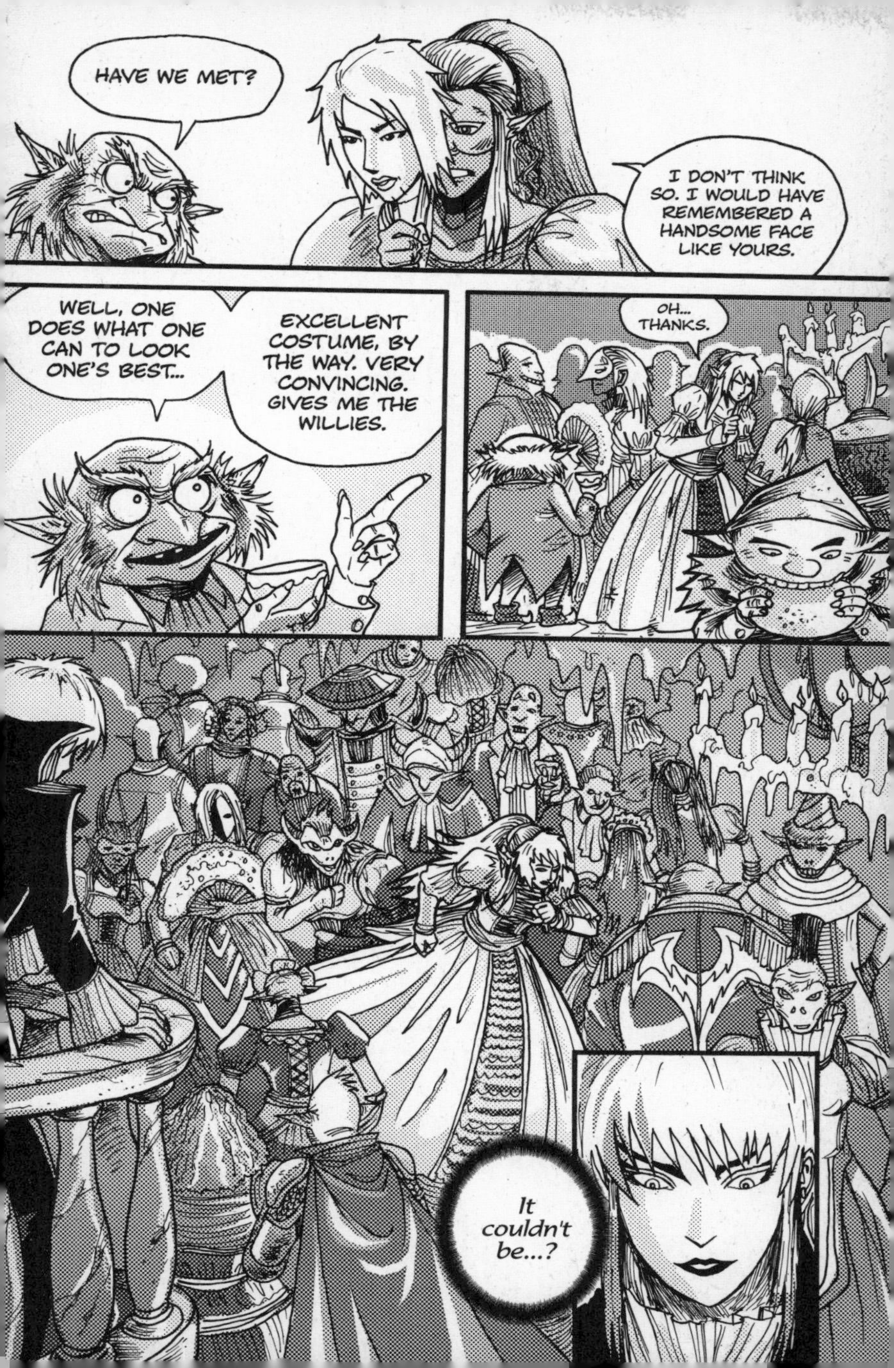
HAVE WE MET?
I DON'T THINK SO. I WOULD HAVE REMEMBERED A HANDSOME FACE LIKE YOURS.
WELL, ONE DOES WHAT ONE CAN TO LOOK ONE'S BEST...
EXCELLENT COSTUME, BY THE WAY. VERY CONVINCING. GIVES ME THE WILLIES.
OH... THANKS.
It couldn't be...?

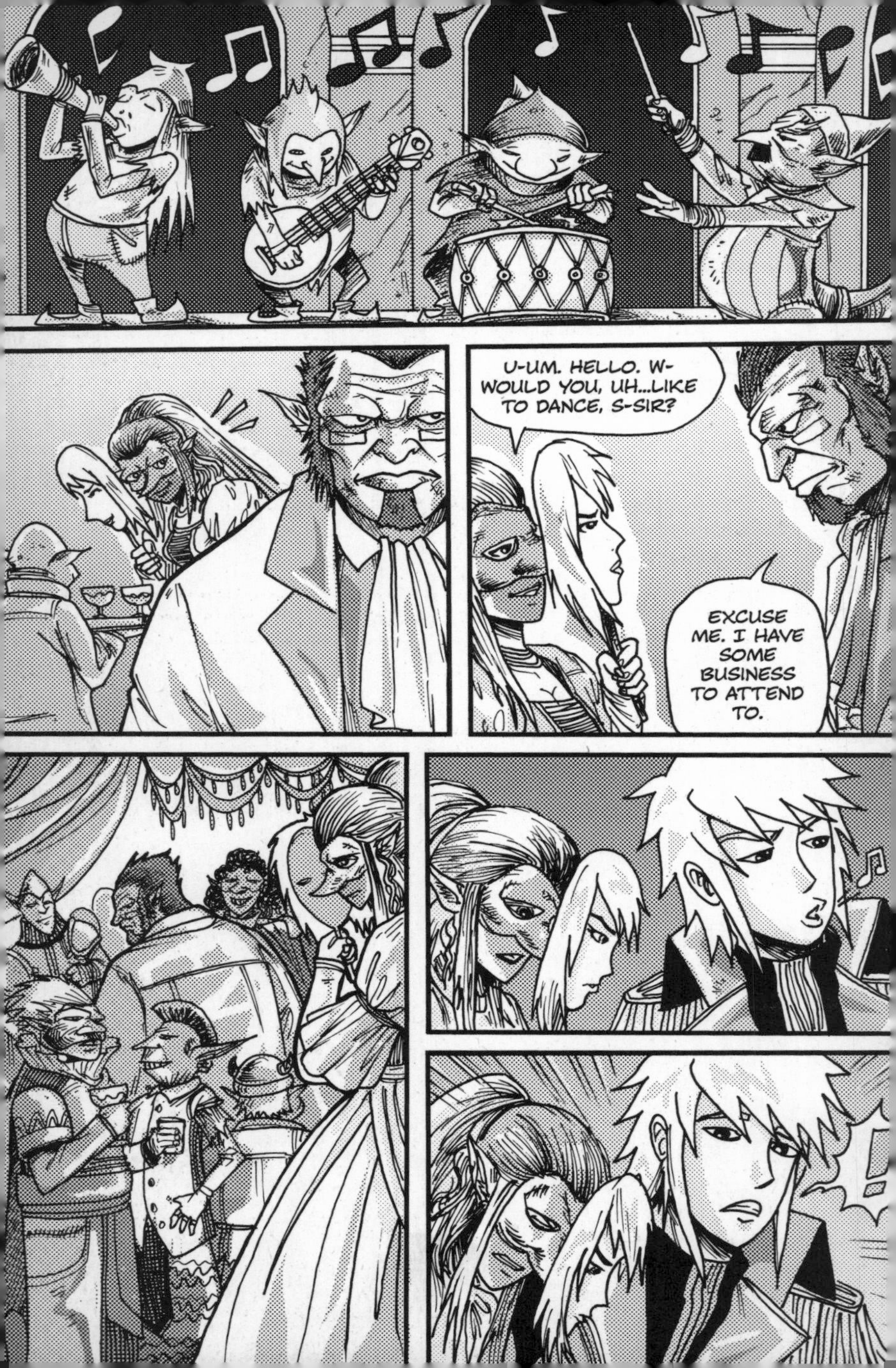
U-UM. HELLO. W-WOULD YOU, UH...LIKE TO DANCE, S-SIR?
EXCUSE ME. I HAVE SOME BUSINESS TO ATTEND TO.
!

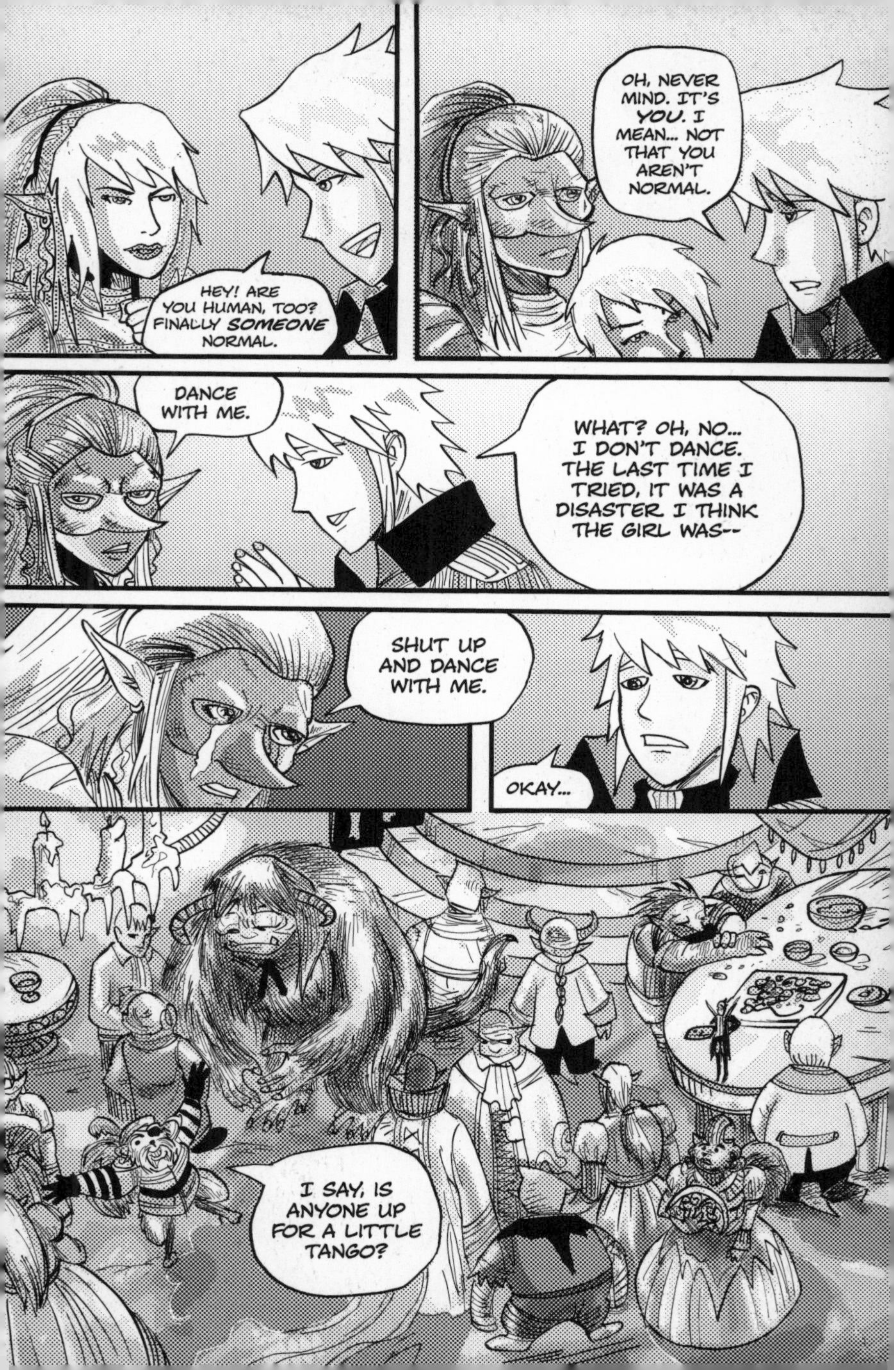
HEY! ARE YOU HUMAN, TOO? FINALLY SOMEONE NORMAL.
OH, NEVER MIND. IT'S YOU. I MEAN... NOT THAT YOU AREN'T NORMAL.
DANCE WITH ME.
WHAT? OH, NO... I DON'T DANCE. THE LAST TIME I TRIED, IT WAS A DISASTER. I THINK THE GIRL WAS--
SHUT UP AND DANCE WITH ME.
OKAY...
I SAY, IS ANYONE UP FOR A LITTLE TANGO?

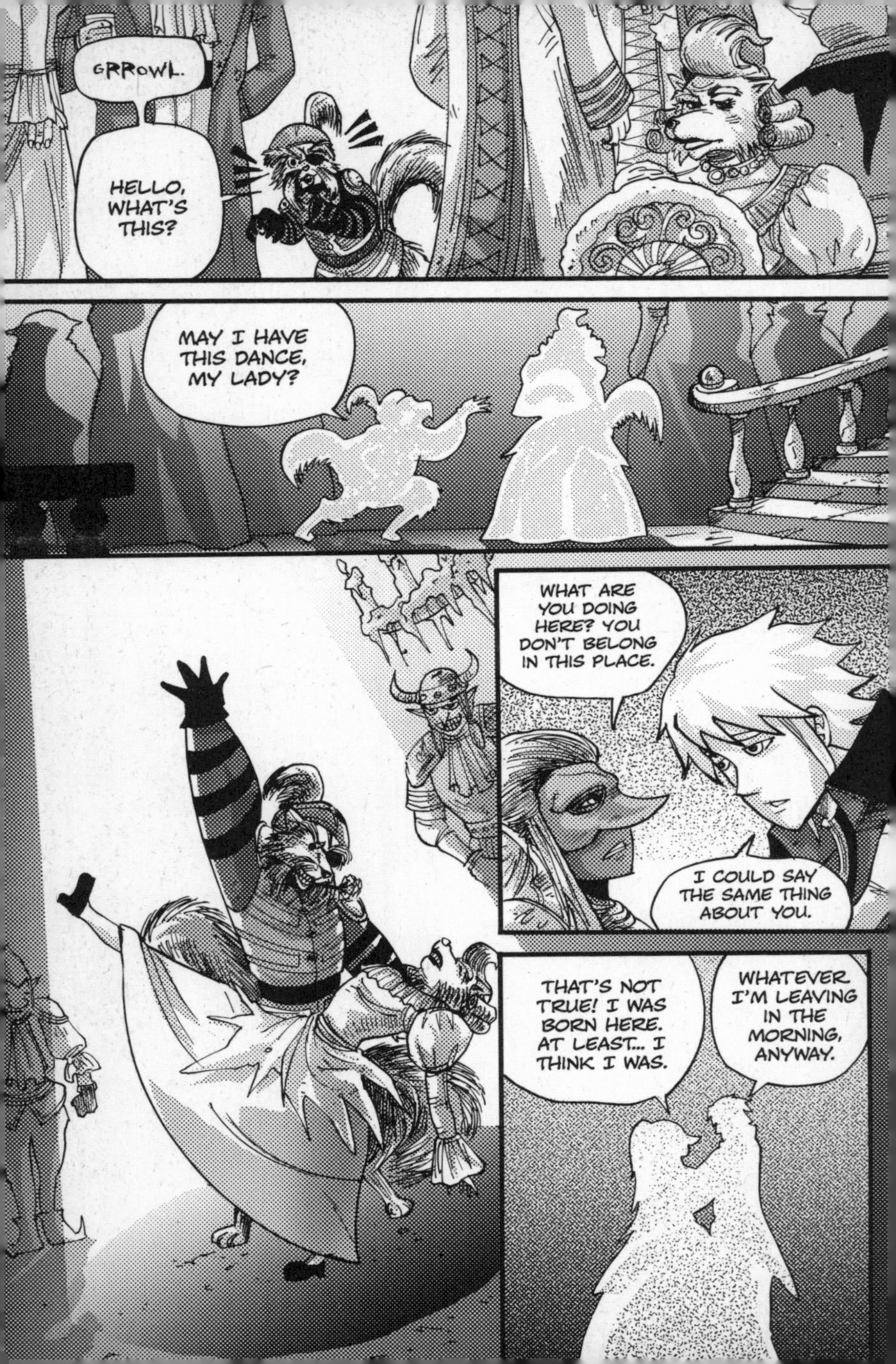
GRROWL.
HELLO, WHAT'S THIS?
MAY I HAVE THIS DANCE, MY LADY?
WHAT ARE YOU DOING HERE? YOU DON'T BELONG IN THIS PLACE.
I COULD SAY THE SAME THING ABOUT YOU.
THAT'S NOT TRUE! I WAS BORN HERE. AT LEAST... I THINK I WAS.
WHATEVER. I'M LEAVING IN THE MORNING, ANYWAY.

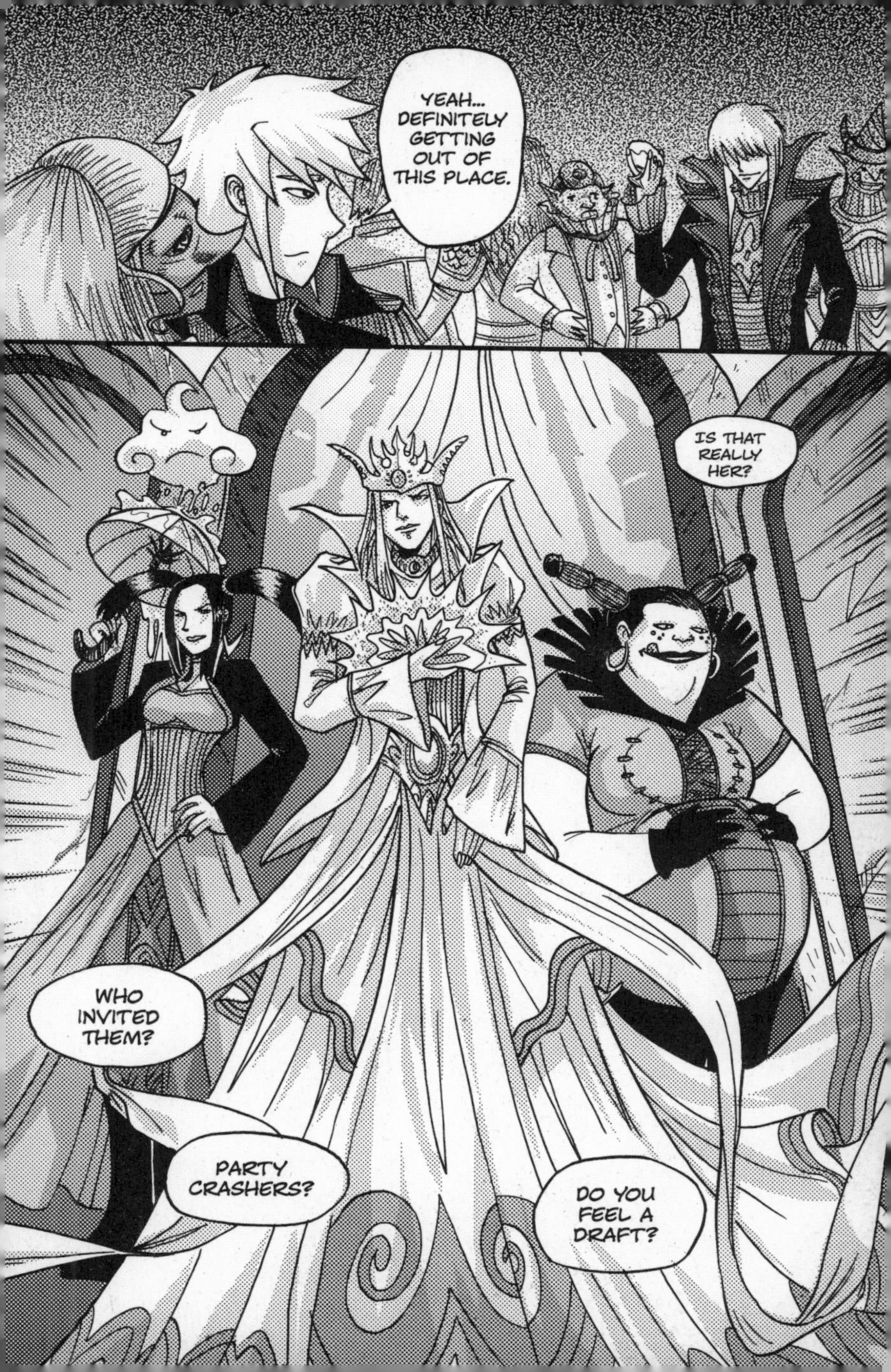
YEAH... DEFINITELY GETTING OUT OF THIS PLACE.
IS THAT REALLY HER?
WHO INVITED THEM?
PARTY CRASHERS?
DO YOU FEEL A DRAFT?

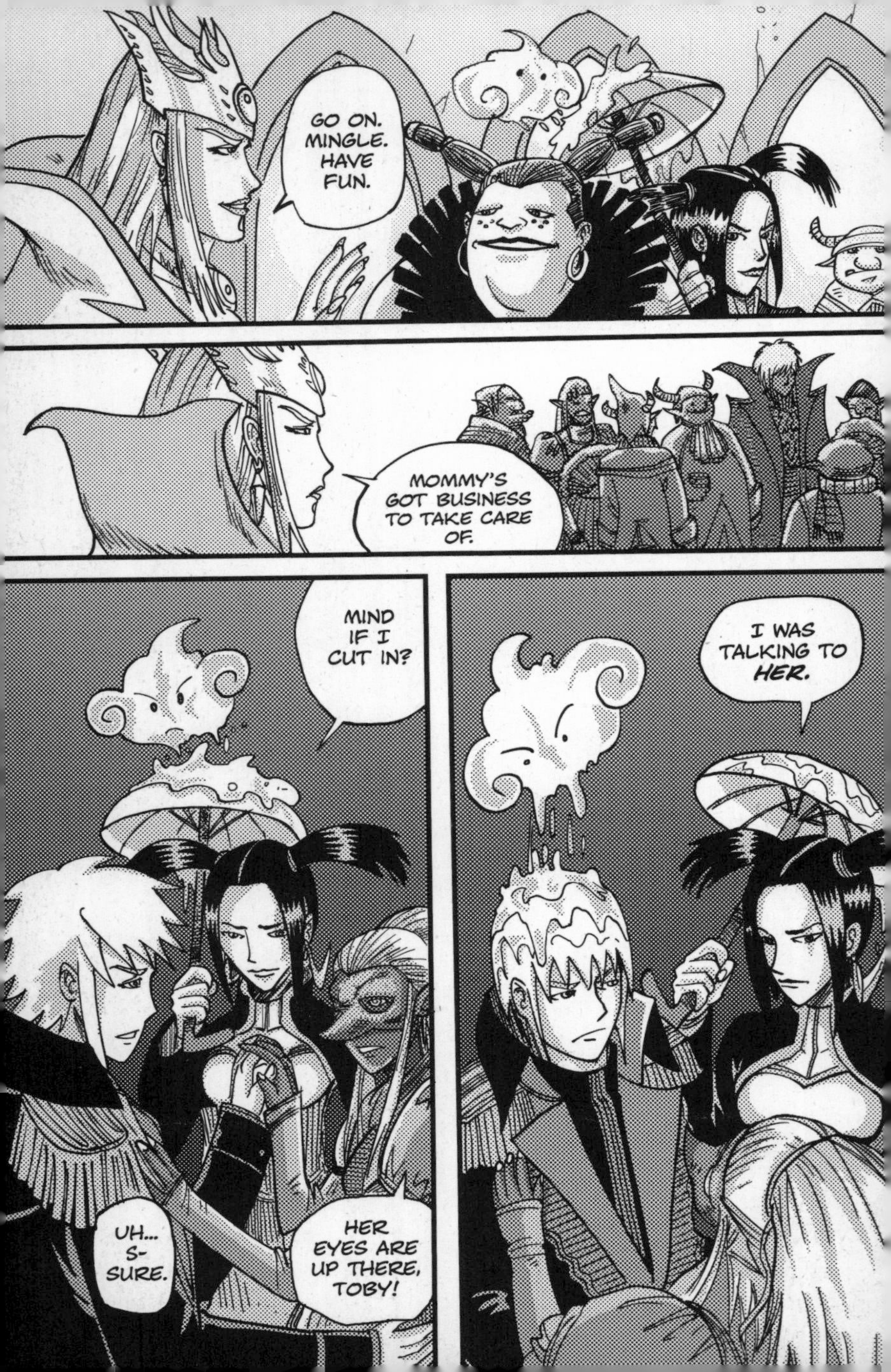
GO ON. MINGLE. HAVE FUN.
MOMMY'S GOT BUSINESS TO TAKE CARE OF.
MIND IF I CUT IN?
UH... S- SURE.
HER EYES ARE UP THERE, TOBY!
I WAS TALKING TO **HER.**

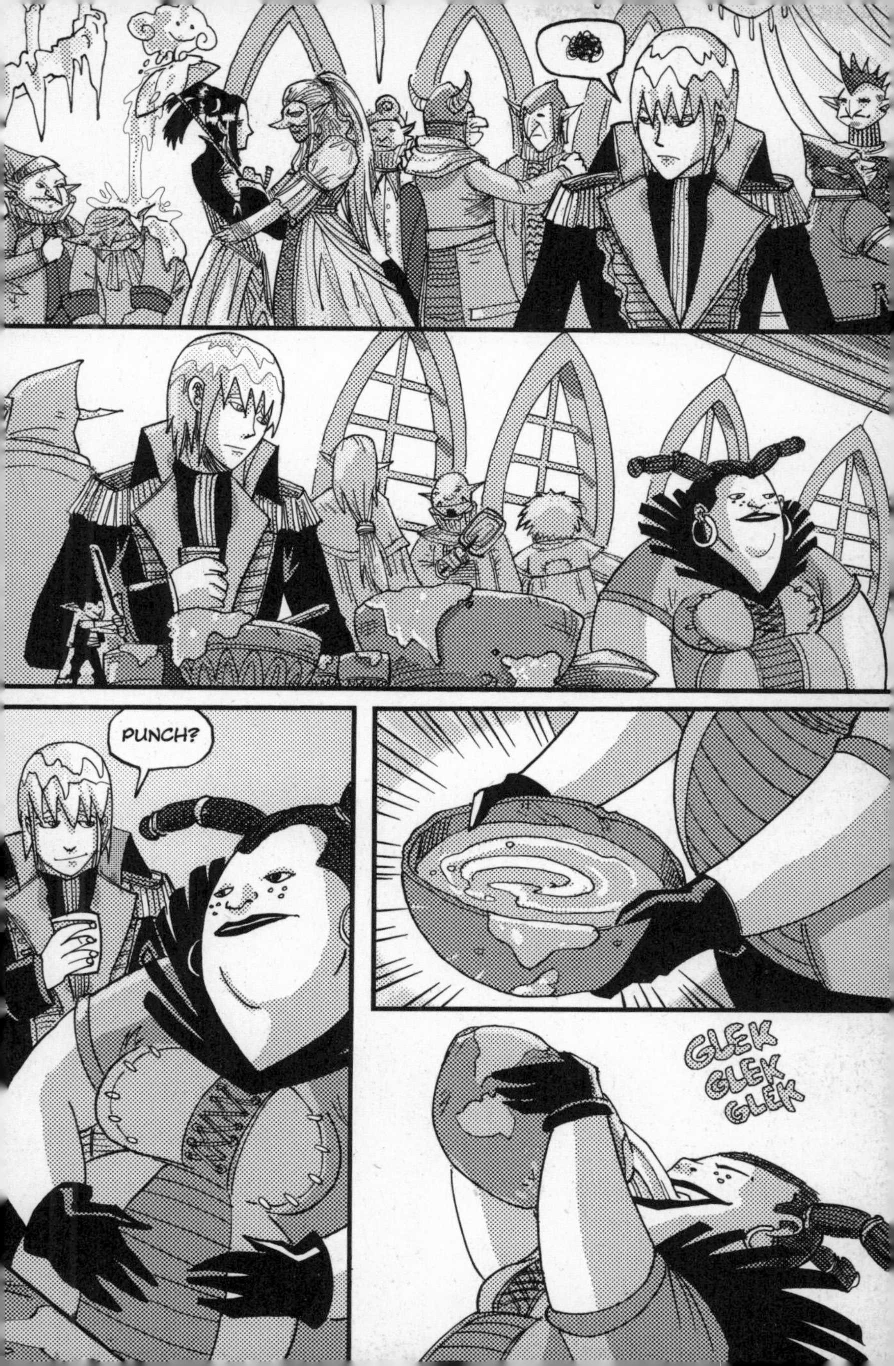
PUNCH?
GLEK GLEK GLEK

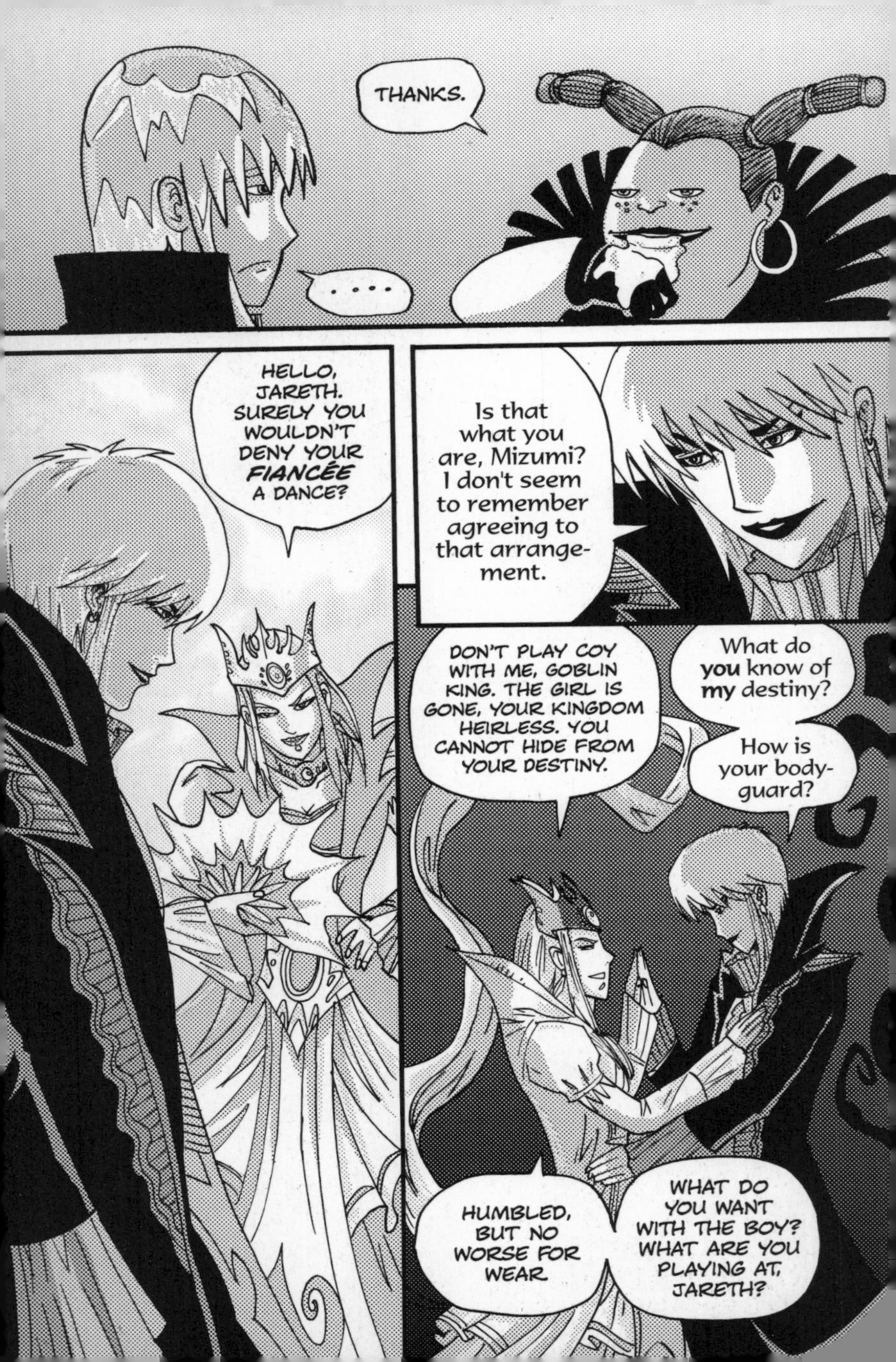

THANKS.
. . . .
HELLO, JARETH. SURELY YOU WOULDN'T DENY YOUR FIANCÉE A DANCE?
Is that what you are, Mizumi? I don't seem to remember agreeing to that arrange-ment.
DON'T PLAY COY WITH ME, GOBLIN KING. THE GIRL IS GONE, YOUR KINGDOM HEIRLESS. YOU CANNOT HIDE FROM YOUR DESTINY.
What do you know of my destiny?
How is your body-guard?
HUMBLED, BUT NO WORSE FOR WEAR.
WHAT DO YOU WANT WITH THE BOY? WHAT ARE YOU PLAYING AT, JARETH?

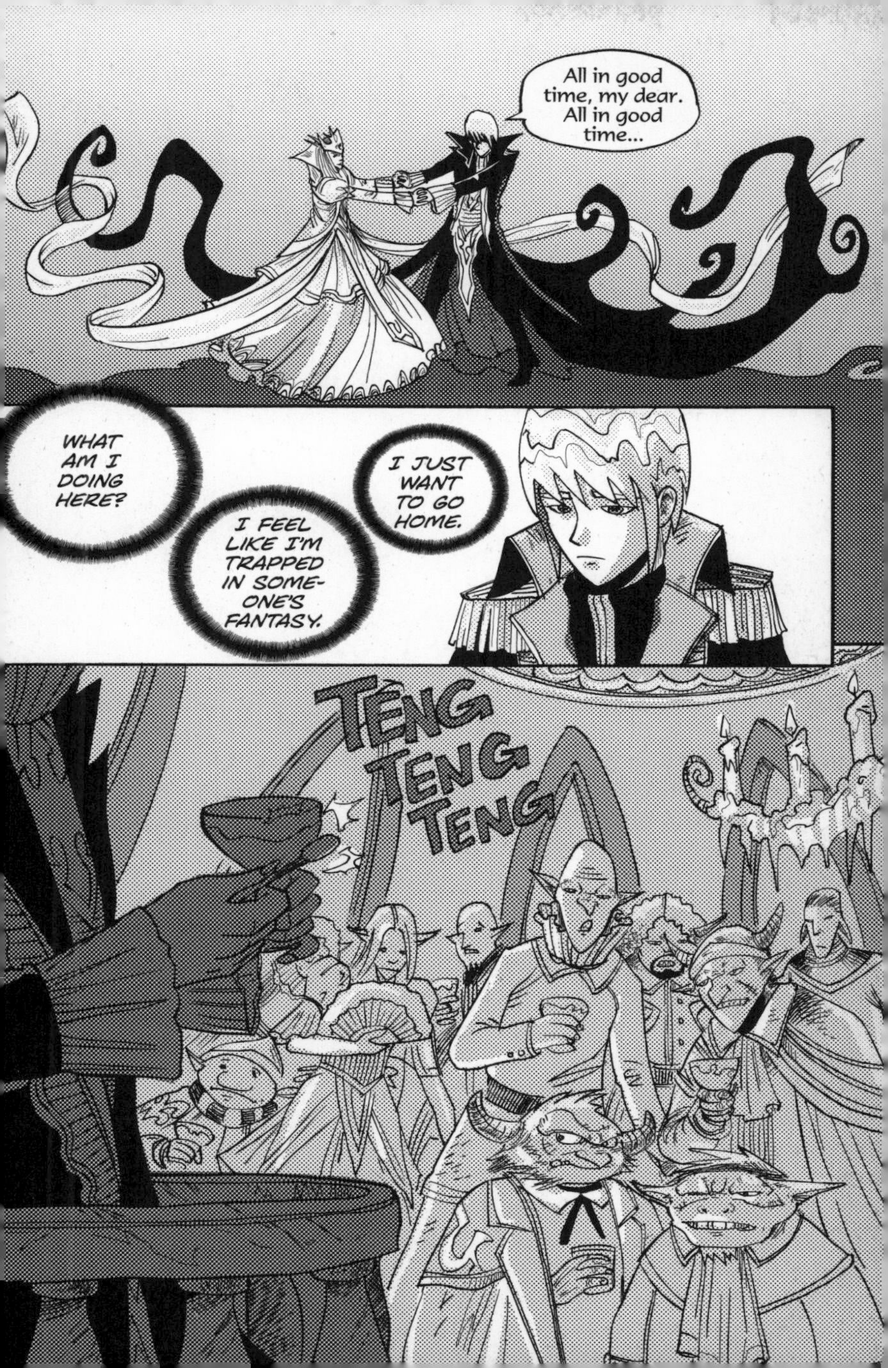

All in good time, my dear. All in good time...
WHAT AM I DOING HERE?
I FEEL LIKE I'M TRAPPED IN SOME-ONE'S FANTASY.
I JUST WANT TO GO HOME.
TENG TENG TENG

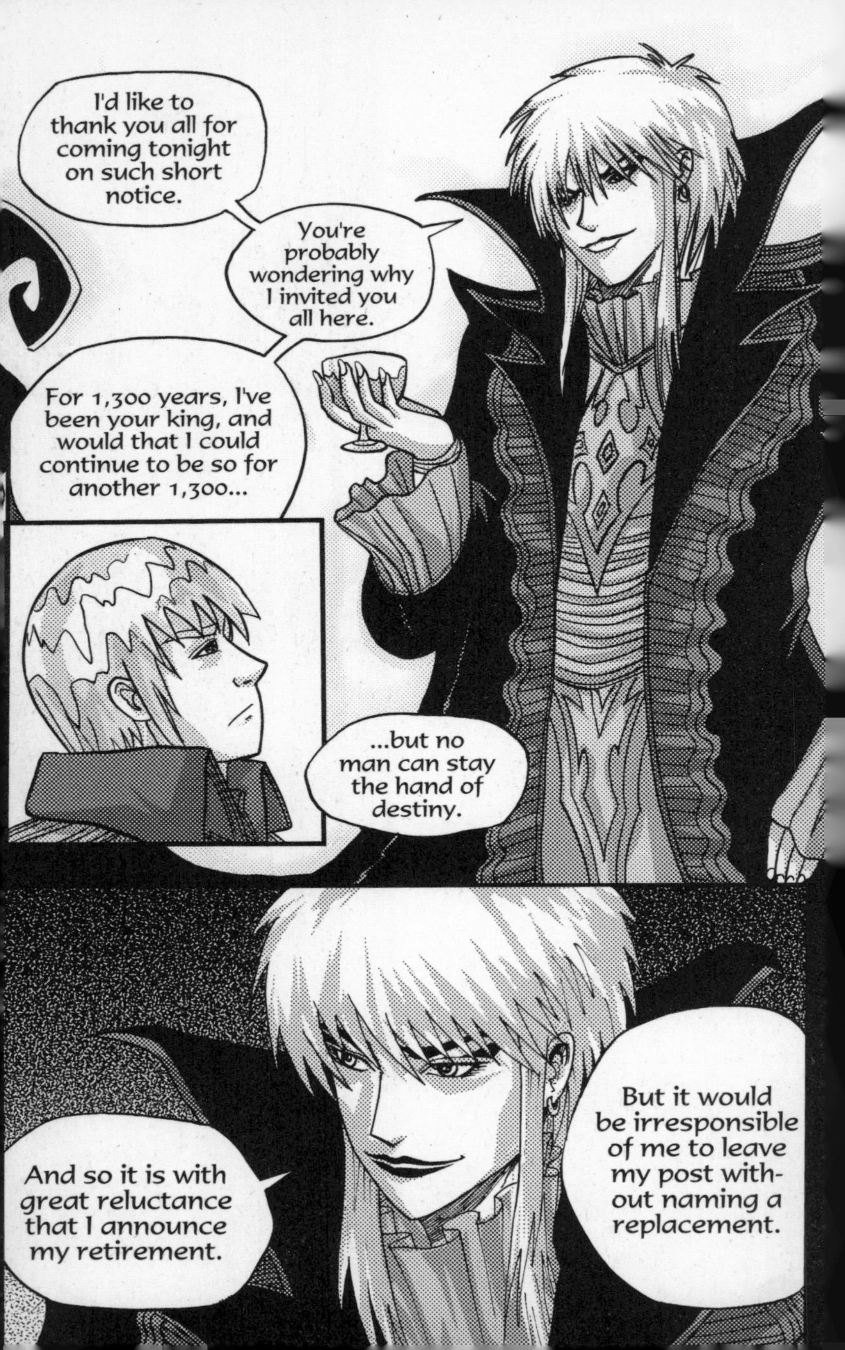
I'd like to thank you all for coming tonight on such short notice.
You're probably wondering why I invited you all here.
For 1,300 years, I've been your king, and would that I could continue to be so for another 1,300...
...but no man can stay the hand of destiny.
And so it is with great reluctance that I announce my retirement.
But it would be irresponsible of me to leave my post with-out naming a replacement.

Ladies and gentlemen...and I use the phrase **VERY** loosely...I am pleased to present to you my **successor.**

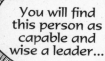

You will find this person as capable and wise a leader...

Y-YOUR MAJESTY! I DON'T KNOW WHAT TO SAY!

ACTUALLY, I DID BRING A *FEW* NOTES...JUST IN CASE.

...and in time, I trust that you will come to love him as you love me.

"HIM"?

The next Goblin King and Lord of the Labyrinth...

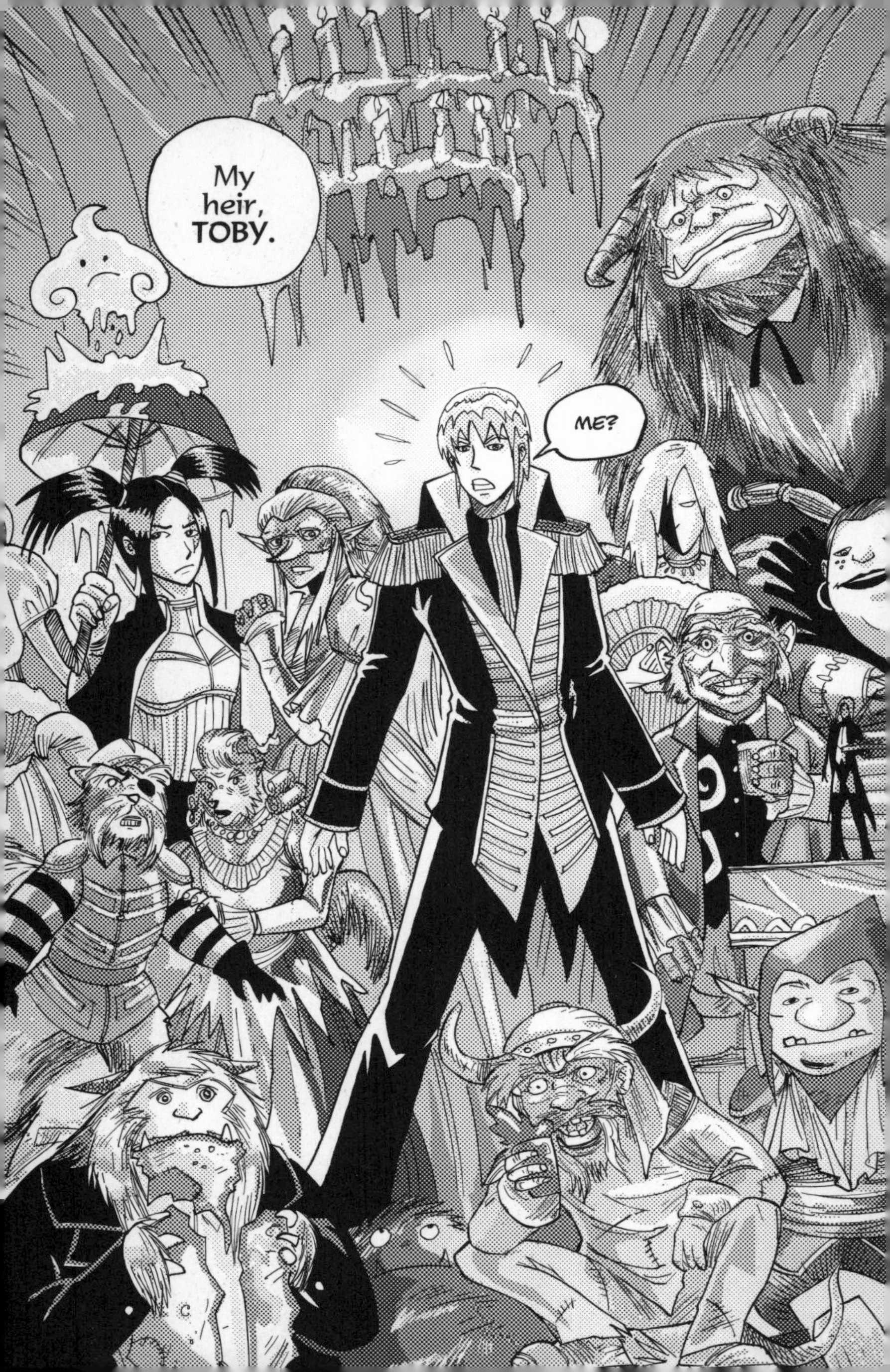
My heir, TOBY.
ME?

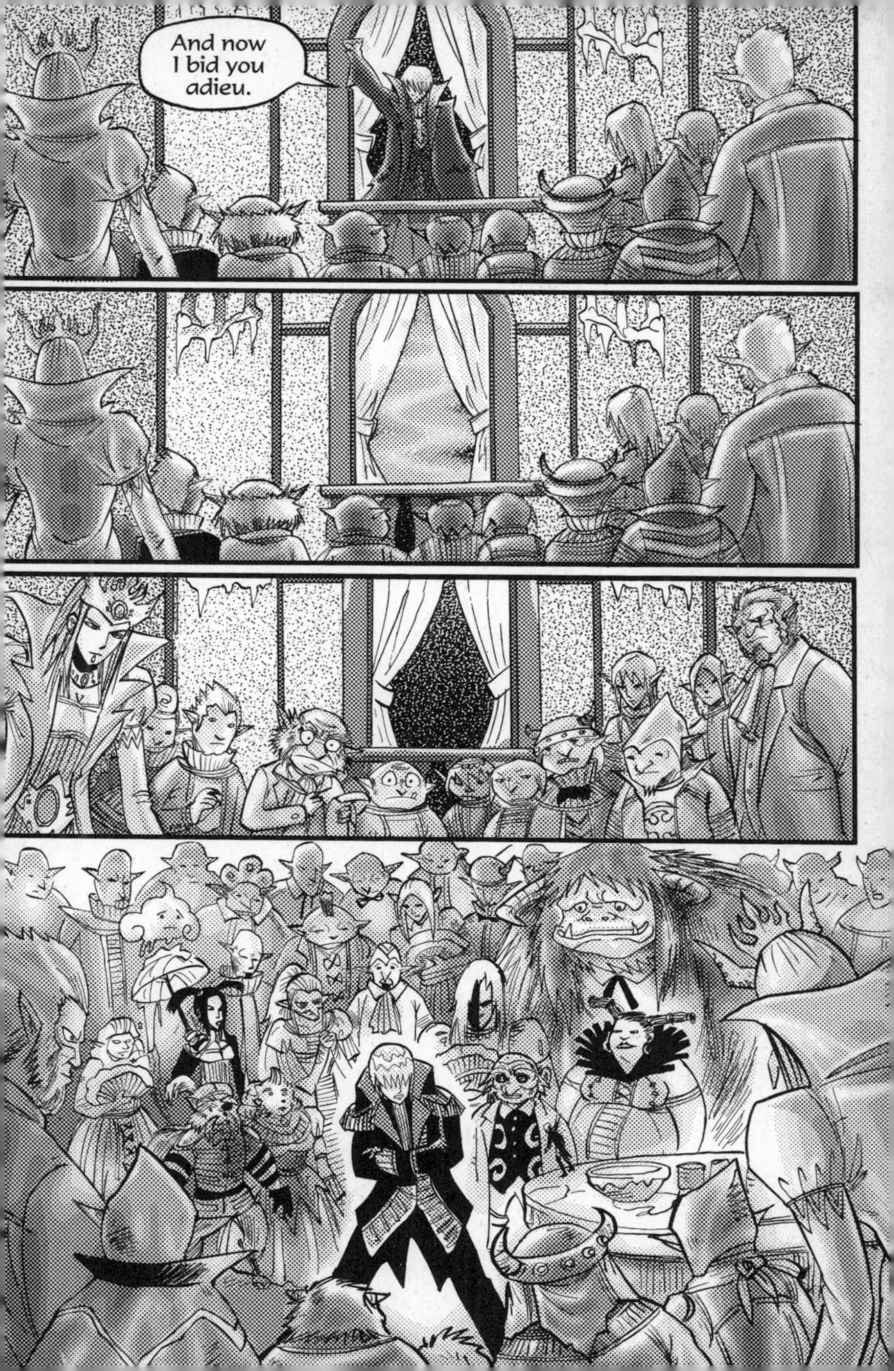
And now I bid you adieu.

In the next volume of:

Jim Henson's

RETURN TO
LABYRINTH

The trials and tessellations of Prince Toby Continue...

What causes the Labyrinth to move?

What do Goblins eat?

Where did Ludo come from?

What is par for the course on hole 18 of the Bog of Eternal Stench?

These are just a few of the burning questions that will be answered in:

*GOBLIN PRINCE OF
THE LABYRINTH*

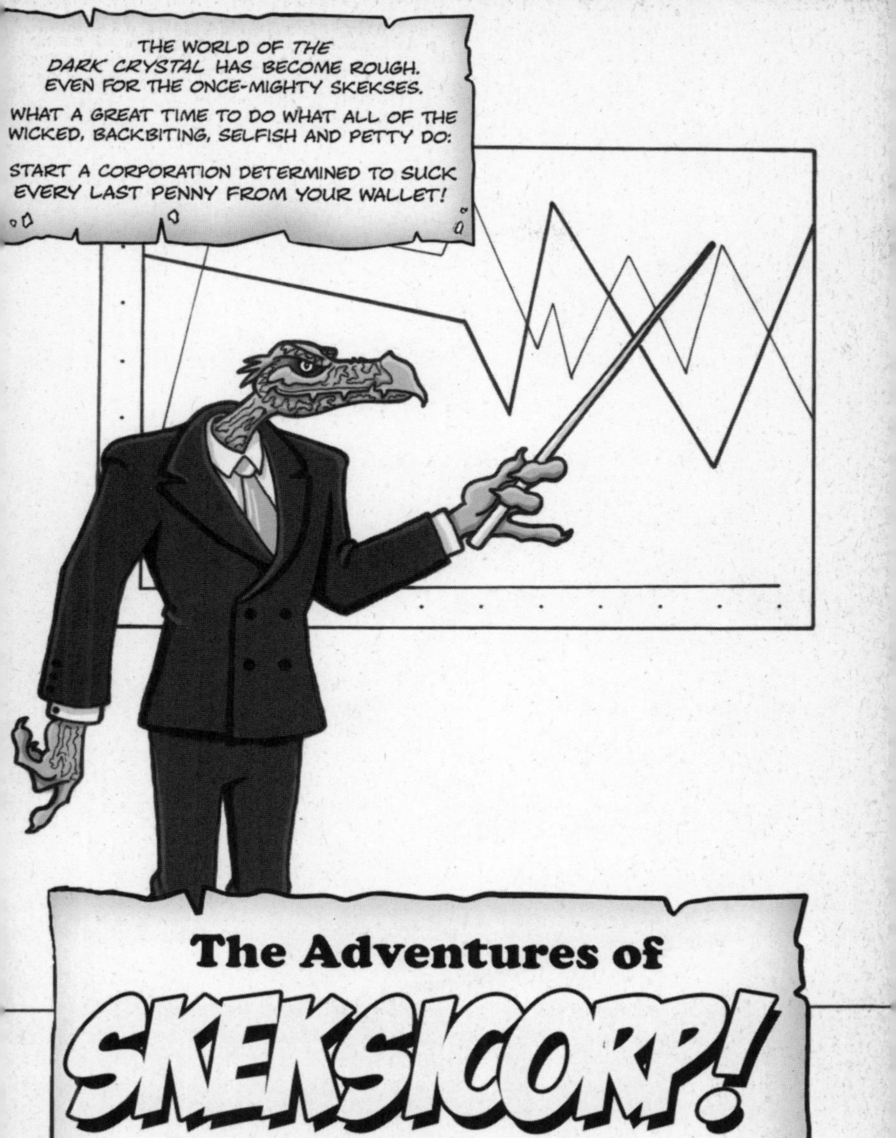
THE WORLD OF THE DARK CRYSTAL HAS BECOME ROUGH. EVEN FOR THE ONCE-MIGHTY SKEKSES.
WHAT A GREAT TIME TO DO WHAT ALL OF THE WICKED, BACKBITING, SELFISH AND PETTY DO:
START A CORPORATION DETERMINED TO SUCK EVERY LAST PENNY FROM YOUR WALLET!
The Adventures of
SKEKSICORP!
"Where quality is a slogan..."

By M. Polis & J. Formanek

Jim Henson's
Legends of
The Dark Crystal

The Garthim Wars

Story by Barbara Randall Kesel

Art by Max Kim

Four years before the release of *Labyrinth*, Jim Henson conceived and directed *The Dark Crystal*, a wondrously imaginative film that told the story of Jen and Kira, the last Gelflings living in a fractured world precariously balanced between the forces of good and evil. The film was released to great acclaim and has since gone on to become one of the most popular fantasy films in history. Yet, epic as the film was, it was only a chapter in a much larger story.

In 2007, that story continues. We journey back to an earlier time, hundreds of years before the birth of Jen and Kira, back before the Great Extermination, when both the gentle Mystics and evil Skekses were plentiful. It is the era of Lahr, a shepherd, and Neffi, a weaver from a nearby village. It is an age where SkekSo the Emperor is still in his prime and holds council with SkekSil the Chamberlain and SkekLach the Collector, while in the Valley of the Mystics, UrSen the Monk offers his wise advice to any who will need it. It is a time where small creatures can become heroes and stories often turn into legends. This is but one of them.

A legend of the Dark Crystal.

The legend of the Garthim Wars.

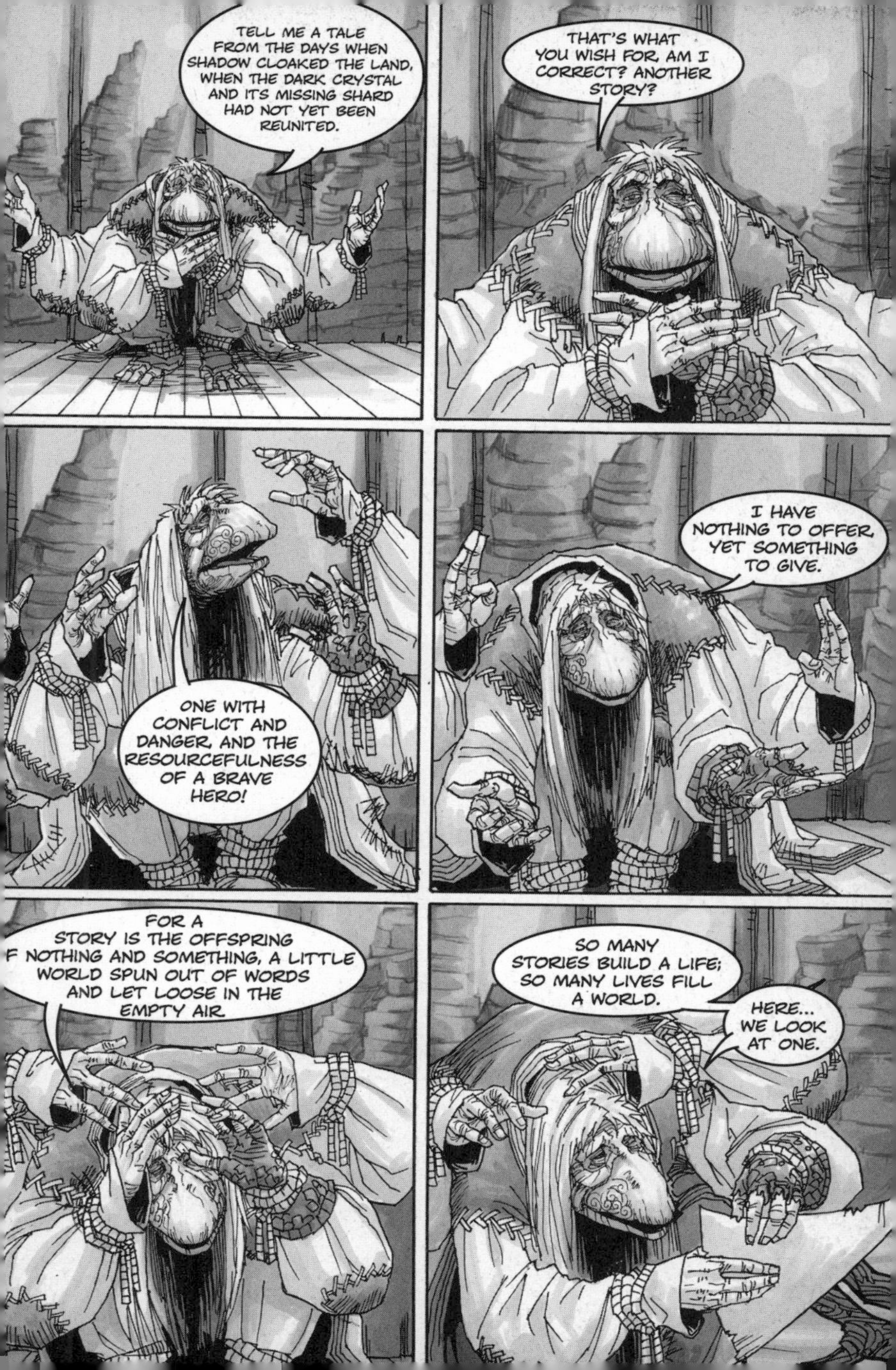
TELL ME A TALE FROM THE DAYS WHEN SHADOW CLOAKED THE LAND, WHEN THE DARK CRYSTAL AND ITS MISSING SHARD HAD NOT YET BEEN REUNITED.
THAT'S WHAT YOU WISH FOR, AM I CORRECT? ANOTHER STORY?
ONE WITH CONFLICT AND DANGER, AND THE RESOURCEFULNESS OF A BRAVE HERO!
I HAVE NOTHING TO OFFER, YET SOMETHING TO GIVE.
FOR A STORY IS THE OFFSPRING F NOTHING AND SOMETHING, A LITTLE WORLD SPUN OUT OF WORDS AND LET LOOSE IN THE EMPTY AIR.
SO MANY STORIES BUILD A LIFE; SO MANY LIVES FILL A WORLD.
HERE... WE LOOK AT ONE.

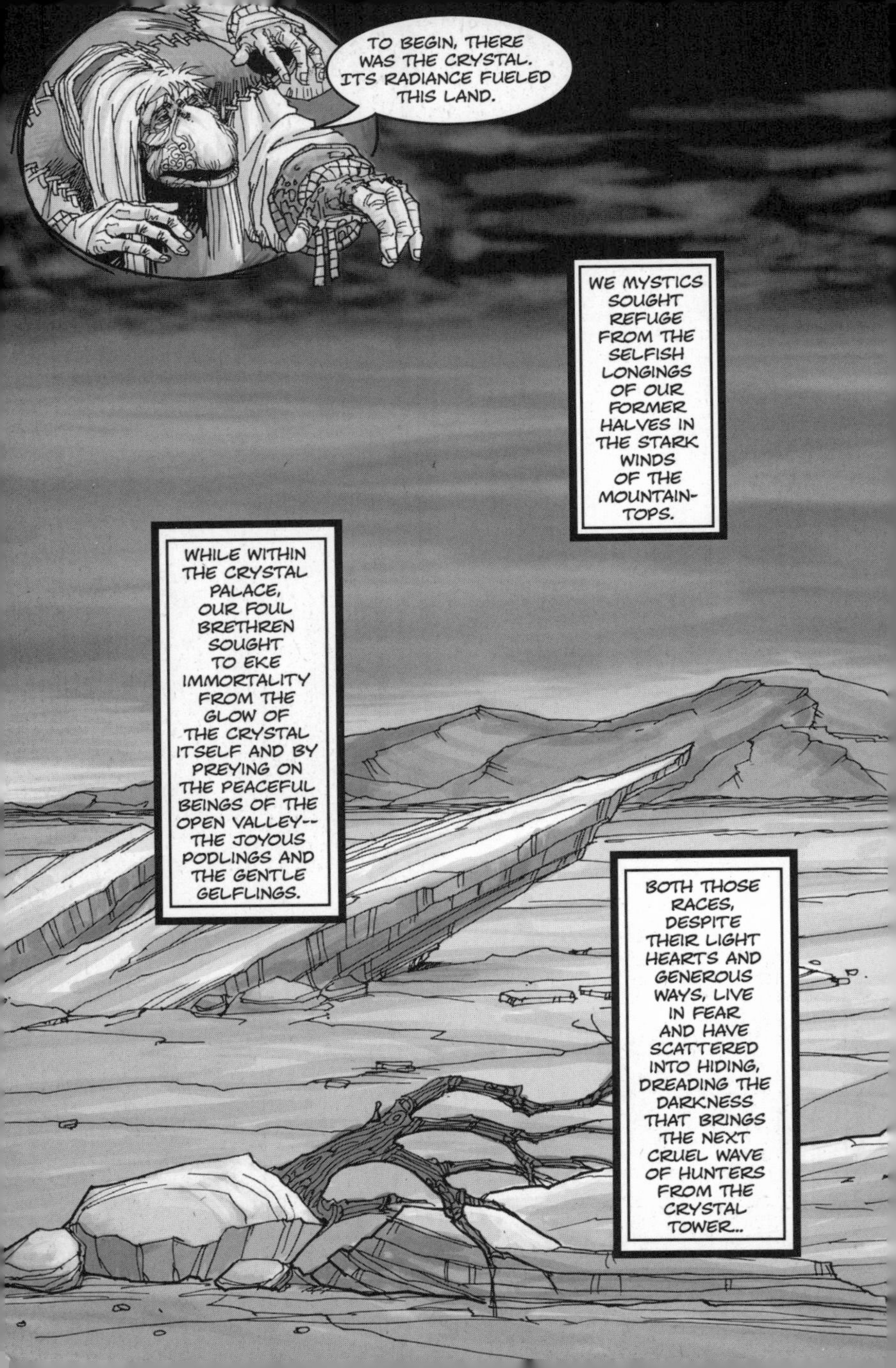
TO BEGIN, THERE WAS THE CRYSTAL. ITS RADIANCE FUELED THIS LAND.
WE MYSTICS SOUGHT REFUGE FROM THE SELFISH LONGINGS OF OUR FORMER HALVES IN THE STARK WINDS OF THE MOUNTAIN-TOPS.
WHILE WITHIN THE CRYSTAL PALACE, OUR FOUL BRETHREN SOUGHT TO EKE IMMORTALITY FROM THE GLOW OF THE CRYSTAL ITSELF AND BY PREYING ON THE PEACEFUL BEINGS OF THE OPEN VALLEY-- THE JOYOUS PODLINGS AND THE GENTLE GELFLINGS.
BOTH THOSE RACES, DESPITE THEIR LIGHT HEARTS AND GENEROUS WAYS, LIVE IN FEAR AND HAVE SCATTERED INTO HIDING, DREADING THE DARKNESS THAT BRINGS THE NEXT CRUEL WAVE OF HUNTERS FROM THE CRYSTAL TOWER...

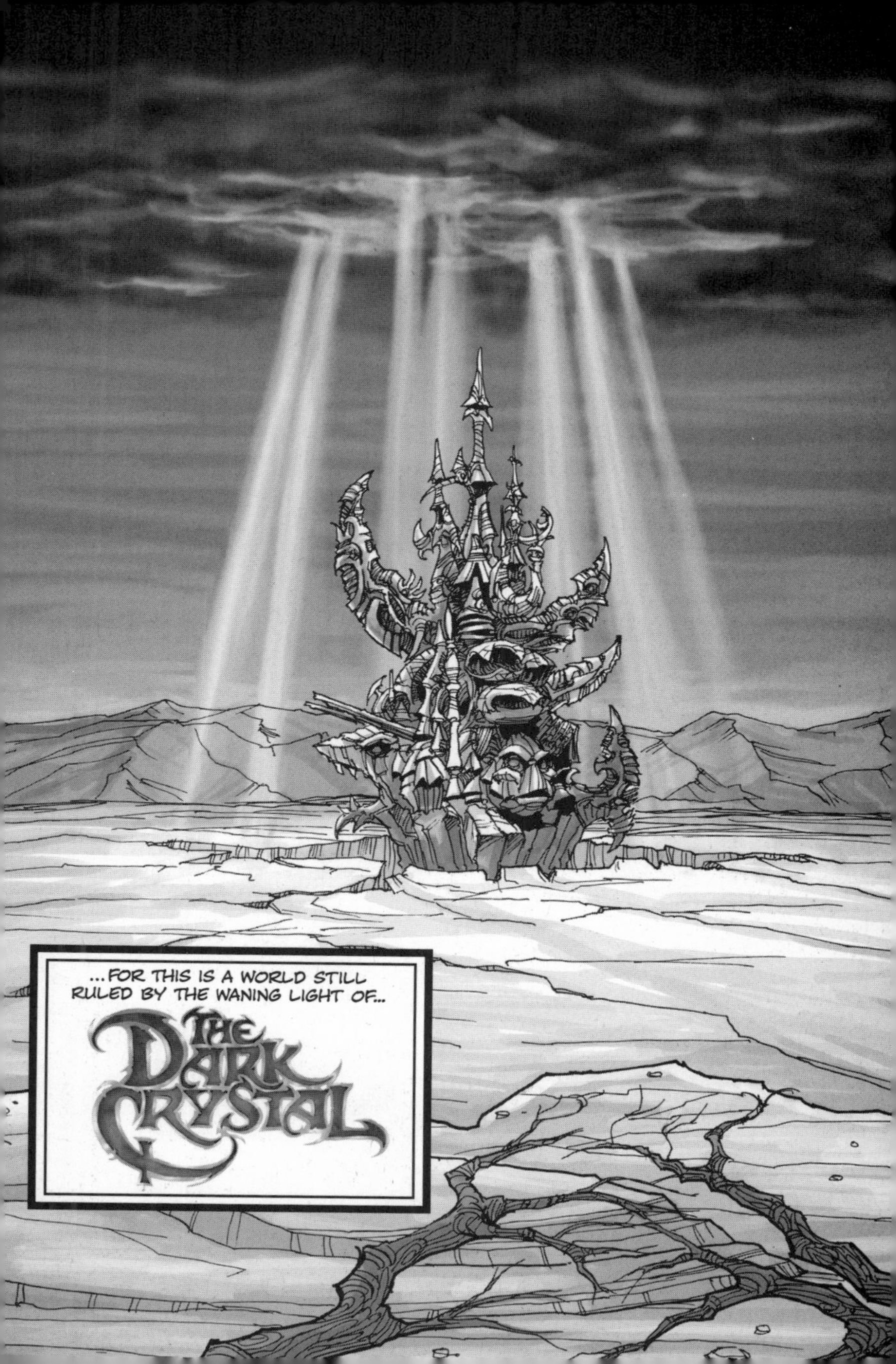
...FOR THIS IS A WORLD STILL RULED BY THE WANING LIGHT OF...
THE DARK CRYSTAL

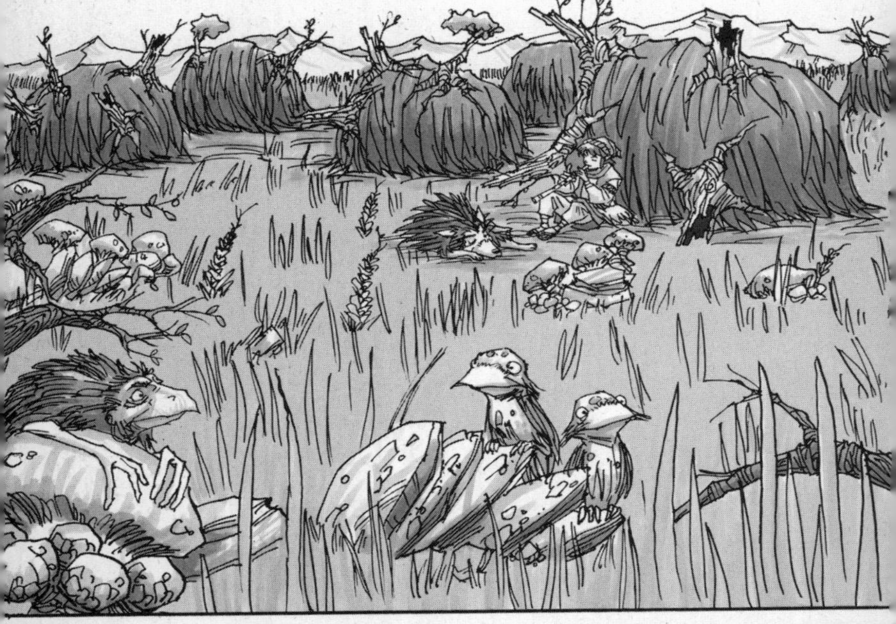

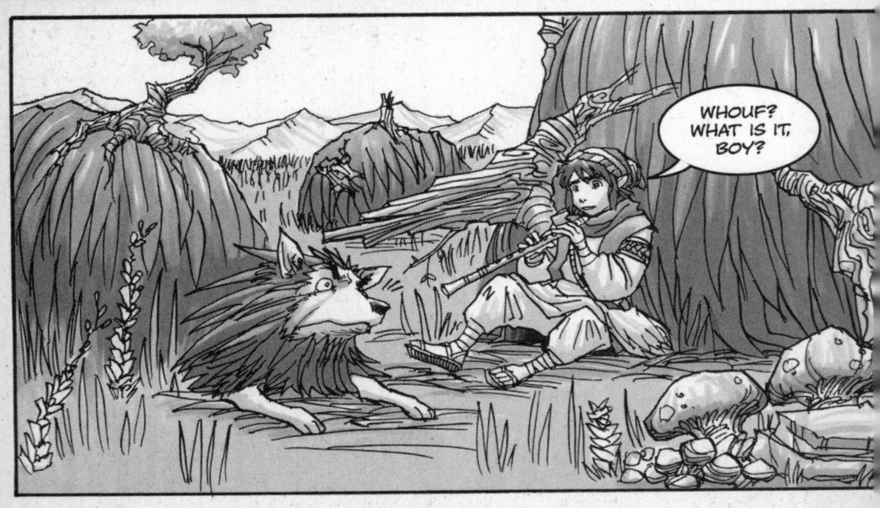
WHOUF? WHAT IS IT, BOY?

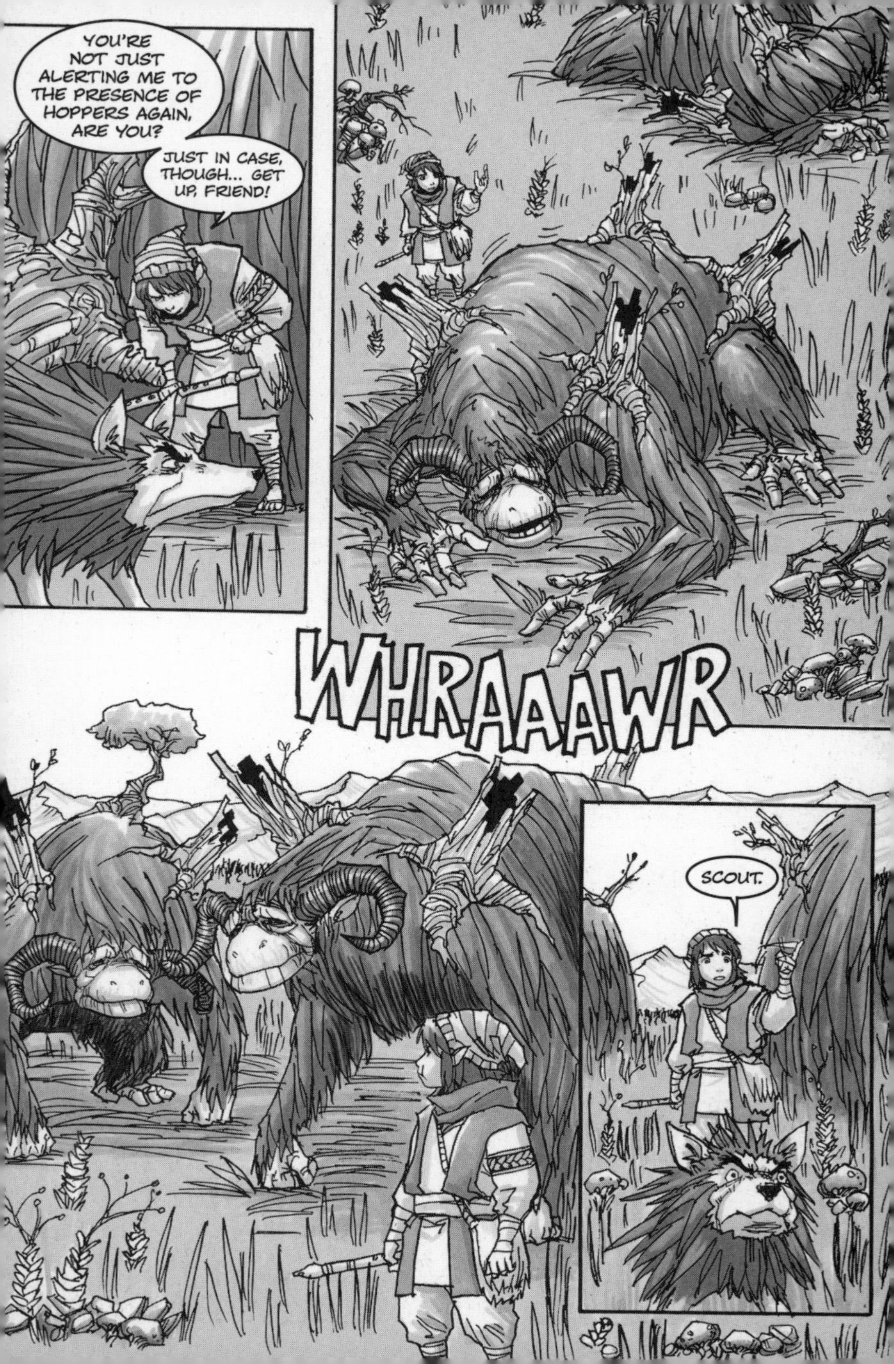
YOU'RE NOT JUST ALERTING ME TO THE PRESENCE OF HOPPERS AGAIN, ARE YOU?
JUST IN CASE, THOUGH... GET UP, FRIEND!
WHRAAAWR
SCOUT.

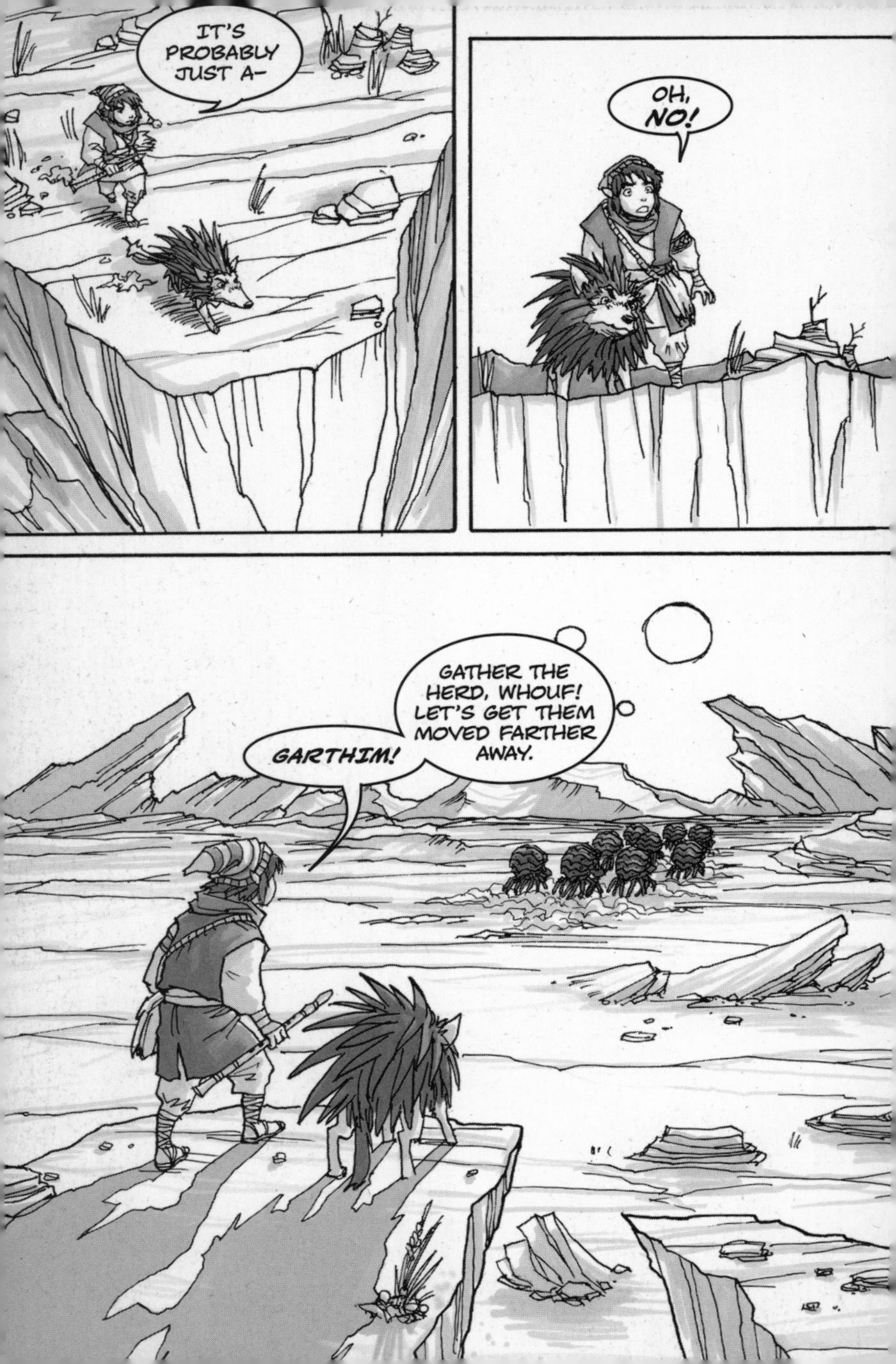
IT'S PROBABLY JUST A-
OH, NO!
GARTHIM!
GATHER THE HERD, WHOUF! LET'S GET THEM MOVED FARTHER AWAY.

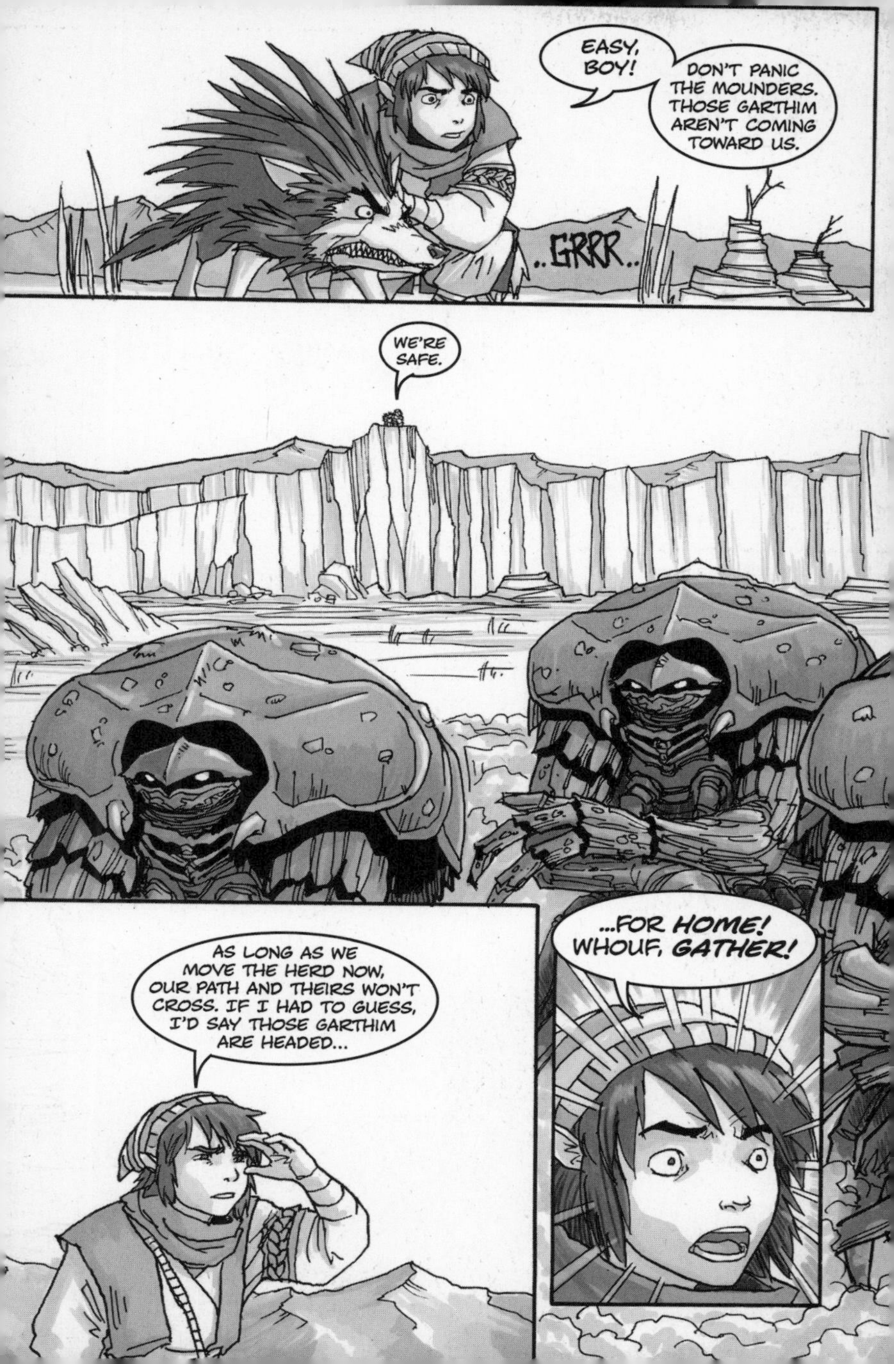
EASY, BOY!
DON'T PANIC THE MOUNDERS. THOSE GARTHIM AREN'T COMING TOWARD US.
..GRRR..
WE'RE SAFE.
AS LONG AS WE MOVE THE HERD NOW, OUR PATH AND THEIRS WON'T CROSS. IF I HAD TO GUESS, I'D SAY THOSE GARTHIM ARE HEADED...
...FOR HOME! WHOUF, GATHER!

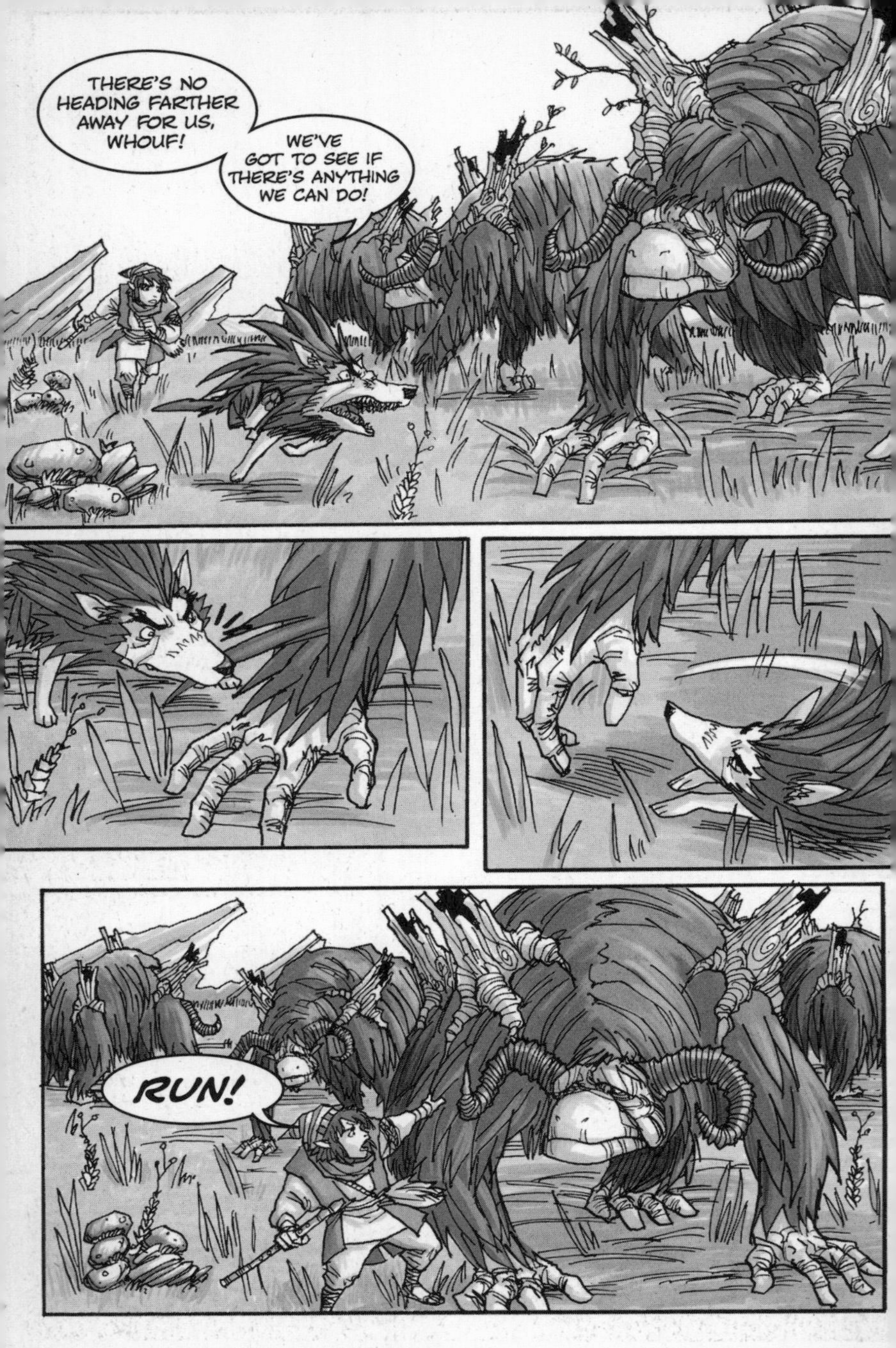
THERE'S NO HEADING FARTHER AWAY FOR US, WHOUF!
WE'VE GOT TO SEE IF THERE'S ANYTHING WE CAN DO!
RUN!

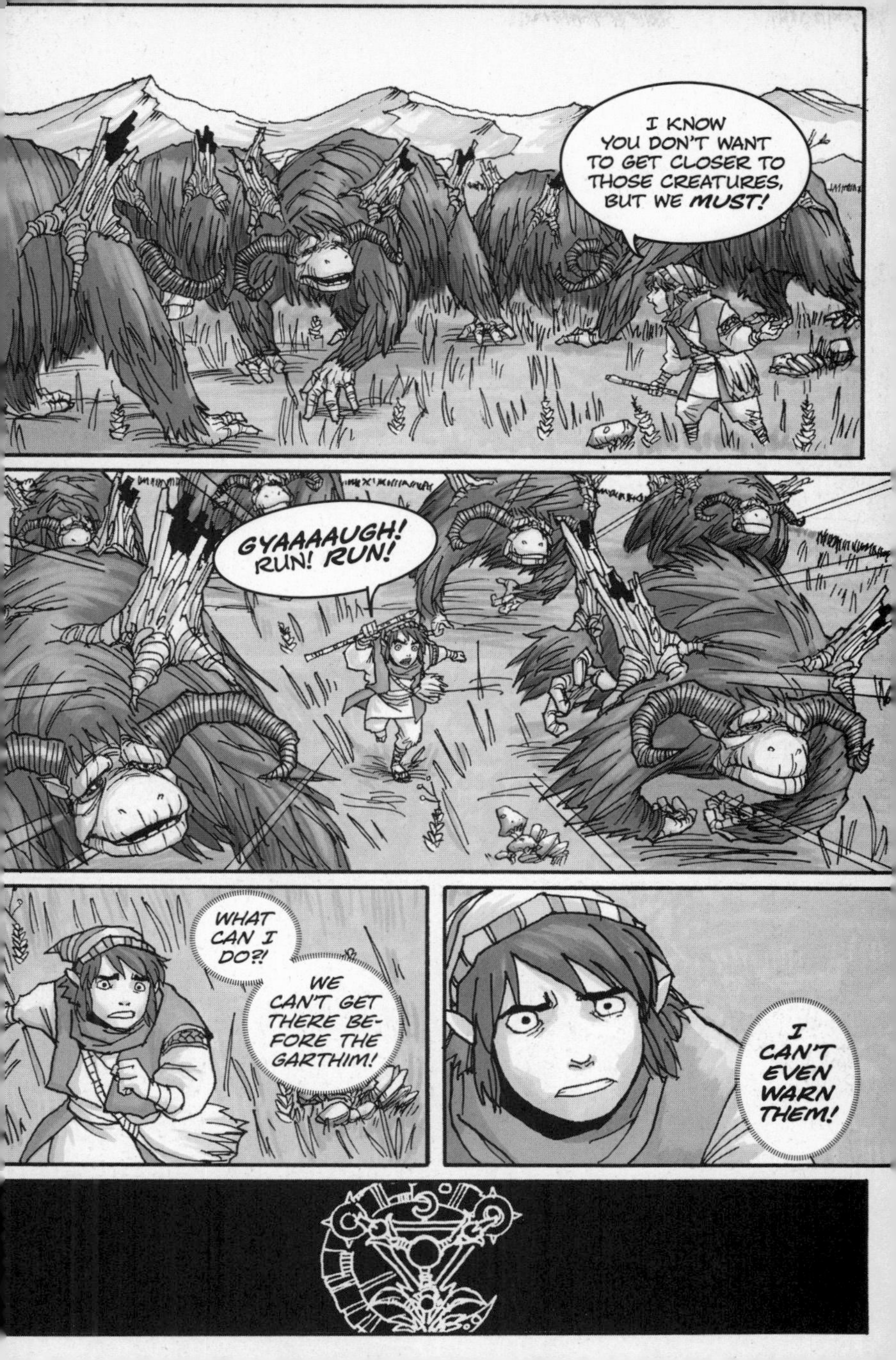
I KNOW YOU DON'T WANT TO GET CLOSER TO THOSE CREATURES, BUT WE *MUST!*
GYAAAAUGH! RUN! *RUN!*
WHAT CAN I DO?!
WE CAN'T GET THERE BE-FORE THE GARTHIM!
I CAN'T EVEN WARN THEM!

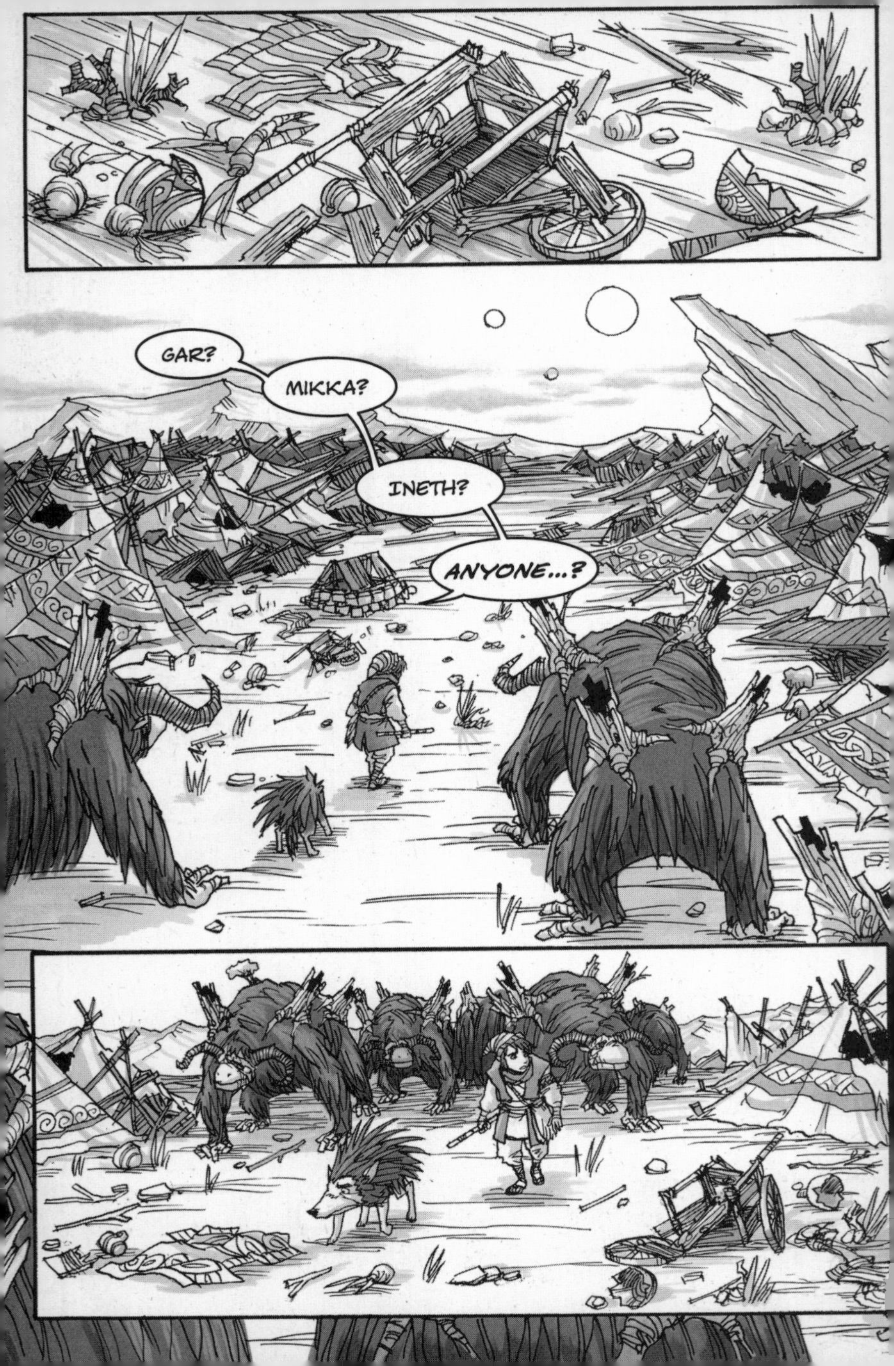
GAR?
MIKKA?
INETH?
ANYONE...?

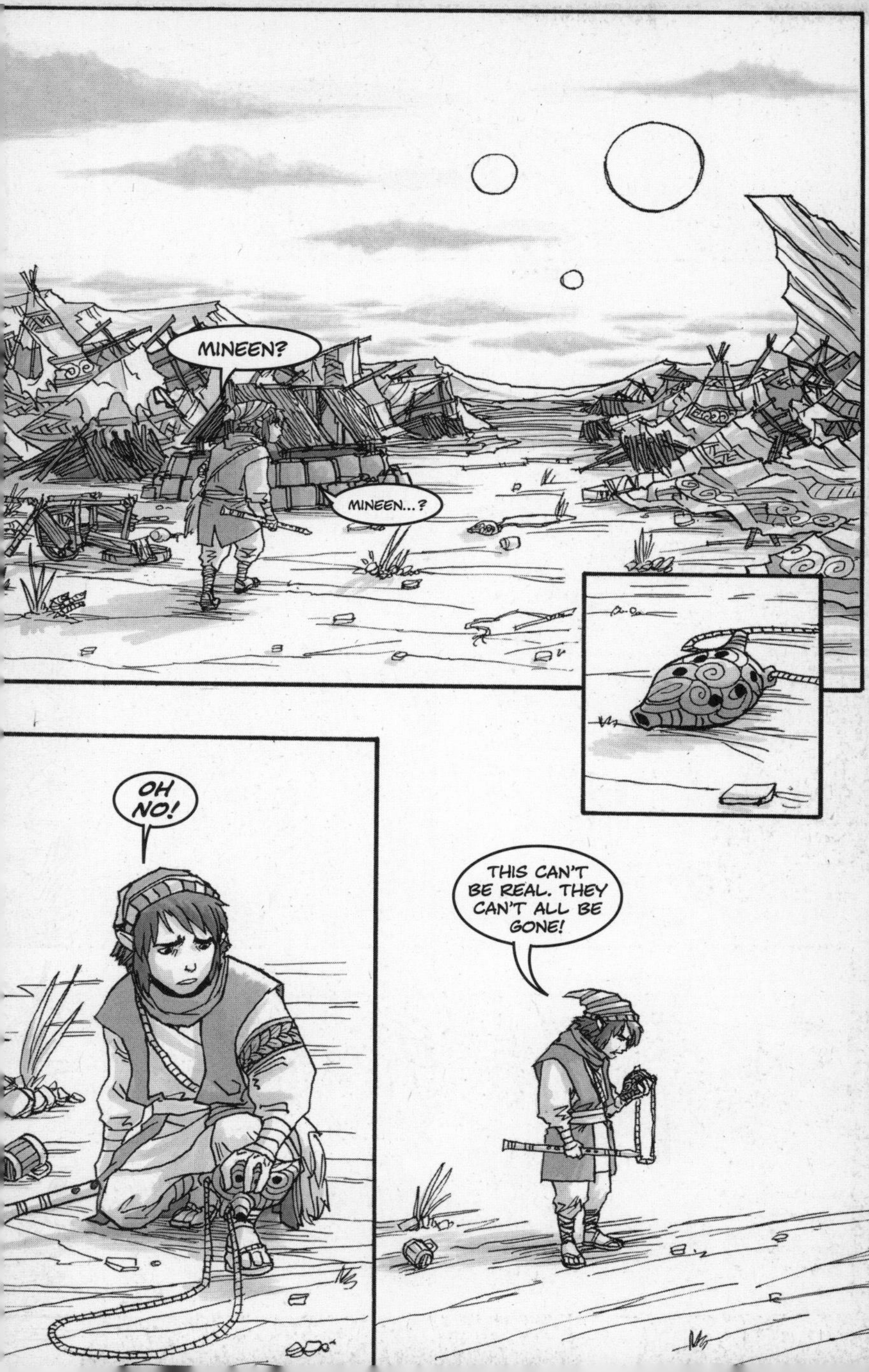
MINEEN?
MINEEN...?
OH NO!
THIS CAN'T BE REAL. THEY CAN'T ALL BE GONE!

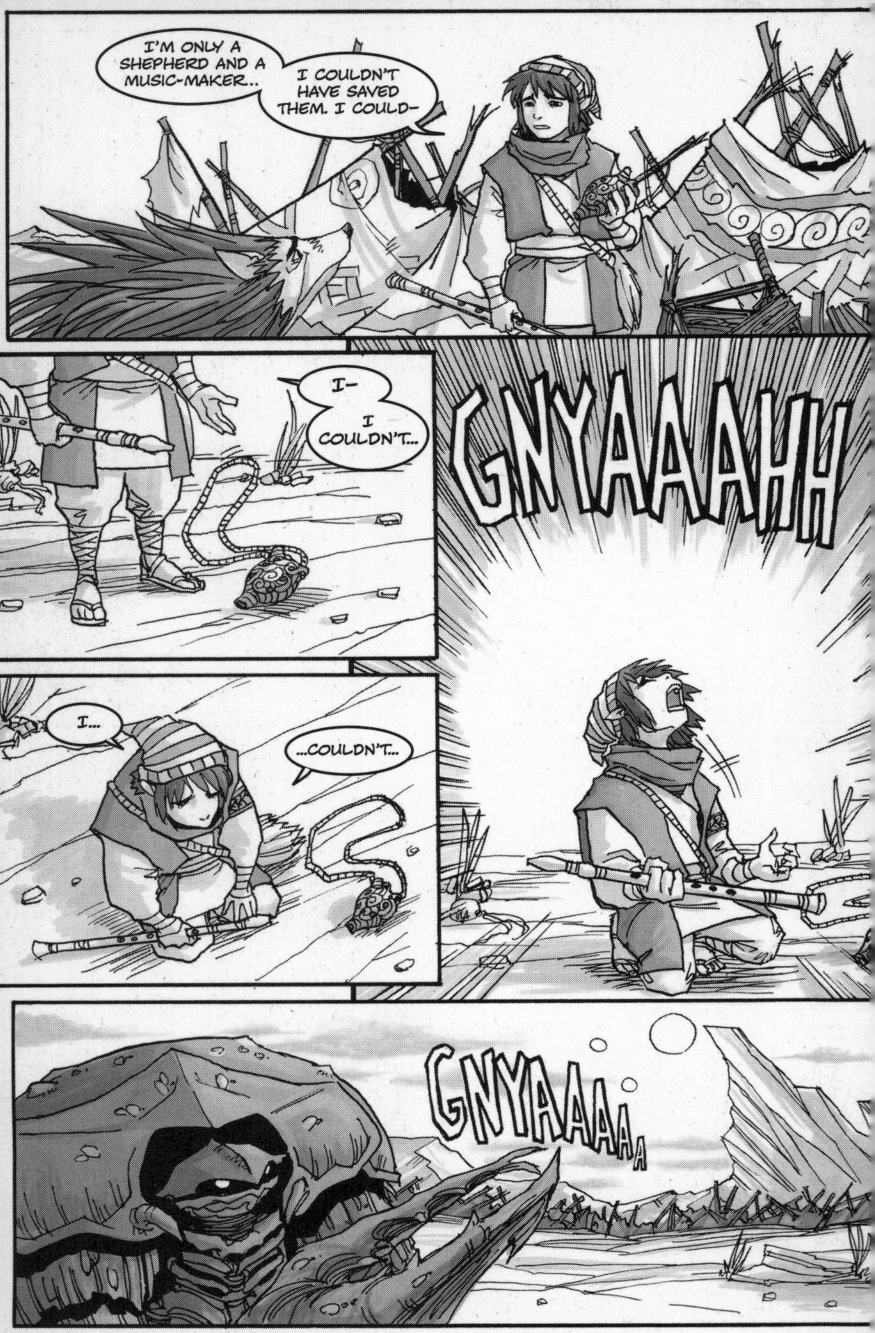
I'M ONLY A SHEPHERD AND A MUSIC-MAKER...
I COULDN'T HAVE SAVED THEM. I COULD-
I-
I COULDN'T...
I...
...COULDN'T...
GNYAAAAHH
GNYAAAAA

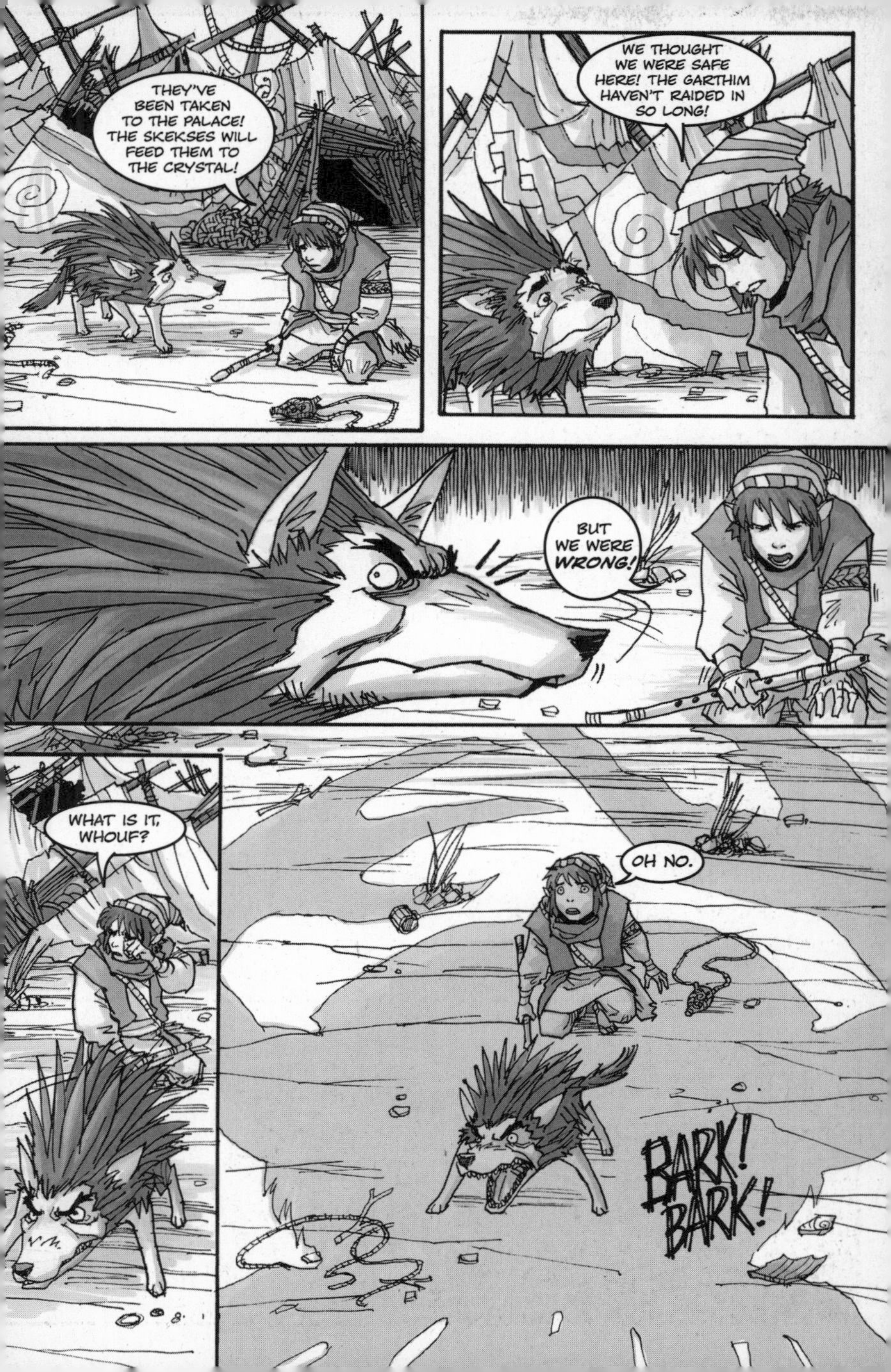
THEY'VE BEEN TAKEN TO THE PALACE! THE SKEKSES WILL FEED THEM TO THE CRYSTAL!
WE THOUGHT WE WERE SAFE HERE! THE GARTHIM HAVEN'T RAIDED IN SO LONG!
BUT WE WERE WRONG!
WHAT IS IT, WHOUF?
OH NO.
BARK! BARK!

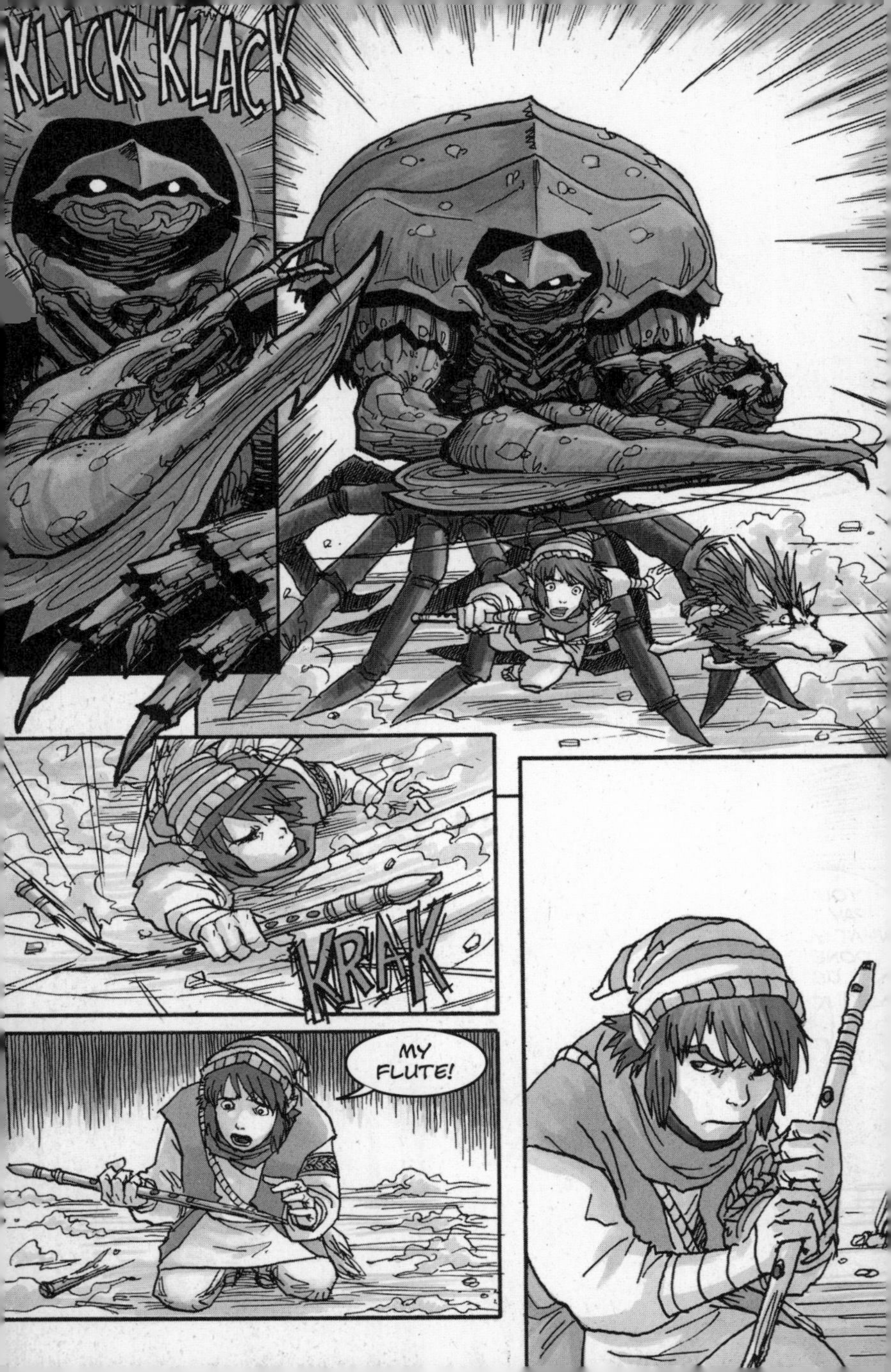
KLICK KLACK
KRAK
MY FLUTE!

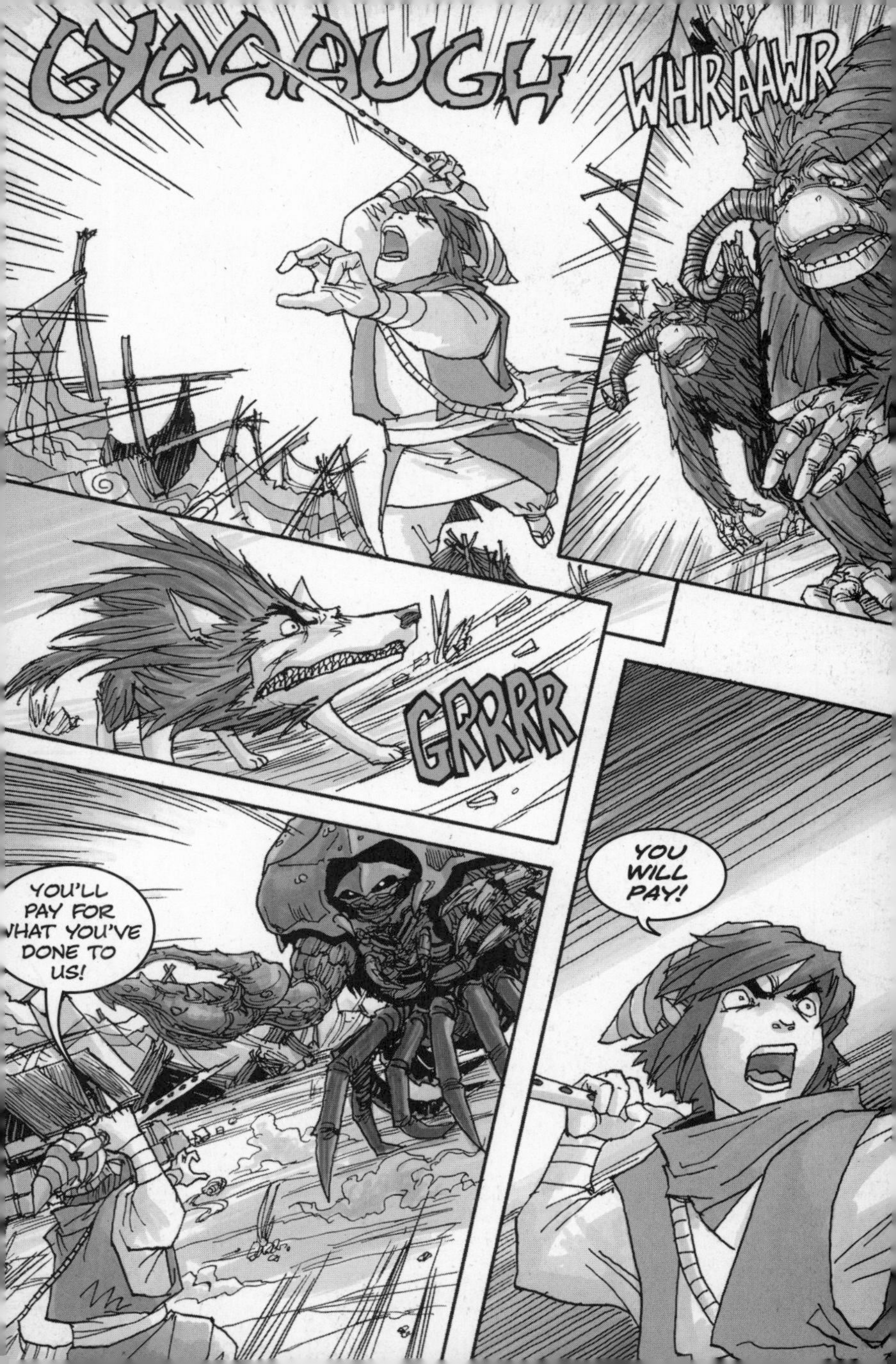
GYAAAUGH
WHRAAWR
GRRRR
YOU'LL PAY FOR WHAT YOU'VE DONE TO US!
YOU WILL PAY!

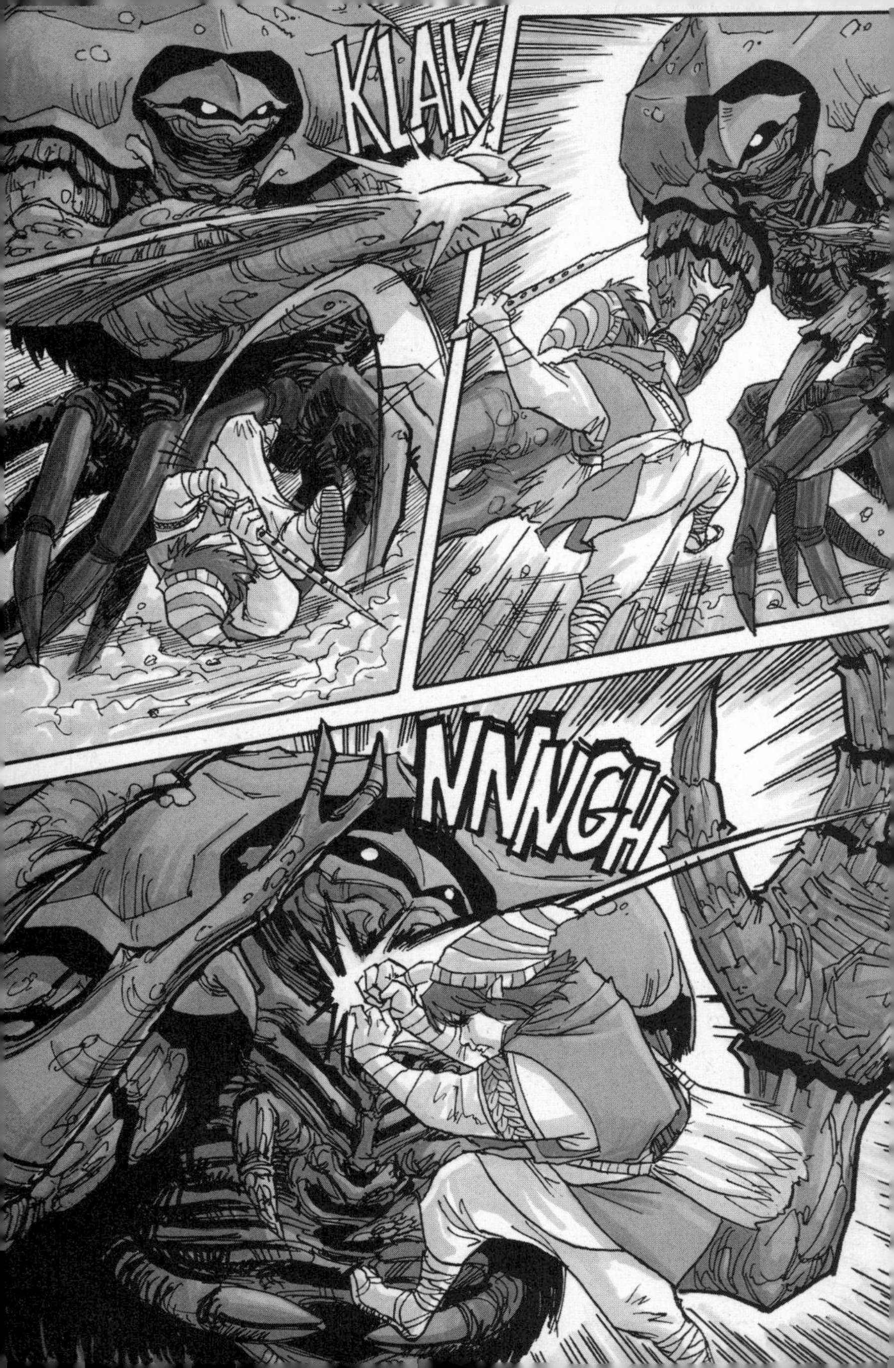
KLAK
NNNGH

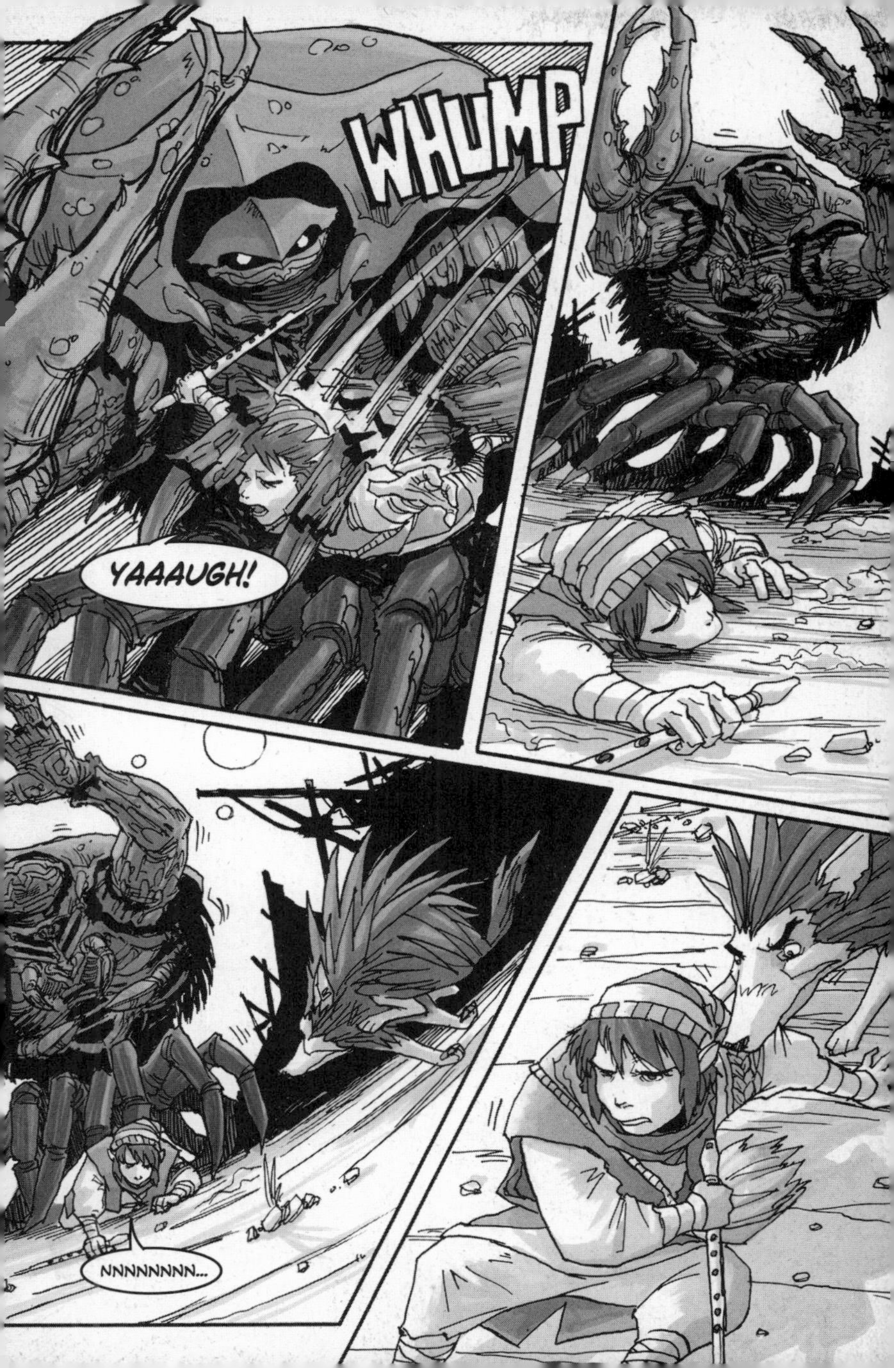
WHUMP
YAAAUGH!
NNNNNNNN...

KRAANNNGG

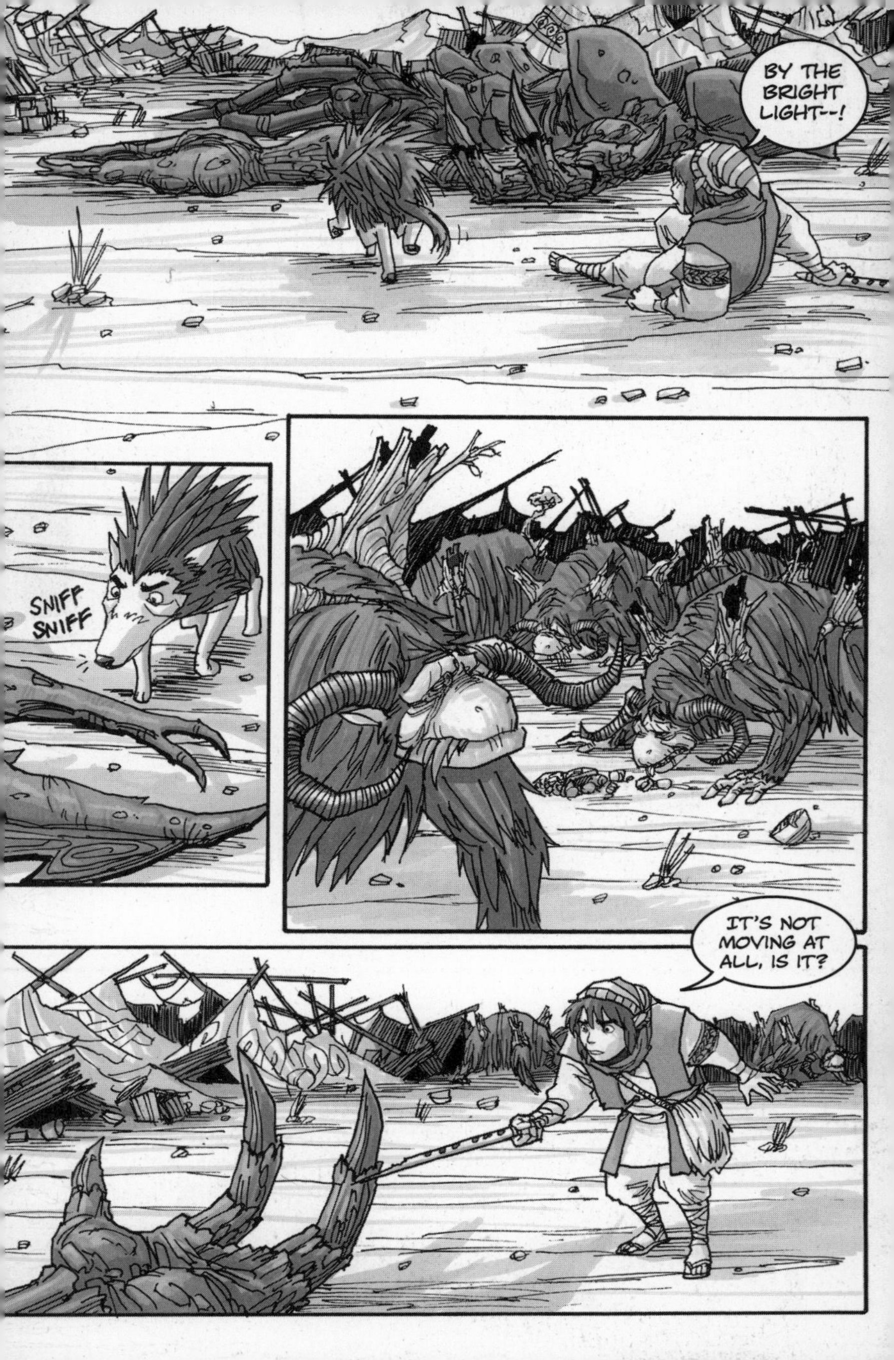
BY THE BRIGHT LIGHT--!
SNIFF SNIFF
IT'S NOT MOVING AT ALL, IS IT?

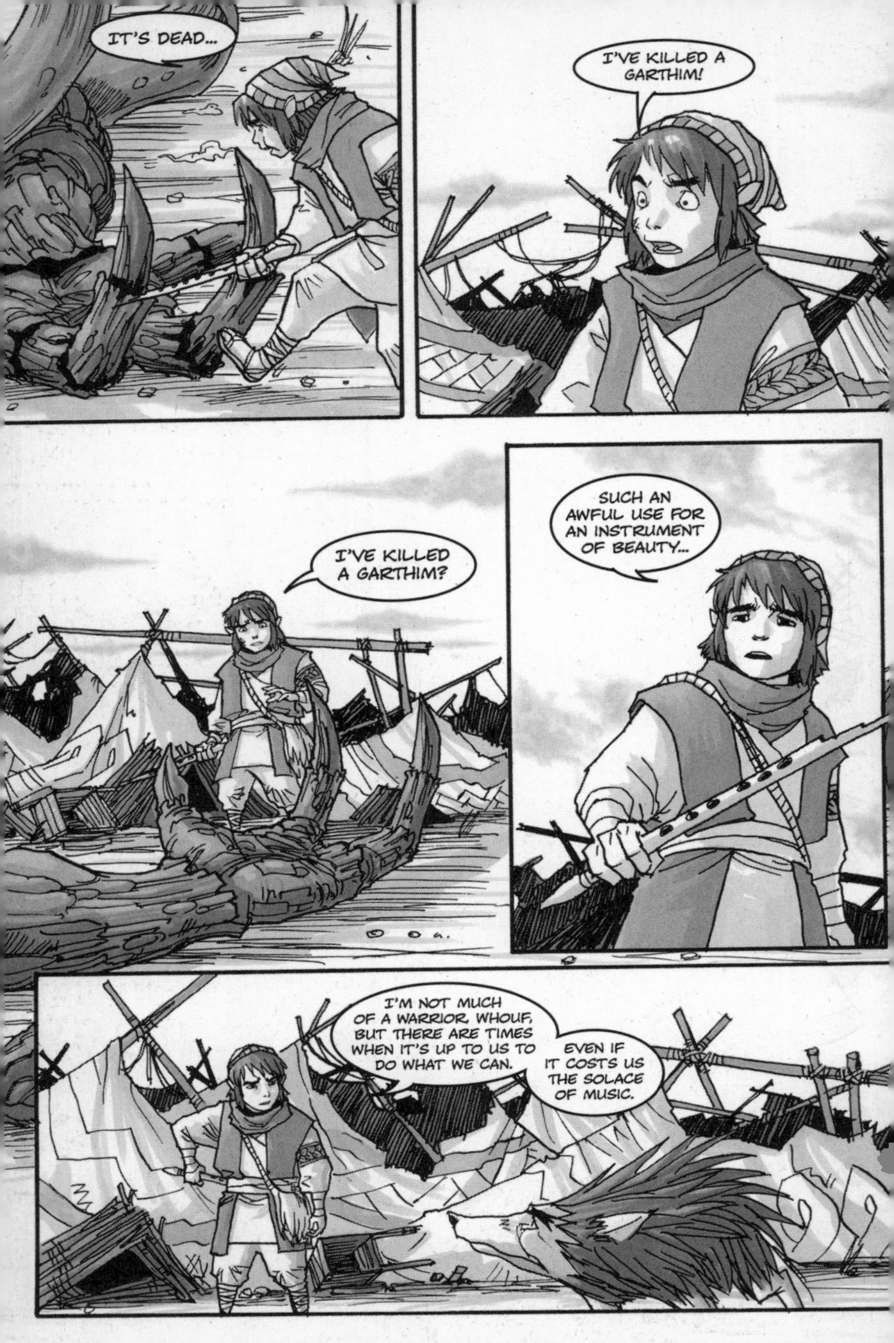
IT'S DEAD...
I'VE KILLED A GARTHIM!
I'VE KILLED A GARTHIM?
SUCH AN AWFUL USE FOR AN INSTRUMENT OF BEAUTY...
I'M NOT MUCH OF A WARRIOR, WHOUF, BUT THERE ARE TIMES WHEN IT'S UP TO US TO DO WHAT WE CAN.
EVEN IF IT COSTS US THE SOLACE OF MUSIC.

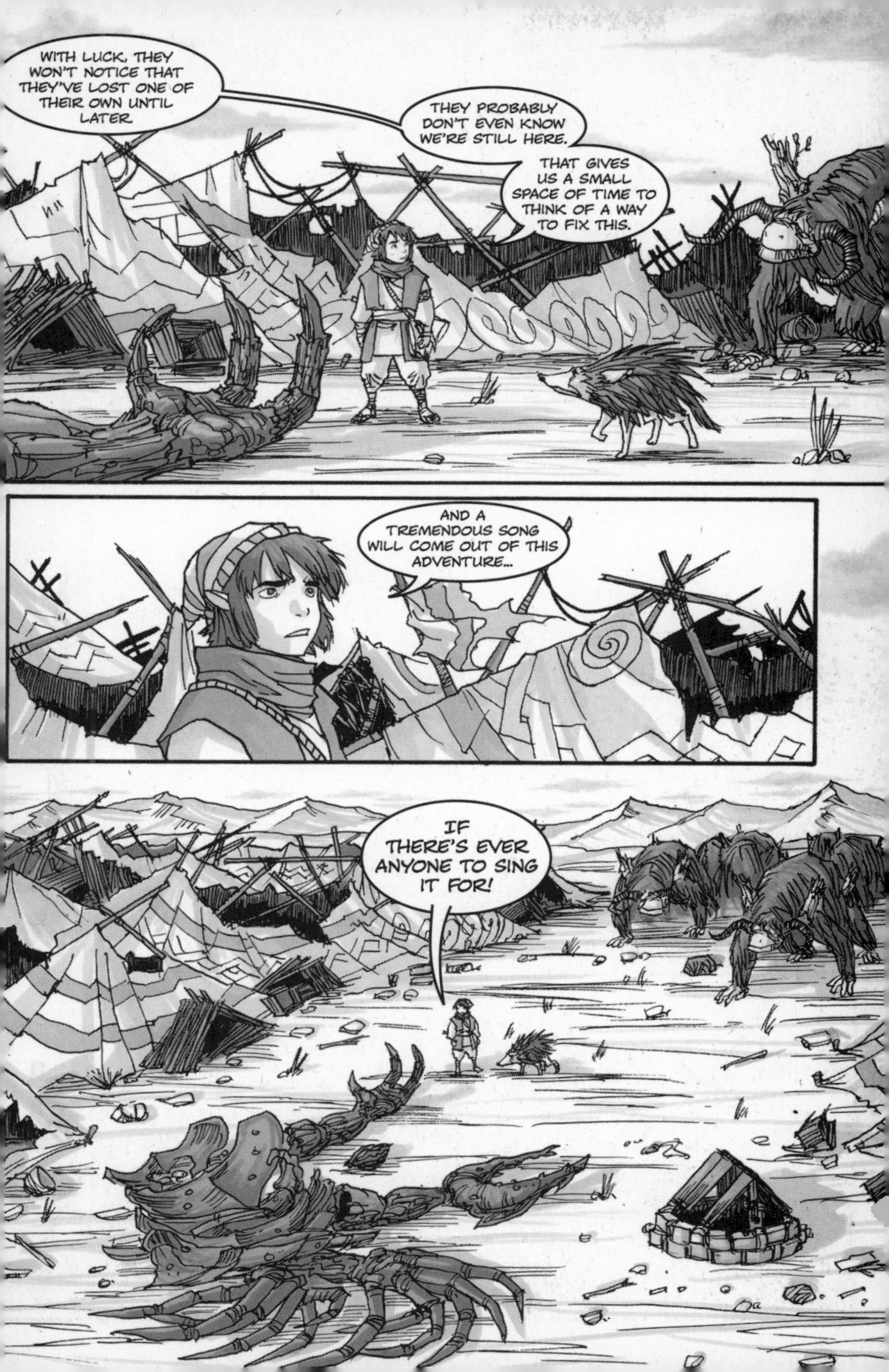
WITH LUCK, THEY WON'T NOTICE THAT THEY'VE LOST ONE OF THEIR OWN UNTIL LATER
THEY PROBABLY DON'T EVEN KNOW WE'RE STILL HERE.
THAT GIVES US A SMALL SPACE OF TIME TO THINK OF A WAY TO FIX THIS.
AND A TREMENDOUS SONG WILL COME OUT OF THIS ADVENTURE...
IF THERE'S EVER ANYONE TO SING IT FOR!

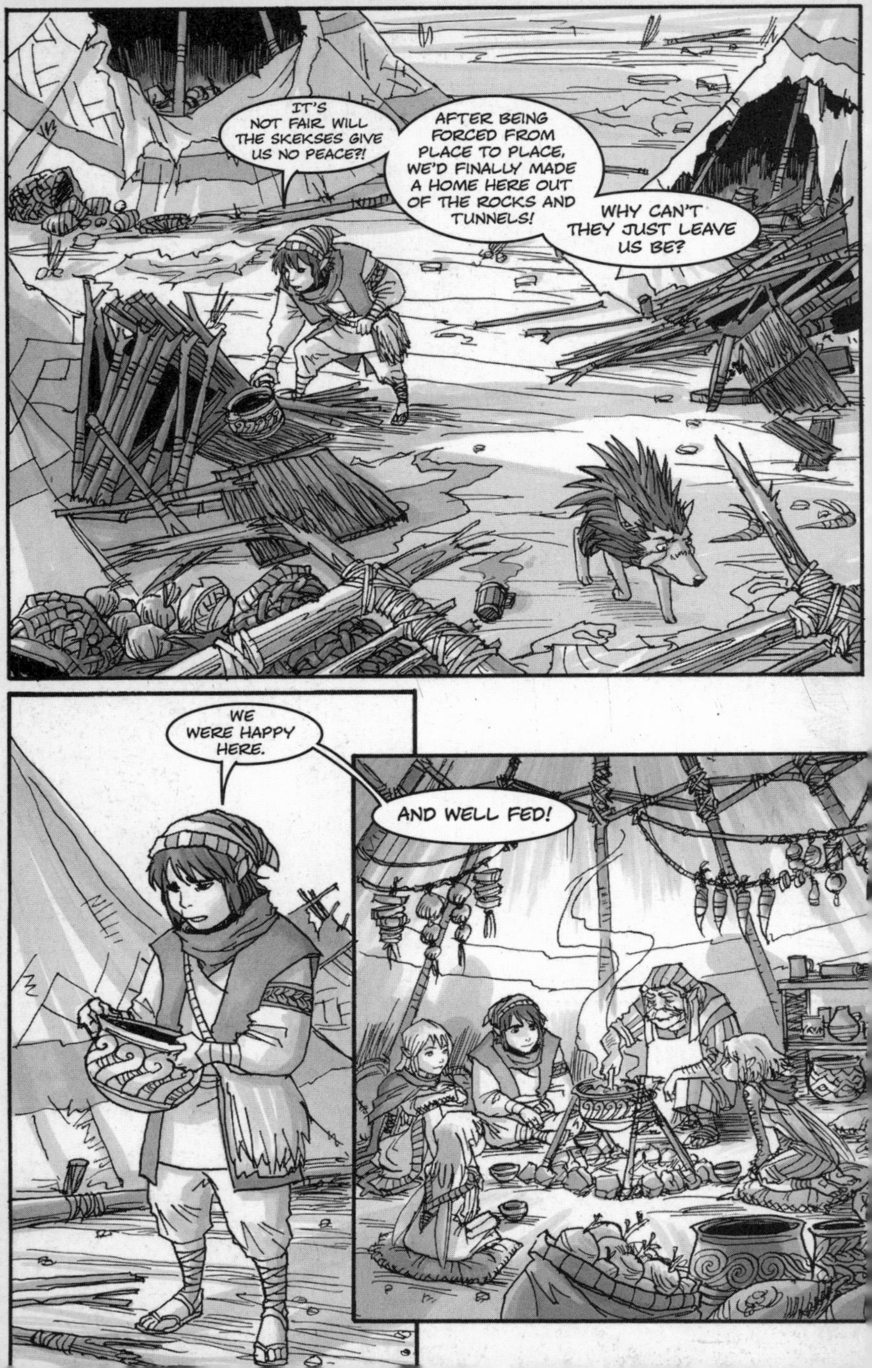
IT'S NOT FAIR WILL THE SKEKSES GIVE US NO PEACE?!
AFTER BEING FORCED FROM PLACE TO PLACE, WE'D FINALLY MADE A HOME HERE OUT OF THE ROCKS AND TUNNELS!
WHY CAN'T THEY JUST LEAVE US BE?
WE WERE HAPPY HERE.
AND WELL FED!

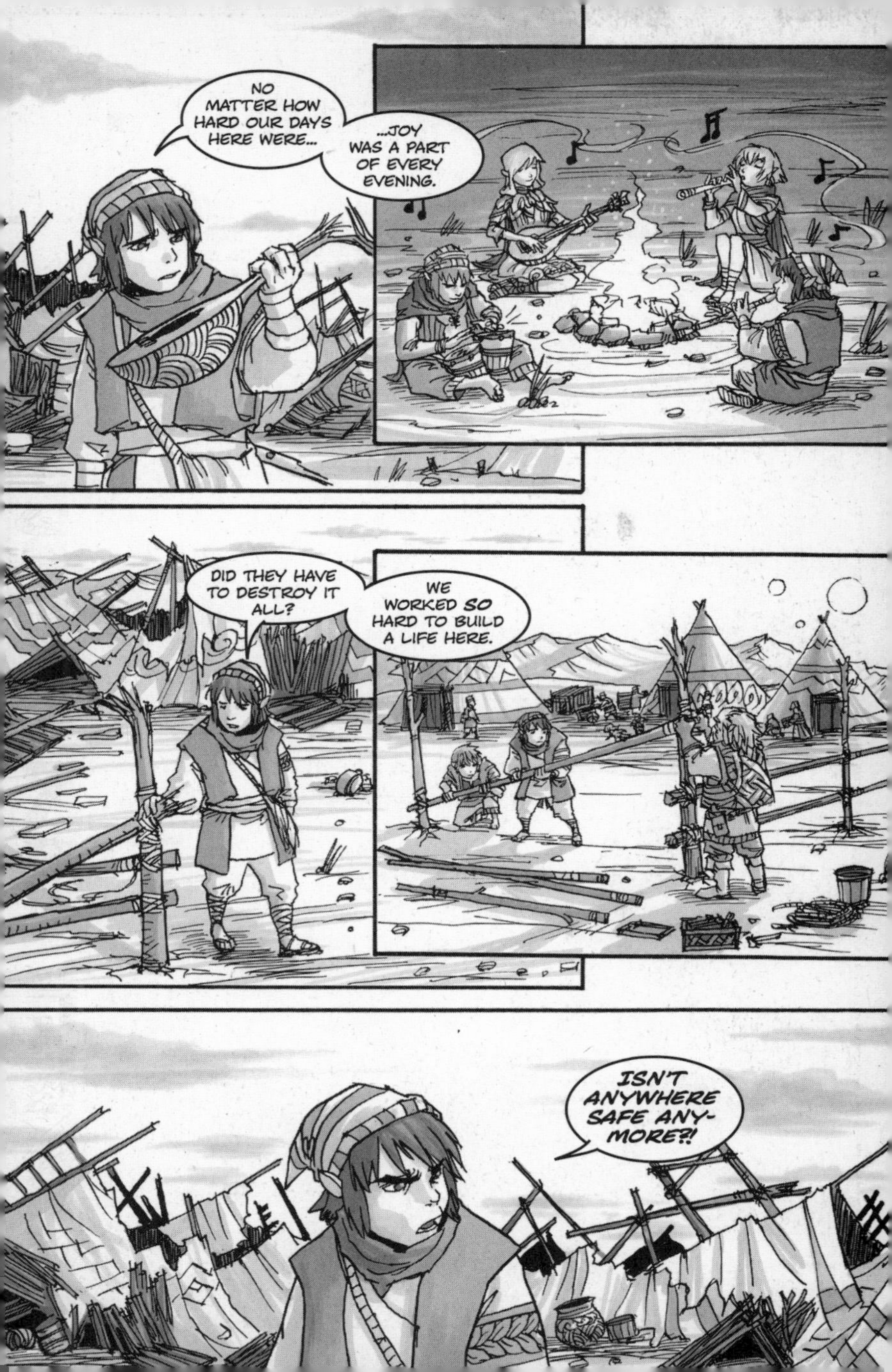
NO MATTER HOW HARD OUR DAYS HERE WERE...
...JOY WAS A PART OF EVERY EVENING.
DID THEY HAVE TO DESTROY IT ALL?
WE WORKED SO HARD TO BUILD A LIFE HERE.
ISN'T ANYWHERE SAFE ANY-MORE?!

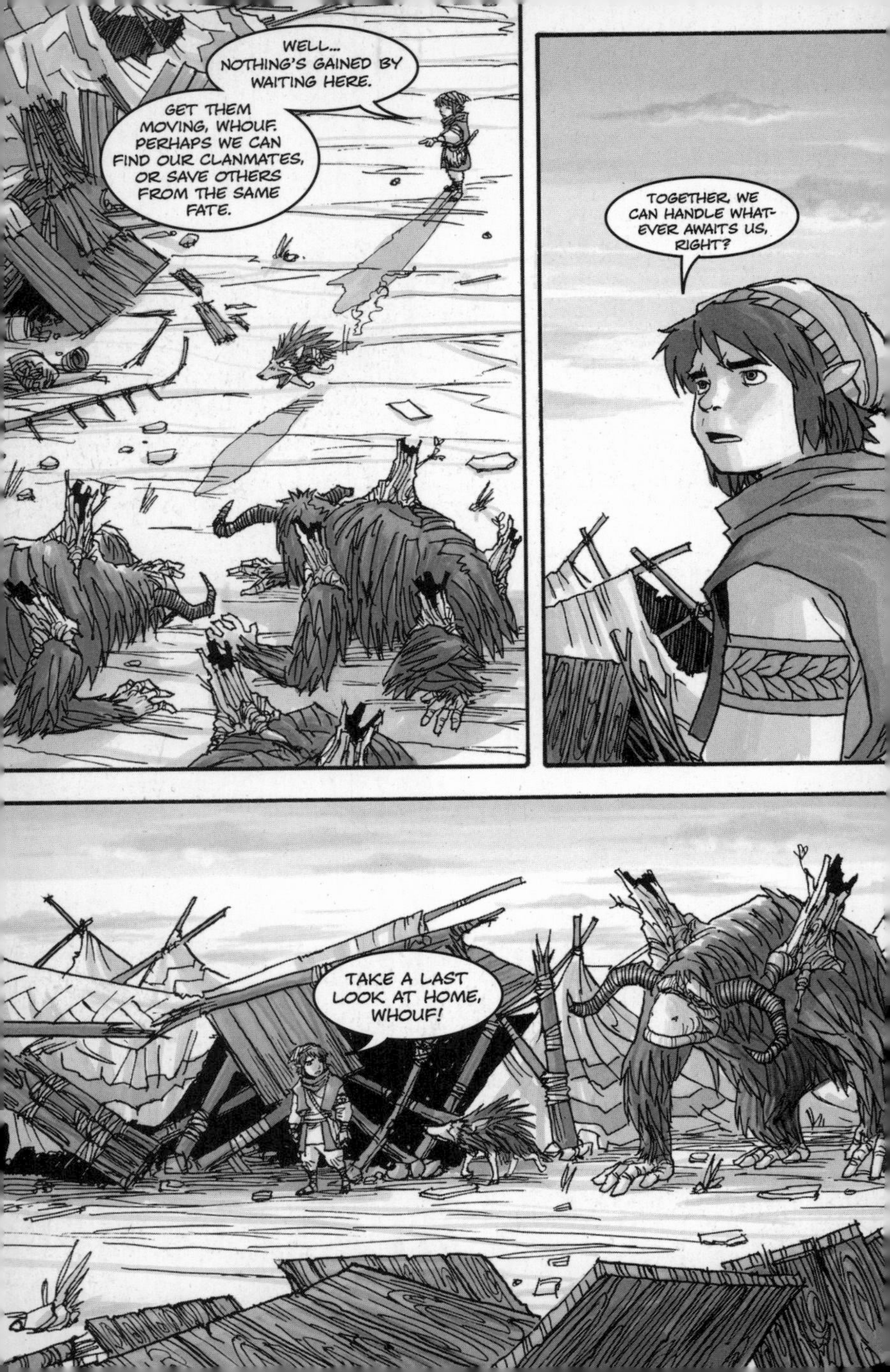
WELL... NOTHING'S GAINED BY WAITING HERE.
GET THEM MOVING, WHOUF. PERHAPS WE CAN FIND OUR CLANMATES, OR SAVE OTHERS FROM THE SAME FATE.
TOGETHER, WE CAN HANDLE WHAT-EVER AWAITS US, RIGHT?
TAKE A LAST LOOK AT HOME, WHOUF!

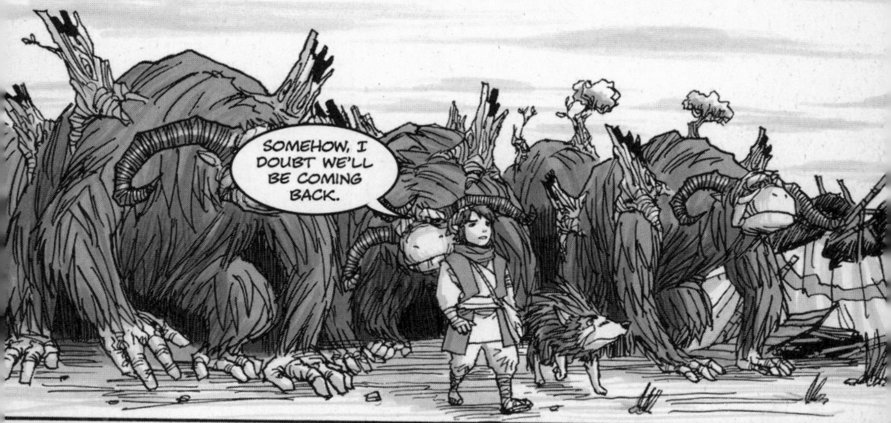
SOMEHOW, I DOUBT WE'LL BE COMING BACK.

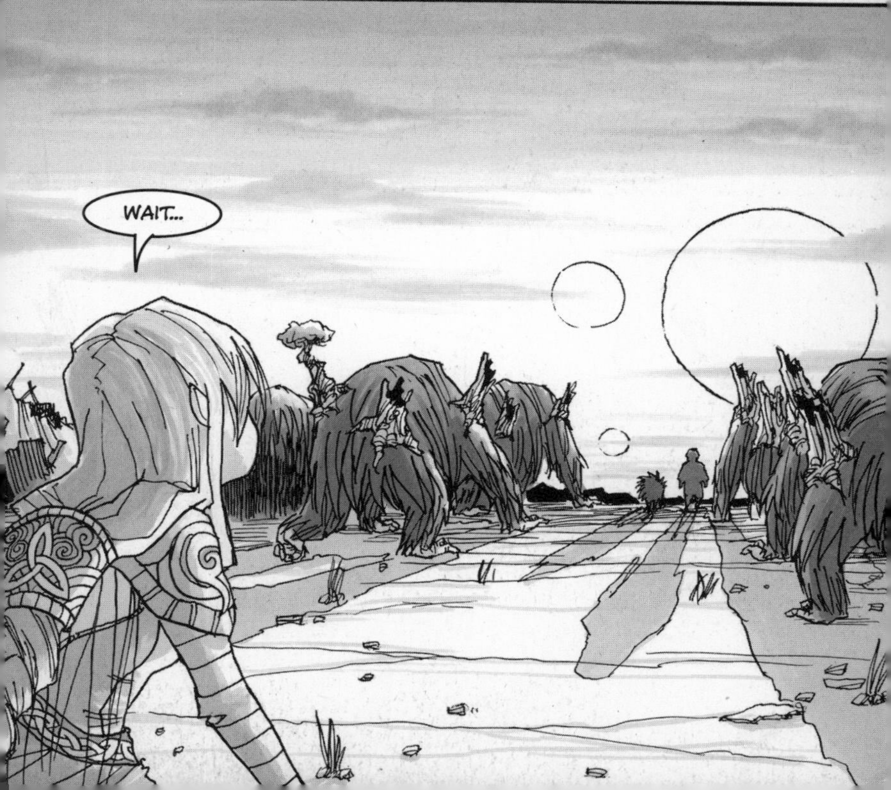
WAIT...